First hardback edition August 2019

Book design by Aggie Bainbridge | petitspapiers.co
Photography by Pierre Carton | pierrecarton.com
Historical photography supplied by Getty Images and Presse Sports
Map illustration by Celine DeMaesschalck | Modern Hobbyist
Original artwork 'Brothers in Arms' © Rachael Dalzell | rachaeldalzell.com
Illustration by Ovalie Bell, Paris

Cover image: Jean-Pierre Garuet-Lempirou and Philippe Dintrans, photographed together in 2018.
Photo by Pierre Carton

ISBN 978-1-9160099-0-5 (hardback)

brothersinarmsbook.co.uk

for

Jo, William, Ollie and Marcus

Mum and Dad

The Loved and Lost

Brothers in Arms

BY DAVID BERESFORD

MY PERSONAL
JOURNEY TO MEET
THE GOLDEN GENERATION
OF FRENCH RUGBY

'Brothers in Arms' by Rachael Dalzell

"When I first met David, I was blown away by his knowledge of France and us, the former players, and of French rugby. After his first sentence, I stopped him and said: 'Hold on, you are English and your French is better than mine!' What he has achieved is magnificent."

« *Quand j'ai rencontré David pour la première fois j'ai été impressionné par ses connaissances sur la France et sur nous, les anciens joueurs, sur le rugby français. Il n'avait pas prononcé sa première phrase que je l'arrêtai : "Attends, tu es Anglais et tu parles mieux français que moi !" Ce qu'il a réalisé est formidable.* »

PASCAL ONDARTS

Contents

Foreword

BY SEAN FITZPATRICK

I t is a great pleasure for me to write the foreword to this book. Beres and I first met in 2003 when he was the host at one of his infamous client lunches in a smart London restaurant on the eve of the Rugby World Cup (RWC) Semi-Finals. I remember it well because the food, wine and company were fabulous, and I quickly understood what a deeply committed Francophile and epicurean he was, and still is!

When he told me about his idea to write this book, I was immediately captivated. This wasn't just because it was my generation, it was the golden generation of French rugby for all of us, and I too wanted to know where they all were and what they were doing. It was a big, ambitious project, and Beres was the man for the job, perfectly qualified who would embrace this labour of love with all the requisite fun, enthusiasm and energy.

Having lived there for many years, working, studying and playing rugby, he of course speaks the French language fluently, which is *sine qua non* to being able to write this book. But more than this, he understands the inner workings of the French mind and their *art de vivre*, especially in the rugby-loving south of the country – the importance of making time to build genuine and strong relationships, understanding their food, wine and local products, and respecting their culture, customs and *terroir*. When it comes to France and their emotions, there are many things that can't be seen or touched. You need to feel them with your heart and soul. Beres is an Englishman who really understands this.

It is a huge credit to his charm, fluency, knowledge and determination that he succeeded so quickly in meeting and getting to know the former players. These weren't simple, perfunctory or transactional meetings either – these were proper lunches, dinners and time spent with them and their families. Life is about people and

les rencontres, and Beres excels at that.

Love for France and French rugby runs deep in the Fitzpatrick clan too.

Dad played centre for the All Blacks in 1954 against a French team that boasted the great André Boniface and Prat brothers, Jean and Maurice. Unfortunately we lost, the first time France had ever beaten us! I played against them twelve times in total, winning eight and losing four.

I won my first cap against them in June 1986 in Christchurch, a game I remember with both fondness, but also trepidation. It was a baptism of fire!

This was the year of the unauthorised New Zealand Cavaliers tour to South Africa and as a result, many of the usual All Black players such as Dalton, Mexted, Haden and Hobbs were banned for two games and unavailable for the test match.

Baby Blacks
We, the Baby Blacks, took our chance.

Eleven of the All Blacks team that day made their debut and our captain was David Kirk. We were warming up in the changing room beforehand while David was reminding us how good the French team were, coming off the back of winning the Five Nations Championship.

"Be prepared, they will come at us hard, they will ruck, punch and stamp on you. Their scrum is a powerhouse so you have to be on your game. No half measures, absolute focus and total commitment."

The 'Battle of Nantes' was
a game of blood and thunder, driven
by unconstrained emotion and ferocity.
They came out of their changing rooms
raging and frothing at the mouths,
their eyes as big as tennis balls.

The team had an array of stars with many more caps and years more experience than us – Dubroca, Garuet, Condom, Haget, Champ, Erbani, Blanco, Sella, Berbizier, Lagisquet. This was both a hard and scintillating team, a beautiful blend of teak toughness and craft.

I had no idea what was in store for me. After a few minutes, we went down for the first scrum and the French put the squeeze on. I remember the feeling of being tossed around as though in a washing machine – we flew backwards at a rate of knots. Somehow, we still won the game.

The Battle of Nantes

There were other memorable games against them too.

We had beaten the French in the scrappy first test in Toulouse on 8th November 1986. The late John Drake, who had played for Bourg-en-Bresse, understood how they scrummaged and wound them up throughout the game. We outwitted them in the scrums and negated a core part of their game plan. They were furious.

The first test was nothing compared to the second a week later - the infamous 'Battle of Nantes'. This was a game of blood and thunder, driven by unconstrained emotion and ferocity. They came out of their changing rooms raging and frothing at the mouths, their eyes as big as tennis balls.

They smashed us at the first ruck and were unrelenting the whole game. We were badly beaten. In separate incidents, Jean Condom cleaned his boots on me resulting in twenty-six stitches. Buck Shelford lost four teeth, was knocked out cold and had his scrotum torn open by a stray boot. I still wince today when I think about it. We lost the game badly.

It was a watershed moment for the All Blacks team as it ushered in some new players. We used the loss by bottling up that awful feeling of failure, and we made sure it didn't happen again for many years. We talked about it a lot in the following few months and used it as motivation for beating them at the RWC final in 1987. 'Remember Nantes' was the cry we used.

After Nantes, I decided to stay on in France for a few months. My sister was importing shoes to New Zealand from the famous brand Robert Clergerie that was based in Romans-sur-Isere. Robert was also the President of Romans rugby club, a first division club at the time, and he invited me to go and play for them, which I agreed to do, but only before Albert Ferrasse, the all-powerful President of the French Rugby Federation, had decided to ban any international players from abroad from playing in the first division!

The first time I walked into the changing room, one of the players threw me an appendage that looked like a cricket box and said, 'You will need this'. It seemed that rugby in France could be pretty dirty back then. I ended up playing flanker for the 2nd team as I was keen to look after my crown jewels!

My wife and I lived in Romans for about five months, until spring 1987. We had a wonderful time, living in a little cottage with great views of the Alps and enjoying the locals' friendship and hospitality. It was simple, but idyllic living.

There was another player at Romans at the same time who would become a great player for France – Philippe Saint-André. It was ironic that Philippe would be the captain of that 1994 team that beat us 2-0 *chez-nous*, including that try from the end of the world that he started.

That try was a great example of how they could turn it on with their French flair. They never thought they could beat us, but we invariably struggled to beat them. I lost more times to France than any other nation.

When I look back at the teams I played against between 1986-1996 and those in the early '80s too, it was a golden generation of fabulous players. They had flair everywhere, but they also had great forwards to lay the platform.

I rated Philippe Dintrans very highly and admired the way he played. He was tough, uncompromising, direct and a great leader. Jean-Pierre Garuet was also formidable, the best tight head I ever played against. He would always attack me, boring into my ribs, occasionally breaking them as he did in 1990 at Eden Park! Steve McDowell and I had to watch him closely.

It was great fun off the pitch too. I loved going to places like La Rochelle and eating at Chez André. Or heading to Moët & Chandon's venue in Champagne with the French team and watching great men like Pascal Ondarts leading the singing and slicing the top off a champagne bottle using a sabre. We swapped blazers after that night and it brings back very sweet memories.

So, sit back, put your feet up and grab a glass of French wine. This book is as much a story about France, life, friendship and the human spirit as it is about rugby. It is bursting with insightful character portraits, great memories, new and forgotten anecdotes, up-to-date information, photos and, most importantly, a deep love and respect for France, its people and regions. It will make Francophiles, humanists and rugby fans across the world very happy.

Vive la France!

Sean Fitzpatrick

Sean Fitzpatrick
Former All Black, 92 caps, 51 as captain
March 2019

Preface

BY DAVID BERESFORD

I am sitting in an idyllic place for reflection, whatever its form, whatever the emotions it evokes in me – nostalgia, dreams, reality, love, fear, loss, pain, regret, hope. There's no science to this, just feelings oiled by lunch, wine and time, that most precious of unmovable constants. Right now, my mind is a turbine of thoughts and ideas, criss-crossing the labyrinth of my fifty years and mapping out the next chapter. Whatever I've experienced, it has always been how I felt that is fixed in my memory, rather than the details. My next adventure would have to be inspiring and memorable, the sort of thing that money couldn't buy.

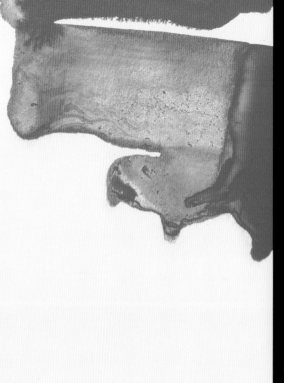

Most of you won't know where I am, in the village of Saint-Savin, near Argelès-Gazost, nestled in the foothills of the French Pyrenees. It has a neat village square, Romanesque architecture and a wonderful hotel called Le Viscos. On this day, the sky is deep blue, the grass embossed in daisies and the air so clean that you can see the fine detail of the mountain contours in the distance. I am captivated by the scene and my own introspection.

I do not know what dreams ask of us, or what we expect of them. I've had this one for thirty years, a collection of fleeting images and fantastical thoughts no doubt inspired by thirty-five years of profligacy, vicarious living and, dare I admit it, adulation. But now is the time. I have to distil all this into an adventure that brings this dream alive and allows you, the reader, to come with me on my journey.

This book is about former rugby players, but it isn't simply about rugby. It is about life and its kaleidoscope of colours.

Where a story has marked me, I have included it in the book. Some are very personal, but most are linked in some way to the heart of the subject matter – the great French rugby team of the 1980s, a team of sporting icons who loved, fought and celebrated their good fortune together for over a decade.

The players were a band of brothers from the golden generation who dazzled the rugby-loving world with their skill and unpredictability. It is their French flair that is woven inextricably into my memory like a first love,

undimmed by the passing of time. The excitement of watching Blanco, Codorniou and Sella flowing gracefully through space, unlocking opposition defences with their pace, pirouettes and passing; or the swashbuckling bravery of the free-spirited and heroic Rives, fizzing, ubiquitous, blood-stained and smashing people with a force belying his size; and the marauding beauty and power of Laurent Rodriguez, the bull from Dax, vanquishing his matador adversaries to create space for the fleet-footed behind. If anything, the memories and feelings are even sharper now, no doubt embellished during the passage of time.

If Wales was the rugby team of the '70s, France deserved that accolade in the '80s. They brought poetry to this sporting battlefield with their mix of flair and brute force.

But the course of true love never did run smooth and theirs is also a story ruptured by rivalry, politics, regret, tragedy and death.

...I had to find closure to my dream. I wanted to meet and befriend them because that would be the closest I would get to becoming one of them.

commentary as I scored in the corner. Back then, my passion for French rugby was greater than I felt for England. However, my talent was limited so I played vicariously, but I had to find closure to my dream. I wanted to meet and befriend them because that would be the closest I would get to becoming one of them.

So, in October 2017, as self-appointed chairman of selectors, I named a coach and thirty-two iconic French players in my squad, and I spent eighteen months getting to know them, experiencing their warmth and generosity, and capturing their spirit.

Part chronicle, part dialogue and part travelogue, Brothers in Arms is a personalised account of my travels to track them down and discover their life adventure. I have gone straight to the source, the players themselves as well as gathered insights and opinions from the *crème de la crème* of former international players and coaches such as André Boniface, Jo Maso, Raphaël Ibañez, Pierre Villepreux, Sean Fitzpatrick, Michael Lynagh, Gavin Hastings, Ieuan Evans, Will Carling, Brian Moore, John Kirwan, Hugo MacNeill and many more.

Overlaying these are my own anecdotes of travelling, working, living, playing and studying in France for over thirty-five years, recounting the richness of experiences that unfolded – working and living in the Alps during the 1992 winter Olympics, experiencing the wild frontier of French gastronomy, tasting wine with their greatest wine growers, watching bullfighting, playing rugby for three different clubs, living at the heart of French families, meeting the godsons of Pablo Picasso and

Albert Gleize, and generally enjoying everything that France has to offer.

In my heart, my inspiration to write this book came from my memories and love of watching them. Based on the anecdotal feedback I've had, the rugby-loving world also wants to remember what they achieved and find out what they have become. What were the great sporting moments and anecdotes, what are the players doing today, what are they like and what do they think?

However, it wasn't simply inspired by my love of the players. There was another personal reason why I wrote it - because deep down I wanted to be one of them; to play and live like them, to seduce the public with the looks, swagger and guile, to bathe in the glory and fame, to taste the Latin camaraderie. Aged nineteen, I remember training in my school playground near Avignon and pretending I was Codorniou, Charvet or Bonneval, my heart pounding and imagining the

The former players had to meet the following criteria for selection, which gave me ample room for discretion:

1. Had to have played in the 1980s. I could easily have extended this to the great players before and after the 1980s, but my waistline couldn't have taken it, and my wife would have shown me a red card. I will leave those for another time...

2. Had to have made a significant contribution to the development of the 1987 RWC squad.

3. Had to fit into my subjective definition of French flair and exhibit some of the following: power, pace, character, impact, audacity, non-conformism... It's a fool's errand to get too scientific about this though. My selection, like so many a French coach and selector in the past, is much more about heart, beauty and impact than the chicanery of statistics.

The French team celebrates their 19-15
victory against Wales at the Parc des Princes,
7th March 1981. *Photo - Presse Sports.*

Égalité, Fraternité, Liberté

To those of us who watched their games, whatever our nationality, it was the French flair that we remember. It was their Gallic expression of this beautiful game, their version of the iron fist in a velvet glove, a *mélange* of brutality, skill, spontaneity and vertiginous runs that conjured magnificent tries. Like the world's great artists - Mozart, Picasso, Shakespeare, Lennon, Zidane, De Niro - their talent was intoxicating, palpable and etched into your memory forever.

But to reduce the book to an account of French flair would be simplistic. While that was the finished product and what we remember, there was so much more happening below the surface, and much has happened since. I wanted to capture this in the book too. Besides the natural talent and coaching, there were a couple of themes that kept recurring:

Firstly their humanity and love of each other and the game. Back then, rugby was a chosen way of life, not a profession, emanating from the towns, villages and farms, played for pleasure and touching every aspect of their lives. It was rugby that enriched them, instilling the values and Corinthian spirit that they still hold dear today – friendship, loyalty, selflessness, sacrifice, discipline, freedom, solidarity, determination, courage, respect and *la joie de vivre*. These values were key to their success.

Secondly their belief in *égalité, fraternité, liberté*. They don't like to single out individual players. They enthuse about the intangibles of equality, brotherhood and freedom, and how the whole is greater than the sum of its parts. When discussing rugby, they emphasise *generosité*, encapsulated by 'the pass', and *partage*, the giving and sharing between teammates. They recognise that without the brawn and courage of the forwards, there would have been no French flair, so the backs can't take all the glory. Other countries may have aspired to this too, but the emphasis is not as pronounced. *Egalité, fraternité, liberté* go right to the heart of the French mindset, first expressed by Robespierre before their revolution in 1789, written into the Constitution in 1958 and now the ubiquitous French national motto.

Brilliance, Brute Force and Bête Noire

After the inauspicious start in 1980 when the French team lost every game except one, and 1982 when Fouroux tested new combinations, France's achievements over the rest of the decade were very impressive.

Fouroux coached *Les Tricolores* between 1981-1990, and France won the then Five Nations' Championship six times (sometimes equal first) including two Grand Slams, never losing more than one match in the Championship between 1983 and 1989, and they were finalists of the inaugural World Cup in 1987.

In addition, they played some unforgettable games: 1981 v England in the Five Nations, the majestic Codorniou at his peak; 1983 v Wales, a brutal match where Rives, Blanco and Dospital were all bloodied and bruised; 1984 v Scotland when France lost the decider and Scotland won the Grand Slam, a loss that still irks the players today; 1986 v New Zealand, the infamous 'Battle of Nantes', a violent match won by France where Wayne Shelford suffered a torn scrotum; 1987 v England when Sella scored a sixty metre try and France won the Grand Slam; 1987 v Australia in the semi-final of the inaugural RWC; and 1990 v Australia, a three-test series that showed rugby in all its brutality and beauty.

Ironically, the French press did not see it the same way even though Fouroux's appointment coincided with France's domination of the Five Nations.

Where France's adversaries and the international press saw beauty and flair, the French press saw discipline and pragmatism, a contamination of their culture and playing style: *'le physique plutôt que la technique'* (brawn over technique) as Le Monde put it, scathing throughout the decade.

I have read many of their articles covering this period and there are very few that give Fouroux and his team much credit. Le Monde referred to him as *Napoléon Fou-roux le premier* (Napoléon mad-redhead the first). Beauty was in the eye of the beholder, and Fouroux was the French press' *bête noire*.

Reality or Illusion?

My own love affair with *Les Tricolores* can be traced back to 1981 while I was at King Edward's School in Bath, the year of the French Grand Slam and Codorniou's magic pirouette to send Pardo to the try line. Dad had died years before so my elder brother, Paul, was my sporting mentor and guide through my early years. He and I idolised Didier Codorniou and Jérôme Gallion. We would practise our sidesteps and passing for hours on the road in front of our house, encouraged by the great Lang Jones, our magnificent schoolteacher who lived nearby. He was a brilliant, witty and loving man who gave us boundless support and happy memories.

My adulation of France and French rugby became serious in 1986, at the age of eighteen. I didn't realise it at the time, but my decision to live there was life-forming and exposed me to the magic of *Les Tricolores*, their fans and the people from Provence. Thanks to Mme Dubarry, one of the teachers at my school in Villeneuve-les-Avignon, I joined Châteauneuf-du-Pape rugby club. This story starts in a nearby village, home to my rugby club.

It is Saturday March 15th 1986 in Châteauneuf-du-Pape, a small village better known for its wine than its rugby team, located in the *département* of the Vaucluse, 100km north of Marseille. We have just won our U20 game against Montpellier and we make our way to the centre of the village to eat, drink and watch France v England on TV. They are playing at the Parc des Princes in Paris and it is the final match of the Five Nations Championship.

The bar, one of several in the village, is near the fountain and just down the road from the famous La Mère Germaine restaurant, a local institution that is still going strong today and a perennial favourite with the local wine growers. It is warm outside and the bar is overflowing with locals drinking *pastis* and wine. The owner has reserved us some tables and we enjoy some freshly cooked *paella* and Kronenbourg 1664, our taste buds not yet sufficiently evolved to enjoy the local wines.

At the Parc des Princes, the French are dominating in the spring sunshine. Against the blunt force of England, France has the cutting edge and has already scored three tries after fifty-five minutes, but the best is yet to come.

In the last minute of the match, *Les Tricolores* break from their 22m and the majestic Érik Bonneval accelerates away covering 40m in a flash. He floats a glorious pass to the other Prince of Centres, Denis Charvet, who evades the touchline and tackler to pass inside to the powerful, bustling Philippe Sella to score his fourth consecutive try in the Five Nations and secure the Grand Slam for France.

If I were to suggest the moment when *Les Tricolores* reached their *apogée* in 1986, this is it. It is total rugby played off-the-cuff and brilliantly executed.

The bar erupts and I, the Francophile *rosbif*, suffer a lot of friendly abuse from my French friends. Their regional *accent du midi* is easy on the ear, but hard to understand, but I have no difficulty in hearing their joy.

Later that evening, as friends drive me home south towards Avignon, along those straight, plane tree-lined roads, I think about that sporting marriage of power, skill and unpredictability, and how France can seduce the rugby purist with its own version of the game. They carry in their genes the ability to run into space, pass and hit the right angles. It is instinctive and devastating for their opponents.

England lost convincingly, but that doesn't dampen my mood as we sweep through the warm, garrigue-scented countryside. In fact, I feel fantastic and lucky to be living and playing in the country.

I remember that day so clearly. Was it really so beautiful or was it an illusion? As with all sporting nostalgia, we live somewhere between the dream and reality, but I am with the dreamers. Nothing encapsulated sporting beauty more than those *Tricolores*.

These feelings and memories are the basis for this book. Meeting the players has been fascinating and a hugely rewarding experience. Their warmth of generosity has been overwhelming and reflects the old Corinthian spirit of which rugby is so proud. Thank you all for your time, openness and friendship.

So readers, please join me on my personal journey to discover France through my quixotic lens. I hope you enjoy all the memories, stories and photos about France, rugby and life.

David Beresford
March 2019

Illustration Ovalie Bell, Paris

A Map of France

FORTY YEARS OF LIVING + TRAVELLING IN FRANCE
1981-2019

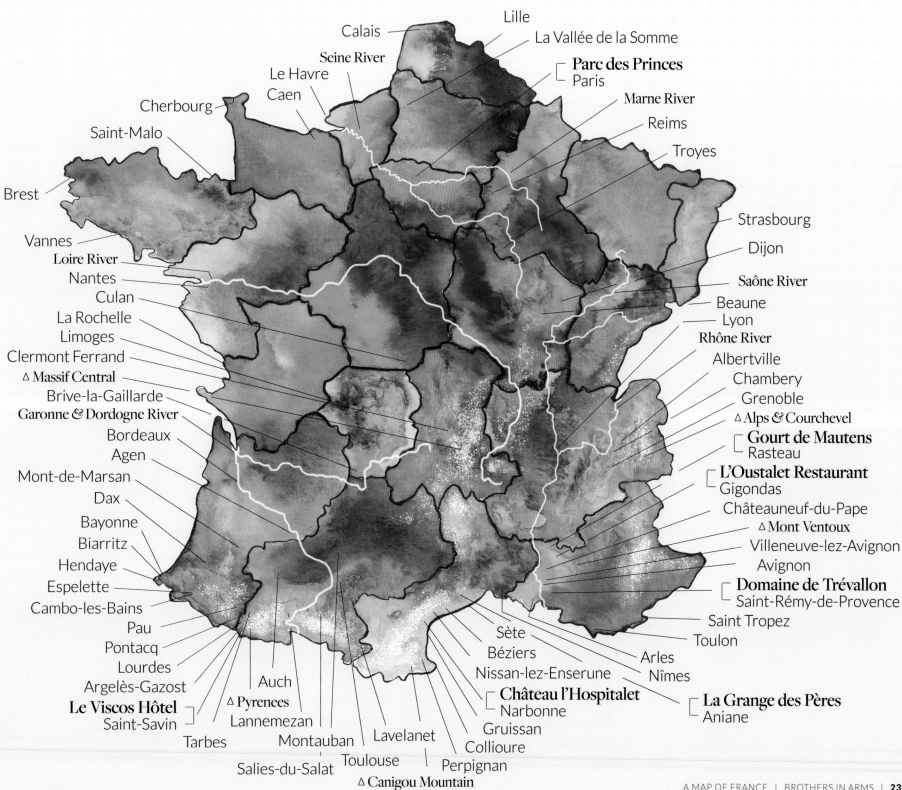

Calais
Lille
La Vallée de la Somme
Seine River
Parc des Princes
Paris
Le Havre
Marne River
Caen
Reims
Cherbourg
Troyes
Saint-Malo
Strasbourg
Brest
Dijon
Vannes
Saône River
Loire River
Nantes
Beaune
Culan
Lyon
La Rochelle
Rhône River
Limoges
Albertville
Clermont Ferrand
Chambery
△ Massif Central
Grenoble
Brive-la-Gaillarde
△ Alps & Courchevel
Garonne & Dordogne River
Gourt de Mautens
Rasteau
Bordeaux
L'Oustalet Restaurant
Agen
Gigondas
Mont-de-Marsan
Châteauneuf-du-Pape
Dax
△ Mont Ventoux
Bayonne
Villeneuve-lez-Avignon
Biarritz
Avignon
Hendaye
Domaine de Trévallon
Espelette
Saint-Rémy-de-Provence
Cambo-les-Bains
Saint Tropez
Pau
Toulon
Pontacq
Sète
Lourdes
Béziers
Arles
Argelès-Gazost
Nissan-lez-Enserune
Nîmes
Le Viscos Hôtel
△ Pyrenees
Château l'Hospitalet
La Grange des Pères
Saint-Savin
Auch
Narbonne
Aniane
Lannemezan
Gruissan
Tarbes
Montauban
Lavelanet
Collioure
Salies-du-Salat
Toulouse
Perpignan
△ Canigou Mountain

Club Abbreviations

Abbreviation	Club
AB	L'Aviron Bayonnais
Béziers	Association Sportive Béziers Hérault
Clermont Ferrand	Association Sportive Montferrandaise Clermont Ferrand
BO	Biarritz Olympique Pays Basque
Boucau	Boucau-Tarnos Stade
Castres	Castres Olympique
Lannemezan	Cercle Amical Lannemezanais
Brive	Club Athlétique Brive Corrèze Limousin
Bourgoin	Club Sportif Bourgoin-Jallieu Rugby
Aix-Les-Bains	Football Club Aix-Les-Bains Rugby
Auch	Football Club Auch Gers
Grenoble	Football Club Grenoble
Lourdes	Football Club Lourdes
Montpellier	Montpellier Hérault Rugby
R92	Racing 92
RCF	Racing Club de France
Narbonne	Racing Club de Narbonne Méditerannée
Nîmes	Rugby Club Nîmes Gard
Toulon	Racing Club Toulonnais

Abbreviation	Club
SJDL	Saint-Jean-de-Luz-Olympique Pays Basque
Pau	Section Paloise
Beaumont	Stade Beaumontois Lomagne Rugby
Hendaye	Stade Hendayais
Lavelanet	Stade Lavelanétien
Stade Montois	Stade Montois Rugby
ST	Stade Toulousain
Tarbes	Stado Tarbes Pyrénées Rugby
Hagetmau	Sport Athlétique Hagetmautien
Agen	Sporting Union Agen Lot-et-Garonne
TOEC	Toulouse Olympique Employés Club
Perpignan	Union Sportive des Arlequins Perpignanais
Bordeaux	Union Bordeaux Bègles
Carmaux	Union Sportive Carmaux
Cognac	Union Sportive Cognaçaise
US Dax	Union Sportive Dacquoise
Montauban	Union Sportive Montauban
La Tyrosse	Union Sportive Tyrosse Rugby Côte Sud
La Voulte	La Voulte Sportif Rugby

Stade de la Méditérranée in Beziers.
Photo - Pierre Carton.

Vines of Ispour (The Appellation Irouleguy).
Photo - Pierre Carton.

Basque Country

"LISTEN TO THE WIND ON THE WATER
LISTEN TO THE WAVES UPON THE SHORE
TRY TO SLEEP, SLEEP WON'T COME
JUST AS I BEGIN TO FADE

THEN I REMEMBER
WHEN THE MOON WAS FULL AND BRIGHT
I WOULD TAKE YOU IN THE DARKNESS
AND DO THE TANGO IN THE NIGHT TANGO"

FLEETWOOD MAC
TANGO IN THE NIGHT, 1987

This region covers the North Basque country in France, such as the towns of Biarritz, Bayonne, Saint-Jean-de-Luz and Espelette. It is a wonderful part of France dominated by its wild Atlantic coast. The views overlooking the Bay of Biscay are stunning – the rocky outcrops, rushing waves, wild flowers and thick, grassy dunes, all flogged by the salty winds. On a bright day, that piercing, Basque sunlight and huge sky enhance the image and your feeling of freedom.

As you travel south through Les Landes to the Basque Country, the scenery changes from pine forests and flat land into lush meadows and rolling countryside, kissed by the humid air and sunshine. It is reminiscent of the picture-perfect Jurançon, only the shapes of the houses, the oxblood and green colouring, and the Basque signs fix your location.

I've been fascinated by the Basque Country (Euskal Herria) and the Basques (Euskaldunak) for years, an indigenous ethnic group characterised by their unique language and traditions. However, my fascination and love for it goes way beyond its obvious attributes of rugby, fine food and wine, breath-taking flora, wild mountains, sumptuous coastlines and its sea, cobalt or black depending on the weather. France is blessed with those riches right across its land, as is Spain. No, what the Basque country has in abundance is mystery. And where there's mystery, there's excitement. Like Picasso's Guernica painting or da Vinci's The Last Supper, the riddles, secrets and questions keep drawing me back to look for answers. I travelled down to Bayonne, Biarritz and San Sebastian to find some.

Notre Dame bridge at Saint-Jean-Pied-de-Port
(part of the St Jacques de Compostelle way).
Photo - Pierre Carton.

I first felt this way about the Basque Country back in 1988 when I was living in Bordeaux and playing for the BEC (Bordeaux Etudiant Club). I travelled south to visit Saint-Jean-de-Luz at the height of ETA's reign of terror, not long after the 1987 massacre in Barcelona. In spite of the fear on the other side of the border, I was struck by how relaxed Saint-Jean-de-Luz was. What marked me more was the Basque language, as strange and incomprehensible as Welsh. Venture inland to the villages of Espelette, Ascain, Sare, Itzassou, St-Pée-sur-Nivelle, or many others, and you frequently hear it spoken, the villagers alternating effortlessly between French and Basque.

On the French side, the 'Northern' Basque country starts at Bayonne near the Adour river, which separates the Basques from Les Landes, that large area of pine forests to the north, and home to many a top rugby team like US Dax and Stade Montois. On the Spanish side, the 'Southern' Basque country ends at the Ebro river near Rioja, the great wine making region, and it extends as far west as Bilbao, bordering Cantabria and the Burgos province. The entire Basque region has a population and surface area of approximately 3 million across 20,000 square km. It covers seven provinces, three in France (Labourd, Basse Navarre, Soule) and four in Spain (Viscaya, Guipuzcoa, Alava and Navarra), what the locals refer to as North and South, as though it were a nation state. Its flag is green, white and red, flying proudly across the Basque homeland from Bayonne to Bilbao.

The mysteries of the Basques are legion. For years, researchers tried to identify their origin, until they realised that they had lived there all along, possibly as far back as 150,000 years. As the years went by, the Cro-Magnon people adapted to their environment and started to develop the physique we think of as typically Basque today, although these characteristics have no doubt been diluted over the years as the gene pool has diversified. However, if you travel to places like Espelette, you will still see that Basque shape – thickset, broad-shouldered, aquiline nose, long ear lobes, lantern-jawed and striking eyebrows.

Far from being an isolated land, cut off by its geographical setting, Euskal Herria has been the opposite. By welcoming people through it as a safe passage, notably the pilgrims to Santiago de Compostela, and adapting to different environments, it has managed to preserve its own identify, language and culture.

Basque is a language *isolate*. Attempts to relate it to other languages have failed. Known as Euskera, it is probably the oldest living European language and has been subject to much analysis and research in an attempt to discover its origin. Unlike nearly all other European languages, Basque is not Indo-European, which is why it looks and sounds so odd to our eyes and ears. In fact, Basque is the only surviving language of Western Europe that pre-dates the Indo-European expansion, evolving organically alongside its indigenous people. There are many theories that relate Basque to the languages spoken in Finland, Hungary, the Caucasus and the Iberian peninsula, but none has established a definitive link.

Bizarrely, in the Basque language, there is no word for Basque. The way you would identify yourself as a member of their group is to describe yourself as an Euskera speaker, or Euskaldun. Language is what defines the Basque.

Pierre Dospital, a proud Basque and fluent in his native

Bizarrely, in the Basque language,
there is no word for Basque.
The way you would identify yourself
as a member of their group is to describe
yourself as an Euskera speaker, or Euskaldun.
Language is what defines the Basque.

Traditional Basque dancing in Cambo-les-Bains.
Photo - Pierre Carton.

tongue, gave me some pointers when we met. I found out that there are no prepositions or articles, no genders, no conventional plurals, and the letters C, Ç, Q, V, W, and Y are not used in writing traditional Basque language, although they have crept in over time. Basque is also an agglutinative language, which means that multiple prefixes or suffixes can be added to a root word, be it a noun or verb, to create phrases or even sentences. Other examples of agglutinative languages are Japanese, Korean and Inuit.

For all its complexity, nearly a third of Basques speak it although the vast majority of those are in the south.

To complete the mystery, there is also a very sinister side. The Basque separatist organisation waged a violent civil war against Spanish governments for forty years, a bloody conflict that killed 800 people, the vast majority of them Spanish. Thankfully, ETA, the Basque terrorist organisation founded in 1959 during the dictatorship of General Franco (although the conflict started as far back as 1936, pre-dating ETA) declared a ceasefire in 2011 and fully committed to abandon violence in 2017 by decommissioning all its weapons.

The most remarkable thing about the Basques is their very survival. Many pre-Indo European tribes that established polities, kingdoms, empires and different republics have disappeared, but not the Basques. And while for some, globalisation and centralisation have undermined individualism, the Basques, strong as ever and determined to hold on resolutely to their identity, are bucking the trend. They have never been backward

or marginal, trying to maintain tenuous grasp on a quaint culture. They have always been forward-thinking, capable of embracing the rapid change of a world without losing their beliefs and way of life. It behaves like a united nation of seven states, but it has never been sovereign. The term 'separatist' is a weak epithet for the Basques.

Some of the best areas to visit for a summer holiday are along the coast, notably Bayonne, Biarritz and San Sebastian to enjoy the fabled Basque hospitality, food and wines, but it is worth the trip to Gernika to see the great Picasso mural and feel the history of the town, which is so central to the Basque identify.

To get there, you head west from Hendaye and into the Southern Basque country, where the road cuts through the rich, verdant pastures and hills that are peppered with steep, rocky outcrops and pine forests. The land and living space here can be so cramped with high-rise

apartment blocks, bridges, factories and railway lines all built along and on the precipitous, narrow valleys. Society is clearly organised around the limited, workable land. I was staying in San Sebastian, but continued west to Gernika for the day.

Back in 1937, Gernika had a population of 7,000, but on April 26th, the day it was attacked, that number was swollen by the weekly market where farmers flocked to the town centre to sell their produce. It has since become synonymous with war atrocities as Luftwaffe bombers, backing General Franco and supported by the Italians, dropped explosives and incendiary bombs, and strafed the fleeing population with machine-gun fire. The town was completely devastated and many civilians lost their lives.

To my ear, just the name Gernika evokes 'warning'. It must be that hard 'k': looK out, the BlitzKreig is coming...

Remarkably, the two most important symbols of Gernika, the Biscayan Assembly and the Gernika tree, both survived. This is where the Lords of Biscay and Basque politicians would meet to legislate and make decisions. It was beneath the branches of the tree where the Lords of Biscay swore to respect the Biscayan liberties and where they established a set of laws known as *'fueros'*, which granted the Basque people some autonomy. For these reasons, the Gernika tree became emblematic of Basque identity and worked as a lightning conductor for Basque independence. Today, the Spanish Basque Country enjoys many privileges of self-government.

The oak tree there today was planted in 2015. The remains of an older tree, planted in 1742, can also be found in the gardens that surround the Biscayan Assembly. This 'old tree', is the oldest one still partially standing. The first documented Gernika tree dates back to the 14th century.

As it is my natural habitat, I spent the afternoon strolling around the squares, eating *pintxos*, drinking a lovely, local wine called Bitxia Txakolina and chatting to a local barman called Txarles in my terrible Spanish. The mural of Picasso's Gernika nearby is made from ceramic tiles and a true copy of his painting. It clearly shows the extent of the tragedy that Gernika suffered on the day of the bombing.

I wanted to know more about Basque nationalism so I travelled to a small town, Hernani, a short drive from San Sebastian and a hotbed of Basque independence.

For many years, Hernani served as a source of manpower, funding and political support for Euskadi Ta Askatasuna (ETA, Basque Country and Freedom). Approximately five percent of the remaining four hundred or so ETA prisoners who are still incarcerated hail from this non-descript town.

I wandered around its streets and was struck by its vibe and friendliness. I saw and heard the optimism and partying on one street in particular where people were out in full song, spilling into the street from the bars and seemingly oblivious to the former troubles. However, perhaps it was the dark brooding skies on the day that made my antennae more sensitive, but I caught a distinct whiff of simmering tension here. Nearby and along the narrow lanes of the old town, the walls were adorned with Basque flags and large billboards displaying photos of ETA prisoners and demanding their release. ETA has moved on, renounced violence and its armed activities, but passions still run strong. Amid the new-found tranquility, there is unfinished business, no doubt, as there was and still is in Ireland, South Africa and Sri Lanka, which have all suffered their own versions of civil war.

I picked a colourful bar with tables outside and ordered an ice-cold beer. The locals spotted this outsider within seconds and before I could say *'bi garagardo mesedez'* I was locked in conversation with them. Most were pro-Basque independence but none supported the violence, and all were very happy to be living without any fear.

Oiled by some good local beers, the group expressed a resounding consensus: *"ETA didn't achieve anything in the causes it claimed. It was a guerra sucia (dirty war)".*

It was Saturday afternoon so I didn't want to spend too long discussing politics. Instead, I moved the discussion onto more familiar territory where we talked about Bilbao football, Basque rugby and where to eat in San Sebastian. I will certainly return one day and get to know the town and area far better.

I had based myself in San Sebastian so headed back to enjoy its hospitality. It was my first visit and it made a big impression – an elegant city, full of foodies enjoying its exquisite cafés, food and wine, architecture and coastline. I was only there one night, but didn't waste the opportunity to eat a marvellous medley of fresh fish at La Rampe restaurant – lightly fried squid, clams in white wine and parsley; grilled mussels, all plump, perky, salty and glistening; then firm, perfectly steamed prawns and grilled langoustines, followed by *cigalas a la plancha*, garnished simply with some local lemons. The whole experience was exquisite, head, shoulders and gills above any fish I have ever eaten.

Anyway, while the food, politics and history fascinated me, that would have to wait for my next book. I was here for more pressing reasons, namely to meet the rugby greats of this magnificent region.

Serge Blanco

BASQUE COUNTRY

"PLAYING AGAINST SOUTH AFRICA
IN 1980 WAS A BIG MOMENT FOR ME.

I ALWAYS WONDERED WHETHER
I WAS SELECTED BECAUSE I WAS
GOOD ENOUGH OR BECAUSE
I WAS OF A MAN OF COLOUR.

I THOUGHT THAT THE ONLY WAY
TO FIND OUT WAS TO GO TO SEE
WHAT WAS HAPPENING."

BORN : 31ST AUGUST 1958

CLUBS : BIARRITZ OLYMPIQUE

INTERNATIONAL CAPS : 93

POSITION : FULL-BACK, WING

GRAND SLAMS : 1981, 1987

NICKNAME : PELÉ

NOM DE GUERRE : THE BASQUE ALCHEMIST

MY VISIT TO MEET HIM : THURSDAY 23RD NOVEMBER 2017

D riving to Hendaye, south from St-Jean-de-Luz in the south west corner of France and deep into the heart of French Basque country, you exit the main road and take the wonderfully named Bretelle de Socoa that heads north-west towards the coast. Soon afterwards, you join the Route de Corniche where the Atlantic opens up in front of you, an expanse of deep, brooding blue. I raced along the coastal road in my cabriolet with Fleetwood Mac booming out from the radio, 'Listen to the wind on the water, Listen to the waves upon the shore'.

It was the 23rd of November, but the sunlight was dazzling and the temperature still 23°c. I had nothing in my diary today, except a long lunch with the great Serge Blanco. *Que la vie est belle*, I thought. This is an experience that money can't buy.

Serge Blanco scores the winning try as Australian Tommy Lawton tackles him in vain. Rugby World Cup Semi-final, 13th June 1987, Sydney, France 30 v Australia 24. *Photo - Georges Gobet, Getty Images.*

On the big day, a few kilometres along the Route de Corniche, I drove into Hendaye next to the main beach, 3km of flat and fine yellow sand. Its edges were decorated by a multitude of trees - magnolias, palm-trees, eucalyptus and oleanders, and there was an assortment of neo-Basque houses facing the sea, characterised by their sloping roofs and whitewashed frontages adorned with colourful woodwork. I called my Francophile friend, Julian, back in London to flaunt my good fortune, but went through to his voicemail where I left him a full rendition of La Marseillaise.

In the weeks preceding our meeting, I thought about what we would discuss. Of course, we would talk about rugby, but I also wanted to get to know the man. He had an inauspicious start in life losing his father at the age of two, but had transformed himself into the greatest rugby player of his generation. I am sure this wasn't down to pure talent and that his mental attributes had played a huge role – the determination, self-confidence and audacity to unleash a scintillating attack from anywhere.

I arrived and was welcomed by Serge's assistant who showed me through to his office. His friendly face and broad smile greeted me, an imposter from *la perfide Albion*, as I gave him my peace offering, a bottle of wine from the fabled Domaine de Trévallon. He took me through to his Spanish-Basque restaurant, the convivial Bodega Cidrerie - La Pinta, which adjoins his hotel-spa, where we sat down at a specially prepared table, alone in a large side room adjoining the main restaurant next to the cider barrels.

As a player, other than perhaps David Campese, Serge Blanco had no peers during his twelve years playing for France. He was that good. But post-career, in the world of *bon vivants*, it was different. I may have been an average rugby player, but he looked at me across the table and he knew, and he knew that I knew, that he had some serious competition, what some of my friends would describe as 'world-class'. Game on, I thought. We clearly both enjoyed friendship, food and wine, two epicureans ready to spend two to three hours discussing rugby, food and life.

Gallic Pride and French Love

We started with a large *plateau de charcuterie*, not French but, near enough to Serge's Basque roots - *chorizo ibérique, lomo ibérique de bellota and jambon ibérique Pata Negra grande reserve*. Spanish ham is incontestably the best in the world with a taste and structure that melts in the mouth. It was served at room temperature, saline, moist and silky smooth, its marbling adding texture and flavour. It was magnificent. He popped open a bottle of wine.

"France has the best wines but we have spread our knowledge and expertise all over the world so quality is increasing everywhere."

As he said this, he had a glint in his eye revealing his Gallic pride. As a Francophile and French wine lover, I nodded in affirmation while taking a sip.

First, I wanted to get into the meat of the discussion about rugby so I started by asking him a general question about the success of the French team in the 1980s.

"We were successful for lots of reasons – we had great players, a brilliant leader of men in Jacques Fouroux and we were great friends. You know David, we really loved each other and that continues today (he stresses the point: on s'aime réellement). And our friendship went back a long

way. Players like Codor (Didier Codorniou), Berbiz (Pierre Berbizer) and I had played France Juniors together, and Berbiz and Lolo (Laurent Rodriguez) had come from the same club, Lannemezan. Jean-Pierre Rives had a huge influence on me on my first tour with France to New Zealand in 1979. I treated that tour as a reward for my season's efforts, but Jean-Pierre taught me what it took to play for France and to win. It was a watershed and after that moment I never left the team. He is a man I really love and I don't mind saying that to him. We would have done anything for each other and we still would today.

"We should have won a lot more though, which didn't happen due to a number of factors – we were inconsistent and were a young team developing."

Serge was being polite, not seeing the point in objecting about the refereeing after all these years. However, in 1983, the French press and team were convinced about the bias of a Scottish referee in the key game against the Irish, which the Irish won, depriving France of the Grand Slam and finishing joint top. Le Monde wrote: *"The players were stitched up. It seemed to them that the referee had been much harder on their errors than the Irish tricks".*

In 1984, a welsh referee was pilloried by the French for his performance when they played Scotland for the Grand Slam and lost, Rives accusing the referee of incompetence and 'spoiling the party'.

French-Welsh relations were still sore from the previous year when Rives, Blanco and Dospital all suffered knocks and blood injuries, even though France won the match. Le Monde described the 1983 game against Wales: *"Apocalypse now... Rugby terreur".*

France won Grand Slams in 1981 and 1987 but just missed out on the Slams in 1983, 1984 and 1986.

I know, I know, I can already hear all the cries of derision out there: 'If my Auntie had bollocks, she'd be my Uncle'. All ifs and buts and maybes... As a committed Francophile, the excuses are my words, not Serge's.

Out of Africa

Ironically for Serge, a player of mixed race, he made his debut against South Africa on 8th November 1980, in the midst of apartheid, France losing by 37-15.

"Playing against South Africa was a big moment for me. I always wondered whether I was selected because I was good enough or because I was of a man of colour. I thought that the only way to find out was to go to see what was happening.

"I saw and experienced some bad things – the townships, the separate toilets and entrances - and I have very mixed feelings about the tour. When I was wearing my blazer and other clothes emblazoned with the FFR badge, I was treated like any white man. However, when I took it off and wasn't associated with the team, it was very different and people's reactions and behaviours to me changed markedly.

"I remember one situation well, when Serge Gabernet

and I went to a park where there was a bowls match - a petanque-type game. Serge (G) and I sat on a bench, transfixed by this Anglo-Saxon game. Suddenly all the players stopped and told me I couldn't sit there. It really hit me hard.

"Serge (G) wanted to leave straight away, but I said no, we needed to stay. It wasn't for very long, but it felt like a long time when people are staring at you and you can see the whites of their eyes. As soon as they started playing again, we watched for a while then stood up and left. It was important for me to leave when I was ready, not because they told to me to leave.

"It was an experience I will never forget. Even though we lost the test match, I had scored a lot of tries in the very hard three provincial games that we had won. I was an idol of all the blacks and mixed race. I said to people: I'm neither black nor white, I am of mixed race and I am a human being."

Serge travelled again to South Africa in 1982. While the team were from the Five Nations, they played under the name of the SARB Overseas XV, ostensibly for the re-opening of the Ellis Park stadium. Dominic Erbani and Serge were the sole representatives from France. Besides them, other players on the tour were Jim Renwick, Terry Holmes and Graham Price. Willie John McBride and Syd Miller were the coaches.

"I remember a few things from this tour such as the amount the British and Irish could drink yet still run like rabbits the next day. Willie Duggan was so impressive! The Irish loved boozing and smoking and would always be

puffing away before the games, and saying 'Serge come on, have a beer'! Their mentality was incredible – they gave the impression they were rubbish before the game but on the pitch they were superb.

"I remember a match I played when Errol Tobias, their only black player, intercepted a pass. I turned around to chase him and I caught him. Tobias shouted at me and was furious. Even to this day, I never understood his reaction.

"After the tour, when I returned to France, I was the first Frenchman to vow never to return or play against South Africa until the system of apartheid had been dismantled. Honestly, when I said that, I didn't realise the impact that it would have or that it would last ten years."

By this stage, we were well into a bottle of Château Haut-Selve 2012 from Graves, Bordeaux that complemented the charcuterie well – enough body and freshness to stand up to the strong flavour and cut through the marbled Iberico ham. We drank it with all the gusto of rugby fans watching *Le Crunch*. The starter was followed by a hearty 'middle' course of tomatoes and asparagus salad.

On 31st October 1992, Serge was asked to select a French Barbarians team to play South Africa in Lille. The stadium was rocking. It was an emotional event for him, ten years after his experience touring there in 1982 with the SARB Overseas XV. He had retired from playing for France but he selected the heart of the great French side from 1987. He, Benazzi and Loppy were the non-white players, and South Africa had none in their

"...I was the first Frenchman to vow never to return or play against South Africa until the system of apartheid had been dismantled. Honestly, when I said that, I didn't realise the impact that it would have or that it would last ten years."

side. Rob Jones, the Welsh scrum-half, was the only non-French player, a sole Celt among the Gauls. All were older, wiser and probably slower and heavier, but they won.

I love the footage for a number of reasons. Michel Palmier, the hit man and enforcer from Béziers and the great 1977 Grand Slam side, was sitting in the stand, sporting an oversized handlebar moustache, looking like he had just dismounted his Harley Davidson. In the changing room before the game were Jean-Pierre Rives with his blond, flowing locks, the great benefactor and rugby fan Serge Kampf and the diminutive and charismatic Jacques Fouroux.

All the quintessentially French characteristics were on show: the affection between the players, the love for Blanco, the *bises* they gave to each other, the perspiration and sheer emotion on their faces. It was the tactile, emotionally-charged France that I love.

Contrast this with the South African's *froideur* on show that day.

As for the actual game itself, there was the noise of the trumpets and drums, the look of confusion on Rob Jones' face when Blanco was giving the team talk in French at half-time, the cheap shot by the Moroccan Massif, Abdel Benazzi, on Muller when he scored, and the dynamic link play between the French forward and backs, a vestige of their greatest days.

At the RWC final in 1995 between South Africa and New Zealand, everyone remembers President Mandela and Chester Williams wearing the Springbok jersey, then the symbol of white supremacy. It was a wonderful moment in South African and Springbok history.

But Blanco, a man of mixed race, had beaten them to it in the 1992 French Barbarians game. After the game in Lille, he swapped jerseys with the late James Small and ran around the pitch wearing the Springbok jersey, celebrating both his retirement and the emancipation of non-whites in the country he had just played.

"The Springboks were very unhappy about losing while we partied hard into the night. The French Barbarians arrived late at the post-match dinner because we had been singing in the changing rooms. Just as we arrived, the Springboks were passing us to leave.

"But what a diplomatic incident! We enjoyed the post-match dinner on our own. Jacques was on brilliant form, performing a one-man show and appointing each player to a fictitious FFR position. Jean Condom, who never said much, was appointed as head of communication! It was Jacques at his best.

"But the South African Federation back home was so embarrassed that they sent me an official invitation to visit them. I said I would go but only on the condition that I could visit the townships, schools and villages to see the kids. The Federation agreed so I went back in 1993 with my wife and father-in-law. We were welcomed like heroes. I saw many old friends – Du Plessis, Gerber, Botha. These people are good friends who I invited to celebrate my jubilee. Unfortunately, I didn't play enough against them because of apartheid.

"Visiting South Africa was a great moment for me. We went to the townships to see the kids. I remember a big group of blacks came to greet the delegation when we arrived and they all said to me: 'We are here to thank you. When we needed you most, you helped us. You were the first person

to say, back in 1982, that you wouldn't play against South Africa again while apartheid existed'.

"When they told me that, it touched me greatly. It was a big thing back in 1982 to tell the French Federation that I would no longer play for France against South Africa. They could have just carried on and not picked me.

"The South African Federation held a dinner where I was the main guest and there were about five hundred people there. I wore a white DJ, next to all their black DJs, and they loved it!

"Those trips to South Africa marked me greatly and the 1993 trip in particular was an exceptional part of my life."

Our Best Enemy

The main *plat du jour* arrived. It was *daurade à la plancha* (sea bream), all plump and shimmering with salty freshness, garnished with some olives and sliced potatoes that had been lightly oiled. It was the size of a small child but Serge and I weren't going to share with anyone else. We tucked in, squeezing words out in the short periods between ingestion.

I asked him about what it was like playing the English.

"They were our best enemies," he replied, an expression I would hear a lot on my travels.

"I found the English arrogant and aloof when we played against them. I never felt the English were genuine. I didn't make many friends, although I did have friendships with players from the other nations. We were brought up like that. The press always built our matches up and we had all this history with Joan of Arc and the hundred years' war. It was drilled into us that we had to beat the English.

"In 1991, for the RWC quarter-final against England at the Parc des Princes, Stuart Barnes told me that there was an 'an anti-Blanco plan' and I was specifically targeted by the English under the high ball. That was my excuse for punching Heslop after his late tackle on me! Champ caught him too. I don't blame the English, but I do blame the New Zealand referee for not protecting me. 1991 was my biggest disappointment in rugby."

When I spoke to Will Carling, he confirmed that England had a plan to target Serge:

"At the first scrum, we planned to not engage and for the scrum to reset, and for our players to look at Serge and point to where the ball was going. We knew that would intimidate them. After the first scrum, the ball went up, Serge caught it and got trampled on badly by the whole England pack. It really set the tone for the rest of the match. Skins and Champ were already nose-to-nose in the early exchanges and the atmosphere was electric.

"Then, after Serge hit Heslop, the referee Bishop spoke to

the French. All their players were shaking with rage. I went back to my team and said 'they're on the edge'. That is where we needed them to be. We wanted them fighting, not playing rugby."

Superhuman

Serge didn't talk much about his own *grandeur* so I will do it for him. Guided by his natural instinct for finding space and making the right decision, he would set rugby stadia alight with his pace, guile and sparkling rugby skills. There are several videos on YouTube that show his flair, but one twenty minute montage in particular sets my heart racing. It shows him in his full glory and encapsulates all his talent that made him the greatest player of his generation – vision, pace, power, chips, running lines and support play. He could do everything.

Regarded as one of the greatest players ever to play the game, he was nicknamed Pelé, after a British journalist watched him play for France B in 1978 when he scored most of the points on his own. Fast, elusive, powerful and naturally gifted, he set rugby pitches on fire around the world between 1976-1992.

I sought out the views and memories of some of his teammates and opponents. The veneration for Serge was universal.

Patrice Lagisquet reminisced with great passion about playing with him:

"His pace was extraordinary, being able to just glide away from the opposition. You couldn't see him accelerate because his legs didn't go any faster, he simply lengthened his stride. It was very deceptive and it took me a while to anticipate it. And he could chip the ball over the opposition at full pace, the ball rebounding into his hands! 'How does he do that?' I used to ask myself. His mental side was very impressive too. If he made a mistake, he just put it behind him. It wouldn't stop him from trying something else as daring immediately. In team sports, the greatest players always find a solution – a pass, kick, try, break, whatever - and he was a truly great player."

When I went to see Nick Farr-Jones at his offices in Sydney, he was smiling when recalling Serge's 100m try against them in the 3rd test in 1990:

"He simply picked up the ball on his try line and ran the length of the field to score, outsprinting our quickest player, Ian Williams. It was a fabulous try scored by a genius. What's more, a couple of hours before, he'd been puffing away on his cigarettes! He was superhuman."

I chatted to Richard Pool-Jones, the former England international, who played with Serge in Biarritz:

"When you played with him, he was so good that he could transform you from team mate to spectator on the pitch. You never knew what he would do or where he would run, but when he was on song, he was fabulous, playing on pure instinct. Franck Mesnel would say, 'When he runs on snow he leaves no trace'.

"In club games he could be ordinary, and in warm-ups he would be at the back with the props as though he didn't have the required fitness, which isn't surprising as he smoked forty plus cigarettes per day! But when it mattered and in the knock out stages of the competitions, he was on a different level.

"Serge controlled everything. When I was signing for Biarritz, I thought I should have been speaking to their President but Pierre Villepreux said to me, 'No, speak to Serge, he controls everything'. He had an aura about him, which is natural for the best player of his generation. When I arrived for the first time in Biarritz, Serge met me at the airport. We were walking through it and he said calmly to me, 'Just stay close to me, I'll make you famous'. He was so reassuring."

Serge Blanco, 15th March 1986, Paris, France.
France 29 v England 10.
Photo - Bob Thomas Sports Photography, Getty Images.

Serge scored and was involved in many wonderful tries but three stand out for me: First the try in the corner to win the RWC Semi-Final in 1987; second the Saint-André try that Serge started against England in the 1991 Five Nations game; and third, that try he scored from his own try line against Australia in the third test in 1990, aged thirty-two. But there are thirty-eight tries to choose from so fill your boots!

He had exceptional athletic qualities. He was tall, slender and powerful, and his running was feline. He could sense space and the slightest gap, and would accelerate away effortlessly, smoothly hitting his top gear. The only other player I saw who could change gear as imperceptibly and as gracefully as Serge was Jerry Guscott.

Other players told me that his warm-up exercises before matches, whether mental or physical, were minimal. Phlegmatic and seemingly impervious to pressure, he knew he could rely on his outstanding natural ability. He loved his cigarettes, charcuterie, wine, a *digestif* and the good life, and that, minus the cigarettes, has continued after his rugby career. He was everything I loved about the amateur era.

Humble Background

We know about his rugby career but to understand Serge, you have to understand the man and where he came from.

Born in Caracas in 1958 to a Basque mother from Biarritz and a Venezuelan father who was a police inspector,

he came to France aged two after his father died.

"I have no memory of him at all. From photos he was a good-looking man with a moustache, and was a police officer in Caracas."

With no brothers or sisters, his mother, Odette (née Darrigrand), came back to Biarritz in 1960 carrying a young mixed-race child. They lived in a small three-roomed apartment with Odette's parents where there shared a bedroom, and the same bed up to twelve years old.

"We didn't have any money and we had no bathroom, so I would go to the local showers in Biarritz twice a week.

"For a long time, each evening my grandmother would heat the water up on the stove and I would use it to wash. That was life back then, we lived very modestly."

"There was lots of work around but you had to move around to find it. But all work was and is honourable work – that is something I really learnt when I was growing up."

Odette worked tirelessly to give Serge the best possible upbringing. He understood the value of hard work and money, and this probably explains his determination and aspiration to succeed in whatever he does.

Having lost my own father very young, I know what it is like to be raised by your mum with whom you have an unbreakable bond and who is the single most important person in your life. Her subjugation to your happiness, her utter devotion and sacrifice can't be over-estimated. In Serge's case, he was the only child so that singular love was focused on him alone.

"At the end of my career, I wanted to take mum back to Venezuela to rediscover a part of our old life and perhaps our old house, but mum died shortly after I had finished playing and I didn't see the point in doing it without her. Mum didn't really talk much about that part of her life. Like a lot of people of that time, she was discreet and didn't really express her feelings. She lived in the present, which consisted of living and bringing up a kid."

Was there a father figure in your life? I asked this question self-indulgently, wanting to know how others dealt with the loss of their father.

"Dominique Perez, my first football coach, an exceptional man who would pick me up and take me home after every match. On the rugby side, Michel Celaya was my spiritual father, but I struggled to 'tutois' him, even when I was an adult!" ('Tu' is the informal version of 'you' in French).

"I was too scared to go and anyway I didn't want to leave my mum." Football's loss was rugby's gain.

A supremely gifted athlete and sportsman, his gym teacher wanted Serge to go to Nantes football club to become a professional, but he rejected the offer, preferring to stay in his beloved Basque country. At that point he changed sports and started playing rugby for Biarritz in 1975.

"I was too scared to go and anyway I didn't want to leave my mum."

Football's loss was rugby's gain.

Leaving school at seventeen, he started work at Dassault as an assembly line worker where he stayed for eight years during which time he graduated from rugby novice to international. There was a world of difference between playing in front of 50,000 fans in Dublin, Paris, Edinburgh, Cardiff or London, and going back to work on the assembly line on a Monday morning.

In 1983, he swapped oil and metal for liquor and glass, joining Jean-Pierre Rives at Pernod, which benefitted from his intoxicating mix of fame and charm, perfect for a large consumer brand. This sustained him during his rugby career, but it didn't fulfil his ambition to become a successful businessman.

In 1991 as his career came to an end, he opened his first health spa. Twenty-five years later, his sporting and commercial tentacles have reached and continue to reach into many businesses and projects – a three-star hotel (Hotel Ibaia), four-star hotel/spa complex (Hotel Thalasso) and Spanish/Basque restaurant (Le Pintos) all based in Hendaye; a five-star hotel (Le Brindos) in Anglet just outside Biarritz; and there are around sixty franchises selling his Serge Blanco clothing range. He has no active involvement in the business now even though it still sports his name.

"If the right opportunities come up, there might be other new projects in and around Biarritz too. Let's see."

In spite of his humble upbringing, he clearly has a formula that works, whether in property or textiles or consumer brands.

Latin American Passion

Serge is a passionate man, driven by the Basque and South American blood pumping through his veins. He was a creator on the pitch and that creativity and determination has never left him, whether in rugby or business. When we discuss rugby, I discern his balanced view on both the club and country debate, understanding the interests of both. Having worked on both sides of the fence – for the club and league, and also the Federation, he is steeped in the Corinthian values of amateur, elite rugby but also understands the needs of professionalism. Perhaps that has made his post rugby career difficult because he is constantly torn between sometimes conflicting needs.

In business, just like when he played rugby, he understands when to take a risk and can see things others can't. He is a very impressive businessman, networker and personality.

However, success can be more dangerous than failure and the ripples can travel further. Those of us in business understand the perils of working closely with friends, and Serge has had strained relationships with a number of them over the years.

A young Serge playing for France B in 1979.
Photo - Presse Sports.

Patrice Lagisquet explained to me: *"He is a very generous and kind man but he doesn't like confrontation and can be a bit clumsy when giving bad news to those he loves. But don't confuse this clumsiness with a lack of love or generosity. He loves the people he played rugby with dearly. We have all known each other for over twenty-five years and we would do anything for each other. One example of Serge's kindness sticks in my mind. I remember him doing some commentary for the Rugby World Cup and he simply told the TV station to send all his fees to my association called Chrysalide (an association that supports parents and kids with handicapped kids). He just did it without telling anyone except the TV company. That is the mark of the man's character and generosity."*

Whatever those reasons and the apparent clumsiness of some dealings, I hope any bruised friends reconnect with him soon. Life is way too short to fall out with life-long friends when you have suffered and celebrated so much together. These ex-players are all great, if imperfect, men, and the fraternity that was built over so many years should last a lifetime.

For all his success on and off the pitch, he strikes me as a simple, local lad from humble origins, and I don't think that human imprint will ever be effaced. I wrote down the following descriptors after I met him: warm, friendly, humorous, open, easy-going, generous, big-hearted, grounded, loving, committed. He was so keen to know that I had been well received by all the players. The image projected by France and French rugby is very important to him.

I loved spending time with him. He took time to chat, build a rapport and answer my questions, all over a wonderful lunch and much laughter. He is a man who clearly loves people and life.

Fat Cats

The lunch was over. We ordered a couple of coffees and talked more, keen to prolong the postprandial discussion for as long as possible (well I was anyway). After a fine, long lunch, we sat there, relaxed and lavishly assimilated like a couple of plump, fat cats. Life was good. This is what they must do every day, I thought.

I thanked him for his time and wished him well, searching for any excuse to come back to see him. As I left the restaurant, my head was giddy with food, wine and wistful affection for Serge's magnificent rugby skills. What a player he was. What a man he is.

I ambled to a nearby cafe where I stayed for a few hours, making calls to my friends Knoxy, Julian and Will in England to pass the time, and slowly drinking a large bottle of St Pelegrino to rehydrate. Basking in the sunshine and rallied by a couple of espresso coffees, I quickly recovered, the benefit of years of experience.

I travelled back to Bayonne via Saint-Jean-de-Luz, a place I have always loved. Back in 1988, when I lived in Bordeaux and played rugby for the BEC, I met a couple of brothers, a prop and a hooker, from Saint-Jean-de-Luz who were studying at Bordeaux University. We discussed the possibility of me playing for

them one day, which of course never materialised. But I also remember them telling me how few restaurants would host their infamous *3ème mi-temps* due to their festivities of excess, which consisted of stripping off down to their undercrackers, covering themselves in olive oil and sumo wrestling as 'entertainment' for the other guests. This was all part of the *bonhommie* and *fraternité* that went on at their Basque club! *Vive le rugby!*

Jean Condom

BASQUE COUNTRY

"AT THE BATTLE OF NANTES,
WE WON THE TOSS AND KICKED OFF,
GIVING THEM THE BALL.
WE DECIDED TO ADOPT SOME OLD
SCHOOL RULES AND SMASH THEM
AT THE RUCK. WE PULVERISED THEM.
THAT SET THE TONE FOR THE WHOLE,
BRUTAL GAME, AND WE WON."

BORN : 15TH AUGUST 1960

CLUBS : BOUCAU-TARNOS STADE, BIARRITZ OLYMPIQUE

INTERNATIONAL CAPS : 62

POSITION : SECOND ROW

GRAND SLAMS : 1981, 1987

NOM DE GUERRE : THE SILENT ASSASSIN

MY VISIT TO MEET HIM : FRIDAY 24TH NOVEMBER 2017

I tracked Jean Condom down via Pascal Ondarts who seems to know everyone and is a central pillar of both the Basque and French rugby community. The day before I met him at Pascal's hotel, I spoke to Sean Fitzpatrick who said, *"Ah, Jean, please say hi and thank him for the twenty-six stitches he gave me!"*

I always thought of Jean as a quiet guy with an amusing last name. After all, you could never forget the famous banner at an Ireland v France game in Dublin in 1985 that read: *"Our Willie (Anderson) is bigger than your Condom"*. But as I discovered, he was indeed a very tough man, a silent assassin on the pitch who could compete with the most dogged of opponents. He was a great example of the Jekyll and Hyde personality that characterises so many sportsmen – as hard as nails on the pitch, but gentle, modest and quiet off it.

I didn't have the balls to call Jean 'The Silent Assassin' to his face, probably because he is very big and it was our first meeting, but I think that descriptor is an accurate term of respect for this man mountain. He was a colossus, both metaphorically and physically, for this great French side, a rock-solid team mate and a towering presence.

Rumours abound that it was Jean who, allegedly and inadvertently, tore open Wayne Shelford's scrotum in the Battle of Nantes in 1986. Ouch. But Wayne knows who the culprit was (I'll tell you later). Someone else thinks it was Garuche. Someone else thinks it was Érik Bonneval (knowing Érik, that is clearly nonsense!). All of them deny it. In fact, everyone denies everything. These things happen in the blink of an eye, the heat of the battle, the maelstrom of a *mêlée*. We may never know.

Ironically, it is the word 'silent' that was Jean's stand-out attribute. He went about his work with extraordinary humility and quiet determination, and this is exactly how he came across when I met him at Pascal Ondart's Hotel Loreak for a coffee at *La Table de Robert*, the high table where I would spend so much time talking, drinking and lunching with Pascal and other players over the following months.

My memory of Jean was as an ever-dependable and unfussy player who delivered consistently for France, what the French would call the '*poutre*' of the team, literally translated as the 'beam' or 'girder'. He certainly was an ever-present rock at the heart of the French pack. I don't remember him fighting or shouting but he

I didn't have the balls to call Jean 'The Silent Assassin' to his face, probably because he is very big and it was our first meeting...

could definitely hurt you, as Sean Fitzpatrick discovered! That calm exterior belied a toughness beneath. His weight and strength gave the scrum great solidity and all the French props raved about him. But he also had great hands, a deftness of touch and natural strength. He would have excelled in the modern game too. He is precisely the sort of person you want next to you in the trenches when the going gets tough because he was so steadfast, resilient and uncompromising.

Pelote Basque or Rugby?

Jean was born just north of the Basque Country in Les Landes where he played for Boucau at Stade Piquessary for the first six years of his career and it was while there that he received his first twenty or so caps. Boucau has never had the status of BO or AB in the Basque Country or US Dax or Stade Montois in Les Landes, but back then, it was an outstanding club that produced some top players such as Jean, Jean Michel Yanci and Henri Gaye.

The last two were notable prop forwards who were revered throughout the first division, but they chose to stay at their more modest clubs rather than seek fame elsewhere.

These great, but nowadays lesser-known clubs, are legendary throughout the length and breadth of France, and there were so many of them, such as US Dax, Stade Montois, La Tyrosse, Carmaux and La Voulte to name but a few. All are a vestige of the romantic days of French rugby, when there were around eighty clubs from the towns and villages competing in the championship. Both Pascal Ondarts and Jean Condom talk with great reverence about Boucau and Hagetmau that were also just up the road. Both provided many teammates in the Côte Basque provincial side that used to play against the top touring sides. Hagetmau is where the late, great Alain Lansaman played, someone who Pascal and Laurent Rodriguez both talk a lot about, stressing his qualities as a man, player and figure of the community.

"In spite of its brutality, I like to think that the sporting principles of rugby still applied!"

Jean told me about his conversion to rugby at Boucau from pelote basque:

"Like so many kids back then, I played pelote basque until I was thirteen years old when my science teacher suggested I play rugby. Dad resisted for a few years but when I was about sixteen, he let me play! I combined both for a while until my hand couldn't take the bare-hand version of the game anymore."

The Battle of Nantes

His first cap against Romania in 1982 was an inauspicious start for him and for the other luminaries who had their debuts that same day (Sella, Estève, Camberabero and Chadbech) as it was France's first ever defeat against them. However, it also revealed the genius of Fouroux as four of these five players would go on and establish themselves as regular internationals and be picked for the inaugural World Cup in 1987.

"It was the force and strength of character of Fouroux that made the team. He was such a great leader and knew how to motivate us. We played and partied hard together, and he usually picked the best team, not necessarily the best players."

'I remember that week before the battle of Nantes when it was a 'now or never' moment for Jacques and many of the players. The Rugby World Cup was happening the following year and we all wanted to go. At the time, we didn't know if there would be another one so we had to get on that plane."

"It was a terrible week for all of us before Nantes. After the defeat against the All Blacks in Toulouse on the first Saturday, Jacques was up against it with the press, being lambasted at every turn. We had to win the second test the following Saturday. It was do-or-die.

"So, Jacques' response was to give us so much shit and make our lives hell. We told him he needed to calm down and his response was: 'No, you need to go and calm the All Blacks down!'. He brutalised us all week and made some players cry. We were told what to eat, what not to eat, how to behave, and we trained our bollocks off. But the effect of all this was that we were incredibly motivated to show him that he was wrong about us, that we weren't weak and that we could beat the All Blacks.

"At the kick-off, we won the toss and kicked off, giving them the ball. We decided to adopt some old school rules and smash them at the ruck. We pulverised them. That set the tone for the whole, brutal game, and we won. In fact, I think it set the tone for the following one to two years when we won the Grand Slam and reached the RWC final in 1987.

"In spite of its brutality, I like to think that the sporting principles of rugby still applied! For example, I remember we stamped, raked and punched the All Blacks the whole match. But there was a moment when the All Blacks did the same to us. They smashed us and Pascal was left wounded on the floor. Gary Whetton stopped and extended his hand to help Pascal up. That really marked with me. I thought 'big respect'."

I spoke to Gary Whetton, who won fifty-eight caps for the All Blacks, about Nantes and playing against Jean.

"Nantes wasn't a violent game but it was brutal. The French had a lot to play for, having lost against us the previous weekend, and the stakes were raised with the inaugural World Cup taking place the following year in 1987. They came at us with everything and they always lifted themselves when they played us. Back then, French rugby was at its best when they combined their Latin free spirit of French flair with their hard-nosed pack, and Condom was right in the middle of it for years. He was quiet but a hard man who always delivered."

I popped down to Sydney on business in October 2018 and took the opportunity to meet Peter FitzSimons and Nick Farr-Jones. Peter played for Brive for four years so knew Jean very well, and vice versa. Jean told me the story of the tests in 1990 in Australia:

"We targeted Peter in those tests because he was always talking to the media, saying that France would concede fifty points, and during a reception at the French embassy, he continued to wind us up. So, Jacques decided to use Peter's comments to motivate us. Jacques loved boxing so he played one of Mike Tyson's boxing matches on a loop before the game, the one where he knocks out Joe Frazier's son Marvis in thirty seconds!"

I also spoke to Wade Dooley about his memories of playing against Jean.

"When I first played for England, we just couldn't beat France. It took me until the 5th game before we won. Up until 1989, they had this immense, powerful pack with players like Rodriguez, Garuet, Champ, Ondarts, Dintrans, Dubroca and Condom. Condom was a quiet man who never let them down, and never caused any trouble. From 1989, many of these experienced players were towards the end of their careers, and they chopped and changed their selection, which meant that I didn't lose to France again between 1989 to 1992.

"I never thought Jean spoke English so we didn't really build a relationship off the pitch. The English and French teams would be mixed in together with their opposite number when we played at Twickenham but the communication didn't get beyond a quick 'bonjour' and toast. And when we played in Paris, then teams would be on separate tables!

"However, I realised Jean's English was much better when Serge Blanco selected me to play in his testimonial in Biarritz for a World XV along with players like David Campese, Danie Gerber, John Jeffrey and Naas Botha, against Berbizier's French squad. We were on the pitch before the game and I heard this voice behind me speaking English with a French accent. I turned around to discover it was Jean! He never offered me that level of English fluency! And of course, I was rubbish at French.

"The other thing I remember about the game was the pre-match announcements. The stadium was packed and one-by-one the players' names were read out as we stood in a line. The French spectators screamed their appreciation for Campo, John Jeffrey, Serge, Naas and all the others. Until my name was read out. Mine was followed by a cacophony of hisses and boos! JJ said to me, 'F**king hell, they don't like you, do they?' Serge apologised but I took it as a compliment. France and England always had a love-hate relationship but we had immense respect for each other. After that testimonial game, I went back to meet my wife and kids at the smart hotel we were staying in. We were due to be heading north to a campsite but the manager, who treated us like kings, offered us a further three nights free, which of course we took up! Being from Blackpool, I sat down to dinner that night and planned on ordering a cheap bottle of wine from the 20-300 € list but Campo joined us and ordered a 300 € bottle. That was vintage Campo back then!"

Jean Condom Five Nations Rugby - France v Wales.
7th February 1987 Paris. *Photo - Mark Leech, Getty Images.*

Love and War

I asked Jean about the other second rows he played
with and against.

*"The toughest French opponents were Sam Revailler,
Jean-François Imbernon and Michel Palmié because
they were tough, hard and knew how to dominate
an opponent and win.*

*"While that team in the 1980s really loved each other,
we were also very competitive and we all had a very strong
winning mentality. I remember playing in a pool game
against Lourdes in 1987 to qualify for the play-offs in the
championship. It took place just before the RWC. Myself,
Haget, Ondarts and Blanco were up against Garuet and
Armary, all teammates in the French side. But we knocked
ten bells out of each other. We were bloodied from all the
fighting, but it was like that back then. After the match,
we had drinks and dinner and partied the night away.
The next day we all headed to la Mongie to train with
the French squad. That was fraternité in action."*

Coffee was over and Jean had to get back to his day job.
I was given a fascinating insight into the French squad,
and Jacques Fouroux's motivational methods, as well
as into Jean's character. Next, I was meeting Pascal
Ondarts, the teak-tough Basque prop.

Pierre Dospital

BASQUE COUNTRY

THESE SEEMINGLY ORDINARY PLACES
ARE STEEPED IN HISTORY AND HAVE
A MAGIC ABOUT THEM. WAITING FOR
PIERRE TO ARRIVE, I SAT THERE IMAGINING
ALL THE GREAT PLAYERS, STORIES
AND MOMENTS OF FRIENDSHIP WHICH
WERE FORMED ON THE PITCH AND IN HERE.
THIS IS WHAT JEAN-PIERRE RIVES MEANS
WHEN HE SAYS: "WE PLAYED RUGBY
LIKE WE LIVED LIFE".

BORN : 15TH MAY 1950

CLUBS : L'AVIRON BAYONNAIS

INTERNATIONAL CAPS : 24

POSITION : LOOSE AND TIGHT HEAD PROP

GRAND SLAMS : 1981

NICKNAME : DOXPI

NOM DE GUERRE : THE BASQUE BARITONE

MY VISIT TO MEET HIM : SATURDAY 9TH JUNE 2018

I had struggled to get hold of Pierre probably because he didn't trust the English telephone number on his phone each time I called or texted him. I didn't blame him. He had spent much of the 1980s twisting and torturing his English adversaries, so why on earth would an Englishman want to speak to him, and vice versa?

I asked his great mate and fellow Basque, Pascal Ondarts, whose generosity towards this unknown Englishman knew no bounds, to facilitate an intro. It worked. Pierre called me back, but I was on a cycling trip to Spain so I couldn't see him this time. Ah well, I smiled, I'll have to come back to the Basque Country for a third trip. The desire was strong and the logistics would be simple enough; it was just a question of seeking yet more approval from my patient wife that worried me... but only marginally. I trusted my powers of persuasion to convince her.

I planned to meet Pierre on Saturday 9th June, and was due to take the train or plane from Paris to Biarritz on the evening of the 8th. This was before I received an invitation that I couldn't refuse from my great friend Bertrand Baret: *"David, 8pm Friday 8th June, dinner with Hugo Denoyer, our place in Paris"*. Those who know me know that I can resist everything but temptation, and this was irresistible. My trip to meet Doxpi would have to be delayed by twenty-four hours.

Bert and I go back a long way, to 1991 to be precise, when we both worked at Andersen Consulting in Albertville for the 1992 Winter Olympic Games. We had done a lot together – I'd skied with him all over the Savoie mountains, been a witness at his wedding, helped organize his stag party in the salacious districts of Paris, lived with him in Albertville and Paris and spent hours in restaurants, bars and various dens of iniquity in Albertville, Courchevel, Méribel, Tignes, Val d'Isere and Paris. I knew he and his gorgeous wife Anne would host a magnificent party in their beautiful house in Saint-Cloud, on the west side of Paris near the Bois de Boulogne. How could I resist this offer? Exactly, I couldn't.

The downside was that I had to rearrange my travel plans and catch the early flight from Orly airport to Biarritz on the Saturday morning, and be in Espelette to meet Pierre by 11am. I knew I wasn't going to get much sleep and that my love for a big party, late night, fine wine and cocktails meant that I might not wake up in time. Nevertheless, I was happy to take the risk.

What raised the stakes even higher was that Jean Courcelle-Labrousse, another great friend and godfather to my twin boys, with his lovely wife, Charlotte, were coming to Bert's party too. Now, Jean is hard core. Brought up near Montluçon in Le Berry in the centre of France, he is a man of the *terroir* where hunting, farming and consuming fine food and wine are de rigueur. He excels at all of the above. Anyway, there isn't anything else to do there other than create mischief.

Jean and I shared a house near Caen for nine months in 1991 during which time I put on 20kg and averaged four hours sleep a night. Along with everyone from the client's office, we would lunch for two hours every day at a restaurant called L'Equitation, head back to the office, take a postprandial dose at our desks for an hour or two, and work until around 8pm. Jean and I, and a few carefully selected others, would then head out to Le Paquebot, a wonderful restaurant in the old part of Caen. We would tuck into *canapés* and *aperitifs* before heading upstairs for a sumptuous, Michelin-starred dinner, accompanied by old Bordeaux from first and second growths, long before the prices were inflated by investors, collectors and the growing middle classes from China.

Anyway, where was I? Ah yes, back to the dinner in Paris. For those who don't know him, Hugo Desnoyer is a well-known butcher and meat supplier to the best restaurants in France – an amazing roster of Michelin-starred chefs and bistro owners. He grew up in Mayenne but wasn't strong at school so he won an apprenticeship with a local butcher and worked his butt off to achieve the success he enjoys today. Clearly determined, he also has a great business sense and knows how to convert hard work into cash, a great skill that many people don't have. He is a real character and fascinating individual, in the style of Gordon Ramsay – funny, quick, direct, sweary, impatient, charismatic and charming.

It was a warm summer's evening and the dining table was set outside in Bertrand and Anne's beautiful, mature garden where the lawn was expertly trimmed, the dry-stone wall was adorned with plump, yellow roses and the peonies were releasing a sweet, citrusy perfume. It was the epitome of Parisian chic. The pre-dinner drinks of Champagne, G&T and cocktails flowed, lubricating my mind and enhancing both my verbosity and fluency in French. The refreshments were accompanied by a mouth-watering assortment of *canapés*, which were of such finger-licking splendour that I had to fight the urge to eat everything on the server's plate. Hugo entertained the guests with his stories and one liners, invariably mocking the English and our food, all in good humour of course:

"Does *ze Engleesh* still boil *ze* chickens and vegetables to destruction?"

Next came his pièce de résistance. His *entrecôte* (rib eye) and *bavette* (Skirt) steak were beautifully cooked, tender, beefy and textured. We raided Bert's cellar and drank him dry of Château Branaire-Ducru 2005 from Bordeaux and various other burgundy wines, the growers and vintages escaping my memory.

Most people had left by 2am but the hard core of Bert, Anne, Alain, Sophie and I stayed up for a late night *digestif* of Japanese whiskey. At 3am, we decided to call it a night. It was two hours before the taxi was arriving to pick me up and take me to the airport. Just enough time to take a power nap...

It was a very painful trip. Exhausted and hot, I thought I must be suffering from male menopause, but then remembered that this is what I always feel like after a skinful. My body was struggling to eliminate all the toxins from the night before. But, more importantly, I arrived in Biarritz bang on time and hired the car to head to Espelette to meet Doxpi.

The Code of Life

I turned the radio and realised that France were about to play the All Blacks in the first test. I stopped off in a village to buy a coffee and some breakfast for some much-needed caffeine and carbs to keep me going. God must be Basque I thought for it was the perfect café: strong coffee, fresh croissants and large TV screen, unencumbered by other customers. I could sit right in front and focus on the game. There were no crying kids, or vacuum cleaners or loud groups of people. France lost, damn it.

At half time, I headed to Espelette. I was meeting Pierre at his eponymous bar and restaurant, Chez Doxpi Trinquet, which has seen many a party and heard many a Basque song. These seemingly ordinary places are steeped in history and have a magic about them. Waiting for Pierre to arrive, I sat there imagining all the great players, stories and moments of friendship that were formed on the pitch and in here. This is what Jean-Pierre Rives meant when he said: *"We played rugby like we lived life. For the code of rugby should be the code of life. I have so many memories in my soul. I don't need the physical things. It is the memories that make me happy".*

All the players reflected the same sentiments – you built your life around your teammates, as much off the pitch as on it. You had a bond of loyalty, respect and friendship with them that would last forever.

When I met Pierre about 11.30am, I was struck by being in the presence of yet another great Basque front row forward. What is it about the Basques that they can produce men of such force and power? Jean Iracabal (AB), Jean-Louis Azarete (SJDL), André Darrieussecq (SJDL, BO), Jean-Louis Ugartemendia, Michel Urtizverea (SJDL), Pierre Dospital (AB), Pascal Ondarts (BO), Jean-Michel Gonzalez (AB and BO), Grégoire Lascubé (Bordeaux). The list of wonderful Basque names goes on.

Pierre was one of France's greatest front row forwards, carrying on the Basque tradition of producing strong and fearless men of granite. He was on the bench during the 1977 Grand Slam season, but then cemented his position

between 1980-85 and was part of the glorious 1981 Grand Slam winning side under Jean-Pierre Rives.

Pierre has a friendly, big smile and is quite tall, with grey hair and chiselled features. Like Pascal, he is broad chested and stocky, and looks fit and healthy, in spite of the fags that he was puffing on. Old habits die hard! What was clear was that he is obviously Basque – the eyes, cheeks, chin and nose collectively declaring a Basque of *pur sang*, just like his mate Pascal Ondarts.

He could see I was struggling from the night before.

"David, would you like a coffee, beer or pastis to help you? I think you need a 'hair of the dog', perhaps." He was grinning and knew exactly how much I was suffering.

You can't kid a kidder I thought. He was a man who had played five hundred times for L'Aviron Bayonnais. I quickly tried to calculate just how many beers and wines and *pastis* he would have drunk in his career, not to mention the next day 'antidote', but my brain wasn't computing fast enough that morning. I simply concluded 'a lot'.

I knew Pierre loved a good night out in Paris in his heyday. When I met Hugo MacNeill, he told me how Pierre and Ginger McLoughlin, the former Irish prop, would spend hours together partying after France – Ireland internationals, neither able to speak their opposite number's language. Only the lingo of mutual love and respect, oiled by booze, could facilitate the communication and it worked perfectly!

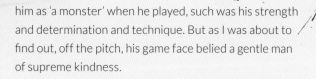

> I plunged a handful of ice into the glass and sipped it slowly, the glacial liquid soothing my throat like a honeyed lozenge. In spite already being outside in the pouring rain with only a large awning to protect us, the chilled *pastis* still reduced my body temperature to somewhere approaching normal.

him as 'a monster' when he played, such was his strength and determination and technique. But as I was about to find out, off the pitch, his game face belied a gentle man of supreme kindness.

I wanted to know all about his background and how a child from the Basque hinterland became one of the best props in the world, let alone France.

"I am born and bred Basque, in the last house in Itxassou, right on the border with Espelette. Mum was from the southern Basque region so only spoke Spanish and Basque, and Dad only spoke Basque. His French was awful! He spoke it somewhere between a pig and a cow! So, we were brought up speaking Basque and had to go to school to learn French. All I knew when I arrived here at school age seven was Basque. My family were all from the southern (Spanish) side.

I hadn't had a *pastis* for a while, at least not to cure a hangover. *"Go on then"*, I said sheepishly, in response to his question, surrendering my pride and showing a little embarrassment for drinking in the morning, although I consoled myself with the fact that it wasn't far off midday.

The *pastis* was sublime. Some may not like its tangy aniseed and muscular palate but the drink was long with minty lemon freshness and the water cold. I plunged a handful of ice into the glass and sipped it slowly, the glacial liquid soothing my throat like a honeyed lozenge. In spite already being outside in the pouring rain with only a large awning to protect us, the chilled *pastis* still reduced my body temperature to somewhere approaching normal.

Pierre was puffing away on his Gitanes and it reminded me that I was carrying a Montecristo No. 3 cigar, a gift that I'd snaffled at the party in Paris. I lit it up and puffed

on this beautiful corona with its woody and earthy flavours. Here I was, a hungover Englishman in Espelette impersonating a Basque Cuban and trying to speak fluent French. I wasn't a pretty sight. I told him all about the night in Paris and my eventful journey to Biarritz before we got into the meat of our discussion. That way, he would forgive my linguistic errors and tired eyes, although I think the combination of alcohol and nicotine improved my fluency somewhat.

I could sit in cafés all day making small talk, but I was here to do a job and I needed to maximise this unique opportunity with the Basque hero.

Basque Thoroughbred

When Pierre played, he looked fearsome with his puckered lips, stony stare and look of menace, sometimes accentuated by the dark beard he grew. Both Jean-Pierre Rives and Philippe Dintrans described

"I started my rugby right here as my school used to be where le Trinquet now is. There was a teacher, Raymond Sanglar, who brought a rugby ball and created a team called Les Gazelles, but parents in this area didn't know anything about rugby even though AB were well known. My parents didn't want me to play because they didn't understand it and thought it was for madmen!

"I knew immediately that I loved it. We played a small match in Bayonne without my parents knowing and I wore rubber boots! I skidded everywhere. I was known as 'The Bear'. I would come back from playing with my clothes all torn only to get shouted at by Mum, but I didn't want to admit that I had been playing rugby, just that I had been playing with mates. 'Were you fighting again?' she would ask me.

It went on and on. I played like this until I was about seventeen years old, when they bought me a pair of proper boots.

" My uncle took me to Jean Dauger's bar in la rue du 49eme, in the centre of Bayonne, which was effectively the HQ, and I signed. Dad finally accepted rugby, but although I played for twenty years for Bayonne, he never came to see me play. He knew and understood nothing about rugby. Mum would watch but was always scared."

"My international career linked the old and new generations. I played with the old stars like Iraçabal, Bénésis, Cester, Vaquerin, Claude and Walter Spanghéro, and also the new group coming through of Cholley, Paparemborde, Garuet and others.

"In 1974, I toured Argentina with Armand Vaquerin and Jean Iracabal but in 1975 I hurt my knee and Gérard

Cholley, Armand Vaquerin and Robert Paparemborde were selected, so I then had to wait my turn, only securing my place in 1980. That's life!"

Pierre's mum, Maria-Jesus Errotaberea, was as Basque they come, the eldest of eight kids. Her whole family were refugees from Spain (like the parents and grandparents of a few players I met on my travels – Codorniou, Rodriguez, Minarro) trekking across the Pyrenees in 1950 in search of food and water and a better life. After Pierre was born, eight of them lived together. But Pierre remembers fondly his youth and how everyone helped across the community – grape picking, harvesting, haymaking.

"These activities brought together the whole community and we worked as a team, laughing, joking, telling stories, and working without realising it. Afterwards, we would party, eat and drink cider or wine, and sing. And then we would give ourselves physical and strength challenges, egged on by drink. This is where La Force Basque came from.

"That feeling of sharing and giving, of team spirit and team work, solidarity, I learnt all of that on the farm. And these values are what underpinned my rugby."

Meat Training

Pierre was feared among his peers for his sheer natural strength and body as hard as stone. He talked me through his weight training regime.

"I started work in an abattoir carrying meat and driving the van. I would start at 2am in the morning and work fourteen to fifteen hours a day. At the same time, I learned how to be a butcher and debone the meat. I remember the heaviest meat I ever carried was a bull, and the smallest part must have weighed 250kg. So, I would do most of my training at work, and my weight training was very natural.

"Once, I missed training with AB because I had the village pig to kill. Fouroux was an ace storyteller and embellished the story to say I missed a French squad training session! He couldn't understand how or why I would risk my place in the team for a pig. But I wasn't mad or arrogant or frivolous. Being an international didn't stop me from being from Espelette and from being Basque. And in the Basque country, killing a pig is a major event."

Basque on Basque

I was keen to know what it was like playing against fellow Basques and especially the local derbies between BO and AB.

"David, I tell you, there was never any violent play. Of course, it was hard and uncompromising but I considered players like Pascal, Serge and Jean Condom as my brothers. And brothers can fight but it was never dirty. Compare that to playing against Béziers when you could take a kick to the head at any point. That never happened in a Basque derby. If anyone got involved in dirty play, they were banished by the family.

> "After the games, we would all party and sing together until the early hours. The bus always went home empty of players, with only the President and medical man on board!"

Pierre was very at ease in this most Basque of French villages. He switched effortlessly between French and Basque, saluting friends as they walked by his fabled and eponymous institution, Chez Doxpi. As someone who can speak French and English fluently, I feel I shouldn't be so in awe of his linguistic mastery, but this is Basque after all, and to my ear, along with Welsh and Hungarian, it looks bizarre and is incomprehensible to anyone but the indigenous population.

"I remember that when my parents first took me to school, I was lost as I didn't speak French. The words and their order in Basque are completely different. In Basque we put the cart before the horse."

Jean-Pierre Rives told me an amusing tale about Pierre's devotion to the Basque identity when he first arrived in the French team.

"He would always wear this Basque shirt. I remember one time just before the shirts were handed out in the changing room before a Five Nations game. I could see Peyo standing there with a red, green and white Basque shirt over his shoulders. I said: 'Peyo, f**king hell, you can't wear a Basque jersey under your French jersey'. He looked at me trying to work out whether I was being serious. Before he got in a huff, I told him I was only joking. He smiled a big, broad Basque smile, easing the pre-match tension. I always pulled his leg, but the reality is I love people with that conviction, who love their country. He always played for France wearing a Basque shirt as his body armour. He was and still is one committed Basque, and a wonderful team mate too."

I talked to Pierre about this and he laughed, but made a serious point too:

"I am very proud to be French and to wear the French shirt and cockerel on my chest, and to sing the Marseillaise. But that didn't and doesn't mean I can't also be a proud Basque. I belong to this special Basque race and I want to contribute to retaining its traditions and protecting its roots."

Voice of an Angel

One of Pierre's great skills is his singing. I am not talking amateur pub singing here, I mean proper, professional singing. He wasn't just a tireless player who crushed opposition scrums with his technique, Basque force and determination. He could outsing his teammates and the opposition too.

Iain Milne remembers Dospital leading the singing after a game around 1980:

"His singing was amazing. I always got the three D's muddled up – Dospital, Dintrans, Dubroca – but one of them could really sing, unlike the rest of us!"

Pierre is a professional singer who still does about thirty concerts a year.

But the singing was a source of some contention, Pierre thinking that he was selected on tours mainly for his singing to provide entertainment for the team.

"In 1980 on the South African tour, I played well in the provincial matches but wasn't selected for the test match. I went ballistic. Michel Celaya was the coach and Elie Peyrebere was the chairman of selectors, and I said: 'Listen, you've taken me for a ride. You promised me things and you've done the opposite. You tossers!'

"I didn't come on tour just to sing, entertain the team and be the court jester. I told them I would be leaving for France immediately, until I realised the cost of the ticket! So, I stayed but said I wouldn't be a replacement or train or be part of the group."

I met Henri Nayrou, the former Chief Editor and journalist from Midi Olympique, who leads the fabulous Les Rencontres en Séronais in the Ariège, who told me that things relaxed after the tour once Doxpi bought himself a harmonica and started to sing to entertain the squad! Pierre continued the story:

"When we all arrived back in France, Jacques Fouroux came in as coach and said 'I need a loose head'.

"I am very proud to be French and to wear the French shirt and cockerel on my chest, and to sing the Marseillaise. But that didn't and doesn't mean I can't also be a proud Basque. I belong to this special Basque race and I want to contribute to retaining its traditions and protecting its roots."

> # "The scrum is all about confrontation with the opposition and our desire to win those personal battles. Our pride comes from not taking a backward step."

"Our physique would be nothing without the mind-set, a key characteristic of the Basques. What is important is our love of challenges, which emanates from a lifetime of struggle working the land. We had to overcome adversity to survive. Resilience and pride drive the Basques on.

"The scrum is all about confrontation with the opposition and our desire to win those personal battles. Our pride comes from not taking a backward step. Across the Basque country, there are challenges everywhere, about anything. Every time, we do our utmost to win."

"I was pig-headed, like Jacques, and said I didn't want to play. Everyone tried to persuade me. Then Guy Basquet, the right-hand man of Mr Albert Ferrasse, stepped in and summoned me to Bayonne. He said, 'Doxpi, do you want to play for the French team, yes or no?' I said, 'If it is you who are asking Mr Basquet, then my answer is unequivocally yes!' From then on, I was the first-choice loose head prop and played continually until I retired in 1985!"

Doxpi is a man of high emotions.

A Source of Inspriation

Pierre told me about losing his second son, Jean-Claude, when he was seven years old, from a blood clot on the brain, and he used his memory as inspiration and motivation on the pitch:

"They were very difficult times. The loss of my son in

1977 was a turning point in my life. He accompanied me everywhere, in the good and bad times. He was inside me for matches and I would say to him: 'Come with me, let's do it together. I didn't need more motivation than that."

Both painful and beautiful in unison, his stories struck me right in the heart. Like water, pain always finds a way to push through the seal.

As we sat chatting, it was wonderful to watch him mingle and interact with his fellow residents. This was his parish and the unconditional veneration extended to him was palpable. He was the ringmaster chatting to people about all manner of local topics - communions, church, weddings, village fetes, rugby, football club celebrations, as well as greeting people and wishing them *'bon appetit'*.

We returned to the question of Basque props and hookers, and how such a small territory produces such strong men.

The School of Hard Knocks

I spent nearly three wonderful hours with Pierre, a truly lovely man who evinces all the great virtues of a human being – loyalty, tenderness, friendship, honesty, humour, thoughtfulness – alongside his teak-tough attitude on the pitch and steely determination to win, Basque traits that will never be effaced.

He strikes me as a man of the people, a religious and simply educated man who understands all the ups and downs of life, and knows what to do when confronted by them. He is a pupil of the school of hard knocks and a graduate of life's university, his wisdom enlarged by his experiences and travels, and not hemmed in by theory or pre-conceived ideas.

What a brilliant role model
for young players, the Basques,
French people and men
of all shapes, sizes, colours
and creeds.

I finally let him escape back to his house for lunch.
I had loved every second of our chat and, as with Pascal
Ondarts, I find I can talk to these Basques for hours
such is their friendship and never-ending flow of stories.
But all good things come to an end.

Bucolic Basque Beauty

After the previous night's festivities and excesses
in Paris, I anticipated heading back to Anglet and going
to bed early. At least that was my intention until I found
a restaurant of such bucolic Basque beauty that I had to
change my plans. Yes, as usual, I couldn't resist. What is it
about my genetic make-up that means I can't say no?
I have never solved that conundrum. *Carpe Diem*,
I suspect, and the fear of missing out. Or maybe I just
like food and wine…

The restaurant was called le Moulin d'Alotz, a former
mill on the river, located at Arcangues, near Biarritz.
Its website is the perfect example of frenchness,
in a creative sense – beautifully designed, retro, cryptic,
intellectual, arty and occasionally random - and it
markets itself under the banner of 'culture, nature and
gastronomy'. *Irresistible, non?* Within ten seconds,
they had lured me in and I was entering the coordinates
into my GPS. I ate grilled langoustines, caramelised
lobster in a creamy bisque sauce, grilled filet of John
Dory and strawberries sprinkled with sechuan pepper
for desert. I washed it down with a bottle of Chablis
2007. The whole thing was so magnificent that I wept
with joy and sang the Marseillaise. I moderated my
consumption by skipping the cheese and *digestifs*,
and congratulated myself on my abstinence.
Yes, I know, there are times when I am deluded.

On the Sunday I was driving to Narbonne to meet
Ieuan Evans to watch the RWC U20 championship,
before heading to Béziers to meet up with the Diego
Minarro, ex-player and now the Sporting Director
of the Academy at Béziers rugby club, Elie Vaquerin,
brother of Armand, and Maryse Lacans, mother of
Pierre. I had quite a bit of travelling to do across the
breathtaking Pyrenees and into the Mediterranean.

John Hall, the great former Bath and England
flanker remembers Doxpi and Phil Blakeway
at the after-match parties:

"They were wearing dinner
jackets and white shirts,
and doing boat races
with bottles of red wine.
Their shirts were covered in it.
They were both bolloxed and
Doxpi was leading the singing!"

Patrice Lagisquet

BASQUE COUNTRY

"ON THE DAY OF THE FINAL, WHEN WE WERE ON THE PITCH TWO HOURS BEFORE KICK-OFF, WE GATHERED TOGETHER IN THE IN-GOAL AREA AND SPOKE ABOUT OUR FAMILIES. MANY OF THE PLAYERS WERE CRYING AND THE EMOTIONS WERE SKY HIGH. I WAS ONE OF THEM. ONLY THE ARGENTINES CAN GET THAT EMOTIONAL AND THEN BE BRILLIANT!"

BORN : 4TH SEPTEMBER 1962

CLUBS : L'AVIRON BAYONNAIS,
BIARRITZ OLYMPIQUE

INTERNATIONAL CAPS : 46

POSITION : WING

GRAND SLAMS : 1981, 1987

NOM DE GUERRE : LE BAYONNE EXPRESS

MY VISIT TO MEET HIM : THURSDAY 8TH MARCH 2018

I met Patrice at the unofficial Brothers in Arms' HQ, Pascal's Hotel Loreak, over a breakfast of two expressos each. Just to be clear, our 'breakfast' was Patrice's choice. This is why he is so slim and fit, I thought. I would have gone for the buffet of eggs, *croissants* and other epicurean delights that were distracting me as soon as I entered the dining room an hour earlier. But once the caffeine had kicked in and we started talking about the Bayonne Express, I refocused. This was going to be no culinary extravaganza though, like the one I had experienced with his Biarritz team mate, Serge.

There is so much I remember about Patrice as a player: the acceleration, that sidestep, the elegance and of course the wonderful tries. He looked like an Olympic sprinter playing rugby with his high knee lift and rapid leg speed, although he was also a wonderful rugby player. He was not just an athlete picked for speed.

The try he scored against Wales in 1990 is just one that is fixed in my memory. Receiving the ball from Lafond on the left-hand side by the halfway line, he cut a devastating line inside off his left foot, slicing the Welsh defence apart and arcing to the left-hand corner. Once he penetrated a defence, he was unstoppable, his chiselled, wiry frame able to outsprint almost any other winger of that era. That's what running 10.6 seconds over 100m gives you, but Patrice also had the ability to change direction and sidestep at pace and in the blink of an eye. Pure speed is a dangerous asset, but the threat is magnified considerably when combined with elusiveness. Patrice had that in spades.

Not Quite Ambidextrous

I asked him about his early career and first selection:

"I was brought up in the Bassin d'Arcachon near Bordeaux where Dad was an oyster farmer. I played first for Club Athlétique Béglais and was spotted by Bayonne when we played them. They had just lost in the 1982 final against Agen.

"My first cap was against Australia in 1983 when I played

on the right-wing against Brendon Moon who was very big and strong. It was a real test for me because I usually played on the left-wing. I could only sprint when holding the ball in my left hand, although I could sidestep off both feet! To defend him, I had to pressure on him very quickly and not simply drift, which would have given him more time to run at me.

"In your first international, you have the impression that everything happens so quickly. But afterwards, once you get used to the speed, your brain is capable of memorising every action, as though you have experienced them in slow motion. I used to be able to speak to the coach about all the situations and moves to check whether I had really understood the situation."

An Eye for Detail

He missed three Five Nations Championships between 1985-87 through injury but he was fully fit for the

inaugural RWC in 1987 in New Zealand. He was one of the key players in the semi-final against Australia, scoring the third try, and was heavily involved in the last try that Serge scored to win the game.

"I can remember all the details – the actions, passes, sidesteps, kicks. I can remember Serge's try in the 1987 RWC final by heart! Berbiz, Serge, me, Alain, Dominique, Éric, Pascal, me, Garuche, Lolo, Denis, Berbiz, me, Laurent's catch with the end of his fingers, the pass to Serge. And it definitely wasn't forward!

"We went back onto the pitch after the game and Pascal led the singing in Basque. The players and staff shared a wonderful communion together.

"We had the final to play in a week's time and Jacques tried to replicate the previous week, one of the very few times he made a mistake. A number of the players were injured or exhausted. We really needed to spend the week

recovering but training was too hard. We had partied hard and felt we had played our final against Australia. If anything, we needed some psychological preparation. The All Blacks were ready to become world champions. They were prepared physically and mentally.

"On the day of the final, when we were on the pitch two hours before kick-off, we gathered together in the in-goal area and spoke about our families. Many of the players were crying and the emotions were sky-high. I was one of them. My wife was back in France and pregnant with our second child, and our first one has Down's syndrome. We had been away for six weeks and I was feeling very guilty. Only the Argentines can get that emotional and then be brilliant!

"On the work front, I had just opened my first insurance business. At the time it was losing money, but the opportunity to play in the RWC was too great, I had to go.

"We received the equivalent of 20 € per day (150 FF) to cover costs. It was never a question for me of not going but it meant we couldn't afford the flights for our wives. We were all under tremendous pressure, personally, financially and from an expectant nation and recalcitrant press."

Little Man, Big Impact

What impact did Jacques Fouroux have on his career?

"He was small but a force of nature, a charismatic man with strong personality who could be both charming and funny but also very hard with players. He had a certain way of working with us. When a new player arrived, he was very strong with you, making sure you understood that he was the boss. He would have read all the newspaper articles about you and he exerted a lot of pressure, testing you all the time. You had to show that you were capable of operating at this level and in unison with the other players. Once you had established your place, he challenged you again to see whether you could become part of the leadership group. He was so knowledgeable and passionate.

"When I arrived, his leadership group consisted of players like Dubroca, Dintrans, Berbizier, Rodriguez, Sella and Blanco. I overcame his challenges and became part of that leadership group too, and he relied on us a lot. Once he knew that he could count on you, he backed off. I found it fascinating to watch his management style in action.

"At the time, people thought he was this restrictive, dictatorial Napoléonic figure, always giving orders. But he was innovative, found ways to beat the opposition and encouraged thinking. Le Monde and other journalists would criticise him but Jacques also encouraged this. It meant he could become the focus of their direct criticism, protecting the team, but he would then use the conflict to push the players to higher standards.

"After the Fijian quarter-final, the press was all over us because we nearly lost, and they gave us no chance against Australia. But we were confident because we knew what we were capable of. Due to the vitriolic press criticism in France, at times we had the impression that no one back home cared or was watching.

> " Berbizier said, 'The press has killed the event and we are going to recreate it'."

Coaching Club and Country

Patrice left Bayonne in 1992 after ten years at Bayonne to play for Biarritz, their rivals down the road.

"I had been in the area for a decade so I wanted to stay here and Biarritz was the other big club in the Basque Country. Over the years, there have been quite a lot of players who played for both clubs but people focused on me because I played for France and was very well known.

"I am very close to both clubs and respect the rivalry that has always existed. People always think of Biarritz as a chic, glitzy town with its hotels, restaurants and tourism, but it is really the working-class areas such as La Négresse and Petricot that are the heartbeat of the club. I didn't really have this image when I arrived because I viewed the club through Serge and he came from the coast."

Patrice retired in 1997, age thirty-five, but a year later was coach of Biarritz, firstly with Laurent Rodriguez, then Alain Paco and Jacques Delmas.

"I stopped coaching in 2008 because I was exhausted. I went back in 2011 to support Philippe Saint-André when he became the French coach.

"In 2011, coaching France was a very interesting challenge but it became frustrating and difficult. Philippe and I are great friends and get on very well but we had different philosophies of how to play the game. Philippe was more pragmatic and quite English in his thinking. I wanted to play more open, attacking rugby. I thought that rugby was too slow and not open enough. I didn't want this. I was so frustrated and nearly left in 2014 but we were only a year away from the RWC so I stayed. It was a very painful period. People thought that we were playing a style of rugby that I supported, which wasn't the case.

"In 2015, after the match against the All Blacks in the RWC where we lost by fifty points, I went back to the hotel and was alone in my room. I felt enormous relief that it was over. I couldn't have stayed on, it wasn't good for my health. At one point in 2012, I was coaching both France and Biarritz.

"I don't know if I will ever go back as a club coach. I am not in the same state of mind as I was in 2008 when I left Biarritz, exhausted and devoid of new ideas. During those ten years at Biarritz, I worked during the day and was a coach in the evenings. I was working sixteen to seventeen hours a day and you can never switch off. I am looking for my balance in my life now."

> **"In 2015, after the match against the All Blacks in the RWC where we lost by fifty points, I went back to the hotel and was alone in my room. I felt enormous relief that it was over."**

Pan-Basque Potential

He opened up about the development of professionalism in France and the opportunities for the Basque region:

"Back in 1995, we adopted professionalism slowly. We think we are revolutionaries in France but we always resist change! Players still had another job for a few years, and we only started using video and stats in around 2001, although the videos weren't compressed so after a couple of games, the computers ran out of space.

"As for the future, there is enough support and rugby and money across the Basque Country, North and South, to fund a great rugby side. It isn't about merging Bayonne and Biarritz, they can continue to exist. In the South (Spanish Basque Country), there are ten teams that play in the first or second divisions, and there are the same number of players as Scotland. There are lots of rugby fans and many players come to play in France. In Fédérale 3 in France, there are many teams from the Basque Country."

It is a project that Patrice likes a lot.

"There is a love for the Basque Country in the North and South. The key question is: do we want a Basque team that can compete in France and Europe? The answer has to be a resounding yes. When Biarritz plays in the knock out stages of the French Championship and Europe, it isn't just people from Biarritz who go and watch and support them. After all, the population of Biarritz is only 27,000 people. When you see all the fans waving their Basque flags in the stadium at San Sebastian, you know the whole region, North and South, is supporting them."

We returned to the great players he played with. I wanted to know more about what it was like to play in that fabulous team.

"The opportunity to play with players like Serge Blanco, Philippe Sella and Laurent Rodriguez was a gift from the Gods. Serge was so strong and fast, and you couldn't see

him accelerate so it took me time to get used to playing with him. Philippe had everything – pace, power, skill, technique, and Laurent was a force of nature with pace to burn. The combinations and moves, which Serge, Philippe and I did, were the happiest and most enjoyable moments of my career.

"I first played against Philippe when we were about sixteen years old. He was playing full-back for Clairac and I was playing centre for Cadillac, and the following year we were competing against each other at athletics. I always won the sprints though, even though he had great pace."

If Only...

He reminisced about his favourite tries and plays such as Wales 1990, Ireland 1989, All Blacks 1989 and of course Australia in 1987. He also talked about what might have been against the All Blacks in the 1987 RWC final.

"Earlier on in the World Cup, I had dreamt about playing against John Kirwan on the left-wing, and that is what eventually happened in the final. In that match, I think I had an opportunity to score but I messed up. Mesnel charged down a drop goal from Fox, and I ran back to get the ball. I saw Kirwan bearing down on me near our try line but I could also see a big gap behind him. I thought 'I'll pick it up and sidestep my way through to their try line'. It was a long way but I had the pace and space. But I got ahead of myself and didn't catch the ball. The error is woven into my mind forever. And they scored quickly afterwards.

"John Kirwan was so tough to play against. He was about 100kgs and so fast and elusive. We got on very well off the pitch and we discussed how we practised our sidestepping, both using trees in the forest as defenders!"

Patrice wasn't just a great player. He is also a very intelligent, cultured man, and does an enormous amount for his community, notably with his Chrysalide association where he is President.

It supports parents of children who have learning difficulties such as Down's syndrome and autism. He started it over thirty years ago, and was inspired to set it up by his daughter Julie, now thirty-three, who has Down's syndrome.

It had been a fascinating interview. Patrice is a wonderful human being, someone who cares deeply about the community, its people and the rugby. I sat there wondering how he has fitted it all in – built a business, played for his national rugby side, coached both Biarritz and France, brought up a family, built a foundation to help others and coaches, *pro bono*, some of the smaller clubs in the region. And he still had time to be

interviewed by me over a coffee or two. I was in awe of his achievements.

Of mind he is razor sharp and a very intelligent and articulate man with a wonderful spirit and heart. His sporting, playing and charitable career impressed me hugely, as did his recollection of events and detail.

Our interview was over. Patrice had other meetings to go to and I had lunch with Pascal, Pierre Berbizier, Michel Celaya and Gérard Murillo. I was glad I hadn't eaten breakfast as I knew lunch was going to be a large one, plus I was heading back down to Hendaye later to see Serge and Lolo Pardo, before heading over to San Sebastian. Being in calorie deficit in the morning was no bad thing.

Pascal Ondarts

BASQUE COUNTRY

"I SPEAK TO MY FRIENDS LIKE
JEAN-PIERRE GARUET AND PHILIPPE
DINTRANS NEARLY EVERY DAY.
WE ARE LIKE BROTHERS.
THAT FRIENDSHIP WAS DEVELOPED
OVER FORTY YEARS AND IS WORTH
MORE THAN THE PRICE OF GOLD."

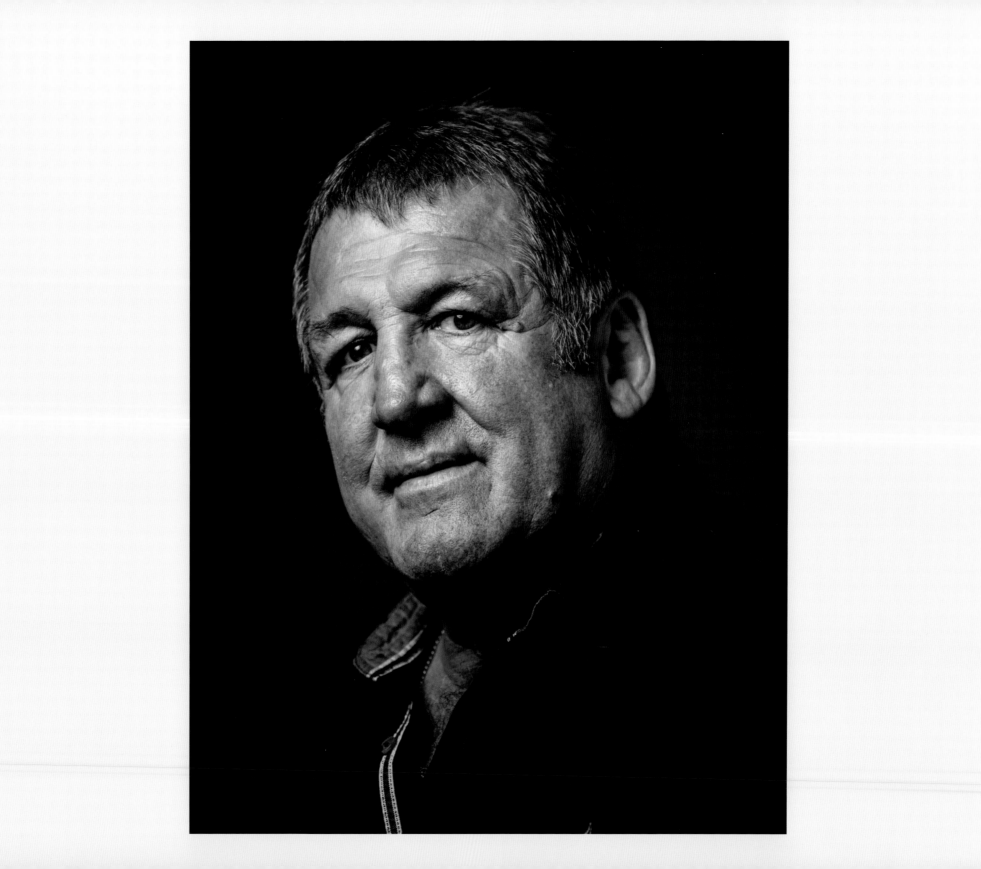

BORN : 1ST APRIL 1956

CLUBS : BIARRITZ OLYMPIQUE

INTERNATIONAL CAPS : 42

POSITION : LOOSE AND TIGHT HEAD PROP

GRAND SLAMS : 1987

NICKNAME : PAXHAL (IN BASQUE), LE SANGLIER

NOM DE GUERRE : THE MAN FOR ALL SEASONS

MY VISIT TO MEET HIM : FRIDAY 24TH NOVEMBER 2017

P ascal was one of the easier players to track down. In 1998, he bought Le Caritz in downtown Biarritz near the old port, a hotel with great views and a fabulous position next to the sea, but he had sold it a couple of years ago and created a new hotel called Loreak (which means 'Flowers' in Basque), 2km outside Bayonne.

Pascal Ondarts. Rugby Five Nations, France 28 v
Scotland 22. 7th March 1987, Parc des Princes, Paris.
Photo - Getty Images.

I have fond memories of the Caritz during a holiday
we took in the Basque Country around 2006/7.
Jo and I had dinner there and we could see Pascal
mingling effortlessly with his guests in the bar and
restaurant. As you would expect, he was and is still
an imposing figure but he radiated warmth and charm
to his clientele, attentive to all their needs.

I recall one warm evening in particular that we spent
with Michael Lynagh (the former great Australian
fly-half) and his wife, Isabella. One of Michael's friends
had invited us for dinner in the picturesque old port.
We ate outside, next to one of the colourful fishing
huts, a prize possession of the locals.

The hut was tiny and the facilities very basic,
but the Basque cooking was glorious. We stayed
for hours enjoying the hospitality, eating local dishes
like *Chipirones à la plancha* (grilled squid) and *Oiartzun
daurade* (grilled sea bream with garlic and red chilli
sauce and vinegar).

We quaffed wine and local liqueurs like Izarra
and Patxaka. It was an orgy of fine food and drink.
I remember the evening so well to this day and that
feeling of deep contentment. We departed late,
handsomely fed and fairly inebriated. Hangover-free
the next morning, we spent all day on the beach in
Anglet playing with our (then) five boys and watching
Michael surf the Atlantic waves like he was back home
on the Gold Coast.

It was one of those evenings that encapsulated
everything you love about the summer in France –
warm evenings and hours *à table* with friends, sharing,
talking, laughing and living. The food and wine were very
enjoyable, but it's the intangibles that you'll never forget.

Blood and Thunder

I arrived at the Loreak where I met Pascal at 11am on
his favourite raised table, *La Table de Robert*. A picture
was hanging next to it to commemorate Robert, a friend
of his who had died recently. His loyalty and friendship
were recurring themes throughout my journey.

His features struck me immediately. Here is a Basque man
of *pur sang*, broad-chested and stocky, with pronounced
eyelids and a face both chiselled and worn by a thousand
scrums. He has a square jaw and gladiator's nose,
but his ears, teeth and hair are all in good shape, and he
has an impressive chin dimple. He is no mammoth though,
as the French describe the modern-day rugby giant, but as

a player he was immensely strong and technically superb.
Pascal opened up with a compliment and some relief:

*"Ah, thank God you speak good French. I was worried
I would have to speak English! In fact, I think you speak
better French than me!"*

To this Englishman's ear, Pascal has a Basque accent that
seems different from the rest of southern France's *accent
du midi*. Lacking the usual nasal twang, throaty notes and
choral intonation, it is both distinctive and neutral, with a
marked guttural pronounciation of the letter 'r'.

It was a bit punchy but I jumped straight in with a direct
question, asking him whether his accolade from the
British Sunday Times as one of France's most frightening
rugby players was justified.

He smiled, shrugged his shoulders and said, *"No idea.
I don't even know what that means. And anyway, you*

needed more in your armoury than handing out a few punches in order to achieve what we achieved."

A testament to his modesty, he didn't use the Sunday Times' epitaph as a platform to vaunt his prowess and hard-nut reputation. I actually think he created this fearsome reputation when he received his first cap playing against the All Blacks.

His first match was a baptism of fire, the so-called Battle of Nantes against the All Blacks in 1986. But to get selected, Pascal first had to play very well for his regional team, Côte Basque against the All Blacks, in the mid-week game under lights and in front of 12,000 people at the mythical Jean Dauger stadium in Bayonne. It was the sort of crowd and atmosphere that epitomised the blood and thunder of rugby in the pre-professional era – a stadium packed to the rafters with people sitting on the walls and filling every available space.

> "The crowd was big, noisy and tribal, lubricated by *pastis* and local wine, the air infused with the odour of Gauloises cigarettes and *merguez*. The Jean Dauger stadium was smoking hot in anticipation.

Pascal didn't disappoint. The first half was very tight, 6-6, and Pascal was playing a blinder, up against the formidable All Black front row of McDowall, Fitzpatrick and Boroevich. But in the second half, the All Blacks imposed themselves. The Côte Basque selection narrowly lost but Pascal's reward was his selection as a replacement for the first test against them on the following Saturday in Toulouse. He didn't get on but with France having lost, he replaced Chabowski for the second test, the fearsome match that became known as the 'Battle of Nantes'.

Nantes was a brutal match. As Sean Fitzpatrick writes in the foreword to this book and has told me many times, the All Blacks were trampled on, beaten up, smashed, kicked and punched. Pascal was rough, tough and uncompromising throughout. That image and reputation would stay with him.

Pascal responded, *"It was all part of the game back then and we had to win. This was the year before the inaugural World Cup and heads were on the line. If we hadn't have won that, many of us may never have played for France again, and I had waited a decade to reach my goal. I wasn't going to give it up without a fight. The All Blacks were also very good at handing it out. They had taught us how to do it. They just happened to be on the receiving end that day."*

Ever the warrior, I loved his edgy, competitive spirit. Once you have it, you never lose it, even when playing your kids at table tennis. If I had challenged him to a scrummage there and then, I am sure he would have packed down and given me a good shoeing.

He spoke at length about the Battle of Nantes.

"The week before Nantes was a nightmare. I had enormous respect for Jacques Fouroux, not really as a technical coach but as a leader of men. He knew how to motivate people, individual by individual. After losing the first test in Toulouse, he was feeling the pressure and did everything he could to work us up into a frenzy. We were scared to come out of our rooms! He told us we were rubbish and fat and stopped us eating certain foods. It was a terrible week.

"I was thirty years old but I would open the door of my hotel room to check Jacques wasn't in the vicinity before leaving my room. He was as small as a dwarf, only 1.63m and 66kg, yet I was scared!

"But Jacques was no fool when it came to motivating men. He knew that by the end of the week, we would be apoplectic with rage and absolutely determined to prove to him that we could win. He was right."

"He had the hotel phone cut off and intercepted messages for the players. He wanted to wind us up. Just before kick-off, he grabbed me near the changing room, holding a letter in his hand. Jacques said, 'The person who wrote this wasn't bullshitting about you'.

"It was a letter from Alain Lansaman, my great friend from Hagetmau who died in 2006. I read the letter with everyone in line behind me. I had known Alain for a long time, he was like a brother and he had written some very emotionally-charged words that had a profound effect on me. Having read it, I was ready to kill! That was Fouroux –

he was like a psychologist and knew how to maximise an individual's performance."

"The warm-up before the game was the most intense and emotional that I have ever been involved in. And Jacques was right in the middle of it, covered in blood and sweat and tears. It was classic Jacques.

"We won the game 16-3 but we should have won by twenty points had Philippe Bérot, our kicker, not had an off day."

I wanted to know the answer to the question everyone has been asking since 1986: who kicked Shelford in the nuts and ripped open his scrotum? Various names have been mentioned over the years: Dubroca, Condom, Ondarts, Bonneval (as a lovely, gentle three-quarter, that would have to be a case of mistaken identity, surely…).

"David, no one knows how it happened. It was simply a rugby incident."

This is as tortuous as identifying who killed JFK, I pondered.

I went in for another punchy question, recoiling slightly in case I hit a raw nerve: what about the allegations of drug taking before the Battle of Nantes? Were they true? In 2015, Pascal and Jean-Pierre Garuet won 16,000 € in damages for defamation against L'Équipe, the French sports newspaper, because they used a photo of them both to illustrate an article called 'Rugby under the spotlight', which claimed there was doping in French rugby and linked it to the Battle of Nantes.

> # If I had challenged him to a scrummage there and then, I am sure he would have packed down and given me a good shoeing.

"I am glad you asked me that, David. Can you imagine a bunch of amateur players back then, all of us with kids and jobs, doing such a thing? We beat them fair and square, motivated by the fear of failure and having been worked into a frenzy by Jacques. I would never want my kids and grandchildren to think that I was taking pills to make me run faster! It's complete nonsense. The only thing we would drink before a game was Guronsan (a perfectly legal, over the counter tablet for treating fatigue), water and, for some players, red wine."

Nature Versus Nurture

I wanted to know more about the Basque culture and what it imbued in him, as a child, man, husband and rugby player.

"I lived in the countryside, in the small Basque village of Méharin about 50km south west of Biarritz, and no one played rugby there. In the villages, we played pelote with our naked hands, and even to this day, it remains my favourite sport.

"I would also compete in the Basque strength tests and I loved them. My record is the cart lifting, nearly 300kgs and doing four turns. We would also lift a 50kg sack of wheat and carry it for over 100m. I was the strongest and people thought I would make a great prop, not a fly-half!"

"You are born a prop. You don't become one. Today they try to fabricate props. I used to play against small, medium and enormous ones and the biggest are not the hardest to play against so why the obsession with them today?"

Amazingly, Pascal only started playing rugby when he was twenty and won his first cap aged thirty. He had just married Mireille, a lady from the nearby area called le Béarn, near the Basque country, and she encouraged him to pick up the oval ball. At twenty, he was working as a blacksmith in Bayonne but due to the competition at the club, he joined BO where he remained loyal to those Basque colours of red and white for his entire career of twenty years.

" Like many of us of my generation, I also worked on the family farm. We worked like dogs. I laugh when I think that I had to get married to discover the great sport of rugby!"

"I learnt to speak Basque at home where I was one of eight children, with four brothers and three sisters, including a twin sister who was born a day after me. We all went to school to learn French. And we love singing. In fact, if you don't sing, you can't be a proper Basque."

Good Things Come to Those Who Wait

By this stage, Pascal and I were in fluent conversation, our repartee broken occasionally by his chuckling and the passing of clients who came up to say 'hello'. The restaurant was buzzing with customers in their element, enjoying the food and company.

Our lunch arrived, which consisted of a goat's cheese salad followed by pork casserole with mushrooms,

washed down with some wines from Jurançon and Bordeaux. It was unpretentious, hearty fare, just what you would expect from Pascal. We were joined by his lovely daughter, Maider, a super-charged, sparky mum of three who runs the hotel day to day.

We returned to his rugby career and I asked him why it took him ten years to win his first cap.

"That is a sore point, David! Jacques wanted to try everyone else but me, so I ended up playing for France B for six years. Jean-Pierre Garuet was the same. In the 80's there was some stiff competition – Dospital, Paparemborde, Chabowski, Crémaschi, Detrez. Jacques Fouroux had been coached by Jean Liénard of La Voulte who indoctrinated him in the value of massive forwards. Fouroux was then captain of France in 1977 behind a pack of monsters, and as coach, he followed the same philosophy. Neither Jean-Pierre nor I were as big as players like Cholley who was 1.93m and 120kgs back then!

"The reality is though that the bloke who is 1.70m and 90kg can be much harder to play than the monster. Technique and intelligence are really important. As soon as I played in Nantes, Jacques said to me, 'I know I have treated you badly but from now on you have proven yourself and I won't do that any longer'. He was true to his word."

Lobster, Lobster… and More Lobster

I asked him about the first Rugby World Cup what it was like to go on tour for six weeks and not be paid a bean. In today's world of professionalism, you have to remind yourself that players used to play for love and fun.

"I worked at Lyonnaise des Eaux for eighteen years and in 1987 when we left for the World Cup, I didn't get paid a penny for nearly six weeks, other than a daily allowance of 150 FF (about 20 € in today's money) to cover telephone calls. I don't think the MD of my company even knew I played rugby for France. I had to take the time off as holiday. At the same time, my wife was working and looking after the kids on her own. It was the same for all the team.

"But we weren't doing it for the money. We were a band of brothers who had grown up together and we were doing it for our families, friends, France and ourselves. The money was irrelevant. We loved it."

What about the semi-final match against the Australians when Serge Blanco scored the decisive try in the last minute and Camberabero place kicked like a demon, I asked? He chuckled and got up on his soapbox.

"Rugby is a team sport where there is a lot of respect but the Australians did not respect us. They were full of themselves and, as we later found out, had already booked the hotel in Auckland for the final! It made us mad. They should have showed us more respect, especially after we had beaten the All Blacks in 1986, won the Grand Slam in 1987 and had won all our group matches at the RWC, apart from the draw against Scotland. How we loved beating them in the semi-final."

In the final at Eden Park, Auckland, France lost 29-9. Between the semi-final and the final in 1987, Pascal would love to have had all the means that are available to players today.

"There were maybe five or six of us who were injured after Australia but we only had the physio and bus driver, to help us get better! Who knows what we could have achieved had we had better medical care. Modern refereeing with TMOs would have made a difference too. Just before half time, we were only six points behind and we were smashing them on their line. We had to play five, five metre scrums. We took them behind their line and then the referee blew his whistle for half-time. We had the team to beat them but it wasn't to be on the day.

"But this is all in the past and whatever the result, playing in a World Cup Final against the All Blacks was an extraordinary thing and I have no regrets.

"The day after the final, the All Blacks players came to pick up their French counterparts, the ones they had kicked the crap out of the previous day! They took us out for the day with their families. What a lovely, classy touch that was. My opposite number was the late John Drake. His family came to visit us last year and it was lovely to see them. I have very fond memories of John as a man and a player.

"More than twenty years later, in New Zealand, people still remember us. That's worth more than any match fee or bonus we would have earned.

"Jean-Pierre Garuet and I went back there in 2011 for the last World Cup, and everyone recognised us, and they remembered Jean Iraçabal from a tour back in the 1970s. We had a great time, always laughing, seeing the things we couldn't do when we were touring and seeing old friends like Steve McDowell and Gary Whetton who both speak some French having played in France."

Before France had left for the World Cup, they met Jacques Chirac at the Matignon who offered them an all-expenses paid trip to Bora Bora for three days should they reach the semi-final. Daniel Dubroca, captain of the French team quickly negotiated this to a week should they reach the final.

But having reached the final, the players were too homesick and exhausted to travel immediately after the competition. They had been away from their families for nearly six weeks and were desperate to see them. Remember, these were the days of amateur rugby when they had taken time off work, invariably unpaid, and couldn't afford to fly their wives, girlfriends and kids out to watch them.

"Upon arrival back in France, there were about 10,000 people waiting for us at Charles de Gaulle Airport in Paris, including many Basques who had turned up with their cars to have a picnic. It was like Twickenham! The Federation had booked Maxime's in Paris for us to celebrate and eat, but I remember that we just stayed at the picnic chatting to all the supporters. It was fabulous, chatting and laughing with all these committed fans.

"About three days later, Jacques contacted us all to tell us that we wouldn't be going to Bora Bora after all, but instead we would be going to Martinique for Christmas and new year to celebrate. Ninety-six people went including all our wives and kids! We loved it – time spent with your family and mates in the sunshine and no training sessions!

"Garuche, Philippe Dintrans and I got stuck into the local food, eating lobster every day! Yves Noé, the team manager/Official Liaison, came over and said: 'Do you need Lobster for lunch and dinner as it is super expensive'. But we thought, 'f**k it'. We had it as a starter and main course, followed by meat, cheese and desert!"

We were both roaring with laughter as he told the story.

"I speak to my friends like Jean-Pierre Garuet and Philippe Dintrans nearly every day. We are like brothers. That friendship was developed over forty years and is worth more than the price of gold. I don't know what it is like now but that is what rugby was like back then. You would do anything then for your mates and you would do so today."

When he was away at the World Cup, friends finished building his house for him.

"Even today after all these years, it gives me goose bumps. Before I left for the World Cup, I was about three quarters of the way through the project. When I returned, my mates were in front of the house and it was finished. There was only the garden wall to complete. They had paid for all the materials from their own pocket."

Friendship and loyalty run deep among these Basques.

"I am not really one for looking back thirty years, but it warms my cockles to think that we were the pioneers of the World Cup adventure. That is why people keep talking

*about us. We had been on tour before, but never to play
against all the best teams in the world during six weeks!
It was extraordinary."*

Pastis or Beer, Sir?

We turned to his former adversaries. Who were his
toughest opponents? He replied without hesitation:

*"Ian Milne of Scotland. He was big, imposing, impressive
and technically excellent. He was about 1.90m and
weighed 130kgs, but he was also very clever. When we
beat them in the Grand Slam in 1987, others had warned
me that he was a very big lad. I bound onto his shorts
with a straight arm so he couldn't move and bore into me.
Then, two months later against Scotland in the first match
of the 1987 World Cup, he had sewn up his pocket and
smeared Vaseline over it, the tosser! It was impossible for
me to get any grip. It was a nightmare, I just couldn't get
hold of him. You see, being a prop isn't just about being
physical. We also need to be intelligent.*

*"There were many other tough opponents – Leonard,
Probyn, Drake, all the Argentines.*

*"Leonard is a top man too. He was hard and tough and
technical but in spite of all that, we were great friends off
the pitch. I respected him as a man and player, not least
because he stood up for himself in his first cap against me.
I smacked him and he retaliated and I thought 'respect'
because hardly anyone did that to me in French
club rugby!"*

I met Jason Leonard and he told me an amusing anecdote
about Pascal.

*"Harlequins were playing in a European match against
Biarritz on a hot day. After the game, we rushed over to the
clubhouse as we were parched and desperate for a beer,
only to be told by the barman that pastis was being served.
F**k that, I thought. I went behind the bar and started
pouring beers for the boys. Out of the window, I could see
the crowd parting on the pitch to let this imposing figure
through. It was like watching Jesus part the seas, such was
this person's status with the locals. He got to the edge of
the pitch when I realised it was Pascal.*

*"He came up to the bar and was red with rage.
He screamed, 'I said no beers until after the pastis aperitif'.
He banged the bar so hard that it bounced up and down
like a trampoline. I said to him, 'Ello Pascal'. He looked at
me, smiled and said, 'Ah Jason, if it's you then that's fine!'
We drank the clubhouse dry. He gave me a lovely bottle of
champagne, which of course I didn't open. I wasn't going to
share that with my teammates!"*

250 Man-Years for Lunch

On the second time I went to meet Pascal, he had
arranged lunch at his hotel for a group of friends and
kindly invited me along. It was an unforgettable lunch
attended by Pascal, Pierre Berbizier, Michel Celaya
(a great player with fifty caps for France between
1953-61, Pascal's coach at BO and coach of France
just before Jacques Fouroux), Gérard Murillo (two caps

for France 1954, very highly regarded coach across the
Basque region in both France and Spain notably
at SJDL) and Albain Lhoste (Lourdes). I quickly totted
up the experience around the table and I estimated
it to be 250 man-years!

Pascal poured us wine from a fine magnum of claret
and I listened to their stories and memories. Michel had
coached Berbizier, Blanco and Codorniou for France
juniors back in the 1970s and realised he had some
special talent on show: the intelligence of Berbizier,
the flair of Blanco and the passing and running skills
of Codor; Gerard remembered the blood and thunder
between Gérard Cholley and Zaza Azarete who would
knock lumps out of each other when Castres played
SJDL; Gerard described the authority and discipline
demanded by Jean Prats when playing for France and
Lourdes, a tough man whose brother Maurice had a
much gentler side; and Berbiz showed us the scar on his
lower right arm, the wound he sustained in Argentina
in 1988 when Alejandro Iachetti, the Argentine second
row, stamped on his arm. I felt very lucky to be in
the presence of the great rugby icons from the older
generations, players who had played with the great
Prat and Boniface brothers from the 1950s and 60s.

Basque Identity

That evening, we headed to watch his beloved
BO play Narbonne, two teams with a magnificent
heritage, which have struggled latterly in the cut
and thrust of professionalism.

Pascal and his lovely wife, Mireille, picked me up and we drove to the Parc Aguilera in Biarritz, the stade Jean Dauger of Bayonne within spitting distance of our route. I threw him a stick of dynamite; what about a merger between BO and AB, I suggested. Surely that makes economic sense and would create a significant, single Basque team, able to compete with the rest of the Top 14.

"I am not against that idea of a Basque team, David, but you can't merge them. You would have to create a regional team above them both, retaining each team's identity, just like we did when we had the Côte Basque selection. The problem is that each team's fans are fiercely loyal and don't want their identity diluted. The reality is that we Basques are all brothers, no matter which Basque side we played for, so creating a regional team should be very straightforward.

"It isn't just a question of getting over the emotions of a merger. It is also about money and we don't have a lot across Bayonne and Biarritz, two small towns. However, we would generate more interest and money across the entire Basque region of France and Spain if there were a regional Basque team covering the seven provinces. Doxpi and I have long thought that for years.

"San Sebastian and Bilbao are both very wealthy, driven by their tourism and industry. Bilbao has been transformed over the last three decades thanks to its mayors. When you see thousands of Munster fans at San Sebastian station and airport giving shirts and pennants and scarves to the Police, and the locals realising that the atmosphere at

rugby matches is completely different from football, you can see the potential for a seven province Basque team.

"But BO has lost its identity. We recruit blokes who don't care about the club or its history, identity and future."

"After the matches, the players leave the stadium and don't even have a drink with the supporters. They are just there for the money. It is the same for the new presidents. They just use the clubs to publicise their name, and when they have had enough, they leave and you go back to square one. Look at how Serge has been pushed aside. He has given everything to that club all his life and never left it even when he was at the summit of his game and other clubs across France were contacting him. One day, he got all the press together and said, 'Tell all the clubs that there is no point contacting me. I started my career at BO and I will finish my life here'."

Pascal parked his car next to the stadium and it must have taken us nearly thirty minutes to walk into the ground, only 200m away. Spectators and friends stopped him at every opportunity to chat. It all comes very easily to Pascal, his big personality drawing the fans in like a magnet. It was a throwback to the amateur era when players were loyal local lads and life was much simpler.

A Long Lunch

The BO v Narbonne match was the perfect denouement of day. We sat in Pascal's box, enjoying time with his friends and hearing about tales of Pascal's loyalty to his mates. Philippe Dintrans once asked him to drive to Tarbes to have lunch.

"I picked up Garuche on the way and arrived in Tarbes to meet Philippe. He got in and just kept saying 'keep going'. These dickheads tricked me into driving over 400km to Carcassonne – for f**king lunch! But we were there for a great cause, to celebrate the birthday of our great friend, Michel Cortal who was paralysed in a scrum playing for Carcassonne against Tarbes in 1983. What a lunch. We ate like kings and must have drunk a barrel of wine each. We stayed over and spent the next day recovering!"

Sitting in the Aguilera, I tried to imagine what it was like watching the giants of the club – Pascal packing down against the great French props Vaquerin, Paparemborde, Dospital, Garuet and Cholley, and Serge Blanco running in tries from anywhere. This was one of the mythical grounds that had witnessed some wonderful players and matches. Like Sauclières (Béziers old ground) or Antoine Béguère (Lourdes) or stade Jean Dauger (Bayonne), you can feel the history when you are there.

After the game, I said goodbye to Pascal, Mireille and their friends. My head was buzzing with thoughts about the Ondarts family and their loyalty to Biarritz Olympique, the Basque community and their friends.

As a player, he was a great stalwart of BO, but now he is a man of the whole Basque *terroir*, a tough guy with a gentle heart. He played for Biarritz, lives in Anglet and runs a business in Bayonne so he transcends any divides. He is a man for all seasons.

He is inculcated with some unassailable attributes – unashamedly independently minded, very determined and fervently loyal to his friends, family, colleagues and region. During his playing career, he was a rock hewn from granite, a pillar of force and dependability who provided the foundations for the team's collective success. He may not have pierced the opposition defences much or scored flamboyant tries, but he was essential to the team's spirit and success. He is a wonderful human being.

This trip to the Basque country was over and I was leaving the next day to head to the central Pyrenees where I would be meeting three more giants of the front row – Louisou Armary, Philippe Dintrans and Jean-Pierre Garuet. I pondered what it was about the Lourdes-Tarbes-Pau axis that created such great front row forwards. Maybe I would find out.

Laurent Pardo

BASQUE COUNTRY   "RUGBY HAS TO BE GREAT FUN.
WE SHOULD STOP COACHING
TEAMS AND A TRY SHOULD BE
WORTH FORTY POINTS. I LOVE
SEEING THE KIDS IN THE STADIA,
I WANT TO DRINK ALCOHOL IN
PROPER GLASSES, SING SONGS,
PARTY WITH OLD AND NEW
FRIENDS AND SHARE STORIES.
BUT ALL COACHES WANT
TO DO ARE TRAINING AND
WEIGHTS SESSIONS FOLLOWED
BY A PRESENTATION.
BOLLOCKS TO THAT!"

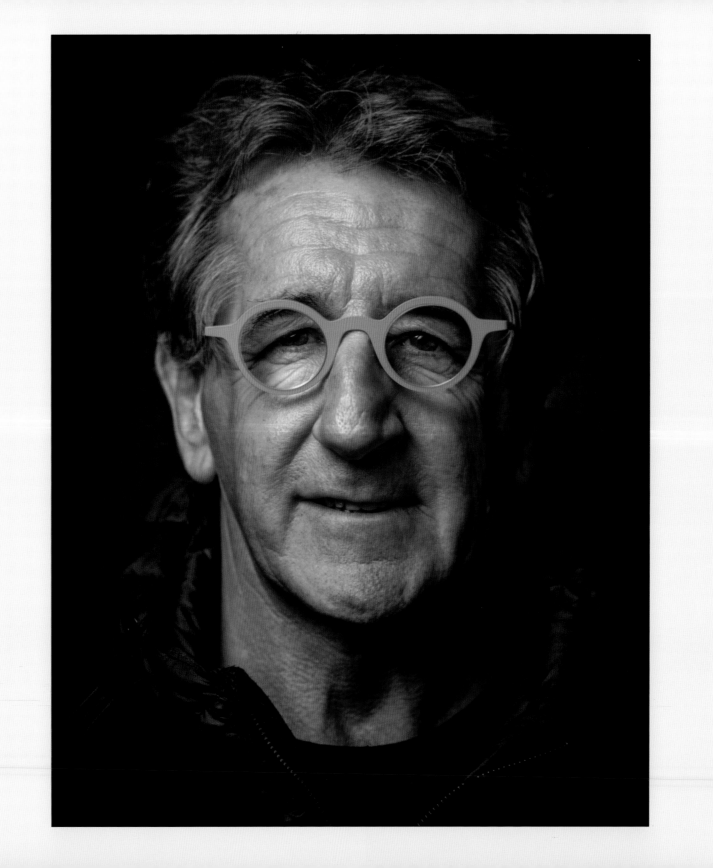

BORN : 19TH FEBRUARY 1958

CLUBS : L'AVIRON BAYONNAIS, CLERMONT FERRAND,
RACING CLUB DE FRANCE

INTERNATIONAL CAPS : 14

POSITION : WING

GRAND SLAMS : 1981

NICKNAME : LOLO

NOM DE GUERRE : THE SILVER FOX

MY VISIT TO MEET HIM : THURSDAY 8TH MARCH 2018

Laurent wasn't part of my original selection of only twenty players, but everyone recommended that I meet him. I don't like to think that my selection was a democratic process or that I bowed to player power, as Laurent certainly made it on merit, but I did extend the squad from twenty to thirty-two players to avoid some difficult selection choices! But he also made it by sheer force of his personality, great humour and team spirit. As I would find out, he is an astonishing expression of vitality and fun.

I found the perfect place to meet him – Maison Eguiazabal, Hendaye's premier wine merchant. I had met its owner, Pierre, a few days before at le Parc des Sports Aguiléra with Pascal, and we immediately hit it off. I mean, what's not to like about any man or woman (or transgender to be inclusive) who loves fine food, wine, sport and rugby in particular?

I arrived ahead of time so I could browse around this treasure trove of love and soul, and select a bottle or two for my interview. The place was full of sumptuous wines, which were arranged neatly on the shelves, glistening like diamonds under the soft lights. I chose Comtes Lafon's Clos de La Barre, a wine I had drunk recently at my birthday at 67 Pall Mall in London.

The Silver Fox

When Laurent arrived, he was sporting his round, pink glasses. The Silver Fox, the *nom de guerre* that I gave him, was looking relaxed, fit and bronzed as he launched straight into a passionate and humorous defence of the essence of rugby: *"Rugby has to be great fun. We should stop coaching teams and a try should be worth forty points".*

"Giving your team mate a pass and scoring a try are the greatest things in rugby, not the coaches. I love seeing the kids in the stadia, I want to drink alcohol in proper glasses, sing songs, party with old and new friends, and share stories. But all coaches want to do are training and weights sessions followed by a presentation. Bollocks to that!"

I sat back and watched him in full flow, this elegant man with a magnetic persona.

"Today, they drink water constantly. You'd think it was Tunisia at the height of summer. I was in the changing rooms recently and there was water everywhere.

" I said, 'you can't drink all that, you won't get through the 2nd half'."

"Back in the day, we didn't earn anything from rugby but we loved it so money didn't matter. We played all the time and partied hard. We didn't rest. Nowadays, at twenty-five years old, they rest. I would have hated that. And there are pom-pom girls dancing at half time now. I would say, 'Don't go back in to the changing rooms – let's stay here'. The players have got the world back to front!

"Yes, sometimes I would get injured back then. I often think that if my nose hadn't had been so big, I would have taken far more punches in the face."

I was belly-laughing and choking on my Comtes Lafon and saucisson when he came out with that great line, one he had borrowed from the great Walter Spanghero. I could see what the other players meant about Laurent's vim and verve.

Rugby Nomad

Laurent wasn't just a great player, he was also something of a rugby nomad, driven by his constant search for fun, friendship and adventure. His grandfather, Leon, played twice for France against Ireland and England, and also played for Bayonne against Stade Toulousain in the Bouclier de Brennus final in 1923.

Like his father, Laurent played first at Hendaye before joining RCF. In Limoges on Mother's Day 1976, Hendaye beat BO to became French Champions for the Colts age group. On that same day, he played against a certain Serge Blanco.

"After Paris, I wanted to come back to the Basque Country and was due to join BO. I knew Serge and had met the Biarritz directors over dinner where I gorged myself on lobster. It was a match made in heaven. However, when I was en route back, I took a detour via a night club where I bumped into a friend who said, 'Don't go to BO, come to AB' so I changed my mind there and then. I said 'adieu BO!' I pissed Serge off for years.

"The reality is that I loved the Jean Dauger stadium because it was where teams like the All Blacks would come and play the provincial matches. Jean Grenet was the President of Bayonne at the time and he was the son-in-law of the great Jean Dauger, the idol of any aspiring player. I couldn't resist."

Laurent was on the tour to New Zealand in 1979, but was on the bench for that famous second test that they won

on 14th July under the leadership of Jean-Pierre Rives.
Laurent would have to wait until 1980 to win his first
cap against South Africa, alongside a couple of other
debutants that day who also feature in this book, namely
Serge Blanco and Pierre Lacans.

*"By 1982, I was bored playing on the wing for Bayonne so I
decided to join Montferrand. I was a victim of the infamous
licence rouge, which meant I couldn't play for another club
for a year so I headed to Wigan to play rugby league. It
would be dark by 4pm so I only stayed five days and played
one game, but I came back with an envelope full of money!*

*"I then went to San Sebastian to play union and had
an awesome time, playing against Wales in the mud
in Gernika. What an experience, playing in the spiritual
heartland of Basque Country.*

*"I stayed at Montferrand for four years. They gave me
a job, a case of money and showed me around the Michelin
factory. I told them I wasn't planning to open a garage so
I never turned up to work. I just played rugby - wing, left
and right centre, flanker - and partied."*

*"Daniel Herrero called me in about 1985 to ask me to join
Toulon. I agreed, but on the way back home to Hendaye,
I bumped into Jean-Pierre at the airport and he was en
route to Ibiza for a break. So, I joined him. We partied
so hard. Jean-Pierre was already at RCF in Paris so
I decided to join him. Daniel was so pissed off! We won
the Championship in 1990 so that justified my decision,
and anyway we were all amateurs back then having the
times of our lives."*

I was in awe of his irreverence and never-ending
love of life.

Laurent's phone is full of photos of his life today, partying
with his old mates, but also supporting younger players
whether for the French Barbarians, which he runs with
his mate Denis Charvet, or playing beach rugby with
the local lads every Sunday on the beach of Hendaye.
He shows me a video of him dressed as a woman and
serving coffee and cakes to his friends who are rolling
around with laughter. He wears the female clothes very
convincingly but his strained high-pitched tones give
him away.

He talked passionately and humorously about his great
mate, Serge Blanco.

*"Serge has given his life and soul to BO and Basque rugby.
He has busted his balls to support his team and create
a Basque-wide club that could compete with the best in*

*France and Europe, but he couldn't get his idea supported.
I say to him 'don't kill yourself for a handful of Espelette
peppers and some jambon from Bayonne'.*

*"Serge has had his health problems and it is well known that
he recently had heart surgery. I tell him, 'Serge, the best way
for you to lose weight is to cut off a leg. It would be easier
than resisting all that charcuterie you love so much'. "*

Hospitality in Hondarribia

We spent the Saturday afternoon watching France beat
England at the Stade de France 22-16. Laurent wanted
me to feel at home so he unveiled an England rugby
jersey, which he draped over the chair next to a couple
of bottles of Champagne that he had opened.

There were no oranges for us at half-time. Instead,
we played pelote basque in his garden where he had
his own fronton or large wall. I tried an assortment of

> "I tell him, 'Serge, the best way
> for you to lose weight is to cut off a leg.
> It would be easier than resisting all that
> charcuterie you love so much'."

> **"*Generosité* was at the heart of everything we did. You shared it all, the ball was the link. As Jean-Pierre Rives says, rugby is a game with a ball in the middle and fifteen friends around it."**

different bats and managed to lose the ball or pelote at the bottom of the road. As usual, I showed too much graft and too little craft.

Laurent is an epicurean *par excellence* so in the evening he took his mate David Beraza and me to dinner in Hondarribia. We visited the superb Ardoka Vinoteka, a bustling little bar so typical of the Spanish Basques and the sort of place you find in San Sebastian. We ate a *smörgåsbord* of *pintxos* such as cod, scallops, calamari, Serrano ham, crunchy toast and garlic tomatoes, washed down with some local beers served in beautiful, fine glasses. Their ice-cold freshness and acidity cut through the food and simply encouraged us to go back for more. If there is a better combination in the world than those flavours on that night, then I am yet to taste it.

The bar ebbed and flowed with noise and movement as people passed through to enjoy the company, warmth and food. It was a picture of societal bliss with locals of all sizes, ages and backgrounds chatting and laughing. I witnessed Spain, France, the Basque Country, the world at its best, watching the way food and wine can be such an equalising, democratising and unifying force.

As I bathed in this sea of conviviality, I concluded that we should all be eating more, not less.

Laurent was keen to ensure that I was being looked after during my time in France and that I was seeing his best friends - Denis Charvet, Érik Bonneval , Jean-Pierre Rives, Doxpi (Pierre Dospital) and Jean-Baptiste Lafond.

"Jean-Pierre was so impressive when you played with him. He showed you the way with his commitment and charisma. He helped you understand the importance of how to live in the moment. He was a great example when he played and still is now. He showed you what égalite, liberté, fraternité meant. But fraternité or brotherhood is the key thing – that unbreakable bond and trust you have with your teammates. He brought a great image to rugby – friendship, family, modesty, leadership, politeness, respectability.

"Generosité was at the heart of everything we did. You shared it all, the ball was the link. As Jean-Pierre says, rugby is a game with a ball in the middle and fifteen friends around it.

"As for Érik Bonneval, we would compete for the same position so when I shared a room with him, I would leave the window open hoping he would catch a cold making him too ill to play!"

For all his rapier wit and chutzpah, Laurent is very serious about the need for players to enjoy the moment:

"Playing rugby is a wonderful opportunity. You have to maximise the lucky hand you have been dealt."

Christian Montaignac, the great writer and journalist, said the same thing to me about Laurent Pardo himself:

"They had the time of their lives and Laurent was right in the middle of this fabulous life, sharing his fortune and vitality with his teammates. He was and still is in love with life."

His point about enjoying the moment is so apt and obvious but it proves elusive to so many of us, time passing quickly before we realise we should be enjoying the moment. Laurent elaborated:

"Today, some players are so self-absorbed and focused on their image. They should focus on expression not impression. We didn't look inwards, we just played and had the times of our lives. We lived in the moment. We loved the moment."

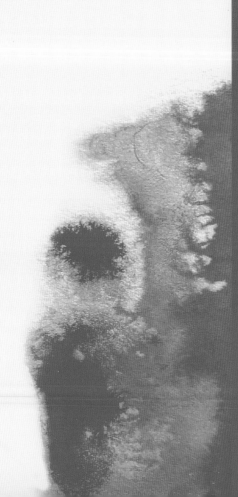

Laurent's humour knows no bounds. Franck Mesnel told me four amusing anecdotes about him:

"I was playing my first provincial game in Brive and Tuigamala was my opposite number. I was nervous, hot and sweating in the changing rooms. Laurent arrived without a care in the world, like this was just another match. He had a tube running from a bottle in his bag to his mouth, and there was a pair of mannequin's legs sticking out of his rucksack.

"Someone said, 'Lolo, what's that?'

"Lolo responded, 'I am a bit tired at the moment so I picked up a new pair of legs'. "

"On another occasion, we were playing a game in Agen but there wasn't much to do so we went to the cinema. Laurent had to get back to Hendaye afterwards so he went back to his cabriolet where he found a tramp sleeping in the back. He just put his bag in the back and drove off. The tramp woke up in the sunshine in Hendaye."

"Laurent called Jean-Pierre Labro, President of RCF, about finding a job and he emphasised how important it was. Lolo got very animated. Five minutes later, Lolo called him back to say, 'About that job, Dad has left the room now, so I don't need one anymore'. "

"Lolo was in a telephone box when a lady arrived and blocked him in, shouting to everybody who will listen that Lolo has nicked her bag! About thirty people turned up to block him in, so he had to call Jean-Pierre Labro to call the police to get him out. Of course, it was a case of mistaken identity."

"He is a genius, a very funny and wonderful man."

Rugby sur la Plage

The next day, we played touch rugby with his mates in the sun, a routine they follow every Sunday morning. I was slow back in my 'heyday' but that was nothing compared to now. The opposition had a couple of whipper snappers who could weave left to right in a nanosecond, long before I could react. I played in ultra-slow motion. Lolo was playing at a similar pace but he still had the guile and class. Afterwards, we went to the local bar for some light refreshments where Laurent regaled us with a rendition of God Save the Queen supported by some improvised percussion involving saucepan lids.

Feeling light-headed after a good work out and a few beers, we returned to Lolo's home where the family were waiting. Patricia, Laurent's lovely and eternally patient wife, had prepared a magnificent lunch of Italian chicken for us all – Jules, Jessica, Lola, Annie, Lolo, Patricia and me. Lolo nipped out to his cellar and casually brought back a couple of stunning wines, a 1982 and 1995 Château Haut-Brion, both of which were the vinous equivalent of liquid platinum. They were silky, fresh, earthy and concentrated, and they cut through the food effortlessly, like Lolo would have cut through a defence in his prime. Lunch was stellar, world class, *magnifique*, just like Lolo.

I had the time of my life with him and his family. He is a free spirit and a passionate advocate for the swashbuckling style of rugby he used to play.

It is no surprise that he is such good friends with the likes of Jean-Pierre Rives, Denis Charvet, Érik Bonneval and JeanBa Lafond. They are all independent thinkers, artists, contrarians and rule breakers. They were born to create, innovate and entertain. They are kindred spirits and encapsulate everything I love in a human being.

"Serge has given his life and soul to Biarritz and Basque rugby. He has busted his balls to support his team and create a Basque-wide club that could compete with the best in France and Europe, but he couldn't get his idea supported. I say to him 'don't kill yourself for a handful of Espelette peppers and some jambon from Bayonne'."

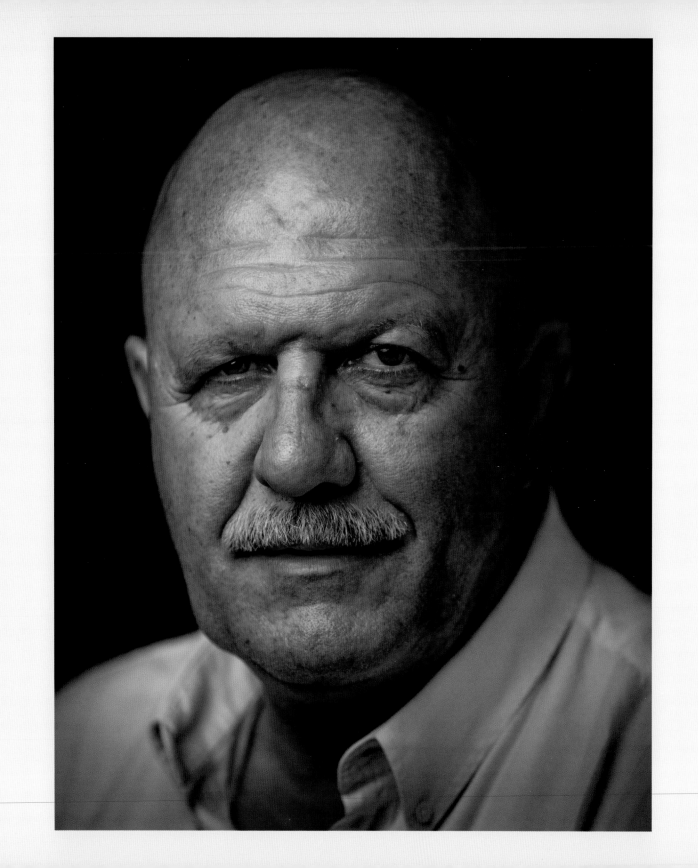

Laurent Rodriguez

BASQUE COUNTRY "ALL THESE STORIES ABOUT US
TAKING DRUGS WERE ABSOLUTE
NONSENSE. IN 1986 IN NANTES,
THE ALL BLACKS SAID WE CAME
OUT WITH EVIL IN OUR EYES
AND SO CONCLUDED WE'D
TAKEN DRUGS. THAT WASN'T
THE DRUGS – THAT WAS A
COMBINATION OF RAW GARLIC,
COFFEE AND ASPIRIN!"

BORN : 25TH JUNE 1960

CLUBS : CERCLE AMICAL LANNEMEZANAIS,
STADE MONTOIS RUGBY, UNION SPORTIVE DACQUOISE

INTERNATIONAL CAPS : 56

POSITION : NUMBER 8

GRAND SLAMS : 1981

NICKNAME : LOLO

NOM DE GUERRE : THE TAURINE WARRIOR

MY VISIT TO MEET HIM : WEDNESDAY 22ND NOVEMBER 2017

L aurent was the first former player I met on a beautiful
sunny day in Cambo-Les-Bains in November 2017.
I was nervous not just because this was my first interview
but he was such a physically imposing man and, in my
view, the greatest Number 8 in the world for much of the 1980s.
I turned up late and his hotel was closed. Damn it, I thought,
before I realised he had sent me a text asking me to call him.
A few minutes later, a huge silhouette of a man appeared. I shook
his enormous hand, its shape and broad fingers were the size
of a baseball glove.

As I drove to meet him, I couldn't stop thinking about it. Did he or didn't he? I'm not talking about an Agatha Christie 'who dunnit'. I'm talking about the World Cup Semi-Final in 1987, about two minutes from the end. Let me remind you...

Moving beautifully with all the rhythm of George Michael, Didier Camberabero was in his groove and kicking everything. With a few minutes remaining, he nailed his second penalty to draw France level. With the score at 24-24, the Australians won a line out in the French 22m and tried to run it, but the French defended aggressively. They won the ruck and shipped the ball to Lagisquet who kicked the ball deep into the French half, and it was this that unleashed the French flair to deliver the *dénouement*. First came Alain Lorieux's kick-chase, showing all his athletic ability to hunt down the opposition. If it weren't for the *Pompier's* athleticism, France wouldn't have scored. So hard and fast did he run that he spanked his head on an Aussie player, thereby missing the rest of the movement and (possibly) the greatest try in French history! There is no justice in the world.

It was the *Pompier's* pressure that meant Erbani, the ever-dependable flanker, picked the ball up and passed it to Champ, the Godfather of Toulon. He popped it up and Pascal Ondarts miraculously fielded the ball off his toes like a great 2nd slipper in cricket. When I watched it live, I shouted 'howzat'. Pascal passed to his great mate Garuche whose quicksilver thought of mind shipped it to Rodriguez who had the brawn of a bull from Dax but the guile of a three-

quarter. He drew his man, swivelled his hips and passed right to the team's Prince of Centres, Denis Charvet, who straightened and accelerated silkily, Porsche-like, before swerving to the right. How did he do that so beautifully? He was tackled but found Berbizier who switched the play back to the left where Lagisquet was in support again. As slippery as an eel and as fast as the Bayonne Express, he tried to flick the ball inside but found Lynagh, who under pressure from the Godfather, knocked on. The bull from Dax picked it off his toes and it was this action that sparked the controversy. Did he or didn't he knock it on? According to this one-eyed Francophile and every Frenchman I met on my journey, it definitely wasn't forward. To use a hackneyed cliché, that's the beauty of sport.

Of course, it is all academic anyway as Serge glided into the corner to score, just out of reach from the giant Tommy Lawton. However, I like telling the story because it was a moment of magic and reminds me of

why I love the game. Back then, the French could play this style of spontaneous rugby and make it look so easy and beautiful – their artistry, pace, lines of running, movement and instinctive search for space. These are the very foundations of the game and what the public wants to watch.

Man Mountain

Anyway, back to my meeting with Laurent. When I came down for breakfast the next morning, his thirteen-month-old grandson, Pablo, was making him work. Running between the tables of the dining room, Laurent had to deploy all his old defensive skills to keep up.

As his family name suggests, and like many of the players I met, Laurent is of Spanish origin. His parents worked on the construction sites for the SNCF, the French national railways, moving around France to follow the work. Laurent was born in Poitiers, hardly known for

> "...Lolo simply said to me, 'watch this'. When he smashed him, the guy's face moved like a boxer's in ultra-slow motion. I remember his grimace, the sweat and the noise! He just fell to the ground."

its rugby, but the family settled in Lannemezan in the foothills of the Pyrenees. It was here that Lolo found his opportunity to deploy his astonishing sporting talents.

"Dad was very strong and used to lift 50kg bags of cement around with one hand. I must have got my natural strength from him. I hated weights and would avoid them like the plague. I had the opportunity of a job through Stade Montois and I wanted to help Mum and Dad so I joined them. I went straight into the first team and learnt to defend myself from a young age.

" I never wanted to play Béziers back then. You either took fifty points or got beaten up, or both. They had a massive pack and players would get stamped on and take twenty to thirty stitches. I would just close my eyes and protect my head if I found myself on the wrong side."

"Back then, you needed two or three hard men in your team to sort problems out. Perpignan had Goze and Imbernon, Béziers had Saisset, Palmier, Senal, Estève and Vaquerin.

"When I started out at Lannemezan aged seventeen, I played with someone who was forty years old and as hard as nails who looked after me. He was a chef and had these enormous hands like buckets. In my first game against Pau, I was targeted so I retaliated and smacked one of their players. The old chef just looked at me, smiled and said, 'Ah, I can see you get it. Good lad'. You had to defend yourself."

I met Raphaël Ibañez who played with Laurent at US Dax and was effusive in his admiration of Lolo:

"The juniors at US Dax became Champions of France and was full of future internationals –Pelous, Magne, Dourte, myself – so we went straight into the first team. Laurent was a brilliant mentor, a fatherly figure who had this incredible ability and strength.

"Back then, rugby was slower and there were a lot of physical confrontations. After twenty minutes or so, the referee would say to the captains, 'Right, how do you want the game to go? Do you want to fight or play?'

'The captains would then decide. It could be quite rough back then! I loved it and would be in the middle of everything but it was very reassuring knowing that you had players like Lolo behind you.

"I remember that the mauls would go on forever. Lolo would watch them, then, after a few minutes, would decide enough was enough. He would arrive and put his huge hand and arm in, followed by the second one. He would literally lift the maul up, rip the ball away,

burst through and be off. It was extraordinary to watch.

"Another time, we were playing Tarbes in January in the cold and mud, and both teams were wearing red and white. Unfortunately, he confused me with one of the opposition players and gave me a very powerful short-arm jab to the jaw. I said, 'Lolo, what the f**k are you doing?' He just looked at me, stroked his moustache and said, 'Sorry young lad'. He ran off to the next breakdown, pissing himself laughing.

"My overriding memory of Lolo is someone who only used violence on the pitch where he felt he had no option. He was usually smiling on the pitch and always remembered that it was just a game. His leadership, speed, strength and hand offs are what stick in my memory. Technically, he was so impressive. He was an inspiration to me."

Quelle Tourte!

Lolo wasn't a violent man on the pitch, but he did tell me a story about how he once had to mete out a hiding to an opposition player. But he paid a price.

"US Dax played Chalon in around 1992, just after I had finished playing international rugby. I wasn't meant to play, but Jean-Louis Bérot asked me because he was worried US Dax would lose. It was a very tough match and I kept getting punched by one of their forwards. I let the referee know what was going on. Then, in a ruck, I got stamped on. As captain, I again let the referee know but he simply told me to be quiet. I responded by telling him that he was no longer required and that I would take matters into my

> "Back then, rugby was slower and there were a lot of physical confrontations. After twenty minutes or so, the referee would say to the captains, 'Right, how do you want the game to go? Do you want to fight or play?'"

own hands. The same player then tackled Jean-Patrick Lescarboura late.

"At the next line out, I simply laid the offending player out cold and walked off before the referee could find his red card. There was a court case that followed. In the court room, I explained the provocation, but the game had been televised so everyone could see the punch. To me, it was powerful and a thing of beauty but to the court room, it looked awful! The judge ignored my pleas and fined me 20,000 FF (about 2,000 €). The department of social security then came after me to fund the repairs to the guy's jaw!

"However, all my international friends around France then targeted him for retribution!"

Jean-Patrick Lescarboura remembers the incident well too.

"After I was tackled late, Lolo simply said to me, 'Watch this'. When he smashed him, the guy's face moved like a boxer's in ultra-slow motion. I said, 'Putain, quelle tourte'. I remember the player's grimace, the sweat and the noise! He just fell to the ground. The changing rooms were behind the posts and Lolo had to get through about four rows of spectators. They just parted like the sea, too scared to get in his way or say anything!

"But this was very atypical of Lolo. He just wasn't that type of player, but this guy really pissed him off."

Laurent secured his international breakthrough in 1981 in Australia when Fouroux wanted big, hard players who could stand up to the opposition. His mate Berbizier, who also started his rugby at Lannemezan, had been badly injured and Fouroux wanted a man to take revenge. As tough as a Spanish bull, at 1.92m, 110kg and running 100m in eleven seconds, Lolo was a force of nature. He fitted Fouroux's requirements perfectly

and that tour cemented his place for a decade.

He was a fabulous player throughout the 1980s but he probably reached his apogee in 1986-1987 when he beat the All Blacks at the Battle of Nantes.

"All these stories from the French journalist about us taking drugs were absolute nonsense. In 1986 in Nantes, the All Blacks said we came out with evil in our eyes and so concluded we'd taken drugs. That wasn't the drugs – that was a combination of raw garlic, coffee and aspirin!"

After he'd finished playing, Serge Blanco asked him to become coach of Biarritz where he had a successful spell culminating in winning the Top 14 title in 2002/3. Following that, he took his business and coaching skills to various places such as Guadeloupe, Pau, Brive, Sicily and then back to Biarritz.

"You know David, I have experienced my greatest friendships and disappointments in rugby."

I could tell that Lolo is a man of great loyalty and principle, and he holds his grudges. He is still emotional about how he was let go by Biarritz when they were relegated in 2014.

On a lighter note, he enjoyed his time coaching in Sicily. When he was appointed in 2007, the team was last in the pool but had to stay up.

"I was given a car and house and had to manage a team of nutters, including a politician's bodyguard who would bring *his gun to training. Once we were training on the first team pitch but the groundsman didn't like it. My bodyguard, in all seriousness, offered me his gun to help resolve matters!"*

I spent a fabulous two days in his busy hotel, listening to him recount his tales.

If you get the opportunity, go to Cambo-les-Bains. Travelling south west from Biarritz, it is set in the heart of the Basque country and every time I'm there, the sunshine gleams like powdered gold over the grassy hillsides.

Patrice Lagisquet played throughout the 1980s with Lolo and they also coached together at Biarritz for six years.

"As a player and coach, he was also a practical joker, which helped reduce the tension. He would squeeze your hand very hard when he shook it so you had to kneel down and ask him to let go. After a while I just gave him 'la bise' instead.

"I remember Laurent once playing against Argentina in Nantes. Madrero was their fly-half who was strong, big and aggressive, but Laurent simply brushed him off with a handoff. He actually lifted him up and moved him to the side, out of his way, and continued running. It was incredible to witness, like watching Obelix.

"He also had great pace. We played together in 1983 at the Mediterranean games in Casablanca and at one point, Laurent was in the backs. He caught the ball and suddenly took off, but his acceleration was so fast that he left me behind, and I was meant to be one of the world's fastest players."

As a top player, Derek White, the Scottish Number 8, remembers him well:

"Rodriguez was fast and skilful and strong, and our plan was to try to stop him getting over the gain line. He was the point of their attack. If you could stop him, you could go some way to stopping France. If not, he could perforate your defence and blow you away."

Vines on La Plaine d'Aniane
in Hérault, near Montpellier.

Blind
Date

I remember it so well. My heart was racing as I turned off the dusty road near the town of Aniane near Montpellier, like I was meeting my lover. I spotted a weathered sign pointing reluctantly in its direction, suggesting that visitors were either unexpected, unwelcome or both. I was on a blind date, but my target wasn't aware of my imminent arrival.

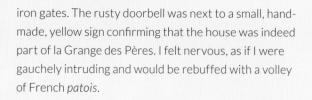

I admit it openly – I'm in love with this Domaine and its region, and I convinced myself that all is fair in love and war.

Ostensibly, Knoxy and I were en route to watch Montauban play BO, but I couldn't resist the lure of dropping in on one of my favourite growers, the fabled Domaine de la Grange des Pères. I remember using the term 'dropping in' as it made me feel more comfortable, like one drops in to an old family friend. Deep down I felt uneasy although the feeling wasn't strong enough to stop me. I admit it openly – I'm in love with this Domaine and its region, and I convinced myself that all is fair in love and war.

Just say it out loud: Domaine de la Grange des Pères. It rolls off the tongue mellifluously like honey trickling from a spoon. Overlay the regional *accent du midi* and the sound becomes even easier on the ear. For me, these sounds personify the south of France and evoke powerful memories of the time when I lived in the Vaucluse, a neighbouring *départment*.

In a little over twenty years, la Grange des Pères has entered the pantheon of great French wine *domaines*, its small stock exhausted swiftly by thirsty and lucky buyers. I had enjoyed their wines over the years (if I could find them), read about Alain, Bernard and Laurent Vaillé, and knew they had a reputation for being reserved and unreceptive to impromptu visits, but this just raised the stakes and piqued my excitement. I knew this would be a test of my character, French language and people skills, but I thrived on situations like this. My elevator pitch was ready.

Volley of Patois

I eventually found the *Domaine*. The grange or barn itself was on the left, signalled by a garnet-coloured sign on an impressive limestone rock. I drove past it and turned left along a narrow track to their house, which was a large but unassuming villa fronted by an imposing set of iron gates. The rusty doorbell was next to a small, hand-made, yellow sign confirming that the house was indeed part of la Grange des Pères. I felt nervous, as if I were gauchely intruding and would be rebuffed with a volley of French *patois*.

I didn't even have time to ring their doorbell before Alain, the father, appeared. He was small with pointed features and dressed in cool denim under the searing heat of the midday sun. He was chewing food. It suddenly dawned on me that I had committed one of France's gravest sins and interrupted his lunch. Life, I thought, was about to get even harder.

"Bonjour monsieur, excusez-moi de vous déranger", I stuttered. *"Est-ce que vous faites des dégustations?"*

"Non", he dead-panned. *"Nous ne les faisons pas."*

I had blown it. In a moment of excitement and nerves, I had forgotten to show empathy or willingness to engage him first. I had reduced the occasion to the merely functional and rather bluntly requested 'a tasting'. As though my very existence depended on it, the adrenaline kicked in. I suddenly remembered my elevator pitch, which consisted of telling him, in my best *midi*-accented French, how I used to live in Avignon, play rugby for Châteauneuf-du-Pape, date a French girl from Avignon and drink copious amounts of French wine. Now, I knew his wine, bought it, evangelised about it, drank it and loved it. I spoke passionately about La Grange des Pères - to its maker for goodness' sake!

My eyes implored him to let me in. And it worked.

"Revenez après le déjeuner et je vous ferai une dégustation", he said smiling.

Built to Last

I was ecstatic. I remember that feeling as I made the short drive to Aniane for lunch. The lunch wasn't memorable for its quality or quantity, but the anticipation had suppressed my appetite. Afterwards, Alain met me at the grange and we spent over two hours tasting his 2006 red in *barrique*, the *cabernet sauvignon*, *syrah* and *mourvèdre* wines all separated.

I drooled over their quality and the setting. They were all rich, powerful and gorgeous even if they were unfinished. His wines, like those of Domaine de Trévallon (where Laurent, Alain's youngest son, had trained under the tutelage of the great Eloi Dürrbach), have a distinct flavour and perfume that I rarely taste anywhere else.

La Grange des Pères is a combination of wild *garrigue* herbs, black fruits, freshness and meatiness. That day, each *cépage* brought something to the wine: the *cabernet* brought tautness and freshness; the *syrah* black fruits, meatiness and *garrigue* herbs; the *mourvèdre* some cherry, spice, earth and gaminess. Typically, the final blend also contains small quantities of *counoise* and *petit verdot* that enhance the freshness, fragrance and complexity.

All this had happened in 2008 so I dropped in again a few years later. There was no point in calling or emailing or tweeting ahead because I knew that wasn't the way they worked.

This time I tracked Alain down in the grange itself and he gave me the same generous welcome he had done five years before. He was again denim-clad, obviously older, but looking slim and very fit for a septuagenarian. Under the high sun, I could feel the sun prickling my head as we walked into the cool grange where we chatted for another two hours.

I bought one of the last cases of their 2010 red for cash, which is now maturing in Julian's cellar in the Pyrenees (although it is entirely possible that he has drunk it), but they had already exhausted their whites. Inside each case, they place a bay leaf and sprig of thyme, redolent of the warm, *garrigue* perfume. Laurent thinks his reds are best after a decade of cellaring, but says people who like them young should drink them earlier as there are no set rules for personal taste.

After a couple of very pleasant and memorable hours, I thanked Alain for his time, promised to return in the near future and drove to a restaurant he had recommended near Pic Saint-Loup. Surrounded by the chattering *cigales* and seated under a glorious *micocoulier* tree, which protected me from the high afternoon sun, I enjoyed a slow, late lunch of prawns *à la Japonaise* (yes, even in the deep south of France), beef from the Aubrac region and local cheeses, washed

down with a bottle of Mas Julien white, only because the restaurant didn't have the very rare La Grange des Pères. Life doesn't get much better than this, I thought.

Like Eloi Dürrbach of Trévallon, La Grange des Pères encapsulates everything I love about this type of wine making – artistry, passion, longevity, simplicity, humility, hard work and determination. The Vaillés represent the very antithesis of the quick-fix, blingy and 'look-at-me' culture. They cultivate wines not publicity. They just want to make great wines with an enduring sense of *terroir*.

Lac Annecy on the edge of the French Alps.
Photo - Pierre Carton.

Mountains

"WELL THE SUMMER TIME HAS GONE
AND THE LEAVES ARE GENTLY TURNIN'
AND MY LOVE I WANNA TAKE
TO THE PLACE HEART-IS-YEARNIN'
WILL YOU GO, LASSIE GO?
AND WE'LL ALL GO TOGETHER
IN THE WILD MOUNTAIN THYME
ALL AROUND THE BLOOMING HEATHER
WILL YOU GO?"

VAN MORRISON,
PURPLE HEATHER, 1973

This area covers both the Pyrenees and the Alps. There is a village in the foothills of the Pyrenees called Saint-Savin, near the town of Argelès-Gazost and not far from Lourdes, which encapsulates the essence of the French mountains, whether there or the French Alps. In the summer, the air can be warm, thick and humid, and you can taste the sweet nectar from the mountain flowers, climb some of the highest peaks and dive into the cold, pristine lakes to cool down. Saint-Savin is close to such iconic places as the snaking Luz-Ardiden climb so the roads and hills are brimming with cyclists and walkers, and the bars and cafés overflowing with tourists and locals soaking up the sun amid the green folds of the summer countryside.

In winter, the locals are still there in force, frequenting the local markets selling *porc de bigorre*, local *saucisson*, bread and cheeses. This is what I love about these places – they are real, not just summer enclaves that become depopulated in winter. On a clear day, the air is pure and the snow-capped mountains razor sharp to the eye with no heat to refract the light and blur the view, and the smell of wood burning fires wafts around the villages. I find that smell intoxicating; it nourishes the soul and reminds me of my childhood.

Chambéry in the foothills of the French Alps.
Photo - Pierre Carton.

Much as I love the Pyrenees, I lived longer in the Alps, from September 1991-Februrary 1992 to be precise, around the time of the Albertville Winter Olympics. I had joined Andersen Consulting in London who offered me the opportunity of a secondment to the Paris office, which was heavily involved in building the information systems for the games. At twenty-three, I was a simple chap with basic needs so I jumped at the chance. All I could think about were rugby, parties, top class food and wine, skiing, the Winter Olympics and French girls, not necessarily in that order, obviously.

However, when I arrived, I was told by Andersen Consulting Paris that all the roles were filled in Albertville. Instead, they would be sending me on an assignment to Caen, Normandy. Damn it! However, after the initial disappointment, I had a blast.

Big Mussels

The weekend in Caen that really sticks in my mind was the stag party of my great mate Steve Meredith (Meres) from Mumbles. A funnier man I have never met. In February 1991, he called me about his stag party and the conversation went something like this (imagine a man with a strong Welsh accent speaking):

Meres: *"Beres, we're not coming to Paaris.*
              We're coming to Son."

Me: *"Son? Where the f**k is that? You mean*
              Somme, as in Battle of the Somme?"

Meres: *"No, f**king Son, C. A. E. N."*

Me: *"Ah, you mean Con, C. A. E. N."*

Meres: *"Aye, that's what I said."*

So, a couple of months later, Meres turned up with his uncles, Chris and Hugh, Carsen Russell, his best man and now CEO of London Scottish, and a bunch of mates in a big red van. They had left Portsmouth around 8am and rolled off, literally, in Ouistreham near Caen at about 3.30pm, driven by another mate, an ex-alcoholic. Yeh, I know what you're thinking but don't worry, he was reformed. Chris and Hugh were sitting alongside the driver in the three front seats. They were fast asleep and so smashed that they were swinging around like rag dolls, only their safety belts holding them upright. I opened up the back door and it was carnage. I could just about make out some prostrate bodies amid the food, newspapers, magazines and bottles of beer.

I was living at the time in a tiny village called Cheux with my friend Jean Courcelle-Labrousse. We were sent to Caen on a 'consulting' assignment although it was more like a 'consumption' assignment, and Jean and I rented a *gite* that was big enough for three people although that weekend we housed about twelve.

The Five Nations Championship was on so we decided to camp out in Cheux's only bar. When we walked in, the owner looked alarmed but soon relaxed when he realised that tripling his annual turnover in a single weekend was a certainty. He even gave up his living room so we could watch a game.

Then, as though the hospitality couldn't get better, a mysterious man turned up on his bicycle with a basket full of fresh mussels. We befriended him and before you could say *moules marinière*, Monsieur Le Capitaine Pugwash was offering to cook us dinner for a fistful of francs and a few *pressions*. 'Carp Diem', I thought. Fish of the Day. They were so good that I still remember them nearly thirty years later. The mussels were plump and fresh and bursting with minerals, acidity and salinity, the sort of food I adore. We ate and drank like kings and amused ourselves with a range of stag-party

games, the quality of which was so low that none feature in this book. Suffice it to say that they took place in the bar and involved paper, flames, beers, human skittles and semi-naked men. At the risk of sounding defensive and to reassure my mother, nothing illegal, immoral, sexual or unethical took place. Only puerile.

Chris and Hugh were the court jesters who humoured us with their (lack of) French, notably at the *boulangerie* where they would ask for three *croissants* each morning: *"try croyssantes por favor"* or some such rubbish. Those two words *'try croyssantes'* have gone down in folklore. If you don't know it already, *'croyssante'* is now Welsh for *croissant* and adopted as common parlance, at least in this family and circle of friends.

Dressed in jeans, which were three inches too short, white socks and training shoes, they would strut about eating their *'try croyssantes'* in the village square, regaling us with stories about Mumbles and referring to me as either 'Dai Beres' or 'C**ty'. Oh, how we laughed. Those are wonderful memories.

Angels

Anyway, where was I? Ah yes, the mountains.

It was September 1991 and I was due to roll off the project in Caen, the client having realised that I was a useless interloper from the Perfidious Albion. Early one evening I received a telephone call from an angel in heaven. The sweet voice said:

"David, you must take the train to Albertville in the Alps at 6pm on Sunday evening."

I almost choked on my oysters. I celebrated like I had just kicked the winning drop goal in the Rugby World Cup Final to beat Australia (ok, that didn't happen until 2003

but you get my point). I still laugh at those words 'must take the train', like the angel had to coerce me.

Maybe it wasn't an angel. Perhaps it was a gift from the Greek God of wine and parties, Dionysus. Or Zeus (Olympics) or Eros (love and fertility) or Pothos (passion) or Imeros (erotic desire) or Aphrodite (beauty and lust). Whoever it was, I thank you.

The omens for my new project were good when I arrived to find a team of a *douzaine* 'consultants' lunching heartily, including my old mate Laurent Parquet. He is a debonair man from Brive but now the archetypal Parisian Frenchman - erudite, urbane, charming and well-dressed although he has never lost his love of the provinces and all its customs, pastimes and sports such as hunting, shooting, fishing, rugby, regional food and wine, whiskey, cigars and bull fighting. He was and is the perfect playmate. Bert Baret and Benoît Papy were also at that first lunch, both of whom would also become lifelong friends.

After lunch, I met my manager, Eric, who introduced me to the 'client'. Holy smoke. *Bon Dieu. Mangetout.* Looking at me were about twenty women aged between eighteen and thirty-five years old - Annie, Gisele, Nathalie – I can't quite remember all their names. I should have been thinking about the job and my career but Aphrodite was blocking out the light.

The work wasn't demanding and the social life was sensational. I was living the dream. We could ski every weekend, wherever we fancied – Tignes, Val d'Isere,

Val Thorens, Meribel, Courchevel. The conversations on Fridays were incredible:

"Where shall we ski this weekend?"

"Ah, I can't be arsed. I've skied every weekend for the last 365 days so I'm just gonna stay in dull Albertville and watch TV."

We became so *blasé* about it.

Jackpot

We lived in a huge house a couple of miles outside of Albertville that had seven bedrooms, seven double beds, fourteen pillows, a large dining room table (with no chairs) and a fridge full of Chablis, oysters, caviar and smoked salmon. Every month, we would hold a big house party and we had only one simple rule: girl invitees only. You could propose blokes but they had to be approved by the social committee of which Marc, the house gigolo, was the self-elected Chairman. Unsurprisingly, not many made the cut. In fact, come to think of it, I don't think a single one did.

To ensure we had enough provisions to last the party, Bert, Laurent, Marc, Benoît and I would visit Auchan where we would fill five trolleys full of food and booze. It was all about excess, on every level.

It was at one of these parties where I met, properly, the beautiful Françoise. I had seen her skip across the floor of the client office but only very occasionally. She would set my heart racing when I glimpsed her but I only managed to say, *"Salut! Ça va?"* Where did she go all the time, I thought? Well, I would soon find out.

Françoise stopped me in my tracks. Her eyes and smile were a proposal, an offer I couldn't refuse.

What's more, she was a foodie, loved wine and was the Assistant Director of Courchevel for the Games, hence why she was rarely in the office. For about six months, we would wine and dine in any restaurant or five-star hotel of our choice in Courchevel – Le Byblos, Le Carlina, Les Airelles. It was like a one-way bet that you couldn't lose.

'Lucky bastard', I can hear you shout.
And you'd be right. She was very lucky...

We also skied the best slopes in France. One of my favourites is the legendary run in Courchevel called La Saulire, starting at 2738m and finishing at 1350m. It is one of the most exhilarating and enduring memories of my lucky life. As I skied through the trees (and sometimes into them) it is the silence that I remember, broken only by distant voices, cow bells and the noise of skis on the crushed, velvety snow. It was magic.

Back in Albertville, we would head to a fabulous restaurant called Les Trappeurs on the Col de Tamié. It was like a scene out of a James Bond movie - darkly lit, sheepskin on the seats, open fires, 007 sitting in the corner. Laurent and I would visit it regularly with Françoise and his girlfriend of the moment, Sophie. Or I would take my great mate Julian Rimmer there when he came to ski, drink and find himself a French beauty to marry. We would eat *tartiflette* and large salads lubricated by some local wines, before imbibing the grog at the end of the dinner to aid digestion. I have no idea what was in it. On the palate it was quite subtle and warming but then it had a kick at the end. The downside was that we had to get back down the mountain. It was a bit of a fairground ride, especially in the snow – road, mountain, sky, trees, road - but fortunately the snow chains never let us down.

For all that I loved the Alps, there is something so raw and naked about the Pyrenees. Perhaps it's the wind and rain that can quickly sweep in from the Atlantic or the lack of outsiders and foreign money, compared to the Alps.

It has a heart and soul that still reflects all those historical, local influences – Béarn, Basque, Catalan, Spanish. Or perhaps it's because Julian has a beautiful house near Salies-du-Salat that has been host to family holidays, stag parties, gastro weekends and other shenanigans over the last twenty years. It has a wonderful garden in front of it nicknamed 'The Field of Dreams' on which many dreams have been broken, much blood spilt and torrents of tears shed.

And look at all the talent those great French sides produced in the past – from Lourdes (the Prat brothers, Caussade, Garuet, Armary), from Tarbes (Dintrans, Crémaschi, Crabos), from Pau (Paparemborde), Lannemezan (Berbizier, Rodriguez), from Lavelanet (Estève) and from Bagnères (Gachassin, Bertranne, Gourdon, Aguirre). In the Alps, the great teams were fewer and represented at the top level only by Grenoble (Lorieux, Kacala, Brouzet, Merle and LAndréau) and Bourgoin (Cécillon), to name but a few.

If you don't know the area, here are a few visits that will make you sing with joy.

1. Amble along the Boulevard des Pyrenees in Pau on a fine, clear day and marvel at the stunning Pyrenean mountains.
2. Visit Le Cirque de Gavarnie, one of the wonders of the world which, Victor Hugo described as 'the Colosseum of nature'. It is a huge horseshoe-shaped rock formation with a waterfall 400m high, formed by a process of glacial erosion. The walk, scenery, flora and fauna will rekindle your faith in mother nature's ability to withstand the onslaught of man*unkind*.
3. Visit the fabulous Viscos hotel in Saint-Savin for lunch or dinner. Owned by the great Saint-Martin family since 1840 (now in the seventh generation), it is one of my favourite hotel-restaurants in the world. It is honest, quintessentially French, gastronomic and lovely. It is an epicurean paradise. Alexis is the culinary genius who has served me some wonderful Pyrenean and Gascon classics over the years – Bigorre pork, Gascony lobster, wood pigeon and partridge to name a few.

When I think about mountains, I always recall John Steinbeck's wonderful prose: *"What good is the warmth of summer without the cold of winter to give it sweetness".*

Go on, sit back and play some Van Morrison. Will you go and smell the mountain thyme, all around the blooming heather?

Louisou Armary

MOUNTAINS

"THE HEARTLAND OF RUGBY
WAS IN THE VILLAGES SO YOU
DEFENDED YOUR PRIDE WITH
EVERYTHING. PLAYING AGAINST
TARBES, BAGNÈRES AND PAU WERE
ESPECIALLY TOUGH BECAUSE THEY
WERE THE LOCAL RIVALS AND
FULL OF EXCEPTIONAL AND HARD
PLAYERS LIKE DINTRANS, PAUL,
PAPAREMBORDE, AGUIRRE,
POURTAL, TOROSSIAN, DUHART,
BERTRANNE, GOURDON,
CIGAGNA, AND MANY MORE."

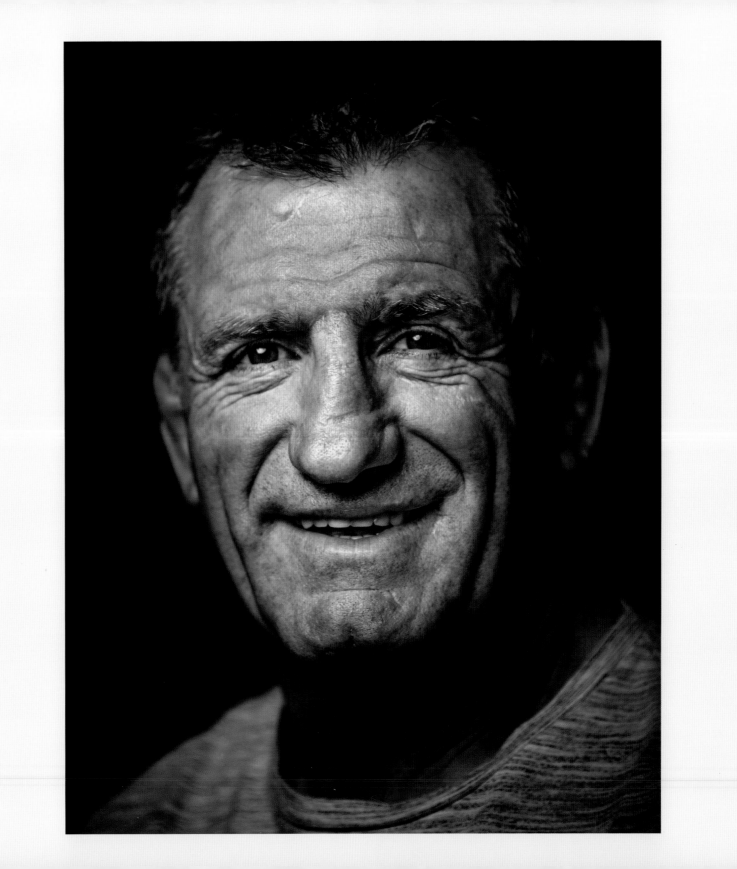

BORN : 24TH JULY 1963

CLUBS : FC LOURDES

INTERNATIONAL CAPS : 46

POSITION : HOOKER OR PROP

GRAND SLAMS : 1987

NICKNAME : GALIPE, LE TOY

NOM DE GUERRE : THE IRON MAN

MY VISIT TO MEET HIM : SATURDAY 25TH NOVEMBER 2018

It was cold and wet on the day I drove into the Pyrenees to meet Louisou, in stark contrast to the sun and warmth of the Basque Country where I had been royally entertained a few days before by the Basque piano shifters, Ondarts, Rodriguez and Condom, and by their pianists, Blanco and Pardo. I had spent a fabulous few days chatting, eating and drinking, but I could feel my trousers tightening around my waist. As I sat at Pascal's hotel, plump and surfeited, I caught sight of myself in the mirror looking tired. However, it was nothing a couple of expressos wouldn't sort out, and within thirty minutes I was off. The fitness regime would have to wait.

I tracked Louisou down via Nathalie Tonon from Bun near Argelès-Gazost, who had hosted me at her charming B&B in September 2017. He lives near Argelès-Gazost, a small town about ten miles south of Lourdes in the foothills of the Pyrenees, and a place I adore. I have wandered around many different regions in France incapable of choosing a favourite place. Like one's children, I love them all equally.

His house is beautifully positioned in a cosy *bourg* with magnificent views across the valley. As I approached it, I could smell the woodsmoke from the chimneys. I love that distinctive, potent smell of wood, thatch and earth. It envelops the mountain air and scatters its soul in the breeze, providing comfort and warmth to the locals. The scent made me recall a quote I once read that said something like, 'Drink, procreate and smoke plenty of cigars'. Two out of three in the previous week isn't bad, I thought.

Chien de Bouchier

To you, the reader, Armary may be one of the lesser known players as he faced some fierce competition in his position of prop and hooker – Dubroca, Dintrans, Garuet and Ondarts – but he went to three World Cups and won forty-six caps.

I arrived and he greeted me warmly. He is as fit as a butcher's dog with a bodily form that looks like it is hewn from Pyrenean granite. His face is scarred and his boxer's nose has been bent out of shape, no doubt from all those dark, close encounters.

Louisou was brought up in the foothills of the Pyrenees and was a good downhill and slalom skier, regularly competing between the ages of six and fourteen. It was an expensive sport lacking coaches and a development structure, and his parents had to buy all the equipment themselves. Money was scarce and as a result, he stopped. However, skiing's loss was rugby's gain. While at school, he started playing *l'ovalie* and his talents were quickly spotted.

" My parents had a small farm holding and they didn't want me to disappear off to Lourdes because I would use my strong arms to help them. Eventually they agreed; I could go and play rugby but I couldn't stay for the *3ème mi-temps*!"

"Lourdes was a big team at the time and had this incredible heritage and backlog of star players – the Prat brothers, Caussade, Garuet, Crémaschi, Gachassin, Mir, Crauste, Rancoule, Lacaze, Campaes, Berges-Cau, and many more. In 1958 against Wales, every player in the backs came from Lourdes.

"I had the fortune of playing with Jean-Pierre Garuet. He was ten years older than me so I played my first match with him when he was twenty-nine. He was a monumental prop, strong and technically brilliant. He was so effective at attacking the opposition hooker. The advantage of being so much younger than him was that he could teach me so much. He was the professor of scrummaging and I was his pupil."

Louisou was a top player too. Nicknamed 'Galipe' by his teammates because of his running prowess, he was the modern-day prop forward – fast, mobile, strong and always available. When I spoke to Daniel Herrero, he talked about the importance of players like Louisou who he described as a *'puncheur'* able to cross the gain line and get some go forward for his team. He certainly wasn't the biggest prop forward but pound for pound he was as strong as an ox.

Sporting Temples

There are some mythical, old rugby grounds that I wanted to visit and the Antoine Béguère stadium was one such ground (the others being Sauclières in Béziers, Jean Dauger in Bayonne and the Guy Boniface stadium in Mont-de-Marsan). I love standing in these sporting temples that are steeped in history and where luminaries would weave their magic to stir the crowd. Where nostalgia incites pleasure, it is a force for good. For me, it evokes excitement and passion and sets my heart racing. These aren't any old grounds and they weren't any old players. They were giants of the game,

an inspiration to thousands of kids, women and men, and a key reason we play and love the game.

When I met Pierre Villepreux and André Boniface, they talked glowingly about their memories of Lourdes in its heyday.

Pierre said, *"I was so inspired by that Lourdes' team of the 1950s. My nan was religious and one day she took me to La Grotte in Lourdes, but I saw this as a great opportunity to visit the stadium of the French champions and try to see some of the stars. I was fascinated by how the team attacked with its speed and high skill level. Lourdes' forwards and backs could interchange and link play so effectively. The whole team played with this collective excitement and fluid style, which no other team at the time could replicate, with the possible exception of Stade Montois that boasted the gifted Boniface brothers."*

André elaborated, *"Having Maurice Prat playing in the backs and Jean in the forwards helped team harmony. If the forwards won the ball and the backs dropped it, Jean would support his brother and not shout at him! At Stade Montois, where I played, the forwards would sulk, and it was even worse when I was at US Dax! Lourdes had a culture of training hard and playing beautiful, running rugby, all under the leadership of Jean. I remember playing a match at the Antoine Béguère stadium and there were 25,000 spectators. It was fabulous. Jean was very tough with his team and would make some players cry because he had exceptionally high standards. I liked him a lot."*

Friends and Foes

I asked Louisou what it was like playing rugby back in his era with this mix of brutality and guile, best exemplified by the French national team under Fouroux.

"Winning at home was very important. The heartland of rugby was in the villages so you defended your pride with everything. Playing against Tarbes, Bagnères and Pau were especially tough because they were the local rivals and full of exceptional and hard players like Dintrans, Paul, Paparemborde, Aguirre, Pourtal, Torossian, Duhart, Bertranne, Gourdon, Cigagna, and many more.

"But the tough matches were all over France. For example, we once played Toulon in 1989/90 when they were at their peak with players like Champ, Orso, Louvet and Melville. Garuet and Toulon's prop, Manu Diaz, were sent off for a fight that took place between the try and halfway lines. But we were all friends afterwards!"

"Bègles was also a force back then. They had Vincent Moscato in their front row who had a fearsome reputation but he wasn't nasty. That role was left for Serge Simon. He would go around smacking you without a care in the world! They also had players who remained fairly anonymous to the press and public, but they were superb, like Mougeot, Berthozat, Conchy, Courtiols and Alibert. Laporte was an average player but a great leader of men, a bit like in the mould of Fouroux."

I remember the test series that France played against Australia in 1989 in France and then the return leg in Australia in 1990. It was a mix of great rugby, wonderful tries and punch ups. I asked Louisou to tell me more.

"Kearns nicked the ball a few times on our scrum so I gave him a little headbutt. In France, you never 'stole' the opposition ball like that, you had more respect! It all kicked off in those tests – FitzSimons, Benazzi, Gallard, Sella, all of us. It was good old-fashioned rugby and a bit of fun and no one got hurt!"

What about England?

"England was always smart and I had great respect for them. Probyn was a clever player and Leonard great fun. Moore was a pain, always chatting and winding us up, usually the week before the game but also at every scrum. Because they beat us a lot between 1989 and 1995, we always felt they were a bit arrogant and disrespectful of us.

> "Moore was a pain, always chatting and winding us up, usually the week before the game but also at every scrum."

"The South Africans would always try and beat you with their size but when they spun the ball out to their back, they could be brilliant.

"Uli Schmidt, their hooker, had a reputation for being a particularly nasty bastard, but didn't get picked for the World Cup in South Africa in 1995."

Old School Lunching

Louisou and I had been chatting next to the wood fire, drinking a pre-lunch beer, but it was noon and time for lunch so we headed to a local restaurant, the Pierre d'Agos in Agos-Vidalos, a typically rustic French beauty serving hearty fare and local wines. It was old school, the sort of place I would have eaten in a hundred times back in the 1980s and '90s, and the type of cuisine that has been handed down from generation to generation. It isn't about fancy stars and trying to be too clever with the food. It is about serving simple, local and seasonal produce at a fair price to the local community and tourists, while earning a decent living so they can feed their family.

It had been a while since breakfast and the beer had enhanced our appetite. We both ordered the *assiette gourmande*. How could I resist? Just saying those words excites me, never mind the flavours. Those words dance with rhythm and flow onomatopoeically off the tongue, overlaid with the regional twangy accent. The *assiette gourmande* consisted of a 'block' of *foie gras*, *jambon de porc duroc* (local pork), *boudin blanc* (white sausage) and *truite fumée* (smoked trout), garnished with a salad sporting a vinaigrette of such salty, briney and acidic balance that I craved for more. Things were going well so we continued with a perfect piece of *filet de boeuf* that arrived tender and moist, its juices oozing like an artist's brush stroke across the plate.

"One of my greatest rugby memories was playing against the All Blacks in 1994 when we won the test series 2-0. That team wasn't simply full of fabulous players, such as Sella, Saint-André, Sadourney, Ntmack, Lacroix, Califano and Benazzi, we also had a wonderful 'etat d'esprit'. We were great friends and we loved spending time together. When you have great players and a real bond, you fight for each other and do everything to win. Our Coach, Pierre Berbizier, also let the players express themselves.

"The clubs today have too many players who play just for the money and don't qualify for selection for France. The result is that you don't create the same bonds of friendship, plus there are fewer young players coming through, which weakens the national side. I keep positive though, because we have such a strong U20 national side. We must give those players time to prosper in the clubs. They still need time to develop their understanding of the game at that level. I want to see dynamic, running rugby, like we played, not slow rugby with lots of collisions, which is what the TOP 14 is mostly like today. We have lots of resources and we should be doing much better at the national level."

I had spent a good three hours with Louisou and really enjoyed his company. He is friendly, articulate and warm. On the pitch, he never had that snarl like some of the other props but appearances can be deceptive. He was a very tough player nevertheless.

We finished lunch and I headed back to the small hotel I had booked in Argelès-Gazost. I didn't book my favourite, Le Viscos in Saint-Savin, because I was trying to be frugal. I knew the restaurant and bar at Le Viscos would be a big temptation, and that Alexis, the culinary genius who runs the place, would provide hospitality of such perfection that I would be indulging by 6pm. But fear not, I had booked a table for dinner and duly arrived about 8pm.

Old School Dining

The quality of his cooking is off the charts. That evening, I ate *langoustes à la gasgogne*, and *suprême de pintade à la graine de moutarde*. Both were exquisite – hearty, rich, decadent but elegant too. Like a great wine, the structure of these dishes has to have texture and acidity to balance the richness, and Alexis always achieves this.

I ordered a bottle of La Grange des Pères 2010, which is hedonistic and rich. Thereafter, I put my palate in the hands of Alexis who whipped up various savoury and sweet gastronomic delights. At about 10pm, after service had finished, he joined me at the table and started pouring a *smörgåsbord* of *digestifs* – Cognac, Calvados, Rivesaltes. So much for an early night. So much for my self-restraint. His brother, Aurélien, and sister-in-law, Maria, joined us and we chatted for hours until only the hardcore of Alexis and I were left. I think it was about 1.30am when I hit the metaphorical wall, only to realise that I couldn't possibly drive back to Argèles. Alexis offered me a room in the hotel but first we had to find one that wasn't occupied, easier said than done when one is inebriated. The front desk had gone home for the night and the computer was off so we reverted to the old school approach of simply opening

each hotel room until we found a bed that wasn't occupied. We may have inadvertently disturbed a couple of guests but I didn't care. I slept like a *gros chat*. Le Viscos is a place that just keeps giving. *Merci* Alexis.

I had the Sunday and Monday morning off before meeting Philippe Dintrans in Tarbes and Jean-Pierre Garuet in Pontacq near Lourdes. I was loving life.

Wade Dooley Didn't Like Uli Schmidt

The name 'Uli Schmidt', the former South African hooker, came up a few times on my travels so he clearly made his mark, legally or otherwise. The best story I heard came from Wade Dooley (read this with a strong Blackpool accent to properly visualise Wade speaking):

"I don't know what he is like now but back then I f**king hated him, and I'll tell you why, David.

"I was playing a game for Quins against Transvaal when Schmidt, the dirty bastard, clocked me from behind. I dropped to my knees and could see about sixty players on the pitch. I wanted to get my revenge, but I couldn't get near him for the rest of the game. So, I marked him and promised myself that one day we would meet again.

"So fast forward a few years and I was in South Africa playing in Rob Jones' testimonial, a World XV v South African XV. There were a bunch of us from England there – Teaguey, Jerry, Deano, Ackers, Winters, Jason. I was looking down the team sheet and I saw his name. I couldn't stop smiling. I thought 'right, you c**t, you're in for it'. There's nothing like holding your grudges is there, David?

"Uli got the ball and went for a trundle up the middle but Jerry dragged him down. Great, I thought, this was the chance I'd been waiting for. I sprinted so I could get there before he got up because I was going to give him the biggest shoeing of his life. But, Teaguey, Winters, Deano and others all beat me to it. They obviously hated him too. We gave him the hiding of his life. Oh, how we laughed afterwards. He got taken off and I haven't seen him since!"

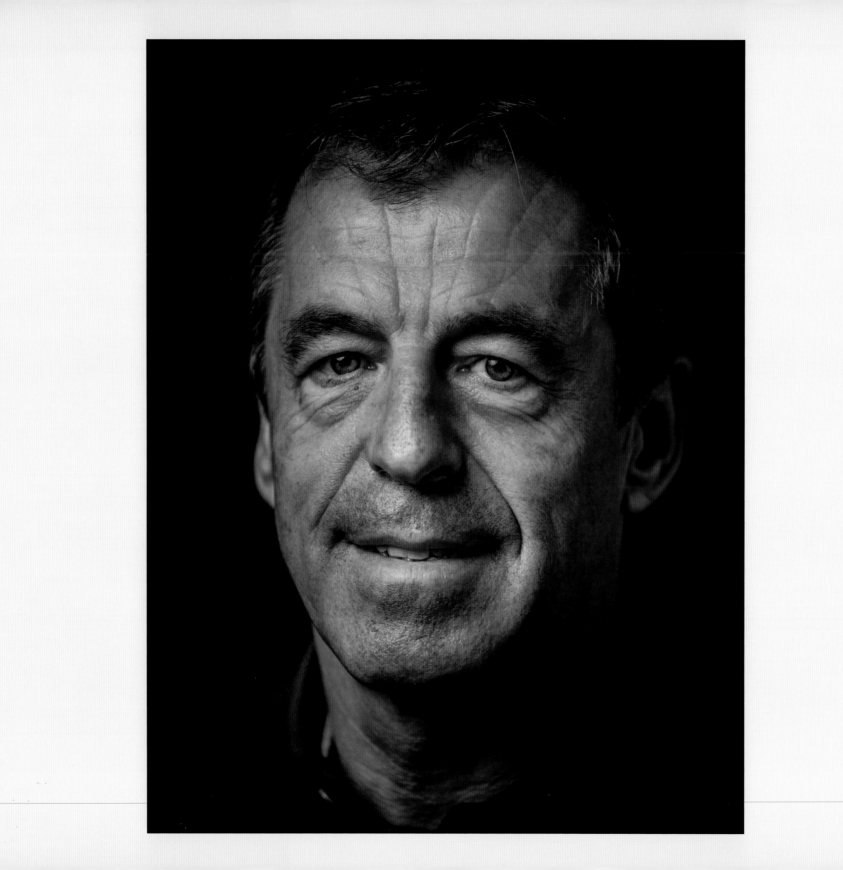

Pierre Berbizier

MOUNTAINS "THE WHOLE DEBATE IN THE PRESS ABOUT OUR STYLE OF PLAY WAS FALSE. THROUGHOUT THE 1980S, THE PRESS TALKED ABOUT BRAWN VERSUS FLAIR, BUT WE HAD BOTH. WE HAD POWER UP FRONT AND SPEED AND FLAIR BEHIND."

BORN : 17TH JUNE 1958

CLUBS : FC LOURDES, SPORTING UNION AGEN
LOT-ET-GARONNE

INTERNATIONAL CAPS : 56

POSITION : CENTRE, SCRUM HALF

GRAND SLAMS : 1981, 1987

NICKNAME : BERBIZ

NOM DE GUERRE : THE STRATEGIST

MY VISIT TO MEET HIM : WEDNESDAY 7TH MARCH 2018

O f all the former players I met, Pierre provokes debate more than anyone. Not as a player. No one questions his ability nor his intelligence. Opinions differed about his style. To some he is authoritative, decisive, strong-willed and focused. To others authoritarian, impetuous, pig-headed and blinkered. As a result, there are some simmering tensions between Pierre and some of his former teammates.

Whatever these subjective opinions are, his success as a player, coach and businessman cannot be questioned. When I met him in his office at the mythical Jean Dauger stadium in Bayonne, where he was Director of Rugby at the time, he was very welcoming and impressive.

Pierre made it very clear from the outset where he wanted to feature in my book:

"I am from the mountains, not the Basque Country. I am from Lannemezan, played rugby for them, went to school there and my friends live there. I played at Lourdes for ten years. The Pyrenees are where my heart is."

I promised him that I would include him in the mountains section, in spite of him being based in the Basque Country, as long as he told me everything he knows about rugby and his former teammates. The warm-up was over and he was off and running.

Sweet Memories of Youth

"Lannemezan has a great reputation for producing top players such as Laurent Rodriguez, Philippe Bérot, Cyril Baille, Antoine Dupont and myself.

"In 1975, when I was sixteen, Lannemezan beat Toulon to become Champion of France for the U16 age group (les cadets). It was one of the best years of my life – the school was right opposite the stadium, the girls organised the parties and we occasionally went to school. After we won, we didn't go to school for two weeks. The town's entire 6,000 inhabitants came out to celebrate with us.

"Normally the game would be one of the curtain-raisers for the final, which was Béziers v Brive that year, but there was a problem with the playing surface so we ended up playing at Stade de la Croix de Berny Antony. This was

> ## "In 1975, when I was sixteen, Lannemezan beat Toulon to become Champion of France for the U16 age group... After we won, we didn't go to school for two weeks. The town's entire 6,000 inhabitants came out to celebrate with us."

where Racing Metro 92 trained when I was coach there. Thirty years later, I was back. That's destiny!

"When I played for Lannemezan, they were a second division side but I wanted to play at the highest level, so, I had to make a choice about which club to join. I couldn't play for Tarbes because they were our biggest rivals. Therefore, I joined Lourdes because they were iconic at the time and had this heritage of great players and success. I played centre to begin but moved to scrum half because I recognised the importance of the position in controlling a game and dictating tactics, and I wanted the ball in my hands.

"I was a PE teacher living in Saint Gaudens and my wife was teaching in Paris. By 1985, we had had enough of all the travelling and complicated logistics. France was going on tour to Argentina but I told Jacques I was finishing at Lourdes so I wouldn't be going. Neither Lourdes nor the FFR believed me. With help from Jacques and the FFR,

I joined Agen, which was much nearer my wife who had found a teaching post in Toulouse. I was sad to leave Lourdes, which had a wonderful team and lots of young players, such as Armary, coming through, but I had enjoyed five seasons with them."

Press Battles

One of the polemics that the press encouraged early on in Pierre's career was whether to play Berbizier or Gallion. Jérôme was an explosive player, a pocket-rocket who was more in keeping with the romantic tradition of French flair. Pierre was more like Jacques used to be – a great leader, strategic thinker and tactician. He really knew how to control the game and win. Over the years, the press loved these apparent conflicts, in battle with the coach, selectors, team or player, or cultivating someone else's grievances. Examples were legion: the French press v Fouroux, the Boniface brothers v the selectors, Fouroux v Astre, Codorniou v Fouroux.

Pierre elaborated:

*"Jérôme and I got on very well. It was the press that
built this conflict up, and Jacques Fouroux encouraged
it. Jacques used conflicts with the press to protect us,
the players, but also to put pressure on us. It was very
stressful but proved very effective at key moments,
such as the Battle of Nantes against the All Blacks
in 1986 and at the RWC in 1987.*

*"However, the whole debate in the press about our style
of play was false. Throughout the 1980s, the press talked
about brawn versus flair, but we had both. We had power
up front and speed and flair behind.*

*"It was one of the greatest French teams ever, but Jacques
was a very strong personality and loved the fights.
France's greatest adversary was itself and we invested
a lot of emotion in these verbal battles, but the team
became a great force."*

*"If you could put our back line against today's,
you wouldn't see many players beating Blanco, Sella,
Charvet, Lagisquet, Esteve, Cambé or Bonneval over
25, 50 or 100 metres.*

*"Jacques was the key man of the 1980s in French rugby.
His preparation for games could be exceptional."*

Self-Doubt

One of the key attributes of a leader is to face
adversity with confidence, and one of the greatest
exponents of this self-belief was Sean Fitzpatrick.

He always exuded confidence and authority, no doubt
buttressed by the men in black who ran onto the field
behind him. Looks can be deceptive, though. He told
me that he would be as nervous as hell before a kick-off,
often doubting himself and his team's ability to win the
game. We think of these playing legends as super-human
but they have the same doubts as the rest of us.
What distinguished them was their ability to get to
the top, stay there and harness their fear of failure.

Pierre talked to me about his own self-doubt:

*"Until the match against England at Twickenham in
1981when we won the Grand Slam, I doubted whether
I had the ability to play at international level. Was I good
enough? Was Gallion better? Did I have the mindset?
Would I make a mistake that would cost us the game?
After that match and in particular my involvement in
the Pardo try, I realised that I was good enough. I made
a break but had to switch play back inside and throw the
ball hard enough into the wind to reach Laporte. The link
play involving me, Rives, Laporte, Codor and Pardo is one
of my greatest playing memories. The team performance
and result were so rewarding because Jacques had rebuilt
the team after the 1977 success. It is amazing what one
game can do to make you believe in yourself."*

It wasn't just the French press who Pierre had to deal
with. The Queensland players targeted Pierre on the
pitch on the French tour to Australia in 1981.

*"They had a free kick on the halfway line and launched
an up and under. Shaw, their flanker, caught me and in the
ensuing ruck, McBain, their hooker, stamped on my head.
I had been on the pitch eight minutes. I received thirty-eight
stitches and still have hearing problems. McBain also broke
Michel Crémaschi's jaw. They were a very tough team."*

Cremaschi, who was a teammate of Pierre and Jean-
Pierre Garuet at FC Lourdes, was France's loose-head
that day. The French didn't forget the incidents in 1981,
and in 1983 when Australia toured France, McBain was
'dealt with'. As Jean-Pierre Garuet told me, *"McBain
went through the mixer and the grass turned red."*

Get Back in the Boat

Pierre was Jacques' first choice at scrum-half in 1981,
but was then in and out of the side for the next few
years. However, from 1986, he cemented his position
and was a key member of the leadership group. While
Dubroca was the anointed captain, Pierre appeared to
be the unofficial captain, dictating the strategy on and
off the pitch. Jacques clearly saw his strong personality
traits (lucid thinker, ability to communicate, great
strategist and tactician, self-confidence) as essential
to the team's success.

In spite of injury, Jacques wanted him to play in the
RWC semi-final against Australia:

*"I knew we wouldn't lose that semi-final against Australia
in 1987. I was injured during the Fiji game, had ten stiches
in the crease below my buttock and was unlikely to play.
Jacques was really struggling with the press, who were so
negative towards us, especially after we nearly lost to Fiji.*

> "Just before a scrum, I pushed Berbizier in his back. He simply looked at me disdainfully and said, 'Don't do that again'. It was like being told off by the headmaster."

Before the semi-final, I was standing at the bar when we had a chat:

Me: *'Jacques, I have watched us in training.*
            We are very strong. We should focus on us
            and forget the press.'
Jacques: *'OK, as long as you get back in the boat and*
            play. Who's your preference at fly-half?
Me: *'Laporte.'*
Jacques: *'Mesnel is playing fly-half. Cambé is the kicker*
            and playing on the wing.'

"That was Jacques – stubborn but very insightful. He knew that to beat Australia, you had to control Lynagh and kick your goals, and Franck and Cambé did exactly that, brilliantly.

"After the semi-final, I played a game with Tommy Lawton, the great Australian hooker who just failed to stop Serge scoring that try in the corner. He said to me, 'I will always

be 5cms too short for the rest of my life'."

A Mix of Emotions

By 1989, things had become more tense between Jacques and Pierre. Jacques had his eye on the FFR presidency but was exhausted. France lost both tests against the All Blacks in New Zealand in the summer of 1989. Once back in France, they played two tests against the Australians in November but Jacques dropped Pierre, Serge and Lolo Rodriguez for the second one. In the Five Nations in 1990, Pierre returned as captain but his team lost to England in the second game, and he was dropped again after a spat in the changing rooms with Dubroca after a club match in Mont-de-Marsan. He declined to tour Australia in the summer of 1990 for professional reasons. They were Jacques' last matches in charge. Dubroca became manager of France, but after they lost twice to the All Blacks in France in November 1990, Pierre was selected again

to play in the Five Nations in 1991 and he performed very well. The coup de grâce delivered to his playing career was non-selection for the 1991 RWC. Dubroca dropped his former team mate and instead selected a young Fabien Galthié. Pierre was gutted.

However, his luck suddenly changed again. Lapasset became FFR President, Jacques was marginalised by Ferrasse and the FFR, and Dubroca resigned after the infamous RWC quarter final against England at the Parc des Princes in October 1991 when he accosted the referee in the tunnel. Ironically for Pierre, the downfall for Jacques and Daniel, two men he had been so close to for years, created the opening and he became the French coach.

"What I didn't like was not being able to choose my own departure as a player. Those who didn't select me for France were the same people who wouldn't let me play for Agen anymore. They wouldn't let me go and play for another club either. After fifteen years of loyal service, I was rejected. It was the end as a player, but not as a coach. "The first couple of years as coach were very tough. I knew that we had a discipline problem in the team and a few weeks before the Five Nations, I told the press I would deal with it. What followed was a nightmare, the debacle at the Parc when Moscato and Lascubé were sent off in the 1992 Five Nations game against England.

"But we then started to improve. We won the series in Argentina in 1992, drew against South Africa in 1992 in France, beat them in South Africa in 1993, drew against the Australians in France 1993 and then beat

the All Blacks in New Zealand 2-0 in 1994, including that try from the end of the world. It takes a couple of seasons to build a team and I could see we were getting stronger.

"We performed very well in the RWC in South Africa in 1995, finishing third, but it was to be Mandela's World Cup, not ours."

When you chat to Pierre, you certainly get the feeling that some of the wounds inflicted in his last playing days have never healed. He was a central figure as a player for most of the 1980s but was continually criticised by the press, seemingly abandoned by some of his teammates at the end of his career, and then allegedly betrayed by the Directors and Board of the FFR and Agen. He did very well as the coach of France, but his contract wasn't extended by the FFR after RWC in 1995.

A Mix of Opinions

The effect of Pierre's strong personality and style is that he seems to have strained relations with some of his former teammates, such as Rives, Blanco, Dubroca and the late Paparemborde. Rives and Parapemborde were like brothers, Rives and Blanco are great mates, Blanco and Dubroca are bosom buddies. Pierre still has lots of friends from the team, players like Dintrans and Rodriguez, men from the mountains.

Valérie Paparemborde told me, *"The conflicts between players were like petty arguments between young girls. In 1992, Pierre had a bad relationship with Robert. Pierre was intransigent and incapable of compromising."*

Nick Farr-Jones and Peter Fitzsimons witnessed Pierre's siege mentality when they were out one evening. Peter told me, *"Tommy Lawton, Nick and I bumped into Pierre when we were out walking in town, just before we were due to play them. Pierre turned his back on Nick and completely blocked him out of the conversation. It was his way of preparing for the game. He had zero interest in engaging in any form of pleasantries with his opposite number."*

Alain Lorieux has mixed feelings about his former teammate:

"I really loved Pierre. At the RWC in 1987, we spoke uninterrupted for an hour before the Australian game. I was very stressed and he was a great help to me. But he can also be very acerbic in front of people, so he has also offended me. At times he is a tortured soul and needs to communicate better. He gives the impression that the world is against him, but we aren't. In 2017, the 1987 team met up in Paris but Berbiz didn't come because he has fallen out with some players. He doesn't need to be like that. We celebrated great times together and we are like brothers. We should stick together. That is what made us a great team."

For all the comments on his personality, Berbiz is passionately loyal to some and clearly appreciates the reciprocal friendship. Finlay Calder told me how Pierre visited him in the Orkney Isles with a host of other Scottish internationals to mark the 25th anniversary of Orkney Rugby Club.

> "He said it was like being on holiday with the sun, sea and sand, only he was also knee deep in mud. He was wonderful company."

In 2014, Berbizier invited his former players from the 1994 team to Archachon to celebrate the 20th anniversary of France beating the All Blacks 2-0 in New Zealand. He asked Sean Fitzpatrick, the All Black captain on that day in 1994, to speak to the team. Sean told me:

"His team from 1994 played a French Barbarians team and I handed the players their jerseys. He then presented me with a Number 2 shirt and told me I was playing! I ran around a little but made no tackles. Pierre was still very competitive on the pitch. We had a fabulous weekend eating oysters and drinking wine with the likes of Pierre, Garuet and Sella. He was a fabulous host. The players he coached clearly have great respect for him."

Lorieux recognised these qualities in him too:

"He was a very good coach, beating the All Blacks twice. He is a brilliant 'stratège' and leader of men."

A Mélange of Colours

As I researched the players for my book, Pierre's journey was the most wide-ranging and complex to cover and understand. I pondered why this was and put it down to four factors: his influence as a player, his longevity (as a player, coach and businessman), his ambition and his personality.

His influence and longevity are more straightforward to chronicle. What's more complex are the politics and intrigue at the FFR that accompany high ambition. The road to the top job can be lonely and fraught with traps. However, I would need to write a whole book to capture properly the politics surrounding Agen, the FFR and the various interlocuteurs! That will be for another time.

Then, there is Pierre's personality and how this has affected the relationships with his former teammates in the subsequent thirty plus years.

As a sportsman, I don't think his personality traits are unique at all, so why the apparent drama?

I have met and listened to many players who also exhibited Pierre's toughness, directness and winning mentality on the pitch. There is nothing extraordinary about these. After all, how else could a top sportsman be successful without that drive and focus? Fitzpatrick, Rives, Dintrans, Ondarts, Champ, Fouroux, Mallett, McCaw and many others all had it. Winning was everything to them. Sean has said to me many times, *"Show me a good loser and I'll show you a loser".*

He states it with utter conviction.

I played alongside a Kiwi prop, Bill LeClerc, at the Athletic Club de Boulogne-Billancourt (ACBB) in Paris in 1991. I remember asking him who his toughest opponent was. As I recall, his response went like this:

"Sean Fitzpatrick. When I played against him, he wasn't just technically an outstanding, hard and brilliant player and captain, he was also brutal, verbally speaking, throughout the game. He psychologically destroyed me and made me question what right I had to be on the same pitch as him. But it was just rugby. He was a winner and he would let nothing get in the way."

But here's the thing: Sean may have been ruthless and stubborn with a win-at-all-costs mindset on the pitch, but now, off the pitch, he is kind, considerate and thoughtful, and an outstanding communicator. He adapted to life after rugby brilliantly, and whatever wrongs he was dealt during his career, he let bygones be bygones. Many other former players are the same.

So, why can't Pierre do that? Why the tense relations between Pierre and some players? Perhaps he can't bite the bullet and adjust his on-field behaviours in the real world?

Or perhaps he has adjusted them but can't let sleeping dogs lie with certain players who he felt wronged him during his career? After all, he is still friends with many of them. We all remember the past differently.

I don't know. I don't have all the facts and am not here to pass judgement on an individual. Whatever his reasons, it got me thinking more widely about human behaviour in rugby and how players adapt afterwards.

Firstly, rugby culture itself. The beauty of rugby back then was that, if you needed to, you could delineate your behaviour, physical or psychological, and leave it on the field of play. Short of maiming an opposition player, you could get away with a lot because it was done 'in the heat of the battle' and it was 'just a game'. Most of the time (but, I accept, not always) players would have a drink afterwards, make up and perhaps be friends for life. The traditional culture and noble values of rugby (solidarity, fraternity, collective sacrifice, and so on) encouraged this. I can't think of another sport or activity that allowed such contrasting behaviour. It was that delineation which allowed players to separate their personalities: one on the pitch, one off it. Not everyone needed to do this, but some could and did.

I write all this in the past tense because modern professional rugby is so different from the amateur era. Nowadays, for the pros, work and rugby are the same thing, and you can't get away with much on the field of play so you have less to apologise for afterwards! Delineation doesn't seem as important.

Secondly, adapting behaviour after rugby. It is acknowledged that adapting to life after any professional sport is difficult for many different reasons. I'm not talking about the emotional turmoil - emptiness, self-esteem, raison d'être, what's next? - suffered by some former pros (I'll touch upon that in the article on the wonderful Denis Charvet). Here, I am talking specifically about how you adapt your mentality and behaviours consistently to a new 'code of conduct' in the real world.

That adjustment is difficult, though. Things aren't as straight forward in life and business as they are in sport. You can't delineate its constituent parts so easily. Life is nuanced and a mélange of colours. They all blend together in life's spectrum that is both multi-coloured and multi-dimensional, and our relationships with people who are not teammates are more complex, outside the rigid structure and laws of the game.

On this spectrum, when does authoritative become authoritarian? Decisive, impetuous? Strong-willed, pig-headed? Focused, blinkered? Cautious, mistrusting? Frank, acerbic?

The differences can be subtle and our own view is very subjective because it is all about context, how things are said and the personalities involved. Oh, for a simple set of laws and a referee to guide us off the pitch too.

Pierre, like so many top sportsmen, may well have been all of these at different points in his life.

I guess it is inevitable that that some fissures exist between some of the former players. We can't expect everyone to get on.

However, what I have never understood is this: in a sport you played for the love, unless you were materially and deliberately wronged, why do people hold long-term grudges against those they have known so long and with whom they have shared such special experiences, often in unique and extreme circumstances? I am not aiming this question specifically at Pierre. It is one I am posing the whole team because tensions exist between other players too.

Perhaps I am looking at this through Anglo-Saxon eyes, being too logical and misunderstanding the Latin mindset, which is possibly more emotional, more prone to overstimulation. However, none of the *"petty arguments between young girls"* (to quote Valérie Paparemborde) that were described to me, seem beyond repair. Words might have been said in the heat of the battle, situations managed clumsily, high achievers competed for the same roles, but surely the strong bonds between the players surmount everything else?

This was a band of brothers in arms who would do anything for each other. I keep thinking about Serge's words 'we loved each other, and we still do'. For the vast majority of them, that love is still very strong. But in some of their relationships, where did all the Latin love go?

I really enjoyed meeting Pierre. He is fascinating – articulate, focused, driven, clever and charming. I had the fortune of meeting him over lunch the next day alongside some other greats of the French game – Pascal Ondarts, Michel Celaya and Gérard Murillo, another very enjoyable and insightful rendezvous.

Whatever the conflict eating away at the French press and team, the opposition was in awe of Jacques' magic and the quality of his players and the influence of Pierre.

Findlay Calder told me:
"Berbizier was probably the best scrum half I played against. He was clever and understood the game, finding space, bringing his back row in, knowing when to release his backs. He ran the strategy and tactics on the pitch."

Ieuan Evans echoed this:
"Berbizier was the 'chef d'orchestre' of the team. They had a phenomenal pack that was physical and abrasive, but Pierre always kept them going forward. I didn't like Champ or Rodriguez running at me and getting caught in the rucks. Fear is a very underrated emotion you know."

Dewi Morris told me:
"Just before a scrum, I pushed Berbizier in his back. He simply looked at me disdainfully and said, 'Don't do that again'. It was like being told off by the headmaster. Berbiz had this air of authority and confidence. He wasn't pacey but he knew where the opposition weaknesses were. He gave those lovely cherry balls to his forwards who would attack the gain line."

Philippe Dintrans

MOUNTAINS   "IT WAS A NERVE-RACKING FINISH.
FRÉDÉRIC COSTES KICKED THE
BALL OUT AND THE WE HAD WON
THE GAME. I WAS SO ELATED THAT
I HUGGED THE REFEREE, JOHN WEST,
FROM IRELAND WHO SAID, 'PHILIPPE,
WHAT THE F**K ARE YOU DOING?'
IT WAS JUST MY INSTINCT IN THAT
MOMENT OF JOY AND RELIEF."

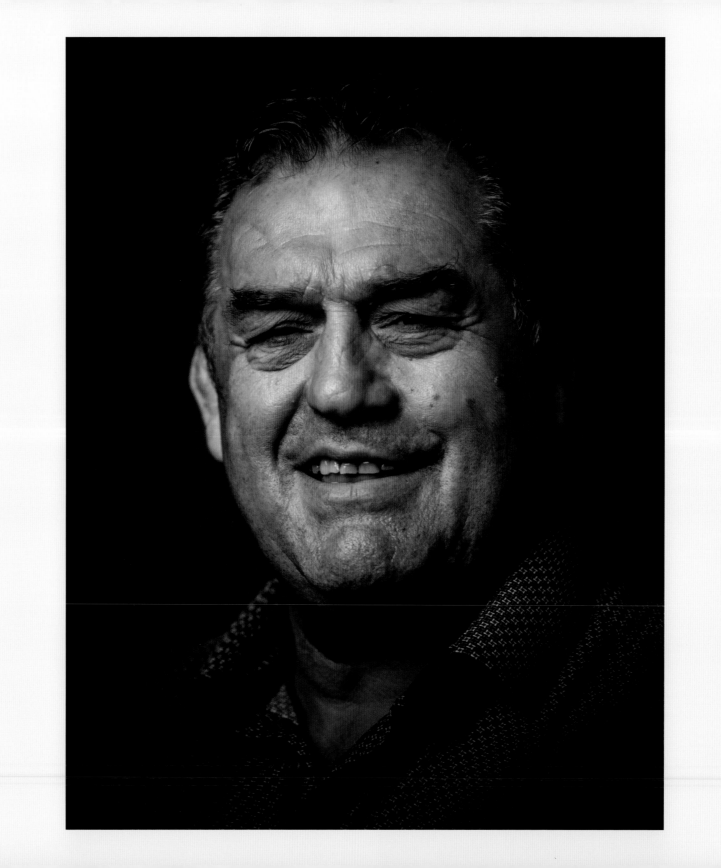

BORN : 29TH JANUARY 1957

CLUBS : STADO TARBES PYRÉNÉES RUGBY

INTERNATIONAL CAPS : 50

POSITION : HOOKER

GRAND SLAMS : 1981

NICKNAME : LE LORRAIN

NOM DE GUERRE : THE WARRIOR

MY VISIT TO MEET HIM : MONDAY 27TH NOVEMBER 2017

I had been in France for nearly a week when I arrived in Tarbes to meet Philippe. I had travelled far but please don't sympathise, it hadn't been any hardship. I had enjoyed the hospitality in the Basque region and was now in the foothills of the beautiful Pyrenees, which separate Spain from France.

After I'd met Louisou Armary, I'd managed to take a day off. Off from what, you ask? Wining and dining with former French greats? I admit that I couldn't describe this as hard work but all the driving and indulging meant that I needed some sleep and some exercise so I headed to the beautiful Lac d'Estaing near Bun on the outskirts of Argelès-Gazost. I got up early and walked some 20km around the lake and up through the trees to the clearing. When I arrived, my lungs were bursting. My friend Julian always points out that *"every bill has to be paid"* and my profligacy was after its money. But *bon dieu*, it was worth it. If you are in search of an area of France that is little known, head to Argelès-Gazost and its surrounding areas. You can walk, climb, cycle, ski and enjoy the fine hospitality. It is peaceful, picturesque, perfect and a pristine pearl of a place.

The Warrior

Philippe Dintrans' name is seared onto my schoolboy memory. He followed in Jean-Pierre Rives' shoes as the next captain of France and did the job brilliantly. He was a great hooker and a fabulous leader – determined, tough, aggressive and talkative, and he never took a step backwards. He was the ultimate competitor. Sean Fitzpatrick talks about him in glowing terms:

"He was a warrior, the sort of player who really impressed me as a tough man and great leader. I liked him on and off the pitch."

I spoke to the great former All Black, Andy Haden, and he told me that he had spent two years at Tarbes around 1973 and saw the young Dintrans play for the colts:

"He was very good but playing flanker at the time so I suggested he try hooker. He possessed all the right attributes – physicality, size, good hands, confrontational. Like many good young flankers, I knew he could become a great hooker."

I tracked Philippe down at his place of work, a large Renault concession on the outskirts of Tarbes, with the beautiful Pyrenees in the background. When I arrived in the car showroom, I saw a beaming Dintrans making his way towards me. He had clearly spotted this Englishman a mile off! We went into his office where we chatted while he kept one eye on his computer screen so he could monitor all the KPIs as they came through in real time.

"I love leading and managing men, David. I have a team of eighty here. It is what I do."

He reminisced about when he broke into the French team for the first time:

"I remember my first tour to Canada and Japan well in 1978. I was selected but those international sides didn't qualify for caps back then. It was a great moment. I departed with the star players from the 1977 Grand Slam winning side – Cholley, Bastia, Rives, Patou. Paco couldn't

go so I took my chance. Jean-François Perche of Bourg-en-Bresse was also selected and he was a great player so I had to play well. I made my mark and was then selected for the 1979 tour to New Zealand.

"I played the first test alongside Patou and Colomine in the front row. I played well enough, leading the line and touching the ball but we were beaten so I was very anxious about losing my place for the second test. Jean-Pierre took over the training that week from Jean Desclaux and he really put us through our paces. He could run and run, and very fast. That week, Jean-Pierre was very demanding and the training crazy. We ran through the woods like Rambo, determined to win the second test. If you couldn't keep up, you lost your place. I made sure I didn't leave his side.

"Christian Béguerie had stitches in his hand that came loose the night before the second test, so he was replaced by Salas. The problem with Salas was that he had been on the piss with the mid-week team the night before the game. At about 5am, he was told he would be playing. He was very reluctant not least because he had been drinking but also because he was being asked to play in the unfamiliar position of Number 8, against the All Blacks! But he tackled everyone and played out of his skin, guided brilliantly by the back row of Jean-Pierre and Jean-Luc Joinel.

"We started the game well and surprised them in the first half. They came back at us in the second half and Mourie had the brain to shorten the line-outs and mix things up.

"It was a nerve-racking finish. Frédéric Costes kicked the

Phillippe Dintrans evades a tackle from Steve Brain. Five Nations Rugby Union, 2nd February 1985, Twickenham, London. France 9 v England 9. *Photo - Mike Brett, Popperfoto, Getty Images.*

ball out and we had won the game. I was so elated that I hugged the referee, John West, from Ireland who said, 'Philippe, what the f**k are you doing?' It was just my instinct in that moment of joy and relief. That evening, there wasn't meant to be an after-match banquet. We were meant to drink some beers and then leave but we ended up in a restaurant with the All Blacks and got wasted. We exchanged everything – shorts, ties, underwear… It was an extraordinary night!"

Injury and Frustration

Phillipe's international career had started well. He had beaten the All Blacks in 1979, played against the Springboks in 1980 (he scored although France lost), won a Grand Slam in 1981 and was the first-choice hooker between 1979 until 1985. However, two events intervened. First, injury struck him down in 1985 when he slipped a disc and was paralysed in his arm, a year or so before the inaugural World Cup. The second was the conversion of Daniel Dubroca, previously the tight-head prop, into hooker.

"Jacques Fouroux asked me who should play instead of me and I said 'Bernard Herrero' from Toulon. Jacques always told me that he wanted me back in the Number 2 shirt as soon as possible, but Ferrasse wanted Daniel from Agen.

"Ferrasse was President of the FFR and also from Agen, as was his great mate and deputy at the FFR, Guy Basquet. They made all the big decisions in a bar in Agen while playing Belote! Daniel was a great tight head prop but I was certainly a better hooker.

"I should have played in the game at Nantes against the All Blacks in 1986. Daniel had been poor against the them in Toulouse in the first test, but Jacques came to tell me that I would only be on the bench for the second test at Nantes. I said, 'So you want me to come and pick the balls up for Dubroca?'

"I left straight after the match because I didn't like the way we had played – it was over the top and violent. It was one of the most violent games I had ever seen."

Ever the competitor, I could feel his pain and frustration, even after all these years.

> " In the 1988 French championship final Agen v Tarbes, I ate Daniel for breakfast. I ran the line, threw in well and led the team."

"I have great respect for him but at the time I wanted that position and missed out badly at the RWC in 1987.

"At the final against the All blacks, Andy Dalton and I were both on the bench and came out of the changing rooms at the same time. We hugged and cried together. We both felt that we should be playing."

It was interesting listening to the players and how they rated both Dintrans and Dubroca very highly, but for their different strengths.

Brian Moore told me: "I once blew a kiss at Berbizier to wind him up. In the next ruck, Dintrans dropped a knee on me. I learnt my lesson and said to myself 'don't be a smart arse'. I always passed this advice down to younger front row colleagues so they wouldn't make the same mistake."

Remembering Jacques

Philippe returned to Jacques Fouroux: "It wasn't Jacques' fault that I wasn't picked as first choice. He was under huge pressure from Ferrasse and Basquet. They wanted their man to pick up the World Cup."

Like all the players I spoke to, Philippe remembers Jacques Fouroux, the coach of that great French squad, with great affection:

"Jacques knew how to motivate people, one on one. He would always find the right words. He could cajole, insult, offend, compliment, whatever it took to motivate the individual. He was a great leader, not so much a technical coach, and we miss him greatly."

> **"You would always want Philippe on your side. I would have followed him into battle. He was inspirational and always suffered for his team but didn't have the career he deserved."**

Local Punch-Ups

I moved the discussion onto the local rivalries in that quadrangle of noble clubs – Pau, Lourdes, Tarbes and Bagnères. The rivalries would regularly spill over into violence back in the amateur era.

"The most violent game I played was against Bagnères in 1976/77. We were playing the two legs of the quarter-final in Lourdes and then Pau, and in the second game it all kicked off. The pitch was flooded and the players took part in a huge boxing match. Anything and everything went, right from the start – kicking, punching, gouging. You name it, it happened. Their forwards were full of nutters. They were stronger than us at rugby but we won the fight! Torossian and Duhart left the pitch bloodied and bruised.

"The referee wanted to send both captains off, but Bertranne from Bagnères refused to go saying that he had nothing to do with it and how would he explain it to

his three kids! In the end, the ref sent off Pourtal from Bagnères and Paul from Tarbes.

"The game was talked about a lot in the media and Christian Montaignac, the great journalist, described it as 'shameful'."

I met Christian at his house near Montpellier overlooking the Mediterranean, and we spent a wonderful two hours chatting about his memories of the great players. He talked very warmly about Philippe:

"You would always want Philippe on your side. I would have followed him into battle. He was inspirational and always suffered for his team, but didn't have the career he deserved."

Andy Haden remembers when he played for Tarbes and the FFR was very concerned about the amount and level of violence among the clubs:

"Ferrasse decided to set up a fines system. If a team was guilty of violence, it would be fined and the money put into a pot. At the end of the season, the pot would be distributed to the teams with exemplary behaviour. The problem was that no team had an exemplary record because every team had been fined! It was a piece of genius thinking by Ferrasse and his friends! I have no idea what happened to the money because there would have been a lot of it in that pot."

Front Row Intelligence

Whatever happened on the pitch and notably the front row, Philippe is another example of someone who destroys this myth that front row players are just large lumps of lard who can't think. Based on my travels across France, Scotland, Ireland, Wales and England, nothing could be further from the truth. Philippe runs a team of some eighty people at the Renault Concession, Louisou Armary is a top politician, Pascal Ondarts is a very successful businessman running hotels and restaurants, Jean-Pierre Gauruet ran a potato business before selling it, Pierre Dospital was a *restaurateur* before retirement, Daniel Dubroca runs a fruit business, Robert Paparemborde ran a shop and restaurant before managing RCF and winning the French Championship final in 1990, and Diego Minarro, the former hooker for Béziers, loves his archaeology, art and history, alongside running the academy at Béziers rugby club. Most have been involved in managing, running or administering rugby clubs. What marks me as well is they all have finesse – the way they think, talk, interact and manage.

I didn't have the opportunity to meet Robert Paparemborde, but listening to his great friends and his widow, Valérie, it is obvious that he was a man of great class and finesse. I love that descriptor. In a single word it manages to encapsulate elegance, intelligence, eloquence, subtlety, smartness, even grace.

You could extend these characteristics of humour and intelligence to many other front row forwards – Fitzpatrick, Kearns, Moore, Chilcott, Sole, Milne, Evans, Windsor.

Who Hates the English Most?

If intelligence and finesse aren't enough, they can also be very funny.

Hugo MacNeill told me how he once saw Phil Orr, the former Irish loose head, in a booze-fuelled argument with a Frenchman in Paris over who hated the English most… pure genius. I'm not sure we English will ever be viewed any differently by any of the countries we have colonised, ruled, invaded or fought over during the past 1,000 years or so!

Micky Skinner also elaborated on the pair of English props, Jeff Probyn and Paul Randell (Judge), and how they would adopt different tactics against the French:

"Judge would build a relationship with his opposite number, probably at the after-match party the year before. They would go drinking and become bosom buddies.

There was never any aggro between Judge and the French or anyone else. Jeff, on the other hand, didn't care about all that. He was like an east-end gangster and would do everything he could to wind his opposite number up. With Jeff, it was always war!"

Philippe was a busy man running the business so I wrapped up the interview. He was everything that his former playing mates and Sean Fitzpatrick had described to me – a great leader, competitive, a player's player, a *Capitaine de Combat*, to quote Jérôme Gallion. I would have loved to spend longer with him but that would have to wait for another day. I was running late for my next appointment – dinner with the great Jean-Pierre Garuet, about thirty minutes away in Pontacq. *Que la vie est belle*, I thought.

Jean-Pierre Garuet said,
"Philippe was hard, fiery, dynamic and aggressive. He had no fear and would always go first, leading by example, in the mould of JPR. Daniel was calmer, more reflective and analytical. Both were great men and players."

Raphaël Ibañez waxed lyrical about Philippe and Daniel:
"I never played against either but I wanted to get to know them, how they played and captained the team. Daniel was clever, subtle, technical, lucid, intelligent. Philippe was like a bomb, explosive, aggressive, physical, all heart and sacrifice. Philippe would do anything for the team and sacrifice himself. He still would today. Daniel would assess the situation and think his way through a problem. Both were different and brilliant.

"Fouroux knew how to put them in competition to get the best out of them. They are totally different personalities and I wanted to be a mixture of them. I wanted to have the courage and heart to fight to the last while being lucid enough to make good decisions. Philippe wanted to be the boss, that's normal for a competitive person."

Jean-Baptiste Lafond said,
"Dintrans was possibly the greatest hooker this country has ever seen. Dubroca was great but Philippe was a beast."

Daniel Herrero said,
"Playing Dintrans gave the team rhythm. He was dynamic, difficult to stop and always gained metres."

Patrick Estève

MOUNTAINS

"MOZART WOULD SAY,
'THE MUSIC IS NOT IN THE
NOTES BUT IN THE SILENCE
BETWEEN,' AND THAT SILENCE
WAS THE PASSING, SPACE
AND MOVEMENT."

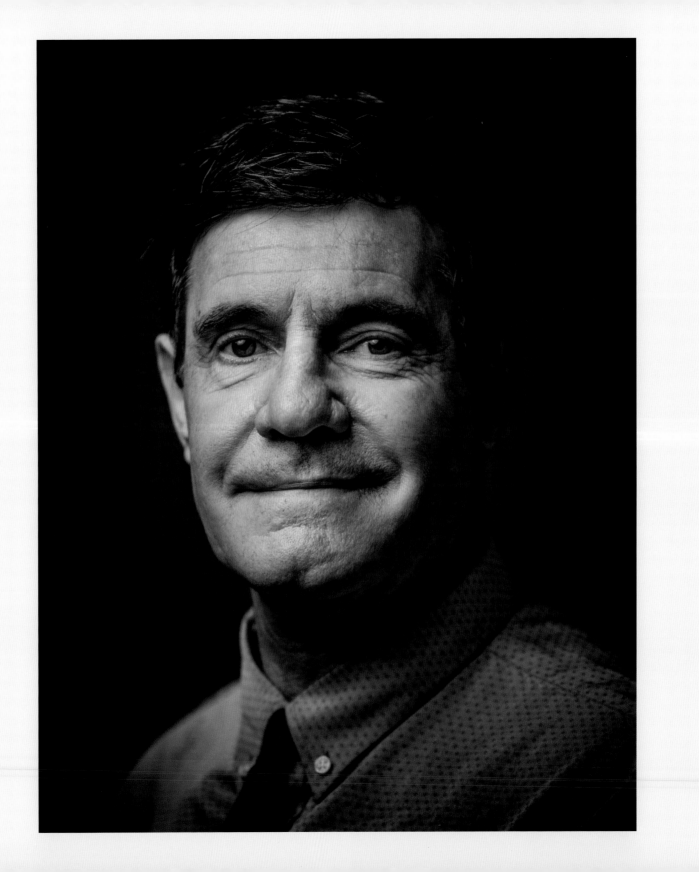

BORN : 14TH FEBRUARY 1959

CLUBS : STADE LAVELANÉTIEN, RACING CLUB
DE NARBONNE MÉDITERANNÉE

INTERNATIONAL CAPS : 25

POSITION : WING

NICKNAME : THE TGV, FLINT

NOM DE GUERRE : THE PROFESSOR

MY VISIT TO MEET HIM : FRIDAY 16TH FEBRUARY 2018

I tracked Patrick down via Didier Codorniou, his team mate at Narbonne where they would conjure some majestic tries. I met him in the quaint town of Foix in the Pyrenees near Lavelanet where he started his rugby career. Based on the other players' feedback, I knew I was in for a very entertaining few hours, but not before I had criss-crossed France seeing Lorieux in the Alps, Joinel in Brive, Sella, Dubroca and Erbani in Agen, Bonneval in Toulouse and Fouroux junior in Montauban. I was staying at Julian's house near Salies-du-Salat, which allowed me to enjoy a short detox en route.

Patrick Estève, 1st April, 1983.

Photo by Patrick Jarnoux, Paris Match, Getty Images.

Patrick and I met in front of La Poste from where we sidestepped our way through the narrow streets of Foix to Le Vertigo, a favourite restaurant of Patrick and a super choice. It is a mix of modern and traditional French, with bright, warm colours, the sort of place you would happily take your family, friends or partner for lunch or dinner. When we arrived, we enjoyed a hearty, warming red from Faugères as an aperitif, as quaffable as an ice-cold cider on a beach in a heatwave. We'd sunk three before we sat down.

Fighter Jets

The memory I have of Patrick is of a beautifully balanced sprinter and finisher who would round off the fluid French back moves with aplomb. He played in a sumptuous back line that featured the likes of Mesnel, Codorniou, Sella, Charvet, Lagisquet, Camberarbero, Bonneval and Blanco. How could one defend against team like that? As Hugo MacNeil said to me, *"It was like squadron of fighter jets coming at you from all directions. It looked chaotic but they knew instinctively where the space was, where to support each other, which angles to hit."*

Patrick elaborated: *"Mozart would say, 'The music is not in the notes but in the silence between,' and that silence was the passing, space and movement. We had such fabulous players so there was no point in taking contact. We had to avoid it, get width on the ball and use our pace. We used miss moves, loops, space, angles and multi-phase rugby to maintain the tempo. Unlike today's wingers who are more like flankers, we were more subtle and could use*

sidesteps, skill and outside breaks to beat players and score.

"But we also needed to be hard and physical up front so we could get the ball.

> "We also had team cohesion. Rugby doesn't tolerate collective or emotional mediocrity. It's a very hard sport and you have to stick together. If you don't love each other or operate as a team, you'll never succeed."

"As soon as the media and money are involved, you forget your values and what makes you successful. We would eat, drink, play and party together. We were like brothers.

"Jacques was also key to our success. He was more of a management guru than a coach. He would wind everyone up in a very individual way. He'd say to Doxpi: 'Make sure your opposite number doesn't score today, because if he does it means you are tired and he is better than you in the scrum'. To players like Lorieux and Garuet, he would verbally and viciously abuse them, telling them they were crap in the last game and their opposition far better than them. It would send them into a frenzy, they would go nuts. To Blanco, he would humbly say: 'Thank you Serge. Thank you for being with us here today'. He was a motivational genius."

"He was like a mad scientist but what a fabulous player. He had a beautiful outside break and was very quick. I loved and feared marking him because he was such a challenge. He could accelerate and change direction on a dime. The French team always had this incredible confidence and nonchalance."

Le TGV

In 1984, they toured New Zealand and while they lost the Test Series, you could see that French flair in provincial matches – the beautiful balance, passing and timing of Codorniou, the pace and balance of Estève, the support lines of Bonneval.

Estève glided like a *'sprinter pur,'* as Jean-Baptist Lafond called him, only he was better than that. He understood space, not just straight lines, he could beat players and finish too.

John Kirwan told me: *"He was like a mad scientist but what a fabulous player! He had a beautiful outside break and was very quick. I loved and feared marking him because he was such a challenge. He could accelerate and change direction on a dime. The French team always had this incredible confidence and nonchalance.*

"For me, players like him and Lagisquet and others were the benchmark for the rest of world rugby. We wanted to play rugby like them."

There was a good reason why the great Roger Couderc (the French equivalent of our rugby commentator *ne plus ultra*, Bill McLaren) nicknamed Patrick le TGV, after France's high-speed train, known as *le train à grande vitesse.*

As a player, Estève developed in Lavelanet and then Narbonne, playing alongside the likes of Codorniou and Claude Spanghero.

"Codor was like a radar, knowing where the gap was and when to pass. He had this ability to fix the opposition and offload the ball before he was tackled. Our whole game plan in Narbonne was calculated to free up the backs. It was all about attacking rugby."

"Playing for France with him made things easy because I knew him so well. We also had Sella alongside us. He had extra-terrestrial, physical attributes – his resilience, strength, pace, skills. I remember in 1984 when John Carleton of England came down Sella's channel and he just smashed him like a back-row forward. In 1984 tour of New Zealand, the All Blacks said that if they could keep one French player, it would be Philippe."

Flint

The other players clearly loved Patrick not just for his rugby ability but also for his wit and intellect.

Flint was the nickname given to Patrick because it was also the name a rugby move when he would took the ball inside from the fly-half.

About half a dozen of the players told me the same, amusing story about Flint when he was negotiating a deal back in the 1980s with the President of Narbonne (yes, in the amateur era... we British were so naive). It goes something like this:

Monsieur le President: "Right Patrick, budgets are tight this year so I will have to pay you in two instalments."

Flint: "That's OK. You can give me half now, and the second half immediately afterwards."

When I saw Jean-Baptiste Lafond, he said to me:

"Have you seen Patrick Estève, le TGV? He's a legend. I'd love to see him. Once, he said to me, 'Courage is about loving life and looking death in the eye, about aiming for the ideal and understanding the real'. It's a quote from Jean Jaurès. It's beautiful and I've never forgotten it. Patrick is a very interesting, clever and funny man. I need to invite him onto the TV show."

The Meaning of Life

At this point, we were well into the lunch and wine. We had chosen a *salade de gésiers* as a starter, a delicious bed of green *mesclun* adorned with juicy chicken gizzards, eggs and tomatoes. In case you're wondering, chicken gizzards are cut from the digestive

> "Once, he said to me, 'Courage is about loving life and looking death in the eye, about aiming for the ideal and understanding the real'. It's a quote from Jean Jaurès. It's beautiful and I've never forgotten it."

You reap what you sow, you make your own bed and lie in it, the end-of-season table never lies, you are what you eat.

Warming Up

The afternoon rolled on, unhurried, as we sat there exchanging stories. We were served an *eau-de-vie*-based drink with fresh vanilla and coconut milk, which was dangerously drinkable, a palate-softening dissembler that made you think you were drinking a milk-shake when it more closely resembled a Moscow Mule, but with a bigger kick.

But it was nothing compared to the terrifying concoction they served me next. It sent my body temperature soaring. It was so hot on the palate that they should introduce some to the Hadron Collider.

"Try this, David. But only a little because it is very strong. It is a home-made chilli-based recipe. We use it for nothing other than to test people's resistance and to sober people up if they have had too much to drink. Once, someone drank two glasses when he was drunk. He cried for several hours afterwards."

They were both roaring with laughter.

What Goes on Tour, Stays on Tour

We had been in the restaurant about four hours and it was time for me to leave and feel the cool air on

tract of a chicken, similar to a stomach. Don't start shouting 'typical French, they eat anything'. Chicken gizzards are a popular food throughout the world, don't you know, sold as street food in Haiti, South East Asia and Africa. Yes, ok, everywhere the French have colonised. We British can hardly talk. We've exported our fine cuisine all around the world too, such as fish and chips, sliced bread, boiled vegetables, Marmite and Spam.

For the main course, Patrick had chosen *riz d'agneau*. Don't be fooled, it has nothing to do with rice and lamb balti. *Riz* are sweetbreads, an organ meat from the thymus gland and pancreas. The texture is smooth, tender and moist, and the flavour mild and they can complement rich and acidic sauces.

I'm at the adventurous end of the epicurean spectrum but I had played it safer and chosen a *faux-filet*, the size of my thigh. If you know me, you'll realise it could feed a family of four for a week but even I could only eat half of it. I am always nervous about ordering a dish in France that has the pre-fix 'false'. I'd much rather have the real thing.

We were knocking back another bottle of the Faugères when Patrick started to reveal his intellect, launching into the importance of rugby's influence on people's lives, and how it links to the philosophies of Jean-Paul Sartre and existentialism, i.e. you are what you make yourself and that things like essence and pre-destination are, well, just self-deception. We determine our own meaning of life. *"Man is defined only insofar as he acts and he is responsible for his actions."*

Hear, hear, I was thinking. It was one for a longer conversation when I hadn't consumed so much wine. At that moment though, my head was full of clichés...

Patrick Estève races past Bleddyn Bowen. Five Nations
Championship, Cardiff. 18th February 1984. France 21 v Wales 16.
Photo - Bob Thomas Sports Photography, Getty Images.

the streets of Foix. I think the chilli-based concoction
must have been cloned from polonium 210.

Patrick ended with a wistful summing up: *"We need to
remember and tell all these rugby stories. They underpin
our lives, family and friendships."*

He said this just before he told me that I couldn't
recount any of his salacious stories about the team
because *"what goes on tour stays on tour."* Haha, I know
the rules Patrick, don't worry.

I'd had a fabulous afternoon with him. He is a great
raconteur with a sharp intellect, as well as being very
funny and generous. I will certainly call him when I am
next in town. I had the fortune of meeting him again at
the end of August 2018 at Les Rencontres en Seronnais,
organised by the great Henri Nayrou as a celebration
of rugby and its fraternity. We smoked cigars and
drank whisky and wine as he regaled me some more
and provoked me with stories about annoying *les rosbifs.*
Mon dieu, quel personage.

Tomorrow I would be meeting the giant Jean-François
Imbernon, followed by Marc Cécillon on Sunday.

Jean-Pierre Garuet-Lempirou

MOUNTAINS

"I STOOD UP AND SAID, 'CHEERS EVERYONE, AT LEAST WE CAN SAY THAT WE PLAYED IN THE RUGBY WORLD CUP FINAL AND DRANK A BOTTLE OF RED WINE TOGETHER'. I THINK WE WERE ALL TOO TENSE TO DRINK MUCH BUT I WANTED TO CELEBRATE THAT MOMENT."

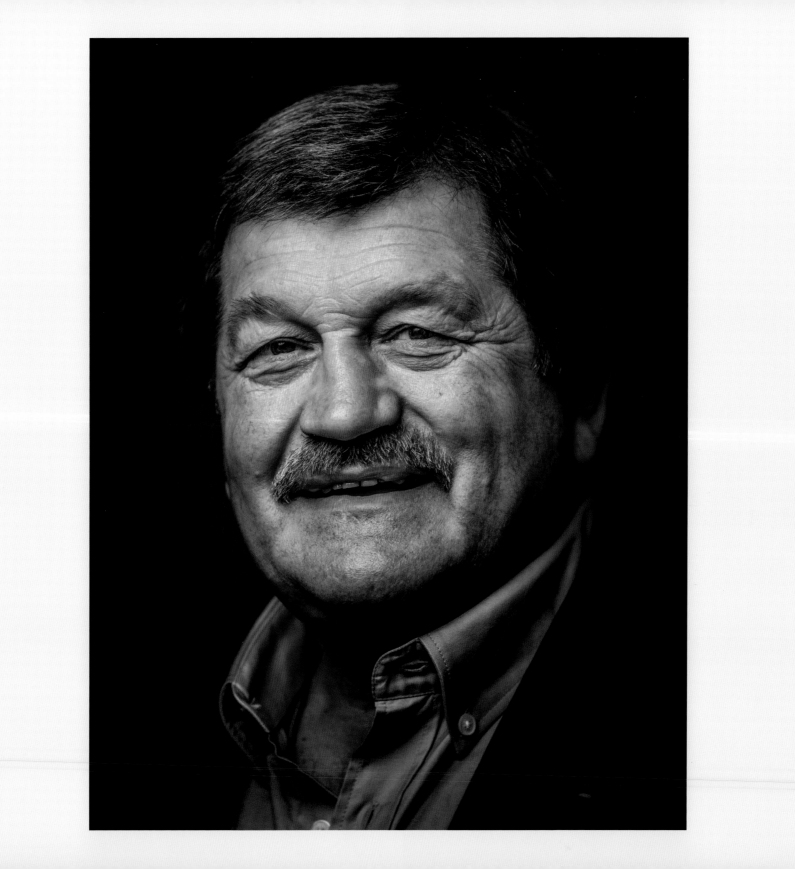

W hat is it about props and their cult status? Is it down to their toughness, personality, wit, generosity, size, shape, strength, (large) appetite or (lack of) pace that makes us love them? Perhaps, it's all of the above. Think of Garuet, but also Ondarts, Doxpi, Leonard, 'Ginger' McLoughlin, Orr, Califano, Milne the 'Bear', Sole, 'Coochie' Chilcott, 'Judge' Rendall, Probyn and many more. They are all unforgettable as both players and characters.

But there's something far deeper and more powerful than these traits. This may come as a surprise to many, but based on my meetings, intelligence is the overriding hallmark of these *démanageurs*, as the French often refer to them. I talk about this more in Dintrans' article. Most have this finesse – the way they think, talk, interact and manage. There's that descriptor again. In a single word, it means intelligence, eloquence, subtlety, shrewdness. Garuet personifies this as well as anyone. You could apply it to many hookers too – Fitzpatrick, Moore, Kearns, Wood, Best.

I tracked down Jean-Pierre or Garuche as he is affectionately known, via Pascal, the commander-in-chief of social activities, and arranged to meet him in Pontacq, about 12km from Lourdes in the foothills of the Pyrenees. I turned up at his farmhouse and he was well prepared for my arrival. The fridge was full of all the requisite French produce – *foie gras, saucisson, boudin, oeuf, jambon*, and *brébis* and *tomme des Pyrénées*, the local cheeses.

Back in the day in France, all of these were acceptable pre-match nutrients, along with a *canon de rouge* and some Gitanes cigarettes. I kid you not. I experienced this type of 'preparation' on many occasions. I remember one in particular when I was a 'ringer' for Bédarrides, near Châteauneuf-du-Pape, back in the 1990s. I have no idea why I played for them on that day, but I did so after a long lunch. When we rolled onto the pitch, the team looked like a herd of hippos, only fatter. We were fairly inebriated and lost by forty points. Our performance was *merde* but memorable for its merriment.

Jean-Pierre's preparation was clearly much more serious than this but he did tell me about the lunch before the 1987 RWC final.

"The team met about 11am, and the final was starting at 3pm. I stood up and said, 'Cheers everyone, at least we can say that we played in the RWC final and drank a bottle of red wine together'. I think we were all too tense to drink much but I wanted to celebrate that moment. Wine is an important part of our culture. My Mum was from Bordeaux and I always drank wine so why break

the habit of a lifetime? After all, it was only another game of rugby!"

Jean-Pierre and I sat down at his kitchen table and he poured me a glass of white Jurancon to whet my appetite. It was fresh and vivacious with aromas of pears and green apples, perfect as an *aperitif*. I had recovered, just about, from my impromptu stay over at Alexis' Hotel Le Viscos in Saint-Savin on the previous Saturday, after I'd met Louisou Armary. I felt match-fit and ready for the next round.

The Price of Spuds

The British press had always referred to Garuche as the 'potato farmer' so I wanted to know whether this was true or part of the folklore.

"It was real, David. I started it by chance in 1976 when we had the drought and there was a shortage of potatoes.

I was chatting to our neighbour who had well-irrigated soil and could grow them so he gave me some. The players at Lourdes rugby club asked me to take them some, which I did in my 2CV. Before long, I was supplying club directors and local hotels from my van. I then acquired a warehouse in Lourdes and started importing from Holland, Belgium, Morocco and other parts of France like Brittany and Montauban. I was in my twenties and had six employees with my brothers, Serge and Éric. We didn't know anything about employment rules so we just worked hard and had some luck.

"I remember at the RWC in 1987, I would be on the phone in the middle of the night with Serge and Éric discussing the price of potatoes. Should we buy or wait, hold or sell, stick or twist, depending on prices and currency movements. I would do this right next to my teammates when they were asleep! We were selling ten tons per day at one point.

> "I remember at the RWC in 1987, I would be on the phone in the middle of the night with Serge and Éric discussing the price of potatoes. I would do this right next to my teammates when they were asleep!"

"We sold it in 1991. Lifting all those bags was a great way to do weight training. I'd get up at 6am every morning including Monday mornings after a game. I never missed a 6am, and I was never ill with a cold or flu."

Garuche opened the fridge and brought the assortment of Pyrenean beauties to the kitchen table.

"Wine has always been around me because Mum was from Sauternes. And of course, we props love eating!

"You know David, I played in a match once against Bourgoin and because we won, Castres didn't get relegated. One of the local butchers from Castres sent us all some charcuterie as a thank you. I love the spirit of rugby!"

Back in the 1980s, he was also known as the world's best scrummager, a *professeur* of the art. How did this come about?

"I played in the backrow until I was twenty-one, and did a short stint at Stade Montois during my military service. There were fifteen of us in the backrow so competition was stiff. When I returned to Lourdes, I told them I wanted to play front row so worked hard on strengthening my legs and back. In 1976, we played Castres in the quarter-finals and I was up against Gérard Cholley, the giant, immovable rock from the French side, but I held my own and never looked back.

"At Lourdes, we had a tradition that if I lifted my opposite number in a match, the directors would buy a round of pastis for the whole team. Therefore, I would concentrate the whole match so I could offer this to my teammates afterwards."

In late August 2018, I had the pleasure of meeting Garuche again with his great mate and fellow scummaging guru, Didier Sanchez, at an annual event organised by Henri Nayrou, once Managing Editor at Le Midi Olympique until 1997 and then a politician for the last twenty-two years. The event is called Les Rencontres en Séronais at La Bastide de Sérou.

Didier told me, "Garuche and I can talk for ever on the subject. People think that the front row is for fat boys and meat heads, that it is all about force and size. But it isn't. It is as much about technique and intelligence, with each position working in tandem. A lighter scrum can dominate a heavier one. It is about impact, individual and collective positions, binding. Everything counts. You have to study your opponents, work out how they bind, crouch, push, angle themselves. You then have to work out a strategy to counter this and then dominate them. It requires a lot of thinking. There are no secrets, just hard work."

I decided to try it out that evening. You know, nothing violent, just unopposed three-man scrummaging. I put down my cigar and scotch, which Patrick Estève had kindly given me, and took up my position. I was hooker, Garuche my tight head and Didier my loose head. When I look at the photo that was taken, what concerned me wasn't my poor binding, it was the fact that I didn't look out of place in the front row. The camera does lie after all, I thought... I was a centre for heaven's sake, admittedly a stocky, slow one. The reality was, I was never hard or intelligent enough to play in the front row.

Back to our meeting at his house in Pontacq.

"I remember scrummaging against Flippie van der Merwe in 1989 who must have weighed 140kgs, and I smashed him. How did I do it? If I told you everything, David, we'd be here all night."

"I used to like playing against players like David Sole. He was young and clever so you had to watch him. You could twist and turn him three times but then he would get you on the fourth, just as I was getting out of breath. And he spoke some French, which helped me!"

Stitched Up Like a Kipper

For all his jovial banter and laughter, I knew there was a very tough and competitive side to Garuche. There were a few 'instances' I wanted him to talk me through, notably 1984 when he was sent off in his first Five Nations game against Ireland in Paris.

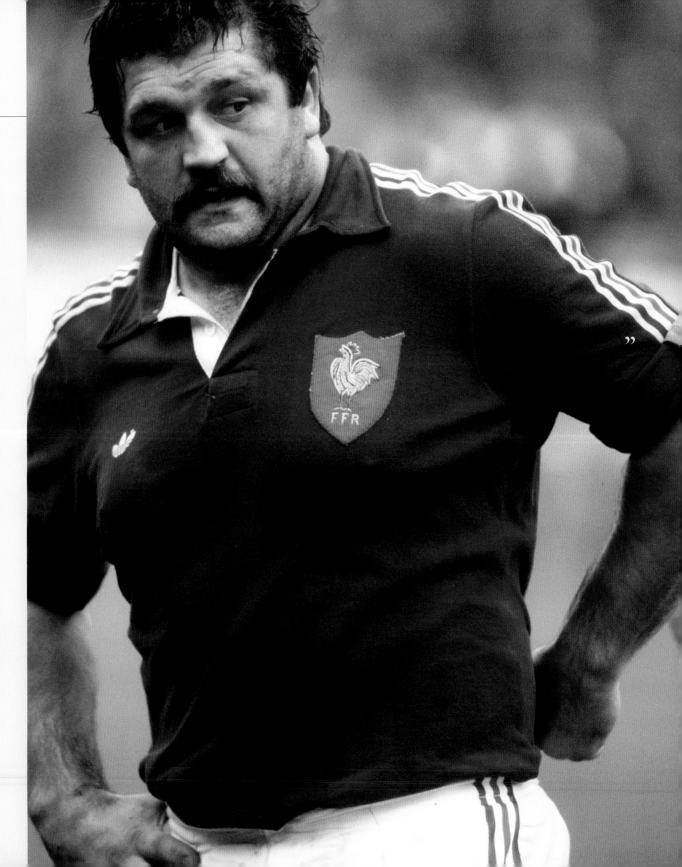

Jean-Pierre Garuet, Toulouse, 8th November 1986.
New Zealand 19 v France 7. *Photo - Bob Thomas Sports
Photography, Getty Images.*

*"I was stitched up like a kipper by those clever Irishmen,
Moss Keane and John O'Driscoll. Keane started the fight
but I was sent off. I was only thirty and it was my first
Five Nations game. Here's what happened.*

*"We had lost three line-outs in a row so we decided to take
Keane out in mid-air when he jumped, what we call
a 'roulette' in Lourdes. In fact, every club in France would
use it back then if they were losing line-outs. We would
then have a 'bagarre générale' and things would calm
down. It was called 'self-regulating rugby!'*

*"But Clive Norling didn't like it, penalised us and warned
me. Because I speak no English, he talked to Jean-Pierre
Rives who said something like, 'It's nothing, what an idiot
for penalising us for that'. Then we started to dominate
the scrum and Orr, Fitzgerald and McLoughlin were
suffering. I could hear Orr blowing. Papa had warned me
before the game, 'I have never really got the better of him,
he's dangerous so watch him like a hawk,' but I felt I was
winning. In one scrum, I lifted him right up with Moss
Keane behind him.*

*"At the next line out, it all kicked off. Keane wanted to take
me out so started a fight and I wasn't going to offer him
the other cheek. John O'Driscoll then starts looking for his
lens on the floor, feigning eye gouging (what the French
call une fourchette). Norling needed a culprit and chose
me. I remember the feeling when he showed me a red card.
I thought 'five minutes ago you were on fire and loving it,
now you're leaving in shame'. It was a very bitter/sweet
experience. I was the first Frenchman to be sent off
in a Five Nations match.*

"I learnt from the British to walk on an opponent, smile and say 'sorry'."

"After the match, we went to the Grand Hôtel in Paris. Albert Ferrasse called me into a huddle with Yves Noué (Chairman of Selectors) and Jacques. Jacques told Ferrasse that he had to save me because the scrummage was strong and there was a tour to New Zealand coming up in the summer, and I had to be on the plane. I was also desperate to get on that plane. If I played in the Five Nations and then against the All Blacks, I would die a happy man! Of course, this was before the first Rugby World Cup in 1987."

At this point, Garuche had had a few drinks, and he started to impersonate Albert Ferrasse, or Bébert La Godasse, as Jean Prat would call him. In rugby vernacular, *La Godasse* means 'shoeing'. Albert would regularly hand out 'shoeings' to the opposition, either on the pitch as a player, or verbally as the FFR President, hence the nick-name. He had another one too, 'Tonton'.

Garuche pretended to light a pipe and started his impersonation, rolling his r's as Ferrasse would: "Right Garuche, you've been a twat and got yourself caught. But I will sort it. To do so, we need to create a charade, like I am really cross with you, so we give them the impression that I am taking this very seriously and that I will punish you myself. I want a minimal sanction. I am going to give you a verbal lashing in front of the Breeteesh. Don't take offence. And you will be on the plane to New Zealand.

"Jean-Pierre Rives took offence though because Ferrasse called me 'un imbécile', but he wasn't aware of the game Tonton was playing! I was suspended for three months but got on that plane to Auckland."

I went to see Ollie Campbell and Phil Orr in Dublin, and we called John O'Driscoll to try to get to the bottom of the incident.

Ollie: "John, it's Ollie, Phil and David. We need a 'yes' or 'no'. Did Jean-Pierre give you a fourchette?"
John: "Jaysus, I think his hand was just in the wrong place. My eye-site was already shite so f**k knows why he would have targeted me."

Sweet and Sour

"I did learn and adapt from the experience. I realised that I could get away with things in the French Championship that I couldn't do in the Five Nations. I learnt from the British to walk on an opponent, smile and say 'sorry'."

What happened in 1983 against Australia?

"In 1981 in Australia, we played a very violent team in Brisbane. I wasn't on the tour but my friend and team mate was, Michel Crémaschi. In a warm-up game against Queensland in Brisbane, McBain, the hooker, broke his jaw. Michel felt hatred because he couldn't play the test matches. So, when McBain and his mates came to France in 1983, Michel and I took revenge. McBain was the same player who damaged Berbizier's ear in 1981."

When I met Daniel Herrero, he raved about Garuet: "He was both 'sweet and sour' in the scrum. He was hard and robust, a gentle man off the pitch with a touch of nastiness on it."

Garuche was a French tight head prop so it was to be expected. Sean Fitzpatrick found that out when Garuche would bore in, occasionally breaking his ribs.

I spoke to Buck Shelford, the former All Black captain, about the Battle of Nantes in 1986 and he remembers Garuet well: *"From the first ruck, I knew we were up against it. They were unrelenting. After twenty minutes, I got kicked in the face and lost three teeth.*

" Then, just before half time, I was over the ball on our try line. I looked up and saw Garuet flying towards me. He was horizontal and moving at pace. He smashed me right in the forehead. He knocked me out cold and it took me about two minutes to come around."

Jock Hobbs told me I couldn't go off because we had no one on the bench. In a third incident in the second half, I was kicked in the nuts in a ruck, which eventually forced me off the field. My scrotum had been split open and my testicle was hanging down."

Who dunnit? You'll have to read the rest of the book to find out.

Primitive but Effective

It may have been the amateur era back then but Garuche was innovative in his preparation methods.

"Today, studs are round whereas in our day they were conical. If you lived in the countryside and had horses, like I did, then you would have owned a file or rasp for maintaining the hooves, which I also used to sharpen my studs. I also created an area where I could lift weights, in the shed, above the tractors. It was primitive back then but it worked!"

It was getting late but there was much more to see and learn. Jean-Pierre took me into his 'museum', a room off the kitchen that was full of photos, catalogued shirts, caps, medals, the RWC final tankard, books and other mementos. It was a treasure trove of memories that span his career and saw him play against the greats such as Jason Leonard, Paul Rendall, Sean Fitzpatrick and Tommy Lawton. We spent an hour poring through the old scrap books and photos and all those precious souvenirs. Like his great mate Pascal Ondarts, Jean-Pierre has a passion for rugby, friendship and life that knows no bounds.

I could have stayed all evening. He is a warm, loyal, generous and an enormously likeable man. I can see why he is so popular with his former teammates and the world of rugby generally. Meeting him is like spending time with your favourite mate, brother and uncle because he is overflowing with funny anecdotes, wisdom and laughter.

He has also aged well. What facial cream does he use, I wondered? Or perhaps it's the magic healing water they have in Lourdes that flows from a spring in the Grotto of Massabielle? Or maybe it's because he's single and has no children to stress him out? Perhaps all of the above! Whatever it is, he looks the same now as he did back then.

I left Garuche about midnight. We gave each other a man-hug but our arms weren't long enough to go around our wine barrel-shaped chests. We'd have made a great front row.

The next day, I was heading back to the UK but I'd be back again in two weeks' time to meet Didier Cambérabero, Didier Codorniou, Éric Champ, Jérôme Gallion, Daniel Herrero and Jean-Pierre Rives. I jumped in the car and turned the radio on. Talking Heads' 'Once In A Lifetime' was on and singing me the words, 'And you may ask yourself, well, how did I get here?' I was wondering that myself, hoping it wasn't a figment of my imagination.

Alain Lorieux

MOUNTAINS

"TRADITIONALLY, THE FRENCH SECOND ROWS WERE BIG, STRAPPING MEN WHO MOVED SLOWLY BUT WERE VERY TOUGH. I HAD A DIFFERENT GAME, ONE WHICH DIDN'T FIT THE MOULD. I WASN'T THERE TO KILL PEOPLE OR 'ENFORCE THE LAW', I WAS THERE TO CATCH THE BALL AND PLAY RUNNING RUGBY."

BORN : 26TH MARCH 1956

CLUBS : FC GRENOBLE, FOOTBALL CLUB
AIX-LES-BAINS RUGBY

INTERNATIONAL CAPS : 30

POSITION : SECOND ROW

GRAND SLAMS : 1987

NICKNAME : LE POMPIER

NOM DE GUERRE : THE ALPINE ATHLETE

MY VISIT TO MEET HIM : MONDAY 12TH FEBRUARY 2018

Laurent Rodriguez is a great mate of Alain so he gave me his phone number and asked me to pass on his best wishes. Alain had ignored my first few messages but eventually called me back once he realised that I wasn't a random Englishman trying to sell him tickets to watch England at Twickenham. I took his call while sitting among the coffee drinkers in Place du Capitole in Toulouse, just as their epitome-of-cool Gitanes cigarette smoke was engulfing me. I inhaled the distinctive odour of third-hand fumes and clicked my brain into French. Alain and I immediately hit it off and scheduled to meet a few weeks later near the Alps.

I flew into Lyon and headed to Belley, a small town about 80km east. The temperature was freezing but it was no chore to drive towards the snow-capped mountains under the hivernal blue skies and bright sun. It was late morning and I was ravenous so I decided to find one of those restaurants *routiers*, the sort of venue where you can enjoy hearty food at low prices.

I found one near Bourgoin called Le Relais de la Maison Blanche, a veritable paradise for the truckers. The car park was rammed and I feared I would be turned away, but they looked me up and down, realised I would be a consumer *par excellence* and found me a table. The place was like a slick food factory, turning tables and serving plates *à toute vitesse* for the peckish punters. I am sure that all the other customers were thin with beards and dressed in dark clothing, a look that made me stick out like a prop in a sprint.

This is a restaurant *routier* for big eaters. Forget doorstops, the chunks of bread here are the size of doors. At my lunch, a couple of slabs were piled on the table alongside my salad of mussels and prawns so it was more like the salad was a garnish for the bread. I ordered fagots for the main course, something I hadn't eaten for three decades or more, since my school days at Batheaston primary school. I have bad memories of them, but when in Bourgoin, eat like the Berjalliens. Out of fear, I didn't dare ask what was in them, but they were delicious. What must these truckers think as they drive through Britain looking for an equivalent *resto routier? Je ne sais pas.*

Champagne and Truffles

I arrived in Belley where Alain picked me up and took me to his house, a beautifully positioned bucolic residence in the foothills of the Alps. He made me laugh en route as we passed a house: *"David, you see that house there on the left? I used to live in it with one of my wives. You see, I've had a slightly chaotic personal life. I've been married three times, twice to the same woman."*

It was only mid-afternoon when we arrived but he quickly cracked open a 2006 and 2009 Comtes de Champagne from Taittinger, accompanied by some *saucisson* and truffle-flavoured crisps. Yes, chips *à la truffe*, a first for me. Were they black or white truffles, from Alba or Burgundy, Périgord or Provence?

I was in the presence of a fellow epicurean, of that there was no doubt.

"Welcome to my house, David. You're the first Englishman I have invited here. After all the rugby we have played against the English, I have never invited one back, perhaps because I didn't want to re-start the 100-year war!"

Actually, I prefer French Englishmen to English Frenchmen who advise the English on how to beat the French."

It was a clear reference to Pierre Villepreux who once spent some time with the English team back in the 1990s.

As he poured the golden nectar, he told me about the 2006: *"This is a blanc de blanc, the Montrachet*

of Champagne. If there's one grande maison to drink, it's Taittinger because it's the only independent house left. We have just planted some vines in Kent in England because we think the chalky soil will produce fabulous sparkling wine."

The seductive aromatics burst out of the glass enveloping the liquid's fine, limestone minerality. It was sublime and elegant with mouth-watering acidity, its creamy mousse releasing notes of fresh, white peach and grapefruit.

It was the vinous equivalent of a chiselled, effervescent seductress dressed in a slinky Chanel dress who left you craving for more.

As I was swirling my champagne in the glass, I was quickly admonished by Alain.

"Unlike still wines, you shouldn't swirl your glass when drinking Champagne. Its finesse comes from the bubbles that have to attach themselves to the side of the glass. If you swirl it, you stop its expression."

Alain walked me around his fabulous cellar, home to wonderful bottles notably from Burgundy and Bordeaux.

All his champagnes were housed in a separate Eurocave.

"My daughter, Mathilde, is also an epicurienne. Not long ago, I opened a bottle of 2003 Egon Muller. She said, 'It's my favourite wine in the world'. I am not surprised because it sells for about 1200 € a bottle, if you can find it at auction!"

Alain is a regional director for Taittinger where he has worked for nearly thirty years, and which affords him the opportunity to visit some of France's greatest restaurants.

"I used to visit Troisgros in Roanne and I asked Pierre to sign one of his books for me. After I had left the restaurant, I took the book out to have a look at it, and he had signed it 'Bon appétit, Jean-François Imbernon!' I can't remember whether I ever gave it to him."

An Athelete, Not an Enforcer

I knew we would be drinking for hours so I moved the conversation back to rugby. I wanted to know all about his journey.

"I played rugby for about six months when I was fifteen, but I gave it up to become a fireman. I also loved athletics and swimming so I wanted to focus on those. Skiing and tennis were expensive sports enjoyed by the bourgeoisie when I was growing up. My family didn't have the money. Even nowadays, I prefer to head up the mountain to eat and drink! When I was twenty-two, a guy who used to bring us beer at the fire station said I should go to play for Grenoble.

He introduced me to Jean Liénard, the former coach of La Voulte who was Jacques Fouroux's mentor. I told him I had only played for six months and hardly knew the rules but he said, 'Alain, if you play for Grenoble, you will be in the French team within two years'. And he was right.

"I played for Grenoble between 1979 to 1985 while I was a fireman, at which point I left for Aix-Les-Bains where I stayed until I retired in 1992. They offered me a job running a camp site and I loved the area.

"In 1992, Jacques Fouroux helped me get a job with Taittinger and that is where I have worked since. It is how I met Sylvie, my girlfriend, who was one of my clients!

" I owe a lot to Jacques Fouroux, for my rugby career and my twenty-six years at Taittinger. Like Jean Liénard, he was *avant-gardiste*, able to see the future. He was such a warm man and a brilliant raconteur. We miss him enormously. He was so passionate and atypical."

"For him, it was never about the money in rugby. He was a brilliant thinker but he wasn't a completer-finisher. He would switch and change his mind but that's the only thing I could reproach him for."

Alain was a very different player to the other second rows who were around in the 1970s and 80s such as Palmié, Senal, Estève, Imbernon and Revailler. He was different in background, skillset and athleticism although, like the others, he was still a very hard man on the pitch.

"I was never part of the traditional rugby milieu because I wasn't steeped in it from an early age. I was a swimmer and athlete, running 100m in twelve seconds. I didn't come through the ranks at Perpignan, Narbonne or Béziers. Traditionally, the French second rows were big, strapping men who moved slowly but were very tough. I had a different game, one which didn't fit the mould. I wasn't there to kill people or 'enforce the law', I was there to catch the ball and play running rugby.

"Jacques put me in the team when I was very young and it created some jealousy among some players in the other clubs. I was accused of not being 'an enforcer' or doing the dirty work. Back then, the forwards played at 3km an hour, hid the ball up their shirts and punched their opponents!

"I didn't have the mentality of a killer. I was an athlete and a well-behaved player with a bit of attitude!

"However, on the pitch it was war. If there hadn't been solidarity with your teammates, you'd have been dead.

Alain Lorieux palms the ball down at the line-out. 20th February 1988, Five Nations Championship, Paris. France 25 v Ireland 6. *Photo - Bob Thomas Sports Photography, Getty Images.*

To play rugby back then, you had to be a bit mad. Players like Palmier and Senal were dirty beyond imagination. Internationally, it was rough and tough too.

"In Australia in 1981, we played Queensland in Brisbane. It was one of the most violent games I ever played. Their hooker stamped on Pierre Berbizier and tore his ear off.

"The upside was that this match paved the way for Lolo Rodriguez's debut. Jacques realised he needed some very hard men and Lolo didn't disappoint. He was only twenty but was so powerful, brave and hard.

"He was the perfect rugby forward back then and would still be today. He was a beast of a player and better than any French Number 8 since. Lolo ran with the ball, made breaks, set up the backs, tackled hard and could hurt the opposition. He was athletic, dextrous and a modern player thirty years ago, but he could also be nasty when required. He would hit people so hard that he'd break his fingers! But you couldn't ask him to take a high ball because it would land 2m from him, and he could only jump 3cm in the line out!"

These two were great team and room-mates, players who were thicker than thieves, and still great friends today, Patrice Lagisquet told me that Lolo once cut the sleeves off Alain's rugby shirt.

"Alain was wearing a shirt with no arms because they had been cut off at the shoulder. It looked like he'd just left a nightclub. Lolo was pissing himself laughing as they ran onto the pitch in a Five Nations game."

"The game today is very different to when we played it. Now the players are managed by their agents, date eighteen-year-old girls and are enclosed in their cocoons. Everything that makes a man such as managing money, buying a house, finding a job, is now handled by their agent. We would play and then work, and the two were intertwined, learning from each other."

I challenged Alain on whether he really was a 'well-behaved player' with a bit of attitude' and reminded him that he was sent off in 1988 in Argentina. He talked me through what happened:

"We played a violent match in the Estadio José Amalfitani in Buenos Aires. It all kicked off from the start. I smashed Iachetti in the nose after two minutes, and we all enjoyed the 'bagarre générale' that followed. Berbizier was on the ground and Iachetti, the dirty bastard, violently stamped on him, breaking his arm. Just as I punched Branca, Iachetti's second row partner, spreading his nose across his face, the referee turned around. He saw and sent me off immediately. As I walked across the pitch to the changing room, the Argentines were shouting abuse, baying for my blood and throwing oranges and other crap at me the whole way! Branca deserved what he got."

"That's what I mean by a 'well-behaved player with a bit of attitude'."

The Champagne was flowing and we were roaring with laughter.

"When you saw Lolo, did he tell you about their hooker, Courreges?"

"No," I reply. Alain laughed harder.

"In the last action of that violent game, Courreges head-butted Lolo in a ruck and cut him open. The match finished so Lolo couldn't get his revenge in. Fast forward twenty-five

years and Courreges arrived with a young Argentine player at Biarritz before a match. Courreges said 'hello' to Lolo on the pitch but when they went into the changing rooms, Lolo punched him and said 'have some of that for 1988!' "

Alain was now wetting himself.

"Lolo is Spanish and always holds his grudges!"

I was beginning to think that Lolo was nastier on the pitch than his former US Dax teammates told me...

Recognition by Martin Johnson

Part way through the afternoon, Alain ran upstairs to find a copy of an interview that Martin Johnson gave to the Midi Olympique. In response to the question: "If you could select a French player in your squad, whom would you chose?", Johnson says, "Without hesitation, Alain Lorieux." Alain beamed with pride that his combination of athleticism, determination and toughness are appreciated by someone from la perfide Albion. Johnson raved about how he took his try in the 1987 RWC Semi-Final against Australia and effused about the other tough and gifted forwards at the time – Rodriguez, Champ and Garuet in particular.

Alain still bristles with anger when he mentions the French press and how they still don't give players like him the credit he was due, especially at the World Cup in 1987.

"In 2007, the newspaper Midi Olympique released a book on the 1987 RWC and there wasn't a single photo of Cambé or Lolo or me, even though we were key in winning the semi-final. They had a photo of Lafond and he didn't even play in the match! Cambé was a fabulous player. In his early career, he may have struggled with confidence but from 1987 he was brilliant. He was quick, skilful and could kick off either foot. The journos are idiots and I told them so."

His strong views extend to current day players too.

"The game today is very different to when we played it. Now the players are managed by their agents, date eighteen-year-old girls and are enclosed in their cocoons. Everything that makes a man such as managing money, buying a house, finding a job, is now handled by their agent. We would play and then work, and the two were intertwined, learning from each other. Because everything is controlled, there are no stories anymore, and their girlfriends and wives follow them around. In our day, the women never came to watch and party with us. It was for blokes only so we could drink, party, fight and get up to lots of mischief!"

It was time for dinner so Alain, Sylvie and I headed into Belley where we enjoyed Navarin d'agneau and pommes dauphinoises. We drank a sublime 1998 Rossignol Trapet's Grand Cru Chambertin. It was laden with cool blueberries and vibrant acidity, and it had a silky, savoury finish. Like the perfect second row partnership, it complemented the lamb beautifully.

Alain was a fabulous host that day. He is old-school, and a warm, funny raconteur. I had taken hours of his time listening to his funny anecdotes and strong views but it was time to leave. I left the next day in the glistening cold sunshine to travel west across the Massif Central towards Brive where I would be meeting the great Jean-Luc Joinel.

The Old Port of Marseille,
Provence-Alpes-Côte d'Azur.

The Armenians in France

What encouraged me to write this piece on the Armenians was hearing all the stories from the former French players of Spanish origin, whose parents and family had walked across the Pyrenees to escape the Spanish war and poverty to find refuge in France. Without France's benevolence, their lives would have been very different and the French rugby team would never have been as strong!

It's weird what sticks in your mind. You spent years somewhere but can't recall the names of the people you met, even if you knew them for some time. Or perhaps it's just me, and the ravages of time have singled me out for special treatment. Whatever, the memory's edges soften, no doubt. I do remember faces well though, even if I can't put a name to them. And I never forget how I feel. Music, words, art, laughter and friendship can have such a powerful, positive and enduring effect on memory, and a fertile imagination can embellish these too, giving you the freedom to reach back and sketch onto your canvas.

The point? Well, there is one name from my time in Paris that I have never forgotten: Aram Tarpinian. I hardly knew him. He sold fruit and vegetables in the local market, and we used to chat about random things – football, family, life, history. He was humble, hardworking and never complained. He was always coy about his past and how his family arrived in France, which led me to do some research on his name and subsequently the Turkish genocide of Armenians in 1915. In fact, as I discovered, Armenians were and are everywhere in France – work colleagues, neighbours, rugby, friends, schools, shops.

The Armenian genocide reminds us of the evil that men can do, but also of mankind's collective generosity and how kindness can triumph over malefaction. France has welcomed so many refugees during its long history – the Spanish, Italians, Jews, Arab-Berber, Africans and the Armenians – even if the initial receptions were sometimes characterised by fear.

All these groups had a big, positive influence on me during my time in France. Aram's interaction with me involved the humdrum chores of daily life but his impact on my inquisitiveness and about the Armenian plight and my quest to understand it was immense. That is why I always remember his name.

What heightened my interest in the Armenians was meeting Virginie Hovanessian in the summer of 1992. I found her singularly beautiful, intelligent and charming, and she was in love and living with her other half, damn it. Tall, dark, vivacious, seductive and exotic, she made my heart beat faster and louder at the music of her laughter. Hopefully, I have painted a beguiling portrait. She was magical and nearly perfect...

When I first met her, I couldn't work out where she was from. French? Italian? Egyptian? It was her name that gave the game away – Armenian, in all its glory.

It was also Virginie who invited me to that restaurant that would become part of my life in Paris: Willi's Wine bar. It is still there, going strong and I always pop in for a drink and/or dinner when I am in town. We would spend hours there chatting. I loved those times.

Much as I liked her, it was her family's personal story about the Armenian genocide that ensorcelled me. I met her again recently in Paris and asked her to re-tell it so I could pass it on to you.

The Armenian genocide reminds us of the evil that men can do, but also of mankind's collective generosity and how kindness can triumph over malefaction.

> # I'm no believer in fate, but what happened to them later tests that conviction to breaking point.

The Walk to Freedom

Virginie is half-Armenian, a quarter-Polish and a quarter-Portuguese, and all her grandparents came to France between the two world wars, in search of peace and freedom, where anybody with the will could find a way to make a decent, safe living.

Both her Armenian grandparents were born in the same village on the Armenian plateau, right in the middle of Turkey today. However, they knew each other only by sight because her grandmother, called Eva, was not allowed to speak or play with her future husband, called Avo. She was born into a family of modest but successful shopkeepers who sold everything from oil for lamps to fabric to food, but Avo was an orphan and deemed an unsuitable match by Eva's parents.

I'm no believer in fate, but what happened to them later tests that conviction to breaking point.

The Armenian genocide of 1915 involved the Ottoman government's systematic extermination of 1.5 million Armenians. Eva, aged six, witnessed the decapitation of her father and three brothers in her backyard. The murders were committed by local Turks wielding axes, the same people who had been customers of the family shop a few weeks before. Only Eva and her mother, Virginie's great-grandmother, survived.

After the killing, the Turks returned in search of the gold and family savings hoping that fear would break them, but they were resolute. Her great-grandmother, called Maria, hid the coins, telling her daughter where they were in the event she didn't survive. After threatening Eva, the Turks eventually left empty-handed. Maria sewed all the coins into the coat's linings and they left quickly, walking south towards Syria.

During the journey, Eva wasn't allowed to take off her coat, whatever the weather. She remembered having

to find some medicinal herbs in order to sooth their sore feet. The journey took time as they made a living along the way, milking cows, harvesting potatoes, doing laundry and cooking so they didn't need to spend the coins. They slept in barns and shacks in towns as long as it took to save enough money, before resuming their journey.

Finally, after a couple of years, they arrived in Aleppo, Syria, where they settled in a small apartment. Maria found a job as a cook in a Christian school, and, as Eva had never attended one, Maria asked the sisters if they could teach her child to read and write. They had no money to spend on education so the sisters said they would teach her if Eva did the housekeeping. Eventually, Maria died there, and Eva was left alone with the coins still sewed into her coat lining.

Not feeling welcome at the school, she decided to leave. Her mother had told Eva to go either to France or America, and she chose the latter. She travelled to Athens from Syria and landed in Pyraeus, and planned to buy a ticket to America with the coins. However, as she was queueing to get her ticket, she saw Avo, (Virginie's grandfather to-be) diving beneath the big cruise liners to fetch the coins that tourists would throw into the sea. Recall, they had never spoken but knew each other. They met up and he told her his story.

A short time before the tragedy happened to her family, Avo came across a businessman in the village. The man was aware of the threat to the Armenians so he took Avo with him and dropped him in another orphanage in Athens. While they were trying to teach Avo to become a shoemaker, he was skipping the apprenticeship as he would prefer swim for coins in the harbour instead.

At this point, Avo was the only person still alive whom Eva knew, so instead of buying a single ticket to America, her budget allowed her to buy two tickets to Marseille. Arriving there, they both lied about their age, pretending to be eighteen, in order to be able to work legally in France. They also pretended to be married. At the time she was fifteen or sixteen.

Back then, there were no registers in Turkey so Virginie never knew their birthdays, and because they pretended to be married, they never had a wedding anniversary either. Their names were also changed, inadvertently. Originally her grandfather was named 'Hovannès Torossian' (Armenians often have biblical surnames), but immigration who granted them the residence permit (and later French nationality) got mixed up and wrote 'Toros Hovanessian' onto the Avo's ID papers. He was so glad to get the permit that he didn't bother pointing the mistake out! Hovanessian has been the family name ever since.

Settling in the South of France, Avo started repairing and selling shoes on the open-air markets of the region while Eva was a maid for a local Armenian family. She helped to raise the young Henri Verneuil, a French-Armenian, who went on to become a successful playwriter and film maker. She told him the story of her life, which Henri used as the basis for a movie called Mayrig (which means mummy in Armenian) in 1991. Virginie went to watch the movie with her family and it was the only time in Virginie's life that she saw her grandmother cry. Eva died aged ninety-seven.

The story encapsulates all the emotions and vicissitudes of a Greek tragedy only this one is Armenian, took place in Turkey, had an escape route through Syria and ended up in France. It has everything: misfortune, hatred, misery, pain, genocide, serendipity, kindness, love, determination, resilience, endurance, survival. Sounds familiar doesn't it, how man*unk*ind has a habit of messing up and repeating its horrors, leaving people desperate, destitute and fleeing repression? Plaudits and immense credit accrue to France for helping them to settle and integrate into its beautiful country.

Scuffle Before Lunch

On a lighter note, but related to the Turkish-Armenian subject, I remember a fabulous lunch at the great Michel Chapoutier's office in Tain l'Hermitage back in 2014. He is one of France's greatest wine makers. Along with my partners in crime, Alun Griffiths, Julian Rimmer and Will Bentley, we enjoyed a wonderful wine tasting at his cellars first. Skipping most of his range, we headed straight to his top reds and whites – Le Méal, de L'Orée, Le Pavillon, l'Hermite, and so on. These are some of France's greatest wines, many of them retailing for well over 150 € a bottle. They were all exquisite, silky and stunning. To round off the tasting extravaganza, we had lunch consisting of a *smörgåsbord* of France's finest meats and cheeses, a veritable *bonheur*.

However, before we had even sat down, Julian, married to a beautiful Turkish lady who was raised in Australia, sparked off a row with our host, by suggesting that he should start investing in Turkish vineyards.

Bon dieu. Talk about the biting off the hand that feeds you.

"Not until Turkey formally admits that it committed genocide against the Armenians," Michel responded.

It was like a *bagarre générale* at the first scrum, thirty seconds into the game. It simmered all lunch. Julian was brought up in Liverpool, attended the local comprehensive, supports Everton and read English at Cambridge. He has all the chips on his shoulders to prove it. He is articulate, funny, sharp-tongued, well-read, convincing and punchy. He is also the only person I know who has been shot on a stag party (fortunately not his) outside an establishment characterised by moral laxity in Amsterdam. He was totally innocent. He is my great mate and I love him.

Will, Alun and I used all our diplomatic skills with Monsieur Chapoutier to bring the situation back under control, so we could enjoy the fabulous food and wine. I doubt he has bought any vineyards in Turkey and I doubt they ever acknowledge the genocide. Few nations do.

An orchard on outskirts of Agen.
Photo - Pierre Carton.

South West

"YOU MIGHT MEET ME TOMORROW
AS ALL THE LIGHTS ARE BLOOMING GREEN
AND YOU'RE FEELING A LITTLE LONELY,
A LITTLE SAD, A LITTLE MEAN
REMEMBER A PLACE
INSIDE OF THAT HOTEL
WHERE YOU COULD DO ANYTHING YOU
WANT TO DO
YOU COULDN'T TELL"

RICKY LEE JONES, LIVING IT UP, 1981

Possibly the heartland of French rugby, this region spans the area from Bordeaux to Brive to Castres to Dax, including such great rugby towns as Toulouse, Agen, Auch, Montauban and Mont-de-Marsan. It is a region of huge charm and the source of many of France's finest exports – wine, prunes, truffles, chestnuts, cassoulet and foie gras. I love the food in the South West, notably the Gascon kind – it manages to be opulent, decadent and cultured all at the same time. I spent a year in Bordeaux playing for the Bordeaux Etudiant Club (BEC) back in 1988 and have always retained great affection for the area, its dreamy landscapes and idyllic villages nourishing the souls of those worn down by the city.

Travelling south and east from Bordeaux to play against clubs from towns such as Auch, Graulhet, Libourne and Sainte-Foy-La-Grande remain some of my greatest memories of living in France – the bus journey, pre-match lunch of foie gras, steak and red wine (oh yes, this is France), the picturesque grounds and the post-match 3ème mi-temps with your mates. Those images are etched into my memory forever.

The Garonne river and valley near Moissac.
Photo - Getty Images.

I'm not sure I developed much intellectually in 1988 (some would say since 1988). I was studying French, economics and rugby at Loughborough University, but I had the opportunity to spend my third year in France 'to enhance my language skills'. Having already enhanced those before Loughborough, some thought it would be unnecessary to do so again. I agreed, so I simply identified other noble reasons, such as the opportunity 'to immerse myself in the French culture, including the language, literature, art and history'. Before you could say '*je prend l'entrecôte, à point, une portion de frites, et une bouteille de Pétrus, s'il vous plaît,*' I was heading to Bordeaux, a place carefully selected for its gastronomy, wine and rugby.

First the rugby. It was without question the most violent I had experienced. I remember one incident in particular when our fly-half chipped over the top early on in the game. As I ran through, I pushed their fly-half out of the way because he had deliberately run into my path. At the next breakdown, he mistook someone else for me, and, acting as if he were the victim, pulled my team mate's head back by his hair and unleashed the mother of all hooks into his jaw. My poor mate lay there prostrate while the rest of us had a *bagarre générale* that seemed to go on for minutes. It was extraordinary, with a level of savagery I had never seen before on the lush pitches of the English West Country and Midlands.

As for the food and wine, *bon dieu*, it was memorable for its decadence. Once, we played a match at Libourne and the bus stopped on the way back to Bordeaux for a team dinner. The place was quintessentially Gascon.

I remember that its food was so rich and enticing that eating it was like being seduced by an ensemble of French maids smeared in goose fat. The *foie gras* was buttery, delicate and luscious, its consistency enriched by the process of *gavage*. The *cassoulet* was copious, meaty and hearty, intensified by the chicken stock and *mirepoix*. It was a dish perfect for hungry men, celebrating victory and preparing for a big night out in Bordeaux.

As for the wines, rather than visit the large *châteaux*, I would visit the smaller ones, just knocking on doors to see whether I could do a tasting. The human challenge of building a relationship and gaining the confidence of someone in the first few sentences was as much fun as drinking the wine. For great food and wine, we could simply visit places like La Tupina, a fabulous restaurant in downtown Bordeaux, which served some of the best Gascon home-cooked food I have ever tasted, plus a stellar *carte des vins*. Years later, I revisited it for Will

Bentley's stag weekend, along with the Unremarkables (Julian's *nom de guerre* for us), a group of dysfunctional friends, blessed with such disparate nicknames as Boy Bentley, Rhinestone, the King of Tonga, Griffalo, Frankie Two Dogs, Bish Bash Bosh, Charlie One Arse, Attila and Shady.

Anyway, 1988 flew by, filled by food, wine, rugby, *femmes fatales* and a solid improvement in my 'knowledge of French culture'. It was definitely a year for living it up. My motto for the year was borrowed from Oscar Wilde: *"Moderation is a fatal thing. Nothing succeeds like excess".*

Érik Bonneval

SOUTH WEST   "WHEN I SCORED THOSE THREE TRIES AGAINST SCOTLAND IN 1987, SOMEONE ASKED THE REFEREE ABOUT A POTENTIAL FORWARD PASS AT THE POST-MATCH DINNER. HE JUST SAID, 'THE ACTION WAS SO FAST AND BEAUTIFUL THAT I FELT I JUST HAD TO AWARD IT!'"

BORN : 19TH NOVEMBER 1963

CLUBS : STADE TOULOUSAIN

INTERNATIONAL CAPS : 18

POSITION : FULL-BACK, CENTRE, WING

GRAND SLAMS : 1987

NOM DE GUERRE : THE DEADLY FINISHER

MY VISIT TO MEET HIM : SUNDAY 10TH DECEMBER 2017
AND THURSDAY 15TH FEBRUARY 2018

Érik was another player whose name and image are stamped indelibly onto my memory. Born and bred in Toulouse, he was a player of both power and craft who joined his home club in the same year as Denis Charvet, both of whom prospered under the talented coaching duo of Pierre Villepreux and Jean-Claude Skrela.

You may have already discovered in my other pieces, but when writing about the French centres, I should declare my bias. I was a centre of average ability so I worshipped at the *crampons* of my chosen quartet – Érik, Philippe Sella, Denis Charvet and Didier Codorniou. Writing impartially about any of them is impossible so, as Editor-in-Chief, please forgive the romance, nostalgia and adulation that permeate these articles.

As Érik was breaking into the international side, it was overflowing with talent. The wings consisted of Pardo, Estève, Lagisquet and Bérot, and in the centre were Sella, Codorniou, and at full-back Blanco and Lafond, who could also excel on the wing. *Pas mal, non?*

Ironically for Érik, he too was a full-back when he joined Toulouse, but he switched to centre. When Codorniou joined ST in 1988, Érik moved to the wing. He was a man of many talents.

Didier Codorniou told me, *"If Érik hadn't been injured, he would certainly been one of the best players of his generation. In fact, he probably was anyway, in spite of his career being affected by a knee injury. He had everything – a piece of both Sella and Blanco. He was supertalented, fast, skilful and powerful. Even when he came back after injury, he was an outstanding player."*

Scottish Trio

You could see all these traits in the three tries he scored for France against Scotland in 1987. French TV described it as *"un match de toute beauté. Détermination, dynamism, fraicheur physique."*

His first try came down the left-hand side after some straight running and a sumptuous pass by the Prince of Centres, Denis Charvet. It was the sort of try that you would expect a top player to score, but that combination of Charvet and Bonneval sprinkled it with pixie dust. It is so easy on the eye.

"Dad loves watching his grandkids play. I'll always ask him how he thought they performed and no matter what, he'll always say 'brilliantly'."

His second try involved a flowing movement from right to left. Mesnel looped Sella and passed to Serge who surged into the line, took out two defenders and passed to Érik who still had to beat Hastings to score.

While the first two tries showed Bonneval's straight-line pace, the last one showed his quick feet and power. Picking up a loose ball after Charvet had drifted and glided past the defender, Érik beat four players to score a hattrick.

I love the TV commentary for the match: *"Trois essais… somptueux, où la vitesse de l'ailier toulousain fait merveille."*

Érik told me more:

"When I scored those three tries against Scotland in 1987, someone asked the referee about potential forward pass at the post match dinner. He just said, 'The action was so fast and beautiful that I felt I just had to award it!' It was great to see French flair winning over the referee."

Finlay Calder told me, *"I managed to touch him with my fingertips for the first try, but he was too fast and strong. He was a fabulous player."*

The other tries that stick in my mind were against England in 1986 and 1987. In 1986, in the last minute of the match, the French broke from their 22m line and Érik accelerated majestically covering 40m in a flash. He floated a glorious pass to Denis, who evaded the touchline and tackler to pass inside to Philippe to score his fourth consecutive try in the Five Nations and secure the Grand Slam for France.

"The funny thing was David, it hadn't been a great game and Laporte had kicked everything. We kept shouting 'give it, give it, pass it out,' and eventually Guy did!"

In 1987, off a scrum, a double switch created space for

> "The game was based on players being intelligent and their philosophy called *intelligence situationelle*. Depending on your position on the pitch, players had to take responsibility. You couldn't simply react based on what we discussed in the changing room."

Champ who sprinted through and passed to Bonneval who used his power to score in spite of two England defenders tackling him.

"I spent many years with Dad watching the Five Nations on the TV and the English invariably won, so there was always a lot of rivalry and the English were the enemy! Those tries against them were particularly memorable."

Strong Genes

Érik exhibits all those classic southern French characteristics that make me yearn to spend time there – that smile, warmth of character, guttural accent, outgoing personality and love of rugby.

I had the pleasure of meeting him twice, once in the bar at the Hilton Hotel next to Heathrow one icy evening after Saracens v Clermont, a European Cup game,

had been postponed. I told him it was obvious who would win that one: "Saracens are just too strong for the men from the Auvergne," I told him. What do I know? Saracens were stuffed 46-14! The second time we met was in the more relaxed surroundings of the St John's Club adjacent to the mighty Stade Toulousain.

I asked Érik to tell me about his background.

"Dad played for TOEC so with Hugo and Arthur, we are now in our third generation of top flight rugby players. Dad was a loose-head prop so I'm not quite sure where the genes come from in the second and third generations! Dad loves watching his grandkids play. I'll always ask him how he thought they performed and no matter what, he'll always say, 'Brilliantly'. Mum might pipe up and say, 'They didn't touch the ball' so he'll always say to her, 'What do you know? Where did you play?' It's his favourite expression!

"In 1982, I joined Toulouse in the same year as Denis. He was a scrum-half and I was a full-back but Pierre saw something in us and paired us in the centre. Our first real glory came in 1985 when we won the Bouclier de Brennus. The year before in 1984, I had made my debut for France in New Zealand as a replacement for Codor and scoring a try.

"We loved playing under Pierre and Jean-Claude at ST. The game was based on players being intelligent and their philosophy called 'intelligence situationelle'. Depending on your position on the pitch, players had to take responsibility. You couldn't simply play based on what we discussed in the changing room. Of course, we had a framework but we had to react on the pitch, based on what we saw. We weren't there to simply implement the coaches' game plan. When I commentate now, I can see things very quickly and can see what a team should do. Teams have to adopt. You have to make choices in real time and focus on where you are winning on the pitch.

> "The French were the gods of attacking play and we wanted to emulate them. They had the ability to turn a game on its head. Bonneval was a fabulous player. He was the back who was most like an All Black - fast, strong, skilful, direct."

When we trained at ST, we loved it. We would often run the sessions ourselves and they would just watch. Robert Bru was the team manager, and he was also a deep thinker and big influence."

Smashed by a Local Bumpkin

Érik was brilliant in 1986 and 1987. In 1986, he played six internationals in a row, against Wales and England in the Five Nations, and then Argentina twice and Australia on tour. Afterwards, the team travelled down to New Zealand to play the Baby Blacks on 28th June, coincidently Sean Fitzpatrick's first cap. But Érik wasn't picked.

"I'd met an Argentine girl in 1985 and asked her to join us in New Zealand in 1986. Jacques went off on one. He told me I was distracted and so didn't pick me!"

In 1986, just before the World Cup started, fate played its hand in a training session in New Zealand.

"There were twenty-six of us picked so we were four players short for a practice match. We asked some of the locals to join us and just as I was scoring a try, one of the rednecks tackled me from the side and cut me in two. I tore my cruciate ligaments so that was the end of the tournament for me.

"I didn't even get a losing medal (a tankard!) after we lost the final. Jacques told me to go up and get one but Ferrasse looked at me and said, 'No'. If I'd played for Agen, he would have let me!"

Nonchalant and Brilliant

I spoke to John Kirwan about playing against this French team and its great wingers, such as Patrice Lagisquet, Érik Bonneval and Patrick Estève, and he waxed lyrical about them as players and men.

"The French were the gods of attacking play and we wanted to emulate them. They had the ability to turn a game on its head. Bonneval was a fabulous player. He was the back who was most like an All Black - fast, strong, skilful, direct. I remember that back line in 1984 in particular because it was my debut, and it was overflowing with talent – Blanco, Sella, Codorniou, Bonneval, Lagisquet, Estève, Lescarboura and Berbizier. I idolised them all and they were everything I aspired to be. And then there was the massive pack. It was like the boxer and the ballet dancer!

"France had this nonchalance and self-confidence. I loved marking players like Érik, Patrice and Patrick because they were so fast and elusive so it was such a challenge. If you weren't on your game, they would turn you and beat you on a sixpence. But if you got on top of the French team, they could become uninterested! Their unpredictability is what made them so exciting."

Talking of Patrick Estève, Érik told me an amusing anecdote.

"Patrick Estève is a funny man. We were playing for France B against England B. England kicked high and Flint caught it before being bulldozered by the England pack. He got up and squealed 'F**k, I feel like I've been through a beehive. I'm stinging all over'. Haha, his hair was all over the place! He was fast and a brilliant attacker, but he didn't like the rough stuff as much."

We ate quite healthily at St Jean's Club, devouring a chicken salad, washed down by a couple of beers, before he showed me around the stadium, one which reflects the glory of their past. I left him in the sunshine, armed with a bottle of Trévallon wine that he can enjoy next time France beat England. It might be a while…

Daniel Dubroca

SOUTH WEST

"WE COMMANDED RESPECT
FROM ALL OUR OPPONENTS
AND WE HAD PLAYERS WITH
A TOUGH MENTALITY WHO
DIDN'T TAKE A BACKWARDS STEP.
PLAYERS LIKE PASCAL, LOLO,
GARUCHE AND ÉRIC WERE
AS HARD AS NAILS."

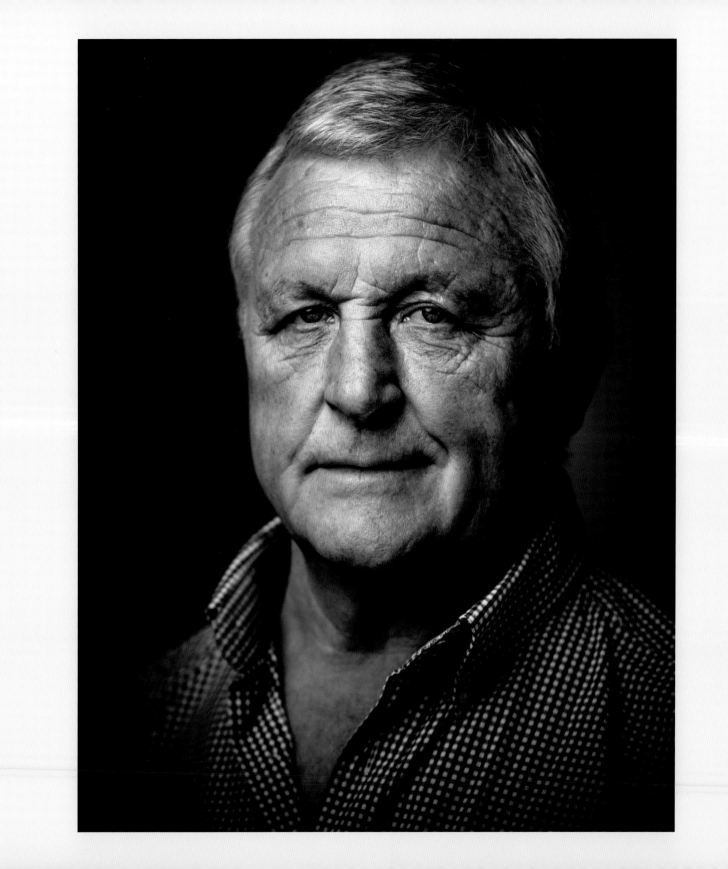

BORN : 25TH APRIL 1954

CLUBS : SPORTING UNION AGEN LOT-ET-GARONNE

INTERNATIONAL CAPS : 33

POSITION : PROP, HOOKER

GRAND SLAMS : 1987

NICKNAME : LA PINTADE

NOM DE GUERRE : THE GENTLEMAN FARMER

MY VISIT TO MEET HIM : WEDNESDAY 14TH FEBRUARY
AND TUESDAY 3RD APRIL 2018

D uring my long lunch with Serge in Hendaye, he said to me, *"Which contact details are you missing, David?"*

I let him know – Didier Camberabero, Philippe Sella, Denis Charvet, Daniel Dubroca and Patrice Lagisquet. Grinning, he picked up his mobile he said: *"Don't move, this is how we do things in France."*

Like the Godfather of his former team, he rang around each one, asking for a favour. His relaxed, Latin style and humour made me laugh.

Here is a synopsis of the conversation with Daniel:

"How are you my little Daniel? Are you taking a siesta? No, I'm not a farmer like you so I can't just have a snooze in the orchard... [laughs] ...Shit, it's twenty-three degrees here today. Listen, I am having a long lunch with an English friend, he is a good bloke, a real 'bon vivant'. He says he used to play centre but you wouldn't think so. If I, a former full-back, am considered a loose head, he should be considered a tight head, like you in the old days. We'd make a very good front row... David is laughing."

The scene was set but it was Daniel who called me back the following week and made me a proposal:

"Let's do a dinner at a great restaurant in Agen called La Maison de Michel Dussau. We'll invite Philippe and Dominique to join us."

I was on the Île de Ré when he called and I almost choked on my oysters and caviar. Fear not, the Chablis helped remove the temporary blockage. Can you imagine the offer of dinner with this great *Agenais* trio including their great captain and leader Daniel Dubroca, Philippe Sella and Dominique Erbani? He could have offered me a bowl of porridge sitting on a spike, and I would have accepted. I started humming some Van Morrison lyrics: this was 'as sweet as Tupelo Honey, just like honey, baby, from a bee'.

Daniel was first to arrive for the dinner, having driven down from Sainte-Bazeille, some 60km away where he runs his fruit business with his brother-in-law and

sister-in-law. They only harvest about 500 tons of apples these days, whereas before it was 4,500 tons.

"We have simplified the business over the years as we have gained experience and aged!"

When I met Daniel, I immediately noticed his assured presence, authority and self-confidence, the same characteristics I discerned in Sean Fitzpatrick when I first met him. Of course, this perception is driven by one's own preconceptions, based on their achievements and sporting stature, but they both possess the essential characteristics of great leaders too – commitment, determination, resilience, steely eye contact, strong and lucid communication, accountability, integrity, clarity of thought, empathy and instinctive intelligence. These are the characteristics that have meant their careers, pre and post-rugby, have been so impressive. Over the last forty years, Daniel has been a businessman, captain of France, rugby coach, club director, father and grandfather.

When we met, he was clear about his plans:

"From 31st December 2018, I am retiring from all the business and rugby activities! I am going to relax, cycle and spend time with my children. I have a grandson of eight months and he already has some mini-rugby balls in his cot."

When talking about his beloved Agen, Daniel was somewhat grumpy because they were languishing in the relegation zone, and needed to win their last three games to avoid relegation to the French 2nd

division, called ProD2.

"I have just been interviewed for an article in Le Petit Bleu (Agen's local newspaper) saying that they need to stop weight training and grow some hormones instead."

As a three-time winner of the Bouclier de Brennus, understandably, Daniel's expectations are very high.

French Domination

I wanted to know the players he played with.

"By the time we reached the final of the Rugby World Cup in 1987, we had been together many years and amassed a lot of caps and experience. We commanded respect from all our opponents and we had players with a tough mentality who didn't take a backwards step. Players like Pascal (Ondarts), Lolo (Rodriguez), Garuche (Garuet) and Éric (Champ) were as hard as nails. The Basques like Pascal weren't just brilliant technically, they were also clever, but looked fearsome and intimidated their opponents. Players like Champ had such self-confidence and became a rallying point in times of adversity, with his Mediterranean chin and chest pushed out. That mix of talent, maturity and physicality meant we were very difficult to beat.

"Garuet would get low, twist his shoulder and attack the opposition's hooker. He was very powerful and would get inside you. I remember many games when he would smash his opponent. It was like a lamb to the slaughter. When you played against him,

Garuet. Ondarts was strong, mobile and fiery, like he was ready to explode. Garuet, the spud farmer, was a brilliant scrummager who went so low that our hooker couldn't hook the ball back. And Dubroca was a born leader, great ball carrier and very skilful player. He would go on these Viking-like charges the whole game such was his fitness."

Captain Invincible

Daniel is a natural leader. Did that come easily to him?

"You need to be able to express yourself, in whatever form it takes. Some shout, some talk quietly, some show by example. Whatever your method, the team soon adapts. We were all motivated by the same goal, to win, and we had the same 'etat d'esprit'. We also had other great leaders like Berbizier who we relied upon."

Raphaël Ibañez talked to me about the different styles of Dintrans and Dubroca, both of whom inspired him:

"I never played against either but I wanted to get to know them, how they played and captained the team. Daniel was clever, subtle, technical, lucid, intelligent. He anticipated situations. Philippe was like a bomb, explosive, aggressive, physical, all heart and sacrifice. Philippe would do anything for the team and sacrifice himself. He still would today. Daniel would assess the situation and think his way through a problem. Both were different and brilliant.

"Fouroux knew how to put them in competition to get the best out of them. They are totally different personalities and I wanted to be a mix of them. I wanted to have the

courage and heart to fight to the last while being lucid enough to make good decisions."

Near-Sudden Death

In 1986, Daniel was playing in the Bouclier de Brennus final against Toulouse when he was knocked unconscious by a kick to the head and swallowed his tongue. Berbizier reacted quickly and he ran to the touchline to fetch the touch judge's flag. He and Daniel's great friend, Doctor Léo Busquet, forced his jaws open and pulled his tongue back. Leo's fingers took about eight weeks to heal because Daniel nearly bit them off.

"I woke up properly at 9.30pm in intensive care. I had started to come around when they put me on the stretcher but I don't remember anything. My wife was next to me, obviously very worried. The first thing I said when I woke up was 'did we win?' I started crying when she told me we'd lost. Life could have ended for me there and then. It was a deliberate kick by someone. I was targeted by Toulouse and they wanted me off the pitch."

Daniel has never admitted who did it but according to his biography written by Martine Loubet-Murgis, the loose head prop Portolan was the chief suspect. He was rested several weeks afterwards for fear of reprisals.

Punch and Judy

Another memorable final was in 1990 against Racing, notorious for its physicality. Franck Mesnel described what happened:

you had the impression he was like a hydraulic drill. If he got the shove on you, it was all over. Furthermore, he was such a clever player. Such was his intelligence, he would study his opponent and attack his weaknesses.

I spoke to Stuart Evans, the former Welsh prop, who played in the first Rugby World Cup, and he told me what it was like playing against Daniel and his French front row mates.

"Playing against those men was like being put through a mincing machine. All of them were rough and tough on the pitch. In 1985, I played against Doxpi (Pierre Dospital), Dintrans and Garuet. Doxpi started gouging me so I gave him by best shot and smacked him on the nose. He just looked at me, growled and said, 'Play on young lad before I knock your head off'. Dintrans had this huge head, about the size of a horse. I smeared my head in Vaseline just so I could slide my head into the scrum.
"Then in 1987, I played against Ondarts, Dubroca and

"Racing lost the final in 1987 because we weren't hard enough. However, in 1990 against Agen, we were much tougher because we had players like Michel Tachdjian, Patrick Serrière and Jean-Pierre Genet. They started smacking Tolot about because he wasn't pushing straight but he didn't care because his face was smashed in anyway. So Michel, who is very clever, started picking on Seigne who said 'Stop it Michel, what are you punching me for?' Michel responded, 'Lolo, stop Tolot boring in, otherwise we are going to target you all afternoon'. And they duly did. Seigne was so badly beaten that he wasn't allowed to go on tour with France the next day. Michel is a lovely man but was as hard as nails on the pitch!"

When I met David Sole to capture his memories of playing the French, he also remembers Seigne from a French Barbarians match against the All Blacks in Toulouse in 1989.

"I turned up and there was meant to be all the other Five Nations captains there as well, but they didn't turn up! I arrived with a broken toe to be met by Laurent Seigne. He was like a villain from a Tintin story. He was on my side but I was still scared of him.

"In the changing room, people started putting on boxes and protective under-garments. On the pitch, I remember that Seigne smacked McDowell who retaliated. If I had been playing for Scotland, I would have gone in for the fight, but there was no way I was going to die playing for a French team, especially as my opposite number was Richard Loe!"

There must have been some residual bad blood from that match because Seigne was fighting McDowell again at Nantes in 1990. Sean Fitzpatrick told me:

"We were up against a tough front row of Seigne, Armary and Ondarts. Seigne wouldn't leave McDowell alone, looking to punch him at every opportunity. He clearly didn't realise that Steve was a black belt in Judo and very capable of defending himself. After a few punches, Steve said to the Australian referee, 'If he does it again, I am going to sort him out'. After the next punch, Seigne lay prostrate on the grass, knocked out cold. There was me, Richard (Loe) and Steve against them and I thought 'oh dear, here we go'. But his fellow Frenchmen just jogged away, not keen on defending their honour!"

Cheese Eaters

As a result of this type of capitulation, Brian Moore would describe the French as 'cheese-eating surrender monkeys'.

Talking of Brian, he likes to rib the French, but based on a couple of conversations we had, I think he reflects some of their characteristics. They are emotional, ardent and passionate like him. I could have seen him playing for Bayonne or Toulon in his heyday! It just so happens that Brian was brought up in Halifax rather than Hendaye or Hyères. He told me a few stories about playing the French. Here's one of them:

"One time, Dubroca stamped on my head when my arms were pinned back and the French had the nudge on.

> " It really f**king hurt but I didn't want Dubroca to know, so I waited ten minutes before we called the medical man on. He stitched it up in the tunnel without an anaesthetic. I was so mad that I didn't need one. I couldn't wait to get back on the pitch to get my revenge."

"Anyway, that night we all went to the Castel Club in the middle of Paris. I was about to leave at 3am but on the way out, I was met by Ondarts and Dubroca who got hold of me, lifted me up and took me back in for a drink."

Crucible of Power

Daniel played for the club where the power base of French rugby resided for so many years. For it was the home town and club of Albert Ferrasse and Guy Basquet who wielded so such influence over all aspects of rugby back then.

"Every day at 12.30, they would play Belote in a bar in Agen. To begin, they played at Chez Dalmolin. When that closed, they moved to Patrick Solé's bar called Le Fair Play.

They would always play at the same table, but against each other, never for the same team. If one of them wasn't there on a day, they had to find a replacement. It was crazy! When they fell out in the early 1990s, Basquet stopped playing against him and they would sit at different tables.

"Guy would say to his table, 'You see the difference between Albert and us? We play at Le Parc des Princes; Albert plays at stade Jean Bouin'.

"At the FFR, Albert was a diplomat, Guy was the enforcer. If they had to execute someone (metaphorically speaking, of course), Basquet did it.

"In 1991, their friendship of forty years ended. Ferrasse made friends with Fabre whereas Basquet had spent years fighting against that faction on behalf of Ferrasse! By supporting Fabre, Ferrasse effectively marginalised Basquet who wanted to remain in post and so joined forces with another Agen clubmate, Albert Moga, in seeking re-election. They failed, and a long friendship turned sour. By this stage, Ferrasse had already ostracised Fouroux. The politics were very complicated back then!"

I tried to locate Le Fair Play the next day, only to find that it has been replaced by a Cuban bar called Havana. I can't describe my disappointment. Cuba? What the f**k has Cuba got to do with Agen? Le Fair Play, a historic monument, has been expunged forever. It is another example of how globalisation has damaged French rugby's heritage. I'll just leave that out there for you to ponder and discuss among yourselves.

The bottom line is this: in this fruit garden of France, there wasn't a prune or a pack of cards in sight.

Le Hold-Up

One of the most infamous France v England games took place at the Parc des Princes during the Rugby World Cup in October 1991. Daniel described it from his point of view.

"That game in 1991 against England at the Parc des Princes in the RWC hurt so much. The ref let England get away with murder. There were so many flagrant referring errors. Serge got smashed, trampled on and abused.

"After the game, I grabbed the referee in the tunnel by the collar and shoved him against the wall and told him he was a c**t. He ran off fast but it was curtains for me as soon as the journos got hold of the story.

"Of course, you regret it afterwards, but it felt good at the time! After twenty-four hours or so, Ferrasse said to me: 'Right, you better resign because you have created a s**t storm with *les rosbifs*."

"The upside was that I could devote myself 100% to running my business!"

Ah, Bollocks

So, the Battle of Nantes in 1986... Who dunnit? Who done what, I hear you ask? I mean, who trampled on Buck Shelford's nuts and tore his scrotum open?

I'll let Buck set the scene.

"From the first ruck, I knew we were up against it. They were unrelenting. After twenty minutes, I got kicked in the face and lost three teeth. Then, just before half time, I was over the ball on our try line. I looked up and saw Garuet flying towards me. He was horizontal and flying at pace. He smashed me right in the forehead. He knocked me out cold and it took me about two minutes to come around. Jock Hobbs told me I couldn't go off because we had no one on the bench. In a third incident in the second half, I was kicked in the nuts in a ruck, which eventually forced me off the field. My scrotum had been split open and my testicle was hanging down. It was Daniel Dubroca'."

Now, who am I to question Buck's versions of events, but I struggle to believe this. Buck was already reeling from the first two incidents so perhaps he was hallucinating? Daniel is a gentleman farmer, erudite, clever and loyal. He wouldn't have done that, surely? Anyway, he denies it, along with everyone else in the French side.

Daniel Dubroca, 1st March 1986, Cardiff. Wales 15 v France 23.
Photo - Bob Thomas Sports Photography, Getty Images.

Extra-Time

It was getting late and we were in extra-time.
We finished off the meringue and pear dessert,
followed by coffee and truffles. The five of us had
enjoyed our Valentine's evening together. Our wives
hadn't, of course, because they were on their own.
On the other hand, perhaps they had? We drank the
remaining Trévallon 2004, a wine of spectacular
concentration with its balance of fruit, acidity and
fine tannins.

I'd had another wonderful evening of stories, laughter
and forceful opinions, not to mention the fabulous food
and wine. I was on a gastronomic and sporting tour
of a lifetime, as good as any Rugby World Cup.

Dominique Erbani

SOUTH WEST   "ROBERT PAPAREMBORDE SAID
TO ME: 'UNTIL YOU HAVE PLAYED
THE ALL BLACKS, YOU HAVEN'T
BEEN PROPERLY TESTED, YOU
DON'T KNOW WHAT RUGBY IS'.
I THOUGHT, HOLY SHIT."

BORN : 16TH AUGUST 1956

CLUBS : SPORTING UNION AGEN LOT-ET-GARONNE

INTERNATIONAL CAPS : 46

POSITION : BACK ROW

GRAND SLAMS : 1987

NICKNAME : THE MAN WITH THE THREE MOUSTACHES

NOM DE GUERRE : THE UNSUNG HERO

MY VISIT TO MEET HIM : WEDNESDAY 14TH FEBRUARY

I always thought of Dominique Erbani as the great bass player in that formidable French pack and XV. Berbizier may have been the *chef d'orchestre*, dictating the strategy and bringing the pack into play, with Rodriguez the lead singer and Champ on lead guitar, but it was Dominique who held it all together in the back row. He was so dependable, the ever-present bassist providing the rhythm, harmony and backbone to the side. You may not have noticed him much but, were he not there, it would have been immediately obvious.

It was Daniel Dubroca who suggested we dine *à L'Agenaise* along with Dominique and Philippe Sella at the fabulous Maison du Michel Dussau in Agen, where we would enjoy a wonderful evening of stories,nostalgia and strident opinions about the demise of the French national side.

Dominique was unmistakable on the pitch with his large frame, mop of curly black hair, bushy eyebrows and bristling moustache. Patrick Estève told me that Jacques Gratton, the former backrower for Agen and France, used to call him 'The Man With the Three Moustaches', such was the prominence of his facial hair.

He did so much hard and unseen work in the rucks and mauls, deploying all the dark arts of a clever flanker to free the ball up for his teammates to score. His mates would occasionally pull his leg that he would be selected when others were injured.

Daniel Dubroca told me,

" In 1986 before the Battle of Nantes, Alain Carminati turned up late to training and he didn't want to play openside. So, he was dropped and Dominique selected instead. Jacques could be brutal!"

If that were the case, he rode his luck, and his dependability and consistency meant that he won forty-six caps between 1981 and 1990. He was also twice winner of the Bouclier de Brennus.

Daniel Dubroca told me, *"He never had a bad game. He was always there when you needed him and he did so much hard work. He was like England's Richard Hill. He was our insurance policy."*

Finlay Calder also rated him very highly. *"He was always in the rucks and mauls, able to slow our ball down or win the ball for the French pack to unleash their backs. He was an underrated player."*

He wasn't all good-natured though, as John Hall told me: *"I can't remember much about the game against the French in 1985 because Erbani kicked me in the head and I had to go off!"*

How to Beat the All Blacks... Once
Dominique played against the All Blacks seven times and I asked him what he remembers.

"Before I played them, Robert Paparemborde said to me: 'Until you have played the All Blacks, you haven't been properly tested, you don't know what rugby is'. I thought, Holy shit. I have played the English, Welsh, Irish and Scots and it was f**king hard. Playing the All Blacks is going to be a nightmare! They were and still are a magical team.

"The only time I beat them was in Nantes in 1986 when we effectively beat them up, just like they would do to us!

"That week was when we saw Jacques at his best and worst. He could be lovely, kind and funny but also very

demanding and hard on players. He pushed the players right to their limits, physically and emotionally.

"In his lighter moments, Jacques had a party trick of stealing your watch while shaking your hand. He would come up to you later and ask you for the time. You'd panic, thinking you'd lost it, and then he'd give it back to you. He was like a magician! After the World Cup Final, Serge Kampf joined us for the banquet and Jacques pinched his watch, which he of course returned, but it gave Serge an idea. Upon returning to France, the whole squad was invited to a dinner in Agen where he gave us each a Philippe Patek watch. He was a very generous man and a wonderful supporter of French rugby.

"Nobody knew Serge back then but Yves Noué, the team manager, was delighted he joined us at the banquet because he paid for the drinks. On tours, the FFR would give money to the team manager to pay for things and if he didn't blow it all on booze, fags and partying then he had a good chance of being team manager next time! Noué wasn't dumb so of course he took up Serge's offer!"

On Tour With Les Breeteesh and Ireesh
One tour I wanted to hear about was the tour to South Africa in 1982 to celebrate the inauguration of Ellis Park. Rives was injured so Dominique went in his place. John O'Driscoll told me that Dominique was very young on that tour so Willie Duggan took him under his wing.

"Willie's preparation for a game was a pint and a fag. I don't think Dominique had met anyone like Willie before."

The touring team was called the Overseas Invitation Team.

Dominique elaborated:

" I loved that tour because we had a brilliant time both on and off the pitch."

"Serge are I were the only two players from France, touring alongside players such as Fergus Slattery, Phil Orr, John O'Driscoll, Willie Duggan, Terry Holmes, Clive Woodward, Les Cusworth and Jim Renwick. The Irish took over a bedroom in the hotel and created a bar for the players. We went out every evening, and the Irish, Welsh, Scots and English impressed us with their ability to party late, drink copious amounts and still get up and play well the next day!"

Irish Craic

Talking of the Irish, I spent three hours with Ollie and Phil in Dublin, and the anecdotes and jokes started immediately. The purpose of my trip was to hear their stories about playing the French and you can see these peppered throughout the book. However, they also recounted tale after tale about the great and late Willie Duggan and Moss Keane. Here are a few of them.

Read or sub-vocalise these in a southern Irish accent.

Ollie: *"Moss told me he went skinny-dipping. I said, 'I thought you couldn't swim Moss?' He replied, 'No I can't, so I only went in up to my knees'."*

Ollie: *"Willie Duggan had a fag at half time and was stubbing it out under his boot. Slatts said, 'What are you doing Willie?' He replied, 'That snail's been following me around the whole first half'."*

Phil: *"Willie Duggan was late for everything, even his own funeral, and he never liked training. He told me it took the edge off his game."*

Ollie: *"Ireland went to Twickenham in 1980 and was greeted by Bill Beaumont who said, 'Welcome to Twickenham, Moss. May the best team win'. Moss replied, 'I sincerely hope not, Billy'."*

Hugo MacNeill told me about a game at the Parc des Princes. Someone from the crowd shouted to Moss Finn, the great Irish winger, *'Vous êtes fini'*. Moss responded, *'Oui, je suis Moss Finny'*.

The Battle of Strasbourg

Dominique also played in the infamous tests against the Australians in 1983 when the French targeted McBain as revenge for breaking Cremeschi's jaw on the tour to Australia in 1981, a tour which Dominique was also on.

"The whole French team was pumped up for the two tests. We drew the first but won the second, and there were some big fights."

Jean-Pierre Garuet talked to me about his memories of the game, which I describe in his article.

I also spoke to Bob Dwyer about what he remembers from the 1983 tour.

"At the line out, it was like a dock yard brawl. I remember a 'warm-up' game in Strasbourg because someone belted Steve Tunyman in the first line out. Those 'warm-up' teams were called 'The Combined Presidents' Team' but there was nothing presidential about them. They always picked a team of thugs to try to soften us up before the test matches.

"Before the match, I warned the players that if there were a fight, we couldn't back away because we'd give them space to kick and punch us. We had to push them back."

" A punch-up started inside our 22m and ended up in their 22m! The French wrote it up as the 'Battle of Strasbourg'."

'Things to Do Before I Go Senile'

I knew Dominique would enjoy the evening in Agen because he works in wines such as Buzet, Lanson Champagne, Bollinger and Gérard Bertrand.

Pierre Carton, my remarkable photographer, and I sat at the table listening to Dominique, Daniel and Philippe reminisce about the times of their lives, all over a beautifully-orchestrated, gastronomic extravaganza of exquisite food and wine. I had to pinch myself. It was another life goal to cross off my list of 'Things to Do Before I Go Senile'. However, I still had plenty left on that list such as a night out with Estève, Lafond, Pardo and Charvet in somewhere like San Sebastian, Las Vegas or Ibiza... I'm not fussy.

We had been at the table for about four hours, consumed several thousand calories and spoken a million words. Dominique is just how I expected him to be – modest, loyal and discreet, notwithstanding his height. I can see why Fouroux selected him so many times for his side. I'm not sure I'll ever have the opportunity to relive that evening, but I'll try to prove myself wrong.

I had a big week ahead, travelling to Toulouse to meet Érik Bonneval , Montauban for Jean-Baptiste Fouroux, Foix for Patrick Estève, Perpignan for Jeff Imbernon and Collioure for Marc Cécillon. I was lost in a world of rugby *rêverie*.

Jean-Patrick Lescarboura

SOUTH WEST "I HAD NEVER SEEN SUCH
AN INTENSE WARM-UP
AS NANTES IN 1986. SERGE
HAD INVITED HIS MATE,
JOSÉ TOURÉ, WHO PLAYED
FOR NANTES AND FRANCE,
INTO THE CHANGING ROOM
TO SEE HOW WE PREPARED.
BON DIEU."

BORN : 19TH JANUARY 1961

CLUBS : UNION SPORTIVE DACQUOISE

INTERNATIONAL CAPS : 28

POSITION : FLY-HALF

NICKNAME : JEANNO, 'LA BOMBARDE'

NOM DE GUERRE : DEBONAIR DAQUOIS

MY VISIT TO MEET HIM : WEDNESDAY 7TH MARCH 2018

I remember Jean-Patrick vividly as a teenager. He was tall, handsome and elegant, and blessed with a massive kick, able to fire those light, rotund French Adidas balls like Howitzers into the distance. Raphaël Ibañez told me how the spectators used to whistle when he kicked it, like it was a bomb falling from the sky, before he and his mates would go and fetch the ball somewhere outside the stade Maurice-Boyau. I tracked Jeanno down via Pascal Ondarts and we met in a bar in Capbreton on a very wet day in March 2018.

I used to love those Adidas balls because they were light and bulbous. On a dry day, you could ping out 'miss' passes some 20m for your full-back to run onto. On the hard, arid pitches around Avignon, much drier than the pitches of the South West with their exposure to the Atlantic, you could chip and chase, and the ball could bounce serendipitously up into your hands to score. I could place-kick them much further than the Mitre balls, especially with the Mistral wind behind me - conversions only of course, because we would always run it. Those balls were perfect for *rugby de champagne*.

I'd left Bayonne in a thunder storm and it was still pouring when I arrived in Capbreton. I knocked back an insipid coffee using a croissant to give it some body. I sat in a sad-looking café thinking wistfully not just about France's glory days as a revered rugby nation, but also about their coffee. What has happened to those rich, viscous, handmade shots that we used to enjoy in any café and restaurant across France? They have been replaced by a machine-made, emaciated concoction of mud-flavoured warm water. There is no body, no froth, and no caffeine punch - even if I drank a dozen of them.

Capbreton is just up the road from the thermal town of Dax, the home club of Jean-Patrick and an array of French rugby stars such as Magne, Pelous, Bastia, Sallefranque, Raphaël Ibañez, Claude and Richard Dourthe, Jean-Pierre Lux and Lolo Rodriguez, among others. The US Dax's stade Maurice-Boyau is very near the centre of town and next to the Les Arènes, which you can't miss because of the large life-size bull outside. The day before I met Jean-Patrick, I sat in a café in the beautifully-appellated square, Place de la Fontaine Chaude, with Raphaël Ibañez while he told me about the players I was writing about. He was articulate, funny, outward-looking, international and hugely impressive. The French team needs Raphaël to help resurrect its success.

French Flair... But Not Always

I explained my book to Jeanno and how, as Chairman of selectors, I had selected him in my squad of Fantasy French Rugby.

Grinning broadly, he said,

" David, many thanks for my twenty-ninth cap."

I wanted to know what rugby was like at US Dax back then.

"I was eighteen when I started and I played there for ten years. Back then, we had a good running rugby culture. Like Stade Montois, we tried to use the backs and score great tries. It didn't always happen, but we had a go!

"The 1980s suffered less from violence on the pitch compared to the 1970s, but it could still be rough. In 1991, we played RCF in Biarritz in the quarter-final of the Championship. I kicked off and put a high one up, and it was quickly followed by a 'bagarre générale'. Normally, it would quickly pass. The forwards would try to intimidate their opposite number, get rid of their adrenaline and then calm down. But this didn't stop the whole game. Franck Mesnel came up to me and said, 'This needs to stop'. They had some really hard men like Tadjean, Serrière and Blond who loved fighting. Two players were sent off.

"US Dax played with the elite for fifty years, but we haven't done that for ten years now. We still have a club culture but small towns can't succeed in the modern rugby world. Just look at towns like Tarbes, Lourdes, Bagnères, Auch, Mont-de-Marsan and Dax."

Stand-Out Players

Who were the stand-out players whom he played with and against?

"I used to love playing with Lolo Rodriguez. Believe me, it was far better he was on your side rather than the opposition's. He was a stand-out player back then because he had so much natural strength. However, he had this habit of squeezing your hand very hard when he shook it. You would have to get down on your knees to beg him to stop! After a while, I just used to kiss him on the cheek instead!

"When we went on tour, we would go to the embassies for various dinners. He had this game of trying to make the ambassador's hand crack when he shook it."

"He hated doing weights so just didn't bother. Anyway, he didn't need to.

"In my position, Christian 'Coco' Delage of Agen was an exceptional player who had an instinctive feel for the game. He saw where the space was and exploited it with his speed, skill and great hands. He would often leave me trailing in his wake. He always impressed me.

"Rives was another who was brilliant. I played with him on my first cap in Cardiff in 1982. He didn't need to speak much because you just followed him. He would put his head where we would put our feet, and he was typically first to every ruck, even if he'd been the last to get up in the previous one. He was so brave and modest, a truly inspirational leader."

Fabulous Mentor

Jean-Patrick had a good run in the French side between 1983-86 but he was blighted by injuries in 1983 and 1987 when he fractured his tibia.

"Just before the Rugby World Cup, I was dropped by Jacques after the game in Toulouse in 1986 against the All Blacks. He told me I was rubbish so he picked Franck to play in the second test in the 'Battle of Nantes!'

"I have never seen such an intense warm-up. Serge had invited his mate, José Touré who played for Nantes and France, into the changing room to see how we prepared. 'Bon dieu'. He is of mixed race but he was as white as a ghost when he saw the warm-up. It was very intense in

there. Our front rowers were head-butting each other! We didn't need to warm-up on the pitch.

"Jacques was very demanding, especially with the forwards. We backs normally preferred to stay calm so we could think straight!"

Franck Mesnel told me how Jeanno had been a fabulous mentor to him when he won his first cap, offering him support and advice. He realised that I wasn't the normal fly-half shape, weighing in at 95kgs.

What about the most memorable matches?

"Scotland in 1984. I will never forget the referee, Winston Jones. We didn't speak good English and you had the impression that they won all the 50/50 decisions. We were penalised constantly and robbed of another Grand Slam. Then of course, there was Jean-Pierre Rives' speech. It wasn't properly translated at the time but it went like this:

'There are three useless things in the world: a priest's balls, a nun's tits and a bad referee!'

"I also remember the first test against the All Blacks in 1984 in Christchurch that we should have won. I put three drop goals wide. I've never forgiven myself for that. It was actually a superb tour. We played Wellington who

had half the All Black backs, and we put thirty points on them. We lost both test matches but we won five of the six provincial matches."

Ironically, the aforementioned Winston Jones refereed this match too.

Jean-Patrick managed his life after rugby well, building a successful business career as a sales director for a business called Menguys, which sells products like peanuts, olives and anything else that accompanies one's aperitif. He also part-owns a restaurant called El Mason in Dax.

He is a charming man, remembering very fondly his great days as the French Number 10, but he is ever the competitor, still remembering those games that hurt him. It is clear that they still gnaw away at his pride. For me, he played in that great romantic époque of French rugby, and for a club that was its heart and soul.

I had been on the road for a few days by now, meeting André Boniface, Raphaël and Jeanno before heading back to the Basque Country where I was seeing Serge, Laurent Pardo in Hendaye, and visiting Gernika and Saint Sebastian.

Jean-Luc Joinel

SOUTH WEST "JEAN-LUC BROUGHT THE FORWARDS TOGETHER AND PROCEEDED TO HUMILIATE US ONE BY ONE. HE SAID TO ME: 'FITZ, YOU THINK YOU'RE SO GOOD BUT YOU SPEND ALL YOUR TIME TALKING TO JOURNALISTS'. IT WAS DEVASTATING AND HE EMBARRASSED US ALL, BUT IT WAS ALSO A BRILLIANT, MOTIVATIONAL SPEECH. AS A RESULT, WE WENT OUT AND SMASHED TOULON 4-3."

BORN : 21ST SEPTEMBER 1973

CLUBS : CLUB ATHLÉTIQUE BRIVE CORRÈZE LIMOUSIN

INTERNATIONAL CAPS : 51

POSITION : BACK ROW

GRAND SLAMS : 1981

NOM DE GUERRE : BRIVE'S BRAVEHEART

MY VISIT TO MEET HIM : TUESDAY 13TH FEBRUARY 2018

J ean-Luc Joinel's elegant-sounding name rolls off the tongue beautifully. It is the quadrisyllabic cluster of soft, alliterative consonants that provides such vocal equilibrium. I tracked him down via Laurent Parquet, a good friend of mine, who was born and bred in Brive-la-Gaillarde and whom I met in Paris in 1990.

Growing up in Bath in the 1970s and 80s, I remember Jean-Luc so well thanks to his euphonic name, athleticism and ability. He was a fabulous player – big, strong, fast and skilful. Capped in 1977, he was ever-present in the side between 1979 and 1986. Laurent told me he was also *un brave mec* so I knew that travelling all the way to Brive-la-Gaillarde would be worth it.

I had visited Alain Lorieux the day before, who had treated me to a wonderful day of hospitality, food and wine, so I had a late and slow morning the next day to rehydrate and recover. When I left Belley and drove east towards the Massif Central, the skies were cloudless and the air bone-dry and freezing, but as I crossed Auvergne into the Corrèze towards Tulle, it started to dump snow. After much slipping and sliding at 20mph along the A20, I arrived in Brive, a small, chic town just west of the Dordogne and the gateway into this rugby-loving south west corner of France. I found my way to the Le Grand Hôtel for a brief power nap before meeting Jean-Luc for another evening of culinary hedonism.

I walked into the bar and he greeted me warmly, his big paws shaking my hand as though he hadn't seen an Englishmen in years, at least not one who is so amorous of France and its rugby.

"David, I love your book. What's not to like? We former players get to sit down, eat, drink and chat to you about how good we were thirty years ago and how we used to beat *les Breeteesh*! I love that!"

Like every good deal, there is something in it for both sides and I too was indulging myself. After all, if you hadn't guessed it already, this whole journey, involving the criss-crossing of France to meet all my childhood heroes, had at its very core my own self-indulgence.

When I first explained my 'project' to my wife, and how it was driven by selfless motives to raise money for charity, she asked me the bleeding obvious question:

Jo: *"What happens if your book is crap, no one buys it and you make no money for charity?"*

Me: *"Ah well, I'll just have to console myself with the fact that I would have had a great time doing it."*

Of course, she knew that all along that my altruistic motives were window-dressing to justify travelling to France twenty odd times in eighteen months.

Bastille Day
I wanted to know all about Jean-Luc's journey to the top.

"I was a student in Bordeaux and played for Sarlat before moving to Brive in 1973. Moving between clubs was very difficult back then because you had to get permission from the club you were leaving, and they weren't typically minded to help you. Therefore, I couldn't play for Brive straight away so played for my university and France juniors. I wasn't able to play for Brive until 1974. That year we reached the final of the French championship losing to Béziers 12-13.

"However, I was picked in the French squad and toured South Africa in 1975. While there, the core of the 1977 Grand Slam team was built. I could see the friendships, solidarity and 'esprit de corps' being formed. I won my first cap in 1977 against the All Blacks in Toulouse, which we won. I played them seven times and beat them twice, the second time on 14th July 1979."

I describe the game on Bastille Day 1979 elsewhere in the book but let me pick out two important, off-the-field facts, which Jean-Luc described to me from that trip.

Firstly, Guy Colomine, the Narbonne prop forward, would eat two chickens a day. I only tell you this because it has made me think about what the modern, professional prop eats. Four, six, eight chickens?

Secondly, the coaching pair of Desclaux and Piquet didn't speak to or pick Jérôme Gallion, a dentist by profession, much on that tour. Jérôme told Jean-Luc, *"Piquet only speaks to me when he has toothache."* Funnily enough, Piquet had terrible toothache on that tour and Jérôme was selected for the second test!

Jean-Luc set up one of the tries in that match. He burst through the middle inside his own halfway, beating four players, and fed Codorniou whose running line, pace and pass were typically sumptuous. Caussade, from Lourdes, took the ball at pace and weaved right then left before passing inside to Averous who caught the ball at the third attempt before scoring. It was another moment of French flair, executed off-the-cuff. All the players were brilliant that day, but Caussade's performance really stood out.

Jean-Luc Joinel leaps above Peter Winterbottom.
3rd March 1984, Rugby Union International, Parc Des Princes,
Paris. France 32 v England 18. *Photo - Bob Thomas Sports
Photography, Getty Images.*

Le Jeu Dur

Jean-Luc's career started in the 1970s so I wanted to
know all about *le jeu dur* back then and whether the
practice supports the myth.

*"Every team had an enforcer back in the 1970s. When you
played Béziers, it was Senal. He was a funny bloke who used
to carry out all the 'obscure duties'.*

"There were no replacements back then so players would be targeted. If you lost a player, it was just tough. People would be kicked in the head."

*"Brive had its fair share of tough guys too, such as Roger
Fite and the late Jean-Claude Rossignol. I remember one
game against Narbonne in 1975 when we beat them
in a semi-final at Toulouse. Jean-Claude kept smacking
Raymond Canaguier in the scrums. He was black, blue
and bloodied at the end.*

*"Jean-Claude could also be very funny. In a game against
Tarbes, their tight-head wouldn't scrummage straight.
Jean-Claude said to him very politely, 'You need to stop
doing that'. Their tight head kept re-offending so he warned
him again, 'Listen, if you keep doing that, I'll stop you and*

then you won't feel anything'. The prop did it once more before he was carried off the pitch unconscious.

"Back in those days, the official guests would sit in the stands, pissed after a long lunch, and Jean-Claude would take advantage of their 'sommeil'. After a player shouted 'out' or 'lost' following a scrum or ruck, you would hear a fist-on-face smack as he anaesthetised one of the opposition.

"His other tactic was to take a player out as he was running to a line out and the ref wasn't looking. You would hear Jean-Claude's whistle followed by a smack a second or two later. He was our enforcer and a very effective one too!

"We had other big fights against Narbonne. Pierre Salettes, their hooker, wanted to take out our Australian second row, Peter FitzSimons. In the end, we just put the ball down and all fought on the athletics track!"

An Outsider's Perspective

Peter FitzSimons played for four years at Brive and I went to visit him in Sydney to find out more about Jean-Luc:

"I loved my time there."

"In 1987/8, we played Toulon away in an evening game. They were fantastic and belted us 63-0. For the return leg about three months later, we all went to a château for some team preparation. Jean-Luc brought the forwards together and proceeded to humiliate us one by one. He said to me, 'Fitz, you think you're so good but you spend all your time talking to journalists. I don't really know how good you are,

etc etc...' It was devastating and he embarrassed us all, but it was also a brilliant motivational speech. We went out and smashed Toulon 4-3.

"After any away game, we would get on the coach and after an hour or so, someone would put the porn on. One evening, the video stopped working in the coach and a black cloud of gloom quickly descended. However, luck was on our side when we stopped at a service station and met the players from Tulle. Back on the road, we drove up close to their coach and watched their porn through the windows. The French didn't blink. That would never happen in the Anglo-Saxon culture!"

Aftershave or Champagne, Monsieur?

Jean-Luc played in the match against England in Paris in 1982, a *3ème mi-temps* that became notorious.

Clive Woodward, who played in that game, told me the story first hand:

"We headed to the after-match banquet at the beautiful Palace of Versailles for a black-tie do, and all the French players were looking dapper and wearing white scarves. There was a box of goodies on the table consisting of a tie, lighter, a record and some aftershave from the French sponsors. Maurice Colclough, who played in France, was aware of French hospitality and he had gone in early, emptied his aftershave bottle and filled it with wine. At the dinner, Maurice stood up and necked the contents of his bottle, and then challenged Smarty (Colin Smart, England's prop) to do the same. Smarty stood up, drank it

but he, obviously, didn't cope with it well. After turning the table over, he fell unconscious and the medics were called. The English medics accompanied him in the ambulance and had to explain to the French medics what he had drunk... he was in hospital for a week! The rest of us forgot about Smarty and ended up at a can-can show with the French players. Fran Cotton went on stage, kicking his legs up and singing. The whole evening was mad!

"In the days of zero social media, it was only when I returned back to Leicester the following day that I heard all the details on the radio. And to cap it all off, the only member of our squad to get dropped for the next game was Marcus Rose, and he didn't even drink!"

Life After Rugby

Jean-Luc has been retired for three years or so, enjoying golf, cycling and reading. His wife manages the Eden Park shop in Brive giving him good reason to head back to Paris, just like he used to back in the glory days of his rugby career.

I had enjoyed a wonderful dinner listening to him reminisce and impersonate various former teammates such as Patrick Estève and Yves Noué. He is a funny, engaging and intelligent man who excelled for France and left an indelible impression on many a rugby fanatic.

Philippe Sella

SOUTH WEST

"MY COACH AT CLAIRAC WANTED ME TO PLAY FLY-HALF BUT I NEVER WANTED TO KICK. WHEN I PLAYED FULLBACK, I WANTED TO RUN EVERYTHING BUT DIDN'T KICK WELL ENOUGH. THEN THEY MOVED ME INTO THE CENTRE ALTHOUGH I WOULD HAVE HAPPILY PLAYED FLANKER. RIVES WAS MY IDOL AND I USED TO TRY TO PLAY LIKE HIM."

BORN : 14TH FEBRUARY 1962

CLUBS : SPORTING UNION AGEN LOT-ET-GARONNE

INTERNATIONAL CAPS : 111

POSITION : WING, CENTRE

GRAND SLAMS : 1987

NICKNAME : SELLOCHE

NOM DE GUERRE : RUGBY ROYALTY

MY VISIT TO MEET HIM : WEDNESDAY 14TH FEBRUARY
AND TUESDAY 3RD APRIL

L ooking through my steamed-up and Gallic-tinted spectacles, my top ten centres of all time are: Brian O'Driscoll, Daniel Gerber, Mike Gibson, Tim Horan, Jerry Guscott, Didier Codorniou, Philippe Sella, André Boniface, Jo Maso and Jean Dauger. And where there is André, there is Guy, so let's make it eleven. That equates to two Irishmen, one Saffer, one Aussie, one Englishman, six Frenchman and NO All Black... Controversial, I know, but it's my ball and my team. As Chairman of Selectors, I can select with freedom, impunity and total authority. I feel like a modern-day Albert Ferrasse.

Sella had everything – pace, power, sidestep, balance and vision. He had this cruising belligerence that could destroy his opponents' defences. I was so excited to meet him, especially alongside the great Daniel Dubroca and faithful Dominique Erbani.

I chatted to Michael Lynagh about Philippe and this is what he told me:

"When came to Saracens, he wasn't used to playing such a structured game. We used to have a move that was simply called 'give it to Philippe' and we just let him find space and run. He was so strong with a low centre of gravity, which meant he could change direction without slowing down. He wasn't really a stepper like Codor or Timmy Horan. Philippe was more like Jason Little."

Jacques Fouroux would say of Philippe, *"Il a la force d'un buffle et le toucher d'un pianist."*

I am sure you can work out the French translation but in case you can't: *"He had the strength of a buffalo and the touch of a pianist."*

Philippe had an astonishing career but against England, it was a career of two halves:

"I beat England in 1983, 84, 86, 87 and 88, drew one in 1985 and then we lost between 1989 to 1995."

Jacques Fouroux would say of Philippe, *"Il a la force d'un buffle et le toucher d'un pianist."*

I Just Called to Say I Love You

Like some other players, Serge Blanco had facilitated the introduction to Philippe over lunch. This is the message, which Serge left him:

"Shit Fifi, it sounds like you are in England... what the hell? I am having lunch with an Englishman who is a top bloke. I know that sounds strange... It isn't usual for an Englishman to be interested in French rugby but this guy really is. He is passionate about it and our era. He is seeing everyone so you must see him too... You will enjoy it... Lots of love."

Daniel Dubroca helped organise our team dinner in Agen at La Maison de Michel Dussau. Philippe turned up looking a little distracted but he was smiling.

"Daniel has just written an article about Agen needing to grow hormones to avoid relegation. That has increased the pressure a little more! Merci Daniel!"

Philippe is the Director of Rugby at Agen and is always keen to hear the advice from his friend and former teammate and captain.

Sella's commitment always impressed me on the pitch and this clearly extended to fine dinners too. Not only had he been at the 'office' all day, but it was his birthday and St Valentines' Day. However, he had chosen to spend it with his former rugby mates and an unknown bloke from England who loves food and wine, speaks a bit of the lingo and is enamoured with all things French.

The upside of having dinner with me was that I had organised a comprehensive display of France in all its gastronomic glory. First, they served us *foie gras* confit, which was rich, decadent and simply melted in your mouth. The figs gave it some acidity and sweetness, and were the perfect complements. This was followed by *Coeur d'entrecôte de boeuf rassis, grillé au feu de*

Philippe Sella opposed by Scott Hastings, Derek White and Peter Dods. 18th March 1989, Five Nations Championship, Paris. France 19 v Scotland 3. *Photo - Bob Thomas Sports Photography, Getty Images.*

bois, chanterelles fraiches, pomme de terre farcies, sauce périgourdinne. I am not going to translate it because I wouldn't do it justice. It was succulent and juicy, and the *chanterelles* gave it earthiness and even more flavour. For a few seconds, I was overwhelmed by the gustatory stimulation. It was like an oral orgasm.

Anyway, where was I? Ah yes, Philippe, one of my top ten centres ever.

Rives Gauche, Rives Droite

His rise through the ranks of French rugby started in Clairac when he started playing rugby league. He first played for Agen when he was eighteen and for France when he was twenty. He had natural strength and was mature ahead of his years.

" **My strength must have come from playing on the farm and eating healthy farm food!**"

Such was his versatility and all-round skills, he could have played full-back, wing or centre.

"My coach at Clairac wanted me to play fly-half but I never wanted to kick, and when I played full-back, I wanted to run everything but didn't kick well enough. They moved me into the centre although I would have happily played

flanker. Rives was my idol and I used to try to play like him.

"When I played with him, we would bump into each other on the pitch. Maybe I just followed him around! He must have thought I was mad. I remember I lent him my tracksuit once because he has given his away but I never got it back. He probably gave it away to a supporter. That's Jean-Pierre, he's a very generous man!

"He could run and run, non-stop. He may not have been the most technical but he was everywhere, left, right, in the middle, at the bottom of a ruck, first to the ruck, first man in support. He didn't have to say much but you understood him. His presence was huge and his speeches were always simple."

Blanco, Blanco

Towards the end of Jacques Fouroux reign as French coach, things were getting political. Jacques was looking to replace Fouroux as President of the FFR, he was making changes to the French side and there were tensions between Dubroca and Berbizier, which had started in 1989.

Philippe seemed capable of rising about all the politics and remaining focused on the sport.

"As a player, I was always 100% 'dans le sportif'. Anything around me that was a problem didn't interest me. On the pitch, it could have an effect though. In 1989, we played Australia in the first test and they beat us 32-15.

"In the second test, Jacques dropped Serge, Lolo and Berbiz, and played me at full-back. He'd seen me play there occasionally for Agen. I ran everything, kicked the ball directly into touch and missed high balls. I missed the first one by a good metre and they scored. Behind the posts, I could hear the crown shouting 'Blanco, Blanco...'

"I was trying to focus on the game but every time I ran the ball, I was thinking about Serge. We were both very professional but we are also great friends. It played with my head the whole match. Ten minutes from the end, I was defending the blind-side and collided with Alain Carminati so I didn't even finish the match!

"Serge was a genius. He didn't need to train much and he liked smoking! I remember playing in a summer tournament called the Mediterranean games in around 1983. It was very hot and none of us was in top shape. At a training session, Jean-Pierre took the forwards off for a long hard run. They all came back sweating profusely. Serge, on the other hand, took us for a gentle stroll where we told jokes and messed around. We found a hose pipe and poured water on ourselves to give the impression we had been training hard! That was Serge for you, the game was easy for him."

I wanted to know about his other teammates too.

Berbiz le Stratège,

"Berbiz was a strategist. He could analyse teams and work out how to win. He's quite a reserved man so many people don't know him that well. He was an excellent

and professional player.

"I am big friends with Patrice, Denis, Érik Bonneval and Thierry (Lacroix). Denis was fast and skilful on the pitch and great fun off it!

"I used to love the front row like Garuche, Pascal le Sanglier, Le Toy (Armary), Califano. Before the match, I liked warming up with them. They were physical and had a great spirit. I loved the knocks and punches and hits, although I had to stay lucid too."

K.O.
Philippe's physicality would occasionally express itself illegally on the pitch. Most of the time he was calm but sometimes the Latin red mist would descend.

"I used to hate my shirt getting pulled. Rob Andrew did it once and I smacked him in the face. Andrew Slack had the same treatment in a different game. And in 1990 against Australia, I punched Peter FitzSimons from behind and it sent him to the floor. I looked up on the screen watched with horror the images of me punching him. I was so embarrassed."

In the Five Nations match in 1992 against England, Philippe had to leave the pitch having taken a ball in his face from a Rob Andrew kick. He was clearly concussed:

"I was totally confused by all the players coming off the pitch – Lascubé, Moscato, Roumat, Sadourney. I kept asking questions: Who has come off? Who was sent off? Who is injured? What, another one?"

In the week before the match, Brian Moore had been winding the French up, telling the media it would be 'a boxing match'. As a source of motivation, Philippe pinned his comments up on the dressing room wall in the France training camp.

Albert et Guy
I wanted to know more about Ferrasse and Basquet, who were both dominant figures at Agen and throughout French rugby.

"Guy Basquet was the President at Agen while Albert Ferrasse was the President at the FFR. I would only see Albert at international matches when I would go and ask him for a cigar. I had the balls to do it! Albert was very hard but he was also very generous, like a father figure to the players.

"Guy was similar but he was much harder. You had to be serious, loyal and well-behaved. If you were lazy but a good player, he would put you in your place but tolerate you. It you were an idiot, he would give you a good kick up the backside. He was close to the players but he could really hand out bollockings when he wanted to.

"You could always ask Albert for advice, especially business. The same was true of Walter Spanghero and Christian Carrère when I set up my sporting association. They are so welcoming and always have time for their friends.

"Albert and Guy were both characters but they were also very effective. They built relationships across the rugby world with people like Danny Craven. Albert's mate, Marcel Martin, would translate for him. He was very smart and would translate selectively and it worked."

Life After Rugby
Philippe set up a sporting association some sixteen years ago, which helps underprivileged kids called 'Les Enfants de l'Ovale'. Over 7,000 children have benefited from it, 40% of whom are girls. The association creates and leads sports and educational projects by leveraging the skills and discipline of rugby. The projects allow each young person to gain confidence in him or herself, to better understand his environment and to believe in their potential.

Based in Paris, it runs activities in Morocco, Mali, Senegal, Madagascar, Niger and the Ivory Coast.

In addition to his role as Director of Rugby at Agen and President of Les Enfants de l'Ovale, he is also a pundit on Canal Plus and Co-Director of Sella Communications, a business he sold to Infront Sports and Media, the global marketing agency. He is as busy and successful off the pitch as he was on it.

He is also a dad to two children who are now both grown up. Geoffrey currently plays rugby for Massy in the ProD2, and Philippine, his daughter, created a rugby team at her business school. Those rugby genes go deep.

The Final Whistle

We had been at the dinner table for several hours,
and Philippe, Dominique and Daniel had enjoyed the
food, wine and lively discussion. Philippe was sparky
and talkative, a natural leader, which made me wonder
why he didn't captain France more.

The Trévallon 2004 was delicious. We'd consumed
the restaurant's remaining four bottles, which had
complemented the food beautifully. I knew Eloi and
Ostiane would beam with pride knowing that some
of France's greatest rugby players had enjoyed it.

*"In the 1984 game against England, Carleton did
a scissors with their centre and he came down
Sella's channel. He just smashed him. I stood there
and watched in awe at his timing, technique and power."*
Patrick Estève

*"Sella was a modern-day player - fast, strong, courageous,
robust, kind, hard, explosive... He had everything."*
Pierre Berbizier

*"Philippe was very focused before matches.
I remember being in the lobby of a hotel in Dublin,
and Lafond and others were joking around.
But Sella was relentlessly focused."*
Hugo MacNeill

*"I always loved the 3ème mi-temps. I remember a party
in 1990 when Philippe and I exchanged jackets. He gave
me his beautiful, stylish Christian Dior blazer, and in
return I gave him my beer-stained wallaby green one.
I think I got the better deal!"*
Nick Farr-Jones

*"Philippe was one of the greatest players of all time.
He was so consistent and strong with lovely balance."*
Gavin Hastings

*"Philippe was one of the finest players I ever played
against. The back line in 1987 was fabulous. Charvet
would ghost around while Sella could do anything."*
Ieuan Evans

La Féria de Nîmes

My friend, Laurent Parquet, loves the finer things in life. Born and bred in Brive-la-Gaillarde in the Corrèze, a remote and relatively unpopulated *départment* deep in the South of France, he moved to Paris after school, attended the prestigious *grande école* called ESSEC, and quickly became the quintessential Parisian Frenchman - erudite, urbane, charming and well-dressed. But he has never lost his love of *les provinces* and all their customs, pastimes and sports, such as hunting, shooting, fishing, rugby, fine food and wine, whisky, cigars and bullfighting.

We met back in 1991 at Andersen Consulting and immediately hit it off. In the May of the same year, he took me on a voyage of discovery to La Féria de Nîmes to see the bullfighting or *la tauromachie* as the locals call it. I wanted to know all about this gladiatorial 'sport' and its origins. We caught the TGV from Paris to Avignon and spent the journey in the bar drinking beer and whisky, and smoking cigars, while he talked me through the key participants and the 'rules of engagement', man against beast. More of that later.

The event still takes place today in the Roman amphitheatre, built in the first century and one of the best-preserved arenas in the world. On the day I was there, Nîmes was buzzing in the late spring sunshine, and the roads around the arena on the Boulevard Victor Hugo were swarming with fans. However, it wasn't boisterous or intimidating like a football crowd. Instead, there was a carnival atmosphere with wine, music, dancing and barbecues, and groups of people were locked in serious debate about the event, its participants and the likely winners and losers, although I remember thinking that the bulls were unlikely to be leaving as winners.

The Spanish influence was everywhere – the bullfighting itself of course, but also the music, clothing and bronzed skin. This part of France received some 500,000 refugees during Franco's reign in the period 1936-39, and it is estimated that about half stayed in France after the war, and that imprint is still very visible today. Nîmes is also near the home of the Gypsy Kings (born and brought up in Montpellier and Arles) and their music

style was being impersonated by every band that day. That Latin sartorial elegance was on show with most people dressed in crisp denim, invariably sporting some type of fancy embroidery. Laurent pointed out that the cloth used to make jeans was, in fact, invented in Nîmes (the term 'denim' is a derivative of *serge de Nîmes*), a piece of trivia that I have used ever since when I want to be a smart-arse.

La Tauromachie

Bulls have been worshipped in the Mediterranean region since Roman times, when they were used in gladiatorial combat and sacrifices to the Gods. Today, the local people see bullfighting as a custom that connects them to the bulls and nature. However, the *féria* or *corrida*, as is it called, is banned across most of France on the grounds of animal cruelty, except where towns can demonstrate a bullfighting tradition. Enthusiasm for *la tauromachie*, like rugby, is well entrenched in large parts of the deep south, and bullfighting is still considered a prestigious occupation.

The day I went, it wasn't all men competing or watching. This sport transcends sex, age, social strata, religion, country, politics and rugby club. It unifies and anchors the people in this Spanish and Roman-influenced culture, not just in Nîmes but also in towns like Arles, Mont-de-Marsan, Dax, Palavas and Béziers. The competitors were clearly all sewn from high-grade genetic material, looking fit, healthy, wealthy and well-dressed. One lady in particular caught my eye. She was (and still is) called Maria Sara and she was the female star of the town.

Known as a *rejoneadora*, a horse rider who fights the bull with a *'rejón'*, a type of spear, she was blond and an extravagantly dressed and beautiful bullfighter with chiselled features. She was about twenty-eight at the time, on horseback and evincing a self-confidence that was intimidating - professionally, sartorially and sexually. I was transfixed but she was too encircled for me to meet her. Damn it.

In the beautifully preserved arena, we settled onto our seats of stone and sat under the dazzling sun, wearing sombreros and smoking Coronas like a couple of Mexican Cubans. Or perhaps Cuban Mexicans. I remember thinking how different life was down here compared to my upbringing in Bath. Both are Roman cities, one with a Roman amphitheatre staging bullfights, the other with Roman Baths staging Morris Dancing, an old English folk dance. Only a 1,000km between them, but culturally light years apart.

Bullfighting isn't a simple killing spectacle though. The Spanish wanted to dramatise it and so created a tragedy in three acts (although it is really six: the opening cape work, the lancing of the *pica* (lance) by the *picadors*, the graceful passes with the large cape, the planting of the *banderillas* (barbed darts) by the *banderilleros*, the dangerous passes with the *muleta* or red cape, and finally the kill, so it is important to understand the key *dramatis personae* in this drama. They consist of the matador, the strutting head honcho, artist and athlete, who administers the final blow to kill the bull; the *picadors* who ride on horseback and look to pierce the muscles on the back of the bull's neck in order to

She was about twenty-eight at
the time, on horseback and evincing
a self-confidence that was intimidating
- professionally, sartorially and sexually.
I was transfixed but she was too
encircled for me to meet her.
Damn it.

At the start of the event,
the 500kg bull rushed out of its pen,
wild-eyed, rampant and apoplectic
with rage, looking for anyone to gore.
The crowd of ten thousand or more ebbed
and flowed to the rhythm of the fight.

weaken them, reduce its stamina and lower its head in preparation for the final stage; and the *Banderillos* who are the assistants on foot who do the initial cape work and place the *banderillas* into the bull in the second act.

Wild-Eyed and Rampant

There was no public address system or referee to start the 'match'. The different stages were signalled by *El Presidente's* waved handkerchief or a musical flourish from the band.

At the start of the event, the 500kg bull rushed out of its pen, wild-eyed, rampant and apoplectic with rage, looking for anyone to gore.

The crowd of ten thousand or more ebbed and flowed to the rhythm of the fight. At times, it was almost silent, happy to concentrate on the unfolding 'tragedy', occasionally cheering '*chapeau, chapeau*' to acknowledge

a show of artistry by one of the collaborators. The spectators sat there, most men smoking a cigar, a picture of concentration until they felt that a *picador* was too strong for the bull. At that point, they would suddenly fire up, booing, jeering and whistling. They wanted a proper contest, not a one-sided one, as if they wanted the *picador* to suffer too.

The acoustics were perfect. When it was quiet, I could hear the *Banderillos* breathing. When the excitement rose, the noise was exhilarating under the pristine, blue sky. It was a magical setting.

Once the bull was tired and the contest entered its final stage, the noise grew much louder and the crowd metamorphosed into a willing accomplice to the killing, spurring on the matador. As a ritual before the execution, the matador kneels before the beast and goes *tête-à-tête* with this bull-mountain of wild, fresh meat. It may be bloodied and exhausted but it

could still easily kill a human. For the spectator, it is a death stare to die for, a short but extraordinary piece of theatre that thrills your bloodthirsty instincts. For the matador, it is just a death stare.

Once the matador has escaped this nose-to-nose confrontation, he or she administers the final blow using a sword called an *estoque*. Plunging it between the bull's shoulders, it strikes through the heart and severs the aorta to deliver a quick death. Although the matador's final blow is usually fatal, it may take the bull some time to die, in which case a *coup de grâce* is administered using a dagger to further pierce the spinal cord. I witnessed several of these on the day, and it was executed with extraordinary precision and speed.

However, when victorious, the matador has no medal or trophy to salute the crowd. Instead, and only if the killing was 'clean', he cuts off one or both ears, or even the tail, which he holds up to acknowledge the fans. Sometimes, the bull's performance is 'rewarded' by being pulled around a circuit of the ring, dragged behind two horses, all to the standing ovation of the crowd.

These primitive traditions live on and are entrenched in the local culture.

There are actually two types of bullfighting that take place. The first is the Spanish style *Corrida*, described above. The second is the *Course Camarguaise*, which does not end with the death of the bull. This type of bullfighting is from the Camargue region of France and involves men, called *raseteurs*, trying to pull ribbons and baubles from the bulls' horns and foreheads. I watched one of these a few years later in Arles but didn't have the courage or pace to participate!

In Nîmes, did I feel any horror at the treatment of the bulls? I must admit, back then, I didn't. Perhaps I would feel differently today. However, I do remember that I appreciated the skill, bravery and undeniable beauty of the spectacle. The arena, the colours, the people, the entertainment and the atmosphere were very memorable. There is much to like that you wouldn't find anywhere else.

Loved & Lost I

"NOW THE SUN'S GONE TO HELL
AND THE MOON'S RIDING HIGH
LET ME BID YOU FAREWELL
EVERY MAN HAS TO DIE
BUT IT'S WRITTEN IN THE STARLIGHT
AND EVERY LINE ON YOUR PALM
WE'RE FOOLS TO MAKE WAR
ON OUR BROTHERS IN ARMS"

DIRE STRAITS, BROTHERS IN ARMS, 1985

There are four magnificent men in my squad who left this world too early.
Rather than simply write about them using hearsay and desktop research,
I wanted to meet someone from their family to get to know them a little.
It wasn't always easy to find a relative but my tenacity paid off. As a result,
I think the articles are much more authentic.

I met the following people:
- Valérie Paparemborde, Robert's widow
- Jean-Baptiste Fouroux, Jacques' son
- Maryse Lacans, Pierre's mum
- Elie Vaquerin, Armand's brother

Thanks to Jean-Pierre Rives, Elsa Paparemborde and Diego Minarro for helping to facilitate
the introductions.

Jacques Fouroux

LOVED + LOST I   "FOUROUX WAS ALSO A HUGE
FIGURE IN MY LIFE, AN ENORMOUS
COMPANION ON THE ROAD AND
A GREAT FRIEND, AS A PLAYER,
CAPTAIN AND COACH. HE WAS
OUR LEADER AND A HUGE
PERSONALITY. JACQUES HAD
A DIFFERENT APPROACH TO
HUMANITY, A PERMANENT CIRCUS,
A GREAT STORYTELLER, A MAN
WHO ANIMATED US AND WELDED
US TOGETHER AS A TEAM. HE WAS
A FABULOUS HUMAN BEING."

Training session in Dublin, 18th February 1983.
Photo - Bob Thomas Sports Photography, Getty Images.

BORN : 24TH JULY 1947

DIED : 17TH DECEMBER 2005

CLUBS : UNION SPORTIVE COGNAÇAISE, LA VOULTE
SPORTIF RUGBY, FOOTBALL CLUB AUCH GERS

INTERNATIONAL CAPS : 27

POSITION : SCRUM HALF

GRAND SLAMS : 1977 (PLAYER), 1981, 1987 (COACH)

NOM DE GUERRE : LE PETIT CAPORAL

MY VISIT TO MEET JEAN-BAPTISTE :
THURSDAY 15TH FEBRUARY 2018

Jacques Fouroux was player, captain and coach of France between 1977-1990. He captained the imperious Grand Slam winning side of 1977 with a brute of a pack, conceding no tries and selecting the same fifteen players for every game.

He became coach in 1981 and his results lived up to his ambitions as he masterminded a fabulous sequence of performances for a decade. He opened his coaching career with a Grand Slam in 1981, and never lost more than one match in any subsequent tournament between 1983 and 1989. He led his team to victory in '81 (Grand Slam), '83 (joint winners with Ireland), '86 (joint winners with Scotland), '87 (Grand Slam), '88 (joint winners with Wales) and '89.

He was a big character and bundle of energy - a wit, charmer, troublemaker, contrarian, devotee and loyal friend. He was a brilliant leader of men and *Le Petit Caporal* is still venerated with great affection by his former teammates.

Aged fifty-eight, he died in 2005 from a heart attack in Auch, his home town, and is survived by his widow, Monique, and his sons, David and Jean-Baptiste. I tracked down Jean-Baptiste, in Montauban, to find out more about his dad.

In answer to the question, 'Whom would you invite to your imaginary dinner party?', Jacques Fouroux would definitely be on my list. He would be in esteemed company alongside Madonna, Robert de Niro, Brigitte Bardot, Nelson Mandela, Laurent Pardo, Diego Maradona and Stormy Daniels. Based on what the former players and teammates have told me, I have no doubt he would be holding court, although he would probably need Brigitte, Laurent or me to help him with the international *lingua franca* of English. I haven't worked out how Diego would understand what was going on, but that's just detail. I'd probably sit him between Stormy and Madonna and let their pheromones oil the wheels.

Jacques was a passionate, articulate, charismatic leader of men and the *chef d'orchestre* of his teams. He wore his heart on his sleeve and was so effective at preparing his players for battle. Like all great leaders, he was fearless and capable of moving his men to another level with his tone and use of language. He had a sociable, unpredictable and demanding brand of communication, and *mon dieu* did they respond, showing unconditional love for him that continues today. As you will see later on and throughout the book, every former player I met is in awe of him and his legacy.

It wasn't as though Jacques was a big, imposing man. He was probably the smallest player on the pitch in that 1977 Grand Slam winning side, although he had some mammoths around him to add ballast and power. He also relied on the sheer power of his personality to command respect.

"He had a profound allergy against brilliant and aesthetic players like Codorniou. He loved hard, agricultural players with big balls."

Bob Dwyer told me that Michel Palmié deemed Jacques untouchable in that great Grand Slam winning side of 1977 because, *'In ze forwards, we were all keellers (said in a very strong French accent)!'*

He had an inauspicious start to his international career and must have thought the gods were against him. In 1968, he was due to partner the great Jo Maso at half-back in the Grand Slam game against Ireland, but when Jo was injured, the selectors decided to select Gachassin at fly-half and he insisted on his club colleague Mir playing with him, so Jacques watched from the bench. He had to wait another four years for his debut in 1972 v Ireland. When he left US Cognac to play for La Voulte, he received a *licence rouge* so couldn't play for them for a year, missing out on La Voulte's achievement of winning the French Championship in 1970.

There were many great scrum-halves at the time – Mir, Barrau, Astre, but Jacques had the self-belief, determination and leadership to rise above them and secure his place. His cantankerous relationship with the French press was notorious. He would prick their egos, mock them and adopt a siege mentality, deliberately provoking them. His brain was like a turbine, a source of ideas that continually challenged conventional thinking. Jacques was never going to sit quietly in a cosy cocoon of traditional reasoning. He liked big, strong men all over the pitch, spurning great creators and technicians like Lacans and Codorniou, picked props as hookers, and adopted the Argentine scrummaging technique called *la bajadita* that adopted unconventional ways of binding and pushing. When I met Daniel Herrero, he made me laugh with his description of Jacques' methods: *"He had a profound allergy against brilliant and aesthetic players like Codorniou. He loved hard, agricultural players with big balls."*

It was a classic Daniel line, using vivid imagery and humour to make his point.

I smile when I read how the French press pilloried Jacques for supposedly ruining French flair. If only they knew that we, in the rest of the rugby-playing world, were in awe of their balance of power and guile. With the benefit of hindsight, you could see that Jacques was a visionary, understanding perfectly where the game was going and what it took to succeed, the balance of power and flair, graft and craft. Like 1977, the pack of the 1980s may have been full of killers too, but there were artisans behind who had extraordinary skills and brought panache and excitement.

Finlay Calder told me, *"France were irresistible in Paris in the Spring. David Leslie would say that the worst place to be at 2.30pm was in the changing room waiting to play them. And the best place to be was at 5pm in the same changing room having played them."*

I wonder what these journalists would make of the French game today, and how the superconductors of high modernity have electrocuted the magic of French flair. The instinctive running and passing skills that were once in the lineage of French backs have been largely extinguished, replaced by body mass, collisions and a meandering, monotonous form of this beautiful game.

By virtue of his achievement as the coach of this great French team of the 80's, Jacques was always going to be in this book. But as I talked to the former players, I became more fascinated by him as a man. I wanted to get to know him – how he led and managed and motivated, his rumbustious relationship with the French press and what he was like as a father. I managed to track down his son, Jean-Baptiste in Montauban, whom I visited in February 2018.

Driven by Passion

As soon as I arrived, it was obvious who Jean-Baptiste was. He had his father's physique but darker skin and hair. Mementos and pictures adorned his shop, notably the ball from the 1987 game against Scotland, which France won 28-22, signed by all the French players. There was also the front page of L'Equipe from 19th December 2005, a few days after Jacques died.

It is a weird coincidence but Jean-Baptiste's opticians is number 630 in the shopping mall in Montauban, the same international number as Jacques was for the French team. Spooky.

> " Of course, I am biased David but Dad was a great person, so loving and affectionate and such a proud family man. "

"He was so charismatic. We would arrive in restaurants - Mum, Dad, my brother David and I - and by the end, everyone would be around our table listening to Dad's jokes and stories. His voice would carry and you could always hear him over everyone.

"He had such a passion for and knowledge of the game. I saw my extraordinary father with all these ideas and energy at all levels of the game. He knew everything – strategy, tactics, leadership, commercial negotiations, people would do anything for him. Through the power of his words and speech, he could get people to scale mountains and realise their potential.

"I was about thirteen when I started to follow Dad everywhere. I remember one time in Grenoble when the Australians were on tour playing the South East of France in a provincial game. I had my picture taken with Jason Little. Dad had this incredible party trick of removing your watch while shaking your hand without you noticing. He always gave them back of course. He presented Michael Lynagh with a Grenoble Number 10 shirt, that's how keen he was to sign him!

"I would travel to home and away games as well as training with Dad to watch Grenoble. We had a great side with players like Kacala, Brouzet, Merle and LAndréau.

"Dad was very superstitious and he loved the number seven. I remember that before the final against Grenoble in 1993, he had to add various numbers up and ensure they divided by seven! We still lost, robbed by the referee at the time.

"Such was his devotion to rugby that he would arrive back in Auch in the evenings after coaching France to help the

guys with their scrummaging. He was the Auch rugby President at the time. He would train the youth teams to the 1st XV. In 1996, we played a youth game against a great Toulouse side, in Toulouse, and lost, up against a ref who was one of their players! For the return leg, Dad prepared us like professional team. We trained for weeks on the scrums, line-outs, kick-offs, everything. Their Toulouse team was full of big blokes who played in regional selections, but we smashed them.

"Sometimes, the floodlights would get turned off before training had finished so Dad would fetch his Mercedes-Benz and turn the lights onto full beam so they could carry on practising. He was so passionate."

The most valuable thing you can give someone is your time and Jacques never withheld his generosity.

"After a match, we would head to the restaurant as a team, about twenty-five of us. By the end, we would be scrummaging and the waiter would be playing tighthead! Dad would be playing hooker and I'd be scrum-half. He would be demonstrating the Baradita, the famous Argentinian scrummaging technique, ramming it down our throats.

"Everyone wanted to buy him a drink in the restaurant so before everyone arrived, he would give some money to the waiter and say: 'When I order a G&T, bring me some fizzy water with lemon in it.' It was the only way he could remain sober!

"But Dad could also be a stickler for discipline. For example, your studs had to be super clean and he would stop players from running out if they were dirty. He once told the referee that a player had the shits and was stuck in the toilet, when in fact he was cleaning his studs! He also insisted that players wear suits and ties, like the English did. He wouldn't accept players today with their headphones. It is a team game and you have to engage and respect the opposition, supporters and sponsors.

"When I look back, Dad was ahead of his time. He realised that you needed regional teams with the best players and you had to entertain the spectators."

"He travelled to Australia and met Rupert Murdoch to see how they did it over there. When I see how rugby has evolved, I think 'Dad advocated all of that'. It makes me happy and proud, even though at the time people rejected it.

"Dad wasn't for full time professionalism. He thought that blokes needed to work and integrate after playing, and lead normal lives."

Le Hold-Up

Jacques was very close to Albert Ferrasse and was regarded as his spiritual son for years, seemingly a natural successor when Albert stepped down. The Machiavellian politics of French rugby intervened though and Ferrasse and Fouroux fell out, with Jacques left marginalised by the French Rugby Federation. Having left the French coaching job, he was coaching Grenoble in 1992 and he took them to the 1993 Championship final to compete for Le Bouclier de Brennus against Castres.

"Two weeks before the final against Castres in 1993, we had played Agen in a thunderous semi-final against the big guns like Sella. The night before the game, Dad brought all the players together in a room, about eight square metres, and he worked them up into a frenzy. Players like Brouzet, Kacala and Merle were crying. That was the effect Dad could have. His charisma was electric."

Grenoble lost the final thanks to a controversial try scored by Gary Whetton. It looked as though Hueber touched the ball down in the in-goal area, but the referee disagreed and Gary pounced to touch down. It was the game's decisive try.

Gary talked to me about his memories that day:

"Apart from winning the game, what I remember is the journey to the Parc des Princes and the police who escorted us. Woe betide any other vehicle that got in the way of our team bus because the police would kick

them and bang their truncheons on the car roofs! When we arrived, we got out of the bus and the boys just hung around. I realised that they didn't know where to go because they hadn't played at the Parc before. I said, 'Come on boys, follow me, I've been here loads of times and the changing rooms are over here!'

"Then, when we were on the pitch for the warm-up, the Castres fans were going mad. Urios, the hooker and his two props, Lafforgue and Toussaint, were crying and waving to the crowd, hyped up on the emotion of the occasion because this was probably the biggest day in their careers. I said, 'Come on lads, we have to go back into the changing room to save our energy'. I loved that Latin temperament. When you could channel it correctly, it made for wonderful, fast flowing rugby."

Jean-Baptiste continued his memory of the final.

"After Grenoble lost the final, the newspaper headline was: 'C'etait un hold up'. I remember because I had the paper in my bedroom. Immediately after the final, I was crying. Dad and I were in the middle of the field while Castres were getting their medals. He had my hand on my neck and was angry with the FFR at the time because they had chosen a referee from Agen! It was as though they had to stop Jacques Fouroux from winning. It was so political back then.

"That rejection of Dad still hurts me today. He just wanted to train and be involved in rugby. From one day to the next, he went from hero to zero and his phone stopped ringing.

"I took him my computer and we listened to the Pilou Pilou chant before a game. We both had goosebumps! He had a new challenge to look forward to. Éric Champ and Toulon had confidence in him."

"I do remember that Éric Champ called him about becoming manager at Toulon. Dad was in bed and not feeling well the day before he died on the Saturday. I took him my computer and we listened to the Pilou Pilou chant before a game. We both had goosebumps! He had a new challenge to look forward to. Éric and Toulon had confidence in him. That was the spirit of rugby and Dad felt that again before he died. It was a wonderful moment together that I will never forget.

"I have some bittersweet memories of a trip to Australia and New Zealand a few years ago. Everyone said he was a star and a god of the sport. However, in France, the press was nasty and said the rugby he coached was crap. But these were the best days of French rugby when we saw Blanco, Sella, Charvet, Lagisquet, Lorieux, Rodriguez, Camberabero and others. Based on all the comments I see on social media about Dad, I think the French public feels the same way."

Aux Larmes

"A few days after he died, the Midi Olympique published a paper and on the front page it simply said: 'Aux Larmes...' After fourteen years, not only have I never read it, it is still in its plastic cover."

"Dad had some wonderful friends – Jean-Pierre Bastiat, Romeu and Rives, and Jean-Pierre Gontier who were unstinting in their support when he died. And since, there have been a huge number of retrospective articles and support for his achievements."

Jacques was admired, much loved and now sorely missed. Jean-Baptiste, David and Madame Fouroux, you must be very proud of his legacy.

I had taken up a good two hours of Jean-Baptiste's time, and during his shop hours. He showed me some of his mementos before we shook hands and promised to keep in touch. I would love to see him again one day as I feel we have much left to talk about.

The next day I was heading to Foix in the Pyrenees for lunch with the TGV, Patrick Estève.

As I travelled around France to meet the players, the unconditional veneration for Jacques is very clear. Each spoke movingly about him as a leader and a man. Here is a selection of the quotes and stories:

"While Pierre Villepreux taught me so much, opening my eyes and helping me polish my game with ST, Jacques taught me about the reality of international rugby. He was a pragmatist and a paradox, mixing brawn with finesse. Jacques was passionate and could be very hard with me but I loved him dearly."
Denis Charvet

"Jacques was a tremendous guy and brilliant leader of men. He was constantly telling stories to humour us or make a point. He could get you up for anything. We were great friends and when he became coach and I was captain, we complemented each other so well. He organized all the training and did all the analysis because I couldn't be bothered with all of that. And I led the team on the pitch. It was a perfect combination."
Jean-Pierre Rives

Franck Mesnel told me a couple of amusing stories involving Jacques, which reveal his wisdom and management skills.

The first involves Jacques at the Tacapuna Hotel in Auckland in 1987 during the World Cup.

"Jacques suspected that one of the journalists staying at the hotel was leaking salacious stories about the players, so he decided to take matters into his own hands. One day after lunch, I returned to my room, and as I went around the corner, I saw Jacques giving a leg-up to another journo, Alain Gex, so they could see through a window. They were looking at the aforementioned journalist engaging in a bit of postprandial sex. I said: 'Jacques, what's happening?' He explained the situation and said, 'Everyone will be ok now. The journo knows why, and he knows that I know his secrets! He belongs to us. He won't write anything bad'. It was classic Jacques – clever and funny."

The second involved a tour to Argentina. Franck continued the story.

"The team arrived at the airport and headed straight to Sheraton. Jacques said, 'RDV downstairs in five minutes, stay dressed as you are'. He took us round the back to the kitchen and said, 'I'm not going to tell you not to go out. This town is beautiful, as are the girls. If you don't want to get caught at the entrance, you come back via this door. The chefs and cooks have been tipped off. You use this knock as a code (Franck knocks the table). You do what you want to do but you make sure you are on the pitch on time'. He had loads of confidence in us. And in return we would do anything for him."

"Jacques did divide opinion. But whether you were for or against him, everyone was at his funeral and everyone knows that he had a huge impact on French rugby in the 1970s and 80s."
Jo Maso

"Jacques Fouroux was more of a management guru than a coach. When he gave the match day shirts out, he would motivate each player in a very individual way.

He'd say to the Basque props like Pascal and Doxpi: 'Make sure your opposite number doesn't score today, because if he does, it means you are tired and he is better than you in the scrum'.

To players like Lorieux and Garuet, he would verbally and viciously abuse them, telling them they were crap in the last game and their opposite number was far better than them. It would send them into a frenzy, they would go nuts.

To Blanco, he would humbly say: 'Thank you Serge. Thank you for being with us here today'. He was a genius!"

PATRICK ESTÈVE

Robert Paparemborde

LOVED + LOST I

"ON HIS BEDSIDE TABLE, THERE WAS A
COPY OF LE PETIT PRINCE BY ANTOINE
DE SAINT-EXUPÉRY. I THOUGHT IF
SOMEONE OF HIS STATURE AND
PERSONALITY IS READING THAT,
HE MUST BE TRULY ASTONISHING.
IT WAS LOVE AT FIRST SIGHT."

19th February 1983, Robert Paparemborde at
Lansdowne Road, Dublin. Ireland 22 v France 16.
Photo - Bob Thomas Sports Photography, Getty Images.

BORN : 5TH JULY 1948

DIED : 18TH APRIL 2001

CLUBS : SECTION PALOISE, RACING CLUB DE FRANCE

INTERNATIONAL CAPS : 55

POSITION : PROP

GRAND SLAMS : 1977, 1981

NICKNAME : PATOU, PAPA

NOM DE GUERRE : THE DIAMOND

MY VISIT TO MEET VALÉRIE PAPAREMBORDE :
THURSDAY 7TH JUNE 2018

Robert Paparemborde is one of those players who is engraved on my memory. I don't know whether this is due to his distinctive name or his playing ability, probably both, but I remember vividly his face, shape, passing, mauling, scrummaging and try scoring.

I contacted Valérie, Robert's lovely widow, via their daughter Elsa, and I travelled to Paris to meet her in the same apartment she had bought with Robert in 1994, and which she now shares with her ninety-nine year-old father, Pierre.

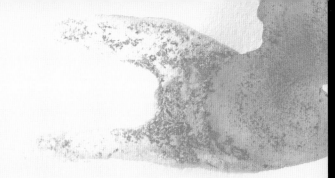

En route to meet her, I was feeling nervous. I only interviewed two women for my book, Valérie and Maryse Lacans. I had chatted briefly to some of the players' wives in passing but none involved in-depth discussions about rugby or their lives since. But the paucity of female input wasn't why I was nervous for this interview. At its core, my nervousness was triggered by my own personal circumstances and of course, the sensitivity of my questions.

My empathy towards Valérie and Elsa is unequivocal, not simply an abstraction. What I mean is that I really feel it. I have experienced the trauma of losing my father. I understand what being *sans père* feels like, and I have seen through my mother's eyes how a widow successfully rebuilds her and her children's lives.

Patou

As a kid growing up in rugby-loving Bath, I admired Robert greatly. He was *la pierre angulaire* (the cornerstone) of the side between 1975 and 1983, feared by so many of his opponents. When I spoke to players, my admiration grew even bigger because he was a shining example of success in sport, business and human relationships.

Robert started with nothing, other than family support, so his successes are all the more remarkable.

The son of a road engineer, he was brought up in humble surroundings in Laruns, a remote town in the Pyrenees. Not far from Pau, Laruns is the last town on the

For the few seconds Elsa and Valérie spoke, I loved the precious mother-daughter moment. The tone, intonation, excitement and expression of Valérie captured exquisitely their bond of both blood and friendship.

D934 road before you reach Spain. It is in the middle of nowhere.

Robert would walk 4kms to school alone through the woods, whatever the weather. There was only one restaurant where they had a great Pyrenean herd dog called Le Patou, a large white species of impressive bulk, which mixed with flocks of sheep to ensure their protection. It's not difficult to see why one of Robert's nicknames was Patou.

He became adept at many sports such as judo, handball, athletics and, of course, rugby, which he only took up because his *lycée* needed a centre to complete its team. Age eighteen, he was playing for Pau in the centre, and at twenty, he found himself selected for the first XV as prop. People said that he had a body shaped like a Perrier bottle, which made him tough to scrummage against.

When his playing days were over, he opened sports shops in Pau and Lourdes before heading to Paris to join his great mate Jean-Pierre Rives at RCF, where he would become Manager and win the French Championship in 1990. He and Jean-Pierre also opened two restaurants called the Black Bear in Pau and Paris. Bear was another suitable sobriquet for Robert, and 'Black' was a reminder of their wonderful victory against the All Blacks on Bastille Day, 14th July 1979.

Le Petit Prince

I was keen for Valérie to tell me how she met him and what he was like.

"I first met Robert when I went to see Jean-Pierre Rives, who I already knew, at his apartment in Paris. They were going out that night and Jean-Pierre said, 'Say hello to Papa, he's there in the spare bedroom'. I thought he meant his dad, but he was talking about Robert! On his bedside

table, there was a copy of Le Petit Prince by Antoine de Saint-Exupéry. I thought if someone of his stature and personality is reading that, he must be truly astonishing. It was love at first sight.

"He really was astonishing. In contrast to his size and look on the rugby pitch, off it he was a man of great class and finesse, with an almost feminine character. He was elegant, eloquent, subtle and smart."

"I can't remember a single time when he made the wrong judgement. He exercised it with a lot of humility, never in an arrogant, categoric way. He was a deep thinker.

"When thinking about rugby, he had a sense of anticipation. He had a vision then of the rugby today.

"He died within two months of being ill. He fell poorly on a plane back from Rome where he had watched Italy-France on 3rd March 2001. When he came back to Paris, he went to hospital a few weeks later for an operation relating to his pancreatic cancer, but he never woke up. Jean-Pierre Rives would pick me up and take me to the hospital every day. He and Robert were very close.

"Robert came to Paris because his international career had finished and he needed a change from Pau where he had spent all his life. Jean-Pierre invited him to join RCF and that's how his Parisian adventure started.

"He adapted to life very easily. In every aspect of his life, he had the ability to fit in and take things on. He had a very human side to him.

"Elsa was only thirteen when he died. She could have crumbled but she uses his presence and memory as an inspiration to give her strength and motivation, which culminated in her studying for four years at Harvard in the USA, and then McGill in Canada. She follows his example of keeping calm, thinking lucidly, being committed and taking the initiative. He really inspires her and all of us. His is still our point of reference and his influence is all around us."

Jean-Pierre spoke to me movingly about his *frère d'armes*:

"Patou was a wonderful friend, someone who didn't speak much but we understood each other well. When Valérie wanted to know something, she would call me! He was a Béarnais, exceptionally strong and gifted outside of rugby too.

"I was there with him right at the end. It is a terrible memory. There was a long corridor and I saw the doctor walking towards me. It was like he had seen the devil. We lost a wonderful friend, husband and man."

A Treasure Trove of Memories

Valérie's lounge is full of books and her father read the whole time I was there.

From the bookcase, she picked out a huge binder full of newspaper articles, documents and photographs, which we spent a good hour poring over. It was clear that Robert was a deep thinker and visionary, writing notes about training techniques and strategies on how to beat the opposition. This original material fascinates me because it is unblemished by the historian's hand. There are other original articles in there too by such journalistic luminaries as Christian Montaignac and Henri Nayrou, two more wonderful men whom I met on my journey around France.

I wanted to know what Valérie remembered about the great Grand Slam side of 1977.

"It was before I met Robert, but that side, for all its strong characters, always remained friends. Jean-Pierre always tells me that for a team to win, you have to love your teammates, and of course, victory reinforces that love. For all the tension in the early 1990s when Robert and Jacques (Fouroux) were having their arm wrestles at the FFR, they never fell out. Robert said that he would always remain friends because they had been through so much together.

"When they had their twenty-year reunion in 1997, they all wanted to get together in one bedroom for an hour, just like they used to before their games. They were and still are like a band of brothers, even though Jacques and Robert are no longer here.

"The French Barbarians and various golfing events were developed on the back of that 1977 success, and created another platform for those players to meet regularly."

Henri Nayrou, once Managing Editor at 'Le Midi Olympique' and then a politician for the last twenty-two years, holds an event each year called Les Rencontres en Séronais at La Bastide de Sérou near Foix in the Pyrenees, which is a celebration of rugby and its fraternity. I had the pleasure of attending this in 2018 along with several hundred others and a galaxy of former French rugby stars such as Jean-Claude Skrela, Richard Astre, Jean-Pierre Garuet, Patrick Estève, Didier Sanchez and the former Irish player, Hugo MacNeill. Valérie attends every year not just because it is great fun but because Robert is one of the former players who is so fondly remembered.

It was wonderful. We ate, drank, sang and laughed all evening, entertained by various singers and speeches including the jovial Pampi Laduche and his band who regaled us with Basque songs all evening. Hugo sang an Irish song, and his wife Jennifer sang one in Basque. Those MacNeills are a talented lot. I drank whisky and smoked cigars with Patrick, before practising my scrummaging with Garuche and Didier Sanchez. It was a cultural extravaganza! Henri was a wonderful host.

Impeccable Judgement

When I met Franck Mesnel, he shed some more light on Robert and his talent as Manager of RCF.

manage the trauma of the past and focus on the future. During our meeting, Elsa called her on the phone. For the few seconds they spoke, I loved the precious mother-daughter moment. The tone, intonation, excitement and expression of Valérie captured exquisitely their bond of both blood and friendship.

Henri Nayrou wrote a wonderful article about Robert in Le Midi Olympique on 23rd April 2001, just after he had died. I have picked out a paragraph that is moving and beautifully written. It encapsulates his character, and why he was the friend of so many, and the enemy of no one.

"Papa was such a smart man. He worked out very quickly how to transform RCF from a sleepy club into the French champions in 1990.

"First, he built the team around talented players such as Baptiste (Lafond) and Éric (Blanc). He knew you couldn't restrict them. You had to give them freedom.

"He also let us perform our 'Show-Bizz' shenanigans. In 1987 when we were planning on wearing berets for the match in Bayonne, Jean-Pierre Labro (RCF's President) wanted to stop us, but Patou said, 'No, let them do it'. Robert realised that it would put pressure on us and improve our performance because we would have to win the game. As players, we knew that we couldn't lose a game wearing berets, that would make us look ridiculous!

"Second, he knew we had to toughen up. He was part of that Grand Slam winning pack of 1977 so he understood that flair alone wouldn't win you trophies, that you needed

hard men too. He developed players like Michel Tachdjian and Jean-Pierre Genet who were both very intelligent and knew, in their own way, how to use their mix of hardness and intelligence for the service of others on the pitch. They were critical to RCF, not just as players but as enforcers. They never took a step backwards.

"For example, Michel would identify the key person in the opposition and take him out! Early in my career, I couldn't understand how some forwards could be so intelligent off the pitch but mad on it. However, I realised that while we might sparkle in the backs, it's the intelligent players in the scrum who are key. Rugby starts up front."

Le Diamant Angulaire

I spent about three hours with Valérie and it was a wonderful privilege. She is bright, articulate, proud, loving, stoical, resilient and such a positive thinker. Like my mum, she knows how to block out the darkness,

"...he was a man of contrasts, at the same time a pure provincial and a true Parisian, big on the eye but adroit on analysis, a leader and follower, fiery and placid, lively and relaxed, dogmatic and liberal, dreamer and realist, committed and reserved, pugnacious and casual, passionate and detached, fluent in 'patois' and competent at golf, able to switch between shepherd and king."

Robert wasn't just *la pierre angulaire* of the scrum. He was *le diamant angulaire* of every team.

"Robert symbolised all the essential qualities of a prop forward – solidity, stability, friendship, intelligence and subtlety. He wasn't talkative but he could tell you what it was like in the front row better than anyone. The looks and groans from his opposite number, who was like a brother in this front row fraternity. The blood, sweat and tears that such intimacy would engender. I could have all the imagination in the world but I will never truly know or feel what it is like in the front row. He was one of these great actors on the pitch who had an enormous presence, both physically and emotionally."
Christian Montaignac

—————————————————————

"Robert had said to a French newspaper that I didn't look at them or respect them in the tunnel before games. Of course, I didn't look at them. I was so short-sighted that I couldn't see twenty feet away!
John O'Driscoll

—————————————————————

"Robert was a great man. He didn't say much but when he did, it meant something. When he got angry, he didn't do it for fun so it made a big impact. He was very kind and a real fatherly figure."
Denis Charvet

"He was one of these great actors on the pitch who had an enormous presence, both physically and emotionally."

CHRISTIAN MONTAIGNAC

Pierre Lacans

LOVED + LOST | "WHEN I LOOK BACK ON
THAT FATEFUL DAY, HE PLAYED,
LED AND CELEBRATED VICTORY
WITH PANACHE, BRILLIANCE
AND ELEGANCE, LIKE HE KNEW
IT WAS HIS LAST NIGHT. HE WAS
AN ADORABLE MAN AND THE
WHOLE COMMUNITY REMEMBERS
HIM WITH GREAT FONDNESS."

BORN : 23RD APRIL 1957

DIED : 30TH SEPTEMBER 1985

CLUBS : ASSOCIATION SPORTIVE BÉZIERS HÉRAULT

INTERNATIONAL CAPS : 6

POSITION : BACK ROW

GRAND SLAMS : 1981

NICKNAME : PIERROT

NOM DE GUERRE : BÉZIERS' PEARL

MY VISIT TO MEET MARYSE LACANS :
MONDAY 11TH JUNE 2018

Pierre Lacans was the captain of Béziers, France's greatest club at the time, and an athletic flanker who played for them between 1977 and 1985, winning the French Championship five times. Competing with some of France's great back rowers of the era (Rives, Joinel, Erbani, Rodriguez), his appearances were limited. He hailed from the Aude, played for Béziers in the Hérault and originated from rugby league. He transcended all the local rivalries.

A fabulous leader of men and immensely popular with supporters and fellow players, he seemed destined for greatness, until tragedy struck. On 30th September 1985, Pierre was killed in a road accident aged just twenty-eight, joining other great French players who had also died on the road: Raymond Albaladejo, Jean Othats et Émile Carrère (1964), Guy Boniface (1968), Jean-Michel Capendéguy (1968) and Rene Berges-Cau (1983) to name just a few. As the great Marcel Pagnol wrote: 'Such is the life of a man. Moments of joy, obliterated by unforgettable sadness'.

I went to meet his mum, Maryse, near Lézignan-Corbières, to find out more about him.

This is a story about a brilliant player but also a human tragedy, and how a parent summons the courage to deal with the grief of losing a child.

Nothing stimulates your emotions like your child. Watching them being born, the first smile, words and steps, the first day at school, the high of watching your son or daughter score the try to win the game. As a father of three boys, I was well aware, and I knew the meeting with Maryse could be a very emotional one. I tried to prepare myself as best I could but didn't anticipate just how stretched my emotions would be.

I remember watching Pierre play occasionally for France when I was a young teenager. Back then, the pictures were intermittent because TV coverage in the early 1980s was poor, with only the BBC featuring the Five Nations. Moreover, in spite of his brilliance, Pierre struggled to get in the side with a back row boasting the talents of Rives, Joinel and Rodriguez. But *bon dieu*, he made a mark. His athleticism, speed and frizzy hairstyle set him apart. He was a pearl of a player.

On that terrible day, Pierre had just played the match of his short life for Béziers away against Narbonne, captaining his side to victory over their nearest and greatest rivals. Didier Camberabero remembers the match well and reminisced about it and Pierre when I met him:

"I only played twice with Pierre, including this match, just before he died. He could do everything. In that game, he made the two breaks to create the two tries. He made it easy for me

and his teammates. He was very intelligent, technically strong and a brilliant player. And most importantly, he was loved by everyone, he was an adorable man."

After the match, Pierre celebrated with his teammates, first at the reception in Narbonne, then in Nissan-lez-Enserune and lastly in Béziers. He drove his Ford Escort back towards his home in Lézignan-Corbières where he ran a well-known bar called Le Conti. He never arrived. Heading west on the RN113 and exiting the dusty town of Coursan, along one of those French roads, long, straight and lined with plane trees, his car smashed into a cattle truck, rolled over and he burned to death.

At the tender age of twenty-eight, this magnificent player was struck down in the prime of his life.

At the time, he was, and had been for several years, a star player. He excelled at everything with his pace, offloading skills, eye for a gap and rugby brain. He was able to react to what he saw in front of him. He exemplified French flair, even though Albert Ferrasse and his friends at the French Rugby Federation seemed to hold a disdain for Béziers because of their dominance and *jeu dur*. This, coupled with the fact that Fouroux's stated preference was for big forwards, meant that Pierre only played six times for his country.

Stretched Emotions

I had struggled to contact anyone from Pierre's family, but Didier Codorniou and Alain Paco had both put me in touch with a man called Diego Minarro, the former hooker for Béziers in the early 1980s and twice champion of France, and yet another magnificent human being whom I met on my travels. We chatted on the phone a few times and instantly hit it off. He talked expansively about Pierre, the Béziers club, its grand history and the local area. He was fluent, articulate and knowledgeable.

Diego and I arranged to meet on 11th June at the Coupole restaurant near Bézier's Stade de la Méditerranée before going to meet Maryse, now aged eighty, in Conilhac-Corbieres in the South of France near Narbonne.

This was an interview I was both nervous and keen to do. Nervous because I understood how raw the emotions might still be. The pain, of course, is unending. Keen because, from personal experience, I am always humbled by how some people can accommodate grief with such grace and dignity, able to deploy their own coping mechanisms. Pierre Dospital, the great Basque prop, lost his seven-year-old son and he used his memory as inspiration and motivation on the pitch, talking to him and taking on the opposition together.

As we travelled, Didier said to me, *"She will shed a tear or two David. Be prepared. But it will pass."*

I was concerned that I too might well up, overcome by the emotion of the meeting. Not wanting my feelings to appear counterfeit or oversentimental, I told Diego about my own personal circumstances and how I experienced the trauma of my father dying in front of my eyes when I was five. My mother, eighty years old like Maryse, had to deal with the fall out but has always shown such remarkable fortitude and resilience in the face of adversity.

When it comes to losing a child though, I can't claim to have suffered like Maryse since Pierre's death in 1985. However, for seven days in 2000, I tasted how 'it' feels with the near death of our own son, William. Admitted into paediatric intensive care at Southampton hospital following a short, undetected illness, he was diagnosed with septicemia and given a mere 10% chance of survival that night. So close to death was he that we were offered the services of a priest. We declined. He was a tough kid and a fighter to the last.

Leaving him on a life support machine, we reluctantly left his side about 1.30am on the first night to find some beds, not that we could sleep. One floor above, we laid down near the nurses' base. I had asked the doctor to come and fetch us if death were imminent. Whenever we heard footsteps on the hard tiles in the corridor, or the nurses' phone rang, we prepared ourselves. We will never forget those sounds and the fear they still evoke. Time and again, we braced ourselves for the dreadful moment when we might be told. Your hope that your child will beat the illness both soothes and destroys you.

We had thunder in our hearts and were overwhelmed by grief. With all the false alarms, it was as though we experienced William dying a dozen times during that long night.

Those feelings are crippling and they tear you apart. Nothing in life can prepare you for them: the pain in the pit of your stomach, your sense of helplessness, your uncontrollable suffering. I can feel those emotions as strongly today as I did eighteen years ago, and can't think, talk, write or read this piece without tears burning my eyes. When I think about William, I always think about this unimpeachable truth: that we can protect our children from harm and that they will always outlive us, is every parent's most cherished illusion.

Thanks to Dr Michael Marsh, the Consultant responsible for the paediatric intensive care unit, William miraculously survived and now lives every day to his maximum, just how we want him to. He and we were blessed on this occasion. Maryse and her family weren't offered that fortune. For her, I have a small sense of how deep the bullet lies.

Gallic Pride

Diego and I arrived at Maryse's house in Conilhac-Corbières and she greeted us warmly. She is a very fit looking octogenarian with tanned skin, deep brown eyes and dark hair. She has an attractively lined face, typical for someone of her age and no doubt worn too by the trauma she has lived through for the last thirty-three

> "As captain and leader, he wasn't a shouter. He always spoke with great intelligence and reflection. As a player he could do everything - transform any ball into attack, offload, find space, read the game. He was magnificent."

years. Her resemblance to Pierre is marked. Her house is adorned with pictures of her beloved son reflecting the happy memories and immortal love for him. One in particular captures his essence beautifully – the frizzy hair, powerful, lantern jaw and thick neck muscles, the look of concentration and steely determination in the eyes. He was adorable off the pitch but a winner on it, and the picture encapsulates that.

We sat down and I explained all about my book. I showed her the collage of all the players I had created, with Pierre alongside the greats of the game. She beamed with Gallic pride. Apart from Béziers fans, former players of the era and some other diehard rugby fanatics, Pierre Lacans' name won't roll off the tongue of many, but it should do. He was a player in the mould of Laurent Cabannes. Yes, he was that fast and skilful. And here was me, an unknown Englishman, rekindling memories of her wonderful son.

Maryse described him:

"Well he loved partying, David. He was never short of friends or invitations. He was very young when he started playing for the infants and juniors at Lézignan, coached by his father. Lézignan was only rugby league back then.

"His dad, Roger, had been a finalist in 1959, a cup winner in 1960 and champion of France in 1961. He had also played for France as a prop.

"He was very sporty and did a lot of cycling as well as rugby. He started playing rugby league age five. After junior school, he went to senior school in Narbonne where he played union with Didier Codorniou, and at age nineteen he played for Lézignan rugby league team in the French championship final against Carcassonne, which unfortunately they lost.

"Béziers came to sign him at nineteen although Lézignan blocked his licence so Ferrasse had to intervene to let him play. So, Pierre had switched from league to union, and then from l'Aude to l'Hèrault to play for Béziers. That was quite controversial back then!"

"He made his debut against South Africa in 1980, in the same match that Serge Blanco won his first cap."

Pierre scored a try against England in 1981, France's Grand Slam year. I remember this game well because Laurent Pardo scored a lovely try after some fancy footwork by Berbizier, Rives and Cordorniou.

"He used to get cross when France didn't pick him although you never saw that in print or when he was interviewed. He had too much dignity to show them he was annoyed. He had some stiff competition and while Béziers was winning everything, the club was out of favour with the fulcrum of power in Agen."

"He opened up a bar called Le Conti in 1983 in Lézignan, and it was always packed because all the teams would come by. It was a great era and players could enjoy themselves without social media and all the controls. All the local teams knew each other and got on well off the pitch, even the big rivals like Béziers and Narbonne."

Stolen Memories, Shattered Dreams

Pierre wasn't married when he died, but he had a fiancée called Cathy about whom Maryse spoke with great affection. Cathy was an athlete and would run around the track at Béziers' old stadium, the mythical Sauclières, when the rugby team was training. Pierre quickly noticed and started dating her.

She reminisced movingly about Cathy and Pierre, of the stolen memories and shattered hopes and dreams, and it was this that triggered her tears of pain and trembling lips, as Diego had forewarned.

I paused my recording and we all took a deep breath to try to contain our emotions. Maryse was so dignified, graceful and beautiful as she strained to speak. Diego touched her on the arm and said, "We don't want you to suffer Maryse" as he helped her regain her composure. It was the moment when I could see into his soul, this magnificent man who has so much love for the mum of his great mate who he has visited every year for thirty-three years. He found the right words and tone and gestures as he touched and comforted her, like only a son or daughter can do to a mother. It was measured and profoundly empathetic, and revealed his class and sensitivity.

It is so hard to conquer one's emotions about one's child, but I didn't want her to relive the horror of the time. I wanted her and us to celebrate his magnificence as a son, man and player. I wanted him in the Pantheon of greats and I had selected *him* in *my* team.

Maryse fetched the family photo album, a huge tome that I went through assiduously with both her and Diego. It is a treasure trove of happy memories spanning a decade and there are some wonderful pictures of a young, fit Pierre. What stands out is that he was always running into space and passing the ball. I don't recall a single photo of him on the ground or being tackled or taking contact. Maryse and Diego provided a running commentary of the 100 or so pictures we went through – the stadium, other players, the results, the fights, who scored the tries.

"He was so skilful that he played fly-half sometimes. In the Championship final against Montferrand in 1978, Pierre didn't get picked in the first team because of the experience of other players, but he got his reward when he came on at fly-half at the end of the match to replace Henri Cabrol. That season, he also played in two more finals – with both the juniors in the B team competition. It was a key turning point in his career."

We moved onto the family and Maryse spoke about how she has coped with the trauma of losing her loved ones: Pierre in 1985, her husband Roger in 2004, and her daughter Pascale in 2014.

"I keep myself very busy David. I have the great-grandchildren and grandchildren and lots of friends, and I go away on holiday. You have to do that, always look forward. The grandkids live next door and they represent the future."

I find it hard to imagine the magnitude of her grief during her lifetime – its length and depth and expression - but her

stoicism was striking. Despite the defensive position
that it pushes you into, Maryse doesn't wallow in any
of the traps of grief like self-pity, loneliness or bitterness.
She exuded positive energy and that was her way of
fighting the demons of the past.

From my own experience, time helps to heal the suffering,
to a degree. But the wounds lie very deep and the scars
never disappear. She was extraordinarily reminiscent of
my mother, always on the go and rarely looking to the
past, other than in specific moments of remembrance.
That connection made the interview even more poignant
and personal for me. Maryse touched my heart and our
rendez-vous pulled very hard on my emotions. Like water,
pain always finds a way to push through the seal.

Mother's Pride

There are moments when time can seem so malleable,
able to quicken or slow depending on your emotions.
We stayed about two hours, I think, but it seemed
a lot shorter. Diego and I embraced Maryse warmly
and kissed her on both cheeks as we said goodbye.
As we walked outside into the brilliant sunlight, I noticed
the pink and yellow roses in her garden, in full bloom,
a strikingly paradoxical example of the bounty of life.
For a moment, I am sure time came to a halt, suspended
by both the sadness and beauty of the scene.

Maryse said, *"When you are back in the area, please come
by and see me."* I felt enormous pride that this project had
brought her happiness and remembered her son in such
rarified company as Rives, Blanco, Sella, et al.

His Last Night

I popped back to see Diego and his family in Nissans-
lez-Enserune in early September 2018. It was another
beautiful day and he put on a sumptuous lunch of roast
lamb, potatoes and *pan con tomate*, all washed down
with some wonderful wines, provided by his great friend,
Ludovic Aventin, of Terra Hominis.

We sat under the lime tree in the bright, dappled
sunlight, listening to stories of rugby, wine, food and the
local history. It was a wonderful Provençal scene, the air
lifted by the perfume of lavender, rosemary and thyme,
our relaxed bodies absorbing the sunshine.

Diego explained the party that the Béziers team had
enjoyed the night before Pierre's death:

*"Before the match, we arrived in Narbonne very motivated
to play well and beat our great rivals. Back then, I ran a bar
in Nissan-lez-Enserune and I said to Pierrot, the captain,*

*that I had a 'fakir' (a showman who performs magic)
coming that evening who would be great entertainment for
the boys. He looked at me, smiled and said, 'Let's win the
game first and then we will see'.*

*"We won and Pierrot had a great match. I mentioned the
'fakir' again to Pierre and he said, 'Let's go!'*

*"We went to the match reception and then headed to my
bar, the Café-Bar-Hotel l'Acropole. The 'fakir' was there
in full flow. We used to get lots of passers-by in Nissans
because we are just off the main road and he just turned
up one day in my bar. He enjoyed the local products and
would regularly get smashed.*

*"That evening, the whole spectacle was very funny. He was
covered in tattoos and lay on a bed of nails, with a wooden
plank on top of him, and invited people to walk on him.
One of the local lads went to get his small tractor to drive
on top of him. The whole evening was hilarious. And this*

guy would also eat glass! Then, he was tied up with some rope and locks and managed to free himself.

"It was a warm evening and the village square was heaving with people. The place was rocking. Back then, the locals loved the big teams stopping off in the village – whether it was Béziers or Narbonne or Bourgoin, en route back from the Basque Country. This was back in the amateur days when all the small towns and villages had teams and would mix and party together.

"After we watched the 'fakir', we all headed into Béziers where we ended up at Alain Estève's night club.

___

"Pierrot was such a great leader of men. He had a rule that after a match, you had to stay with your mates and couldn't wander off with any girls before 3am."

___

"He was big on the team ethos and he prioritised team cohesion above all else. Some of the guys were desperate and had difficulty lasting until 3am. There were lots of girls around and the players struggled to comply with his orders!

"As captain and leader, he wasn't a shouter. He always spoke with great intelligence and reflection. As a player he could do everything - transform any ball into attack, offload, find space, read the game. He was brilliant.

"The Béziers club took his death very badly because we lost the heir to the throne. He was the link between the old and new generations because he transcended both. He was central to the core of the club, the foundation on which everything else was built. That core had started back in 1968, before Pierre arrived, when the Béziers juniors had won the national title. This team then created the basis for success in the 1970s. Pierrot arrived in 1977/8 and would take that 1970's success into the 1980s. That knowledge and experience was suddenly lost, and it is no coincidence that Béziers rugby declined afterwards.

"He was a magnificent man and player, known for his fair play, humility and friendship, He may have played for Béziers but he was close to many of the other teams' players too, especially Narbonne. We all fought like rivals on the pitch, but off it, the affection for Pierre was deep and enduring.

"When I look back on that fateful day, he played, led and celebrated victory with panache, brilliance and elegance, like he knew it was his last night. He was an adorable man and the whole community remembers him with great fondness."

It was a fitting way to end the lunch. We drank some strong coffee to recharge our batteries and ambled around the large garden, before I left for Narbonne

to stay at Gerard Bertrand's hotel vineyard, Château L'Hospitalier.

These moments in the sun, eating and drinking, are so enjoyable and reminiscent of the time I lived in the south, way back in the late '80s. Some British friends don't understand the long lunch, thinking that it is just a question of eating and drinking to excess. But that misses the point. The food and wine, while immensely enjoyable, are the means to the end. The end is the friendship that lasts a lifetime.

The Fragility of Life

I regularly think about Pierre, the precariousness of life, and how he went from ecstasy to death within a matter of hours, expunged indiscriminately from this world. I ponder over all the combinations of timings and circumstances that had to exist in perfect alignment for Pierre to lose his life that night. What if he had left Narbonne, Nissan-lez-Enserune or Béziers a littler earlier or later? Why did the cattle truck have to be in that exact spot on the road at that time? Why not one minute before or after? The probability of all these events moving in sequence would have been minuscule. None of this will bring him back of course so in that sense the detail is pointless.

These strange quirks of fate move in mysterious ways and can have devastating consequences.

Some British friends don't understand the long lunch, thinking that it is just a question of eating and drinking to excess. But that misses the point. The food and wine, while immensely enjoyable, are the means to the end. The end is the friendship that lasts a lifetime.

Armand Vaquerin

LOVED + LOST I

"OUTSIDE OF RUGBY, HE WAS A THUNDERBOLT. HE PLAYED AND PARTIED HARD, AND WOULD HAVE WON A LOT MORE CAPS FOR FRANCE IF HE HAD BEEN MORE FOCUSED ON HIS RUGBY! HE WOULD GO OUT ANYWHERE, AT ANY TIME, AND HE WOULD BE OUT AND AWAY FOR DAYS SOMETIMES WEEKS AT A TIME. HE ALWAYS BURNED THE CANDLE AT BOTH ENDS BUT THAT WAS HIM. HE LOVED LIFE. WE ALL STILL MISS HIM GREATLY."

11th November 1972. Playing for a South West France Selection.
Photo - Presse Sports.

BORN : 21ST FEBRUARY 1951

DIED : 10TH JULY 1993

CLUBS : ASSOCIATION SPORTIVE BÉZIERS HÉRAULT

INTERNATIONAL CAPS : 26

POSITION : PROP

NICKNAME : LE GRAND

NOM DE GUERRE : THE FREE SPIRIT

MY VISIT TO MEET ELIE VAQUERIN :
MONDAY 11TH JUNE 2018

Armand Vaquerin is a legend in France and the most celebrated French rugby player in the history of their game, winning the Championship ten times between 1971 and 1984. Tough on the pitch, he was also a big character with a huge heart, a man of unstinting generosity and loyalty to his friends and the rugby community. On 10th July 1993, tragedy struck when he allegedly killed himself playing Russian roulette in a bar in Béziers. There is some mystery about exactly what happened but I wasn't really here to explore that. I wanted to find out about Armand, the man and player, who was idolised by the fans and players across the country. I went to meet his brother, Elie, in June 2018.

Diego Minarro from AS Béziers Hérault rugby club had helped arrange the meeting in the usual café restaurant, La Coupole, near the Béziers stadium. When Elie arrived, I recognised him instantly. He is thick-set, moustached and looks remarkably like Armand, but it was the sadness in his eyes that struck me. I could see immediately that time had only partially healed the wounds. Twenty-five years after Armand's death, his pain is still visible.

I started by asking Elie about his family:

"Armand and I were very close. We were two of seven kids – François, Manu, Daniel, Florial, myself, Armand and Rose-Marie, in that order. Three of my brothers have died. Most of us were born in Sévérac-le-Château, Aveyron, where Mum and Dad had settled after fleeing Spain as refugees on foot in 1939 during the Spanish war. Other members of our family who fled also joined us there. It is our home village so we talk about it with a lot of emotion. We moved to Béziers when I was seven years old and Armand five.

"We started playing rugby for AS Béziers quite late, aged fifteen or so, because we both played a lot of football until then. AS Béziers was a good team in the early sixties, but it had lost three out of four finals (1960, 1962, 1964) and had won in 1961. We lived opposite one of the players from that era, Emile Bolzan, who encouraged us to play rugby. That was how we started. Armand played for the first XV when he was about seventeen.

"In 1970, Armand played for Béziers against a Romanian side and performed very well. When Jean-Louis Martin was injured for the 1971 final against Toulon, his loss became Armand's gain, and he played. We won 15-9."

"I played hooker that day against Gruarin and their immense front row. Armand did everything he could to keep the scrums up and help me so I didn't suffer. He was an immense player, brother and teammate."

Hard and Loyal

At twenty years old, Armand Vaquerin won his first title as Champion of France. He won his first cap for France against Romania (in Béziers) aged twenty years and ten months. It had already been a dazzling trajectory since he was fifteen years old but a lot more was to come. Alongside his teammates and under the tutelage of the Béziers coach, Raoul Barrière, known as the Sorcier de Sauclières, they dominated rugby throughout France for fourteen years, their success based on rigour, solidarity, power, preparation and mental strength. It was the beginnings of what we call today 'professionalism'.

Between 1971 and 1984, Armand played in eleven finals and lost only one, against Agen in 1976.

Elie elaborated:

"Raoul Barriere was such a smart coach. He tried to copy how the All Blacks played – great on the basics, win your ball, strong in the ruck, great link play. He built upon his success with the juniors who were champions of France in 1968, and he had outstanding players in his side like Astre and Cantoni. Cantoni was one of the greatest players I have ever seen."

Béziers had a fearsome reputation for their physicality and, occasionally, violent play. I asked Jean-Pierre Rives what it was like to play against them at their mythical, former stadium, Stade de Sauclières.

"They had some very tough players. Their Number 6, Saisset, didn't like me because I took his place in the French

side. Estève, Buonomo, Saisset, Senal, Palmier – they were brutes who used to hand out beatings wherever they could – they would stamp, scratch, punch, kick. They would target me, who they referred to as Le Blond, hence why I always had cuts and bruises. I was never happy afterwards. Players just covered their heads and hoped for the best.

"I used to receive hate mail at home in Toulouse the week before we played them so my mother would ask me not to play! But on the pitch, my mate Armand Vaquerin always looked out for me. In rucks he would lie on me and say:

"**Don't move – they want to kick the s**t out of you but I'll protect you.**" Chuckling, he impersonates Armand who spoke with a slight lisp.

Alain Lorieux told me:

"He was the daddy of French rugby. I remember playing in a cup match for Grenoble against Béziers on neutral ground in Toulon. Vaquerin and a couple of his Béziers mates trapped me in a corner and I had to fight hard to look after myself. I'd only been playing for a couple of years. After the match he said to me, 'You know how to defend yourself. Well done'.

"For his testimonial, I arrived in Béziers and was greeted warmly by all the local players. It still gives me goose bumps that players of that stature welcomed me into the sport. I had to find my place among these hard, physical players, but I felt they had accepted me. To be alongside players like Armand was a huge source of pride for me."

Thunderbolt

I asked Elie what he was like off the pitch:

"Outside of rugby, he was a thunderbolt. He played and partied hard, and would have won a lot more caps for France if he had been more focused on his rugby! He would go out anywhere, at any time, and he would be out and away for days, sometimes weeks at a time. He always burned the candle at both ends, but that was him. He loved life. We all still miss him greatly."

"He married his second wife, Laurence, in 1982. She was of American origin and had a house in Mexico so they would spend time there before he finished playing. He would fish, sometimes catching 300kg of fish a day and sell them to the local restaurants. After he'd retired from the game in 1984/5, they lived there for a while. He timed things well because the Football World Cup took place in Mexico in 1986 and he celebrated with the French football team who reached the semi-finals! He returned to live in Béziers in around 1990 as Mum and Dad were getting old. They had sold Le Mondial in 1988."

Armand was a man of many projects. When he returned to Béziers, he enjoyed all the *férias*, opened a fish

Armand and teammates, 13th May 1974.
Photo - Presse Sports.

restaurant, Lobo de Mar, in the Costa Brava in Spain with an old school friend, and then a bar called Le Cardiff, a symbol of his admiration for Wales while he was playing. However, Armand always needed to be on the move so he was rarely at either. He had to discover other places and people. He was a man of *liberté*.

Several of the players told me about the night outs with Armand:

Jeff Imbernon remembers the nights out in the USA:
"In 1976, we were on a tour to the USA, staying in New York. We ate in a French restaurant somewhere and returned to the hotel. I was sharing a room with Michel (Palmié) when there was a knock at the door. Armand was standing there smiling, telling me he was going to Harlem in the Bronx and asking me whether we wanted to go. It was 1am in the morning! He had on him a fistful of dollars and his watch. He returned the next day with neither, but he'd had a great time and made some new friends.

"Nothing frightened him. The greater the danger, the more he liked it, the more fun he had. He lived life on the edge."

At the time, Le Mondial Café was one of the centres of rugby in Béziers. It was owned by Pierre Danos (former French and Béziers scrum-half who played in the 1950s and '60s) from 1956, before being bought by Armand's parents in 1972 who ran it until 1988. The club's HQ was on the first floor. On the face of it, these are ordinary, nondescript places, but below the surface, they are steeped in history. You can imagine all the great players and stories and moments of friendship that took place

there. Le Mondial reminded me of places like Le Trinquet in Espelette, which Pierre Dospital owned, or Le Café des Amis in Agen where Ferrasse and Basquet would play cards, or Le Bar de Jean Dauger in la rue du 49ème in Bayonne, which served as Bayonne's HQ for a while. They were an integral part of life for the players, club and local community. They and rugby were part of the 'code of life' that Jean-Pierre Rives spoke to me about.

Elie elaborated:

"Our parents managed it and were friends with everyone. They had huge hearts and it was a lovely environment. They were always so kind to everyone and never let us leave hungry."

Jean-Pierre Garuet told me:

"Le Mondial was such a warm, friendly place to visit. Armand was friends with everyone, and everyone called his mum 'La Mama'."

Armand could also be very funny on the pitch. I spent a couple of days with Diego Minarro talking about the great Béziers team back then, and he remembers Armand fondly:

"Once, we were playing a Romanian team at Sauclières and it was so violent that they stopped playing and started to walk off. Armand was captain that day and shouted to them, 'You can't leave. It's the féria and we're going partying together afterwards'.

"He would love the féria season. He would go away to watch one and we'd not see him for three weeks."

The Rock Star

Armand died about midday on 10th July 1993 in an obscure bar called Le Café des Amis in the centre of

> "Once, we were playing a Romanian team at Sauclières and it was so violent that they stopped playing and started to walk off. Armand was captain that day and shouted to them, 'You can't leave. It's the *féria* and we're going partying together afterwards'."

Jeff Imbernon told me:

"Armand and I first met when we were eleven years' old when Prades played Béziers. I was his 'témoin de marriage'. If he did kill himself, I can't believe he did so deliberately. He loved life too much. Perhaps the bullets weren't meant to be in the gun when he fired it. We will never know.

"Some would say that he had a dissolute life but he was just restless. He needed to move around, make new friends and see new places."

Jean-Pierre Garuet told me:

"As you can imagine, there must have been two thousand people at his funeral. His mother spotted me and asked me to join the family. She wanted me to see him before the coffin was closed. "

Béziers, in the same *quartier* where the boys had grown up. To some, his death is mysterious even if the official thesis remains that he killed himself playing Russian roulette.

Elie told me:

"I was one of first to arrive. It was a nightmare. I saw him lying there on the floor, dressed in white like an angel. He had his big chain around his neck. It hurts me too much to speak about it."

Over the years, the drama has been told, re-told and no doubt embellished. Based on quotes and newspaper reports, you would think everyone who lived in Béziers was in that small bar when it happened. They all have their own story.

There were rumours about Armand's life at the time, the sort of things you would associate more with a rock star

- sex, drugs, rock and roll, and raucous all-night partying – which seem quite normal because he had (and still has) the status of a rock star.

Then there are the conspiracy theories that raise a number of questions about the circumstances surrounding his death and its build up: a mysterious *légionnaire* who was in the bar when he died, Armand's friends from the underworld in cities such as Toulon and Marseilles, the fact that he was left-handed but the bullet hole was on the right side, why he always carried a gun in his car, and how he allegedly tapped the gun on the bar at Le Café des Amis first to empty the barrel. One bullet didn't fall out - the one that accidentally killed him.

Elie said to me, *"I don't want to know all the stories and rumours and bullshit. I want to remember the good things."*

The wound is still very deep and on the surface.

Romantic End

There are athletes, musicians and artists who remain eternal in people's hearts, and Armand Vaquerin is one of them. It is easy to see why he has such a cult status. He was a towering monument of generosity, friendship and humanity, a free spirit and artist, all of which he forged both on and off the pitch.

Other than perhaps Jean-Pierre Rives (for very different reasons), I can't think of another rugby player who approaches his standing.

Armand was the sort of player and character who

couldn't exist today in professional rugby. His lifestyle was based on the game being amateur and the freedoms that it afforded the players.

But let me be clear: it wasn't the drama of 10th July 1993 that created the legend. He was already one because of what he had achieved long before he died. This was the era of the *hégémonie Biterroise* and Armand was right at its heart.

I would have loved to party with Armand for a month, right across France, preferably during the *férias* and taking in Mexico too. I don't know if I could have lasted but I would have made a good attempt. I will never know. This is one fantasy on my list of 'Things To Do Before I Die' that will never come true. Perhaps I can choose a stand-in such as Vincent Moscato or Christian Califano...?

Beyond his extraordinary rugby career, it was his appetite for life that I admire. He knew it was great to be alive and he was going to make the most of it. When I look at his life through my Béziers *bleu-et-rouge*-tinted spectacles, his death had to be accidental, surely.

Like other rock stars, his end was tragic and romantic, but the legend lives on.

'Live fast, die young' seems a fitting motto for him.

"In 1987 in Australia during the Rugby World Cup, Armand arrived by boat from Mexico with his wife Laurence. He came as a rugby fan and supporter of all his mates in the French team. After we had won the semi-final, I remember that we partied very hard in Kings Cross in Sydney – mainly booze and clubs, and trying to speak to the locals! He made new friends everywhere he went. He always had a wodge of cash on him to help oil the evening. That evening, I had to leave him because I had a World Cup Final to play a few days later, and I knew that with Armand you could be out partying for days."
Jean-Pierre Garuet

"Another time, he came to watch France play Scotland at Le Parc. His pocket was bulging with a load of 500 FF notes. We used to call them 'pascals'! He looked at me with a glint in his eye and said, 'On va s'amuser ce soir'.

"We did our first tour together to Argentina in 1974. Armand, Iraçabal and I were the props. He was a super player – very technical and fast. He was quite straight on the pitch, but would punch and take punches. If you cheated, he would look at you and say, 'Punition'. You didn't want him to say that to you because if he did, you were f**ked for the rest of the game, always looking over your shoulder, more focused on protecting yourself than thinking about the match."
Pierre Dospital

"Back in the 1980s, Elie, Armand, my brother and I went on a Club Med holiday to Kamarina in Sicily. After three days, Armand still hadn't been to his room. His bag was on the floor next to the bar! He was so sociable, lively, loving and generous that he preferred partying to sleeping!"
Laurent Pardo

Loved & Lost II

As I wandered decadently around France indulging myself and my passions, there were nonetheless some very poignant moments that affected me deeply and tested my emotional mettle. As you can read in the chapter 'Loved and Lost I', as well as some other player articles, not every interview involved food, wine and laughter; some touched the trauma of the past, a past that is always there, as T.S Elliot reminds us in Burnt Norton.

Time present and time past
Are both perhaps present in time future
And time future contained in time past
If all time is eternally present
All time is unredeemable.

When I was planning the book, I was in two minds whether to visit *les familles* Paparemborde, Lacans, Fouroux and Vaquerin who had suffered so much. I know from personal experience that when you dig into the past, you risk reopening old wounds. However, I didn't over think it. I believed that their inclusion in the pantheon of great players would bestow far more joy than pain, which was certainly the case. I trusted my sensitivity to manage the topics with delicacy and tact.

Even if they and I both felt some pain, sometimes it's good to reminisce and cry. It sharpens the senses and lets us remember how lucky we are to be here. That may be a cliché but the humdrum activity and challenges of daily life can make us forget to do exactly that.

Loved and Lost II is a collection of thoughts and moments about losing loved ones that I left out of the player articles – sometimes due to space constraints or because they didn't quite fit, usually where it would have come across as self-indulgent, more about my personal circumstances than the players'. However, injecting some personal history into some of the player articles can enhance the story. For example, when I discuss William in the article on Pierre Lacans, it is because I want the reader to think 'only someone who has actually suffered the pain of losing a child (or in our case thinking we had lost one) could write that'. I want to convey my most profound emotions and make the reader really feel my empathy for Maryse, not just experience an abstraction.

Death

Beyond the obvious emotion of heartbreak, it is the brutality of nature (or fate, if you believe in that) that hits me when someone so young or in his or her prime dies naturally. Death is nature's way of eliminating the unlucky in its cruel and unemotional way. As nature coldly imposes itself, our world falls apart, while beyond our circle of friends and family, everyone else carries on as though nothing has happened, or near enough. Those suffering are caught between nature's law of natural selection and the world's ignorance. Nature waits for no one, and the world, oblivious to our suffering, has no time to stop and empathise.

I felt all these emotions when I went to the burial of my great friend's sixth-month-old son, Férreol, who had died from cot death in June 2006. Jean and Charlotte Courcelle-Labrousse had five children and Férreol was their fourth. As I travelled first to Paris for the funeral and then onto Culan, near Montluçon, to the family church for the burial, I fixated on the cruelty and chilling banality of his death. Férreol's beautiful young life had been expunged before he was six months old for heaven's sake. The impact of his death was devastating but the process so matter-of-fact. I wanted the whole world to stop what it was doing and mourn for Jean, Charlotte, Paul, Eugénie, Laetitia and all the family. Stanislas, their fifth child, was born in 2008.

Jean had already lost his brother and sister, Xavier and Florence, in a car accident on Christmas day 1986, brutally taken in their youth. When we buried Férreol under the bright blue skies in June 2006, he was leaving us for the same grave as his auntie and uncle. I watched Jean and Charlotte and Jean's parents, M-C and Philippe, suffer so terribly as the tomb stone was pulled back to receive Férreol. It was a moment of unfathomable pain and grief. I felt again those crippling feelings that Jo and I had experienced six years earlier when William was on his death bed.

All this reminds me about the precariousness of life, how at any moment our sunny lives can be turned upside down by nature's natural selection or plain bad luck, as was the case for Xavier, Florence, Pierre and Armand. Whenever I am preoccupied by some relatively petty issue in life or work or whatever, I remind myself of Xavier, Florence, Férreol, Dad and William. I now add to that list: Pierre Lacans, Jacques Fouroux, Robert Paparemborde and Armand Vaquerin.

When my great friend, Julian, says to me in a moment of lightness, "Dave, your relentless positivity is your least redeeming feature," I think this is why I am who I am, *mon ami*!

My parents, Michael and Jill Beresford on their wedding day, at Batheaston Church near Bath, 2nd September 1961.

Mum

During my interview with Jean-Baptiste Fouroux, he understandably became animated and emotional as he spoke about his late father, Jacques. Losing a father takes its toll. We spoke a little about life without them and how it affects you.

As I too lost my Dad young, I have profound empathy for him because such a loss can incite intense emotions at times – in my case, vague and painful memories, and an indelible image and scar on your memory at the moment of death. Dad's death is constantly on my mind, sometimes in the background, regularly in the foreground, even after all these years.

However, for me, the effect of losing my father is to forge an unbreakable bond with my mother, the person who has subjugated her whole life and happiness to me and my siblings. However, it isn't only her devotion to us that matters. It is also because she represents the umbilical cord to our father, the person who knew him better than anyone, save his own parents. Our Mum is his photographic archive. She is the only person alive who can recount, first hand, the stories and memories. As she grows old and approaches her twilight, it feels like our love for her gets stronger, if that's possible, or maybe we just think far more about life without her. We fear losing her not just for her passing, but because it will be like reliving Dad's death all over again. With her death, her photographic archive of him will die too.

The thing about nature is that it operates in perfect equilibrium. A death hurts exactly as much as it's worth. If it weren't important, it wouldn't be important. Perversely, the pain isn't pointless because it sharpens the colour and taste of memory. Of course, you have to find ways of using the pain as a source of strength and motivation, like Pierre Dospital did when he lost his seven-year-old son.

I asked Jean-Baptiste about his mum and whether she had met anyone else.

"Mum always said that no one else would ever equal Dad."

My own mother has never said that to me or my siblings but I know that is how she feels too. The unspoken is sometimes so obvious.

As it was our first meeting, it didn't feel quite right to delve deeper with Jean-Baptiste. Perhaps next time. I often wonder whether other children who lost a father so young feel the same way as me or are these just my own demons at work.

Dad

Dad died sitting next to me while drinking a cup of tea, one grey Monday in September 1972 when I was five years old. A heart attack killed him instantly, a man of thirty-four struck down in his prime. Another example of nature's brutality.

My siblings, Clare (age five) and Paul (age seven), were there too, and Mum was in the kitchen. I can remember the scene so vividly, as though it happened yesterday – the image of Dad slumped on the table, the colours, the smell, the voices, the crying, the look of fear in Mum's eyes.

His death has impacted me in different ways all through my life. Based on my own self-analysis, I have developed many idiosyncrasies – my struggle with male authority, my self-reliance, my fear of failure, my admiration for life's 'street fighters' who have suffered and come out the other side, my contempt for whingers, my disdain for those obsessed with style over substance, my positivity, my need for love and physical touch… Maybe these would have existed anyway, but I associate them all with Dad's death, probably because I feel it justifies them all!

We all grieve differently and in character. The day after Dad's death, I recall asking Mum if I could go to school the next day wearing all white. Weird. It was several months after Wimbledon had finished so I have no idea what inspired me! I took anything my father owned (cameras and photos in particular) from my mother's bedroom and hid it in mine. I wanted to gather every hint of evidence that he had left behind. I needed his photographic archives.

After he died, Mum struggled to talk much about Dad to me, Paul or Clare, such was her suffering. Nan did though, and I loved the stories and photos and memories. I relished and still relish hearing the slightest new thing about him – any unreported memory, flashback or anecdote.

Nan would also talk about Paul's 'sad eyes' in every photo of him for the following few years, until the pain had subsided and he could see the future again. When I met Elie Vaquerin, I recognised his sad eyes because they reminded me of Paul's. The eyes give everything away.

Mother and Daughter:
Valérie and Elsa Paparemborde

When I met Valérie, I loved her stoicism and positivity, and how she interacted with her daughter, Elsa, on the telephone. Valérie said to me about Elsa at the time of Robert's death:

"She was thirteen and was away on holiday staying with Ken Kennedy and his family. When she came back, he had died. She could have crumbled but she was so strong. She has such a strong will and determination to succeed, which she inherited from Robert."

Losing a father had an impact on me at five years old but I felt it much more in my later years, at key moments in my life such as my twenty-first birthday, my university selection, my graduation, our wedding day, the birth of our children. I can't imagine what it is like for a thirteen-year-old. I have never met Elsa but I wanted to give you an extract of what she said at her father's funeral, as reported by Jacques Verdier in the Midi Olympique on 23rd April 2001:

"How do you measure the importance of a man if not, perhaps, by the memory he leaves? 'He was Patou to you, he was Papa to me,' said Elsa, magnificent in her pain, her striking resemblance to her Patou de papa, in a moving moment that was extraordinarily strong and left the audience reeling, distraught, grieving."

What powerful words from a thirteen-year-old. The scene was beautifully captured by Jacques.

Brothers:
Guy and André Boniface

The name Guy Boniface is etched onto the mind of many rugby fans, in France and elsewhere. Along with his brother, André, he was a magical player, *un petit prince*, whose pace and dancing feet brought both fear and joy on the pitch, depending on your national persuasion.

Terrible misfortune took the life of Guy Boniface in a car accident at Saint-Sever, 30km from Montfort-en-Chalosse on 1st January 1968.

I met his brother, André, in Hossegor March 2018 to find out more about Guy, as well as capture his memories of playing rugby back in the 1960s when he was at his peak. André and Guy were the epitome of French flair and are still revered by the former players I met.

"Mum and Dad never played sport although Dad was fit and athletic-looking. They bought a house in Montfort-en-Chalosse right next to the rugby stadium and we could see the posts from it. Mum only had to walk 40m but she never went! After we had played at different stadia around the world, I said to her, 'Go and see the pitch. It's the same in Cape Town, Auckland, Buenos Aries, Sydney, Twickenham, Cardiff, Edinburgh…it's the same size everywhere and there are fifteen players on each side who play on it!' She never went. She never saw us play other than occasionally on TV.

"Guy and I also had a little brother but he died when he was five months old for no apparent reason. There were two years between us all. We were very sad. Guy and

I always said that he would have been a fabulous full-back. Dad never saw his third son because he was a POW in Germany and only got out in time for the burial.

"Mum would cry a lot but she was so proud of us. She had a few lovely friends in the village who supported her. Mum and Dad died in around 1983.

"Our wonderful Grandad lived nearby in Mugron. He never saw us play either and knew nothing about rugby. He would go to the local café called Chez Nenette managed by a lady who had large breasts. He would sit at the bar and watch her! She would say to him, 'Don't you want to watch your grandkids playing on the TV (which was on behind her)?' He would reply, 'No, I'm going to see them at the house later'. He was very funny and Guy was the same. Both were free spirits.

"I was lucky enough to have played with players as brilliant as Guy and Jean Dauger. I played with Jean against Cliff Morgan in Dax in one of Jean's last games. I was only seventeen, and I had the impression that I didn't do much that day because Jean made things easy for me – his movement and timing of the pass. He could beat a player without the ball, something which the public wouldn't necessarily see. He was the greatest player I ever knew. After he finished playing, he would travel up from Bayonne on Sundays to watch Guy and me play at Stade Montois.

"I was faster than Guy because I did a lot of athletics. Guy feared nothing. He was so dedicated, courageous and impressive physically. When he had the car accident, his insides were all smashed up. The doctor who operated on him said he had phenomenal abdominal muscles.

"Guy's death has never left us. We would sleep in the same bedroom and bed sometimes. In New Zealand, we asked for a double bed, we didn't want two singles! Guy had no kids, which I regretted, but then thought it was better that way after he died. We were brought up in a loving family environment, and had great fun playing with all the kids of the village.

"He was killed driving back from a game. None of us would normally return by car. He wasn't the driver. The driver was a team mate of ours who survived and was obviously very sad. We have never resented him. He is a nice guy. I said to him, 'Go and live your life'.

"Part of me is still very sad. I have never fully recovered from Guy's death but I manage on my own, especially in Montfort where I feel best. You can see the stadium when you arrive in the village, which evokes lots of happy memories for me. Both my brothers are buried there in the cemetery. I try to mow the lawn around their graves regularly. If I don't go for a while, I miss it. I often do a tour of the village to see where we lived, the rugby pitch, where we played, and so on.

"We were a very close family in spite of the sadness that we experienced. Guy and I shared everything, the good and bad moments. His death has never left us."

André is a warm, generous man whose suffering is still palpable. He spoke with great pride and emotion.

"Our wonderful Grandad lived nearby and would go to the local café managed by a lady who had large breasts. He would sit at the bar and watch her! She would say, 'Don't you want to watch your grandkids playing on the TV ?' He would reply, 'No, I'm going to see them at the house later'. He was very funny and Guy was the same."

Paris

"CARNIVAL
THE WHEELS FLY AND THE COLOURS SPIN
THROUGH ALCOHOL
RED WINE THAT PUNCTURES THE SKIN
FACE TO FACE
IN A DRY AND WATER LESS PLACE"

U2, UNFORGETTABLE FIRE, 1982

C ulturally, Paris can seem a million miles away from the rugby-loving south where the sport's roots are so deep. However, Paris is the home of the great Parc des Princes that is so synonymous with French flair and the icons of that 1980's team. Back then, Racing Club de France was the dominant force here, a sporting club known for its exclusiveness and traditions, and therefore more British in its character than the clubs of the south that were deeply rooted in the land and *terroir*.

I was based for two unforgettable years in Paris in the early 1990s straight after university, working for Andersen Consulting, a management consultancy, which wasn't a bad way to help transition me from a testosterone-driven and casual university student to (semi) serious professional. But it was one helluva ride – the intellectually challenging work, 100% immersion in professional (not colloquial) French, weekends away to the mountains, sea and countryside, exquisite food and wine, nights out to bars and clubs, Sundays spent chilling and recovering in those old-school Parisian cafés, the sport, museums and culture in this princely City of Light.

I have many happy memories of my time there so I will tell you a rugby-related one.

Parisian oyster bar. *Photo - David Beresford.*

France played the Springboks twice in October 1992, a team they hadn't officially played since 1980 because of the South Africans' sporting isolation. The Springboks won the first test in Lyon and the French won the second at Le Parc des Princes winning 29-16.

I remember the second test because I was there. I don't remember much about the game itself, but I do recall my eventful journey to the ground, on the back of my friend Dave Anderton's moped, bereft of a helmet and trying to cover up the offence by using a large hood and an even larger parka coat emblazoned with 'Albertville 1992', a souvenir from when I had worked at the winter Olympics earlier that year. We were travelling at c40 kph along one of the Boulevards near the Parc, when I spotted some Police on the other side of the road. 'Bollocks', I thought, especially as we had spent the previous three hours 'warming up' at Willi's Wine bar, my favourite Parisian watering hole.

I put my head down and hoped for the best. After a few seconds, I felt someone tap me on the shoulder in mid-transit, namely the aforesaid policeman, who gestured for us to stop. For a split second and in an alcohol-induced frenzy of bravado, I fancied our chances of a getaway but it was a fleeting impulse. We got off and feared the worst, but I quickly spotted his strong *accent du midi*, the sound of rugby-loving southern France. 'There is a God,' I thought. I explained who we were and that our destination was the rugby at the Parc to watch the reintegration of that great rugby nation, South Africa. He smiled and we got chatting about the match, players, South Africa and his own team, Auch. After a

minute or two, he wished us well and we were on our way. How I love France, I reflected.

Incidentally, Willi's wine bar can be found at 13 Rue des Petits Champs in the heart of the 2nd *arrondissement*, a *mélange* of regal architecture, Parisian arts, shabby-chic restaurants and irresistible watering holes. I must have eaten and drunk and got drunk at Willi's dozens of times during 1992. It has become an institution and destination restaurant over the last thirty years but it was very much a neighbourhood restaurant back then.

At the time, its wine focus was on Rhône styles such as Côte Rôtie, Hermitage and Châteauneuf-du-Pape, and McLaren Vale and Barossa Valley in Australia. For French restaurants, that was quite pioneering back then.

I loved it. I would turn up with ten or so friends without any reservation and George, the Manager, would always find a solution. Then we would head to Les Bains Douches, a veritable den of iniquity on the Rue du Bourg-l'Abbé in the 3rd *arrondissement* and frequented by the beautiful Parisians. We fitted in perfectly!

Paris has changed hugely since the early 1990s but it's the memories that are so powerful during my formative years there. These days, I don't so much visit it as wistfully revisit it, hoping to re-discover the past.

Denis Charvet

PARIS

"YOU CAN'T IMAGINE TO WHAT DEGREE A PLAYER NEEDS CONFIDENCE, WHOEVER IT IS. WHERE IS HE GOING TO FIND IT? THE COACH. PIERRE, WOULD GIVE ME THAT LAST PIECE OF INSPIRATION BEFORE WE WENT ONTO THE PITCH."

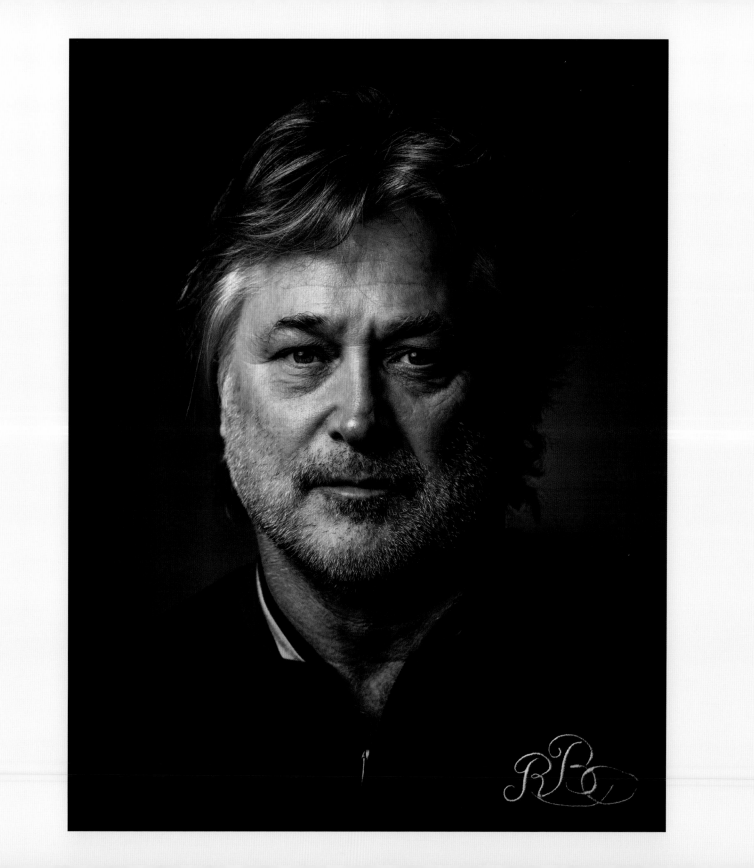

BORN : 12TH MAY 1962

CLUBS : STADE TOULOUSAIN, RACING CLUB DE FRANCE

INTERNATIONAL CAPS : 23

POSITION : CENTRE, WING

GRAND SLAMS : 1987

NICKNAME : LAFLEUR

NOM DE GUERRE : RUGBY'S 007

MY VISIT TO MEET HIM : TUESDAY 23RD JANUARY 2018
AND WEDNESDAY 18TH APRIL 2018

Denis was a player of eye-catching beauty. At first, you noticed the square jaw, floppy hair and dark skin, looks that would have been well-suited to the cat walk or a James Bond movie. Then, you noticed the sportsman. He was a supremely talented player, creator, finisher and stepper, with pace to burn and a turbocharged outside swerve.

In particular, I will never forget one try scored for ST v Toulon in the 1989 French Championship Final. Receiving the ball from Didier Codorniou in his 22m, he sliced instinctively through the gap and ran a devastating arc to the right-hand corner to score. It was a breath-taking moment of sporting glory and an exquisite example of Denis' talent, vision, pace and opportunism. Like Gareth Edward's great Barbarians try in 1973, I have watched it a thousand times and it still triggers an adrenalin rush.

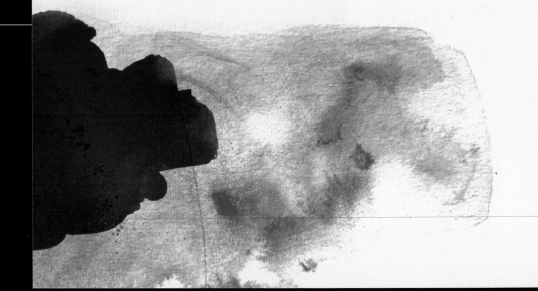

When writing about the French centres, I should declare my bias. I was a centre of average ability so I worshipped at the *crampons* of my chosen quartet – Denis, Philippe Sella, Érik Bonneval and Didier Codorniou. Writing impartially about any of them is impossible so, as Editor-in-Chief, please forgive the romance, nostalgia and adulation that permeate their articles.

It wasn't just Denis' playing ability that fascinated me though. Here was a man who has seen the world from every opposing angle – the free style expression of Villepreux v the pragmatism of Fouroux, the cruising belligerence of Sella v the subtlety of Codorniou, the backwater of Cahors v the megacity of Paris, the glory and celebrity of professional sport v the grieving and obscurity of his real world.

Denis had to fight off some demons, just like most of us have to.

I tracked him down via Serge who called him over our three-hour lunch in Hendaye. He went through to his voicemail and left him a message that went something like this:

"Denis, it's Serge... I am going to give your number to an Englishman. It's odd because he's actually a good bloke... He played the same position as you, however, while you can still be taken for a centre, he definitely can't... Lots of love."

The path was clear and Denis called me back a few days later when I was in *La Ville Rose*, his former home town of Toulouse where he achieved so much on the rugby field.

We arranged to meet a few weeks later for breakfast at the iconic Brasseie Lipp on Boulevard Saint-Germain in Paris.

I arrived early amid a bustling service and grabbed a table upstairs. Denis had called me a few days before to say that Bernard Laporte would be joining us, someone I hadn't seen since 1988 when I lived in Bordeaux.

Back then, I was playing for the BEC and Bernard was playing at Bègles. Both were good teams, but mine was primarily full of charlatans and drunk students while his was full of semi-pro players with a mindset to match. They were on the climb and would win the French Championship in 1991 with players such as Laporte, Moscato, Simon, Gimbert, Conchy, Courtiols, Alibert, Téchoueyres and Sallefranque, most of whom were unheard of in 1988. We had a friend-in-common who arranged the lunch and said to me, *"Come and meet two friends who play for Bègles. They are called Bernard Laporte and Vincent Moscato. Vincent is highly rated and destined to play for France. He's a hard bastard and brilliant player."*

My sketchy mind (oh, the ravages of time) can recall a few images and memories. First, Bernard looked the same then as he does now – an atypical rugby player, his small head and Harry Potter glasses giving him a slightly nerdy look. I've always loved his fluent speech, lifted by his choral, southern French accent. As a coach, I know he tried to emulate Jacques Fouroux with his eloquence, charisma and emotive language. Vincent was stocky with an impressive cranial ridge. He had bumps and bruises all around his cheeks, forehead and eyes. He ordered steak

and chips, which he seemingly devoured in seconds, and his face was covered in perspiration. It was a lunch to remember and helped me cement my conviction that I had found something I could really excel in – the art of lunching and chit-chat.

The Young Upstart

Back to the meeting in Paris. Bernard didn't stay long as he had a few burning challenges to resolve at the FFR, namely how to rekindle both the romance and success of the *Les Tricolores*, the very theme of this book.

I asked Denis to tell me about his upbringing in Cahors and his rise to the top.

" Rugby was always part of my life. My uncle, André Melet, was champion of France in 1947 playing for ST against Agen. Both Albert Ferrasse and Guy Basquet, the two key men at the FFR for so many years, played for Agen in that final. André then played rugby league professionally for Montpellier."

This final became infamous because Guy Basquet of Agen was sent off for kicking a player. However, the Agenais complained so vociferously that the then President of the FFR, Monsieur Eluère, left his seat in the stand to intervene and resolve the matter. It was agreed that Basquet would leave the pitch but could return for the second half! The Ferrasse-Basquet axis was influential with the FFR even back then, some twenty years before Albert himself became the President of the FFR.

> "I loved football too, but I felt it was my destiny to play rugby. It was in my blood and I was born a competitor."

"I joined Stade Toulousain in 1983, the same year as Érik Bonneval. Jean-Pierre Rives had already left for Paris but he took me to a British Barbarians match against Major Stanley's XV in Oxford November 1985. I had played a couple of games for France against Japan and toured Argentina but I wasn't yet capped or well known.

"Jean-Pierre told them he had brought a young upstart along. Willie John McBride, Ian Milne and Andy Ripley were all in the changing rooms having a beer before the game. I thought 'what is all this?' Luckily, I had a great game. The next day, The Times' headline for the match read, "Who is Charvet?"

"Jean-Pierre was another of my idols when I was young. He took me under his wing and made me his apprentice.

"Cahors was and still is my 'club de coeur' so when I played for the first team, I thought I had reached the summit. I never intended to sign for Stade Toulousain. While I was at university there, I was contacted by Narbonne and Brive. Didier Codorniou, one of my idols, was playing for Narbonne then but when I went to see them, Didier wasn't there. If he'd been there, I would have signed. I came back to Toulouse and met Pierre Villepreux, another great man.

"Pierre had never seen me play. I met him after a university match and he invited me to play with some of the youngsters. It was France who made me sign for them, but they already had some great players in the centre such as Salsé and Melos! I had to be mad to sign but I was a determined young man. I feared nothing. I was 'un enfant de balle', born into the trade. It was never about money.

It was about the game and the ball and the friendships. I was so passionate.

"Pierre is the 'éminence grise' and his brand of rugby mirrors how I wanted to play the game. It is very utopian. He taught me so much. I was a rough diamond and he polished everything. He also understood that you had to enjoy yourself. He was the greatest coach I ever had. It was a magic time. You can't put a price on that.

"He really thought deeply about how to play the game and he communicated those ideas so effectively. I loved the way he and Jean-Claude Skrela thought about space, contact and player responsibility. He coined this term 'intelligence situationelle'. The idea was and still is that a player can find himself anywhere on the field and he needs to adapt to the situation. It requires more thought and a good understanding of the game, i.e. intelligence. You also need a strong defence that is capable of recovering the ball. The difficulty is, once you have the ball, you have to make the right choices. Back then, we had that ability at ST and in the national team. It is what the English call French flair.

"He is a fabulous teacher. When I played, his 'discours sur le jeu' was so informative, constructive and sometimes revolutionary. It didn't always work so you had to be pragmatic. We couldn't dream all the time. He gave me freedom, encouraged me to take responsibility, to enjoy myself and be audacious. He wasn't just saying it, he really believed it. It can only work if someone tells you that with conviction, then it is credible and you feel supported.

"Jean-Pierre told them he had brought a young upstart along. Willie John McBride, Ian Milne and Andy Ripley were all in the changing rooms having a beer before the game. I thought 'what is all this?' Luckily, I had a great game. The next day, The Times' headline for the match read, 'Who is Charvet?'"

"You can't imagine to what degree a player needs confidence, whoever it is. Where is he going to find it? The coach. Pierre would give me that last piece of inspiration before I went onto the pitch.

"He always kept his distance between player and coach believing you couldn't be mates. You can love them without being friends with them.

"My misfortune was that he wasn't coach in 1991, I would have had many more caps, maybe a hundred! Perhaps, I would have played another four years with Philippe. It's not a regret, it's life.

"Jean-Claude Skrela was also fabulous. He and Pierre were extremely complementary. He was gentle and understanding. He had great love and empathy for the club and players. I was living a dream. I would ask myself 'did that really happen?'"

How did Pierre's philosophy compare to Jacques'?

"Jacques was a bit of a paradox. He loved the game so passionately and he loved beautiful rugby, but he enclosed himself in a different philosophy. The press couldn't always reconcile their desire to see flair with Jacques' desire to win, and to do that you had to be pragmatic. Of course, the narrative that we were all brawn and no flair was nonsense. We had power up front and flair behind, but we were also pragmatic and could win difficult games, as Jacques' track record shows.

"He was so animated by the game. I loved him, even though he was hard with me. He gave me the greatest human gift once at Rob Paparemborde's golf day. We sat down, just us two, and he said, 'I was hard with you and I regret it'. I said, 'It isn't the number of selections that I miss. It is the memories that I couldn't share with you."

The Mozart of Rugby

Denis had the fortune of playing with some of France's greatest centres including Didier Codorniou and Philippe Sella. I wanted to know how they compared.

"Codor was my idol but I effectively took his place in the team because of Jacques' selection.

"When Codor came to ST, it was the greatest rugby time of my life. I lived a real dream. I was playing with the player I wanted to be. He was the best player

I ever played with. He had everything - the innate sense of the game, vision, anticipation, technique. He was a magician. Yes, when you take everything into account, he was the strongest. CODOR!

"He was the Mozart of rugby."

But how did Sella compare?

"If you are talking about the understanding of the game, Codor was stronger but I adored playing with Philippe too. There was an alchemy that was fabulous.

"Comparing Sella and Codor is so hard because they played a different form of rugby. It is delicate to compare!

"You are drawn to a player like Codor when you are young and so passionate about the game. He was Le Petit Prince. I loved his philosophy - his intelligence, wisdom, generosity,

understanding of space, exquisite passing, love of the game, our complementarity. For three years together, he really helped me develop. My regret is that he could have stayed longer at ST. I really progressed with him and he took me to a higher level."

As Denis spoke, I felt I was asking him the impossible. These were two players for whom he has such fondness. It was like asking someone to choose their favourite child. He loves them both equally and appreciates them for their different skills.

Dreamland

I asked him to describe the feeling he had after he scored his wonderful try at the French Championship final in 1989 against Toulon.

"When studying the video footage of Toulon in the weeks before, Villepreux noticed that they positioned themselves badly when we were in our 22m. He said to us, 'Don't hesitate to play it'. Codor passed and I took the gap and sprinted to the corner. Gallion and Melville were chasing me but I was flying.

"When I scored, the whole ground stood up and cheered, whether you were supporting ST or Toulon.

"I jumped over the barriers, put my hands together and looked up at the sky, as though I was praying, even though I am not religious. I thought 'what have you done to me?' For a few seconds afterwards, I felt my spirit leave me.

"It was like someone had given me this mission, that it was my destiny."

It was the day to do it, the biggest club match of the year, a few months after Jacques had dropped me and with the New Zealand tour coming up.

"When I ran back to my own half for the restart, and in the changing rooms afterwards, I felt a bit embarrassed. It was a very curious feeling. I can't really explain it.

"The Toulon fans still talk to me about that try today. They forget that I scored three tries in the final in 1985!"

From Toulouse to Paris

Denis had a stellar career with ST but in 1990 he took the decision to move to Paris to play for RCF.

"Jean-Pierre recruited me. He called Patou, the Manager of RCF, and then me. It happened in two telephone calls.

"I had loved my time with ST but I had achieved everything there. I had won the title three times and needed a new challenge. Toulouse is a provincial town, neither big nor small, and I felt hemmed in. I was pampered but I needed to explore and meet

other people, experience another culture. There is a frustration in the provinces of not knowing Paris.

"I knew Paris wouldn't be comfortable but I never regretted it. It was very hard at the start. It took me out of my unreal world into a real one, and I wasn't programmed to deal with it. In Toulouse, everything was done for me. In Paris, I had to discover everything, restructure my life and adapt.

"I had some great friends like Jean-Pierre so I wasn't cut off but it wasn't structured. It was hard but was fantastic in the longer term. I built a new life and I love Paris."

Denis lives near Le Parc des Princes and according to Jean-Pierre, he is now more Parisian than Parisians.

"I have no regrets other than I probably left ST a year too early because there was the Rugby World Cup in 1991 for which I wasn't selected. I would have prepared for it better in Toulouse. I played with some great players at RCF and we had a good season. We should have made the final but we lost in the semi to ST, 13-12!"

Ever the competitor, that rejection in 1991 still prickles him.

"I still hold it against Trillo for not picking me."

Denis' First Death

Denis stopped playing rugby in 1996 and struggled to adapt to normal life afterwards. One of the ways he dealt with this was by writing a book called La Dernière Passe.

When I first met Denis at Brasserie Lipp, I hadn't read the book and was unaware of his suffering when he finished playing. I called him again and we met at the chic Hotel Molitor in Paris' 16th *arrondissement*, appropriately near Le Parc des Princes. We sat on the high tables overlooking the legendary summer pool, its pièce de résistance. Denis arrived looking cool in his white linen shirt and sunglasses.

"Sorry, I'm a few minutes late. I was out with Jean-Pierre last night and we had a late one."

I wanted him to tell me everything about the five years after his rugby career finished.

"In October 1997, when I was thirty-five, I played the last game of my career for the French Barbarians at Lansdowne Road. On that day, I experienced my first death. You know you are going to be replaced but you can't prepare your exit. That only happens when everything stops and things suddenly change.

"People admire a champion when he or she is in the limelight. But afterwards, it is in the look of others that you understand what you have lost. The price is terrible - the loneliness, lack of self-worth, lack of recognition, anonymity.

> "You can't leave a professional sports career unscathed. Anyone who tells you that he or she handled their end of career well is in denial. There are no more changing rooms with their distinctive perfume. You no longer experience the grounds, friends or fame in the same way. The magic that you built your whole life around is no more. There is nothing left."

"No one accompanies you and says 'right, that's over so this is what you must do'. You are left to the world, to its reality, which you have never experienced because you were always wrapped in cotton wool."

Denis was talking like it was a Greek tragedy.

"The page was so heavy to turn that it crushed me. It requires an immense amount of courage to continue along the road to recovery. I suffered and lived very badly for about five years.

"During that time, I was cocooned in this Parisian bubble. I was immersed in this false world of showbiz and booze and nightclubs. Drink became my friend, to help me gloss over reality and deal with my demons.

"Nobody could help me because I couldn't hear anything, I was deaf and blind. When you are weak, you only see people who enjoy you. You open your arms up and say 'take what you want'. These people were willing accomplices during my troubles.

"My real friends didn't like what they saw. This period of my life was pathetic.

"Fortunately, I had some friends who have always been there. Jean-Pierre Rives, Richard Bohringer (actor and my spiritual brother), Serge Kampf (businessman in love with rugby who died in 2016) and my friend Charles Melman, a psychiatrist and one of the greatest people I've met. I had nothing to give them except the misery. And they gave me a lot. I thank my lucky stars that they were there.

"I was given a book, Passeurs de Vie, by Jacques Salomé and it was a revelation. It explains that you have to protect yourself from the people who draw on your energy and give nothing back. I saw a psychoanalyst for three and a half years. Little by little, I came out of the night. There was a tremendous effect of reincarnation, of wanting to be something else. Nothing could stop me anymore.

"I told myself that I had to kill Denis, the former rugby player. I wanted to be respected, to see myself as I am inside, like the little kid who played rugby in the garden

in Cahors, imitating the voice of Roger Couderc. For years, I had lied so much to myself that I did not know myself.

"The psychoanalyst changed the man I was. Bernard Laporte was also part of this process. He helped to drag me back up the hill. With all his energy, he is key to the balance of my life.

"I wrote my book because somewhere I had to exorcise all this. I had to go through a sort of mourning and grieving. My greatest achievement was killing the player I was."

Hearing Denis speak and looking at all the rugby, business and personal successes in his life, it has been some turnaround. He is a superb role model for today's players who are faced with similar challenges.

On a lighter note, I congratulated Denis on his outstanding marketing. I bought his book 'La Dernière Passe' that I read in about two days. It is part autobiography, part fiction, and describes the glory, depression, friendship and love during his life. I enjoyed it so much that I bought his next one called 'La Mort Debout', only to realise it was the same book, renamed! Brilliant. I need to recruit his marketing guru.

Now, he appears regularly on French TV and radio. He loves the radio in particular because it gives him freedom to express himself and he loves working with Vincent Moscato. He is also a Director of the French Barbarians, as well as having various business interests.

"Working with Vincent is great fun. He is a big character and a brilliant, energetic, funny communicator. He knows how to capture people's attention and make them laugh. You just wind him up and let him go, and we follow in his wake."

I spent a good four hours with Denis, and I found him and the topics we covered fascinating. Like some of the other players I met, notably Jean-Pierre Rives and Lolo Pardo, he is everything I love in a person – friendly, open, reflective, romantic, charismatic, charming, funny, vulnerable, independently-minded, opinionated and sensitive, but with a resilient streak running through his character. Laurent Pardo might call him 'The Flower' but this man is no pansy. He has a steely determination and clearly doesn't suffer fools lightly. His confession about his troubles and defects took real courage and is a sign of his strength. It is as much the imperfections in a character that renders him or her attractive because it means they are real, something which Denis spent five tortuous years searching for. He is a wonderfully engaging and strong man, and I loved chatting to him.

We gave each other a big man hug, kissed *à la bise* and he strolled back to his house nearby.

It was time to celebrate this fabulous encounter. Fortunately, and unsurprisingly, I already had a plan. I was travelling in style that day to Reims, Champagne, to meet Will, Alun and Hugh - two Welsh men, two English men, four drinkers - for two days of bubbles and fine dining.

"He had great pace and always wanted to run with it."
Pierre Villepreux

"He is a beautiful man, then and now."
Valerié Paparemborde

"We had to watch Charvet like a hawk. He would just take off with great pace."
Will Carling

"Charvet was classy and silky, a brilliant stepper with quick feet."
Ieuan Evans

Jean-Baptiste Lafond

PARIS

WHEN I MET FRANCK MESNEL,
HE TOLD ME THAT JEAN-BA WAS
UNTRACEABLE, LIKE JASON BOURNE.
LACKING THE RESOURCES OF THE
CIA AND WITH ONLY MY PHONE,
TENACITY AND CHUTZPAH TO RELY
ON, I DIDN'T FANCY MY CHANCES
OF FINDING HIM. HOWEVER,
THAT DAPPER SILVER FOX, LAURENT
PARDO, CAME TO MY RESCUE.

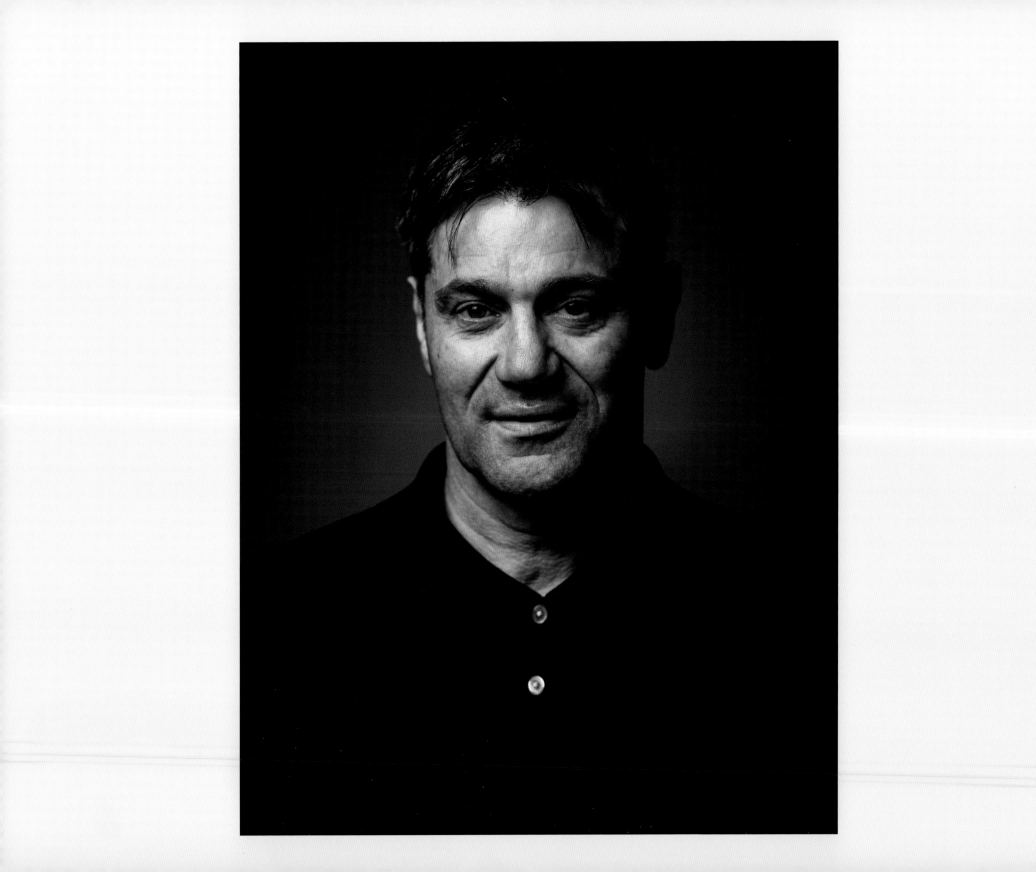

BORN : 29TH DECEMBER 1961

CLUBS : RACING CLUB DE FRANCE

INTERNATIONAL CAPS : 36

POSITION : WING OR FULL-BACK

GRAND SLAMS : 1987

NICKNAME : JEAN-BA

NOM DE GUERRE : THE SMOOTH OPERATOR

MY VISIT TO MEET HIM : WEDNESDAY 18TH APRIL 2018

W hat is it about players from Racing Club de France and their Hollywood looks? There must be a golden gene running through the club, producing players of such grace and class. A player of sublime skill and audacity, scoring tries from his own 22m for fun, Jean-Baptiste stands tall amid that group.

When I met Franck Mesnel, he told me that Jean-Ba was untraceable, like Jason Bourne. Lacking the resources of the CIA and with only my phone, tenacity and chutzpah to rely on, I didn't fancy my chances of finding him. However, that dapper Silver Fox, Laurent Pardo, came to my rescue. Over a lovely bottle of Comtes Lafon's Clos de La Barre at the Maison Eguiazabal in Hendaye, we called Jean-Ba and made a *rendez-vous* in Paris.

Jean-Ba's image is such that I was hoping to meet him in one of those chic boutique hotel bars, like the Hoxton, Lutetia or Molitor. But no, we met at a small, noisy café-bar-restaurant in the 17th *arrondissement* called Le Celtic, on the rue Courcelles. *"This'll do for le rosbif,"* he must have thought.

Freedom

He jumped straight in and was keen to know whom I'd seen so far.

"Have you seen Denis? Did you tell him you were seeing me? I haven't seen him in ages. I'm fifty-six and I am still working hard in the wine trade, unlike Denis. He's a dosser. He was a great mate of Serge Kampf who must have spoilt him, which is understandable. I am a free man. I always have been, beholden to no one."

He was grinning as he said it, deliberately provoking his great mate Denis whom he knew would read this.

"Denis and I were each other's wing-man on tour. We messed around, drank, partied and dated girls together. We had a great time. The players today can't do that sort of thing. There are too many cameras and social media. Professionalism has killed the 3ème mi-temps. We lived through a wonderful era with a lot of freedom. I loved playing rugby with him. We had the same idea of how to play the game and how to celebrate afterwards.

"On tour, we once shared a room at the time he was besotted by Princess Stephanie of Monaco. Every time she called, I had to leave the room. When she didn't call, I'd have to put up with his dejection. He soon forgot all that romantic stuff when we went out partying!"

Jean-Ba was smiling, enjoying the nostalgia. I could immediately hear his free spirit, his predilection for fun and adventure.

> **"Jean-Ba was unmanageable, as a person and player. In rugby, he always wanted to attack from his own try line and play with freedom."**

Franck told me more about what it was like playing with Jean-Ba:

"Jean-Ba was unmanageable, as a person and player. In rugby, he always wanted to attack from his own try line and play with freedom. Robert Paparemborde, understood that he was very talented and that, as team manager, he had two options: 'I either force him into a team structure or I give him freedom to play and build a structure around him'. It was obvious that it had to be the latter. Robert knew that the team had to adapt to the 'mad ones' and that there was no point going against the grain of natural talent. That decision was one of the key factors to the success of the team.

"Training could get heated and Jean-Ba could be so annoying. When we'd play touch, he'd beat you and score, and when passing you on the way back say, 'Take the trailer off and you'll run faster'. You could feel your blood rising! He pricked and provoked in a semi-humorous way, but you knew that he often meant what he said.

"When we did tackle practice, the boot was on the other foot. I would be so angry that I would smash him and cut him in two. Once, a few days before the Scotland game, I broke his shoulder but he never held it against me. He told me that he deserved it.

"He was a brilliant player – elusive, balanced, flowing. He is an artist and 'libre penseur'.

"His brother also played for RCF and we called them 'Les Frères Lumière' because they were always up to mischief and a drama happening. When they were younger, Jean-Ba threw a petanque ball at his brother's head so maybe that explains some of the madness! Jean-Ba was always battling to get his brother in the side on the wing but we already had two great players there in Philippe Guillard and Yves Rousset. It all made for some good battles and arguments."

Jean-Baptiste Lafond, 19th November 1990, Paris. France 12 v New Zealand 30. *Photo - Bob Thomas Sports Photography via Getty Images.*

Size Doesn't Always Matter

We both ordered salad to start, followed by *confit de canard* for me and salad again for Jean-Ba, lubricated with an ice-cold *pression*. It was a simple *formule du jour* but it worked.

There is something very distinct about Jean-Ba, both physically and emotionally. He isn't like the others. First, you have the salt and pepper hair, neatly cut but styled in a showbiz way, coincidently how someone like Matt Damon would. Then there is the tan, perhaps natural for a man with Aquitaine blood running through his veins, but almost certainly deepened due to the time spent on the golf course and tennis court. He was wearing an aging, soft blue-grey blazer with subtle grey stripes and a blue polo shirt, both embroidered with the Eden Park logo. The sartorial elegance is effortless and his clothes hang off him with ease, suggesting he still keeps in shape, and the strong jaw line is still there.

His eyes are brown and, on the day I met him, betray some fatigue, as though he'd been at a fiesta all night, which, based on the testimony of fellow players, was more than possible. I would attribute this to the Gallic casual, though. He speaks calmly and humorously, sometimes straightfacedly, in a style that really struck me. He talks with passion but serenity, without the exaggerated movements and expressions that you would typically see in others, especially those of Latin temperament. His eyes and mouth show no stress, simply delivering his lines in a deadpan way, sometimes accompanied by a smile and a chortle. I'm not the first to say this but he has an enigmatic Mona Lisa smile.

We switched back to the 1980s and the journalists who had a love/hate relationship with the team.

"They would come on the bus and in the changing rooms with us. If you were a replacement, like I often was, they would push you and give you a hard time for not being in the team. On the whole we had a great relationship with them – Denis Lalanne, Jean Cormier, Christian Montagniac, Alain Gex.

"We got on well with the journos on a personal level back then but they would assassinate Jacques and the team. Jacques was the key man to our success."

When I met Christian Montgaignac, the great French sports journalist and writer, he was glowing about Jean-Ba and the times they spent together.

" He is a great friend. He appreciated that he was having the time of his life and he wanted to enjoy it. He is an artist, seducer and comedian with an offbeat sense of humour. He is different but I like him very much. He has a big heart."

I asked what Jacques Fouroux was like. I already had a good insight into his character having met Jacques Junior, also called Jean-Baptiste.

"He was small," he chuckled.

"He was fantastic. He understood every one of us individually and he built a rapport with us. He always said, 'Coaching is great but engaging is better'. He influenced players because he got to know them well, understood what made them tick. He knew that a coach had to be both in front and behind us. When it came to size and physicality, he was ahead of his time. That's why he played the players he did.

"The 1980s were a pivotal decade for rugby, which led to how the game is played today. It was a huge step up from the 1960s and '70s, with the exception of that Grand Slam side in 1977. It really made an impression on him and he knew it was a formula for success. It was Jacques who understood that the powerful forwards were the basis for success and he repeated that approach in the 1980s.

"I loved Jacques because he was great fun, a great motivator and raconteur. He couldn't make his mind up about me as a player though. I would be selected, dropped, selected again, dropped again, replaced and be the replacement. I was the only substitute to be dropped in 1986 after the first test against the All Blacks in Toulouse, which we lost. I think Jacques thought 'let's not mess around, we need big guys'. He wanted to take the preparation very seriously and probably thought that didn't fit my persona."

He's a Lover Not a Fighter

As I travelled around France to meet the players, in response to my question, *"Who are the biggest partygoers?"* I heard the same response every time: Lolo Pardo and Jean-Ba Lafond. Doxpi and Pascal's names would also be cited because of their prowess as *chanteurs*, but Lolo and Jean-Ba were in a different league when it came to gallivanting and mischief-making. Jean-Ba flew to New Zealand towards the end of the RWC in 1987 just to help keep the team's morale up, such was his popularity with the players. He went under the pretext of replacing Érik Bonneval who had injured his knee in the first training session, but Jean-Ba wasn't fit enough to play either.

He saw the tour as one big *fête*. Being well-known to the Kiwi public, no nightclub owner ever made him pay. He could drink and party for free for a few weeks.

"Sophie, encore deux pressions s'il te plait." He shouted out to the waitress as only a regular could.

"On the tours I went on, I was invariably in the mid-week team, playing in the toasts (mid-week dirt trackers) rather than the tests, so I used to go out and party a lot. I slept a lot in hotel lobbies because I didn't want to wake the players up in the middle of the night."

He suddenly tacked left, indicating that this admission reminded him of one of his partners in crime on those tours.

"Have you seen Patrick Estève?

"He was another exceptional man and athlete. I remember a quote he told me from Jean Jaurès: 'Courage is about loving life and looking death in the eye, about aiming for the ideal and understanding the real'. I'll never forget that. We definitely loved life"

"Have you got his number? I'd love to see him again. I need to get him on the TV programme."

I asked him what he remembers about playing with and against the British.

"I loved playing with the British Barbarians. They were some of my greatest memories. The British would give the impression that they took everything seriously but those matches were very relaxed."

Will Carling told me a funny story about Jean-Ba when he arrived to play in a Babas game in Cardiff.

"He arrived and said that he had an injury so wouldn't be able to train. He disappeared each evening and on the Saturday of the match, he turned up with this very attractive girl and asked if she could travel with the boys to the game. 'Of course', I said! I thought it would help the boys to relax and take their minds off the game!"

Jean-Ba remembers it well.

"Back then, the fun was unrestrained. She was my girlfriend and she turned up in my bedroom while I was in the bath.

She jumped in and stretched out, still wearing her mini-skirt. She was lovely and it was magic."

To quote Michael Jackson, Jean-Ba is *'a lover, not a fighter'*. Sugar-coated in French charm, married twice and father of six, he has to be.

"I play sport every day in the week, usually tennis or golf. I stick to cards at the weekend. I play golf with one hand because with two hands it is too easy."

For a second, I thought he was being serious, the deadpan delivery fooling me again.

"No, I have a bad back so find it easier with one hand. I play off sixteen and can drive about 150m, but I can still putt with two hands."

I asked about life at RCF and how the *Show-Bizz* idea came about:

"We were just a band of brothers having fun. One night, Franck, Éric Blanc, Yves Rousset, La Guille and I were in a nightclub and Éric said, 'If we get to the final, we'll play in bow ties'. It was as simple as that."

"We were just a band of brothers having fun. One night, Franck, Éric Blanc, Yves Rousset, La Guille (Philippe Guillard) and I were in a nightclub and Éric said, 'If we get to the final, we'll play in bow ties'. It was as simple as that."

"The backs were in 'le Show-Bizz' team, the forwards in 'le Gros-Bizz' team."

It was a classic Jean-Ba line, the sort of thing that used to wind them up.

"That year we had five colours in the RCF team – (Xavier) Blond, (Éric) Blanc, (Philippe) Roux, (Christophe) Brun et (Yves) Rousset."

Things To Do Before I Die
It was an interview that finished too soon. I really needed more time to dig and get to know him and his past better, ideally over a round of golf followed by dinner, drinks and

a night club. Moreover, I would love to be his wing-man for a night out. In fact, a night out with him, Denis, Lolo Pardo and Patrick Estèveis on my list of 'Things To Do Before I Die'.

Our conversation jumped around quite a lot and I pondered why this was. Possibly because we had a lot to pack in but he too was keen to hear news of the other players. However, I also put his quick-fire Q&A down to his ability to process lots of information at the same time, just like he could on the pitch as he scanned the field for playmaking options. One discussion at a time was too one-dimensional for him. He needed to see different angles, options and passes to assess the space and find his way to the line. He is an amusing and genial man. He was a mercurial player.

With his looks, elegance, nonchalance and *joie de vivre*, he personified the flair and audacity of the French team back then. That independence of thought still predominates today, his *fil conducteur* and path to eternal freedom. When he appears on TV or in the press, he eschews clichés and vacuous replies. He just says what he thinks.

"We are at a stage where French rugby is a disgrace. We need to throw everyone out except the young guys. We speak about the great rugby family but there isn't a big family. It's war!

"It is the fate of disunited families to only meet at funerals and communions. Rugby is the same. We can't meet in

friendship. Meanwhile, who is paying? The national team."

I had to follow that line of thinking carefully. The French love their poetry and philosophy – Sartre, Camus, Rimbaud, Baudelaire, Vigny – and they can all quote it. Can you imagine Jerry, Manu, Tins, Skins or Teaguey coming out with such lines?

When talking about the older players, he then quoted a verse from Paul Verlaine's Autumn Song, which sent me searching for my French poetry anthology.

All breathless	*Tout suffocant*
And pale, when	*Et blême, quand*
The hour sounds,	*Sonne l'heure*
I remember	*Je me souvien*
Former days	*Des jours anciens*
And I cry;	*Et je pleure;*

He sees things simply, like all great sportsman do, because their natural ability allows them to. He is like the brilliant businessman who can just see the way forward without pages of analysis, fake products or financial engineering. His instinct just guides him.

I can see why he complements the likes of Denis Charvet, Lolo Pardo and Patrick Estève so well. They are all colourful characters, contrarians and mavericks. They were born to create, innovate and entertain. They were evangelists for French flair and great exponents of it.

Lunch was over. He took me 20m up the road to the very first Eden Park shop and gave me a beautiful Polo shirt. *"A 3XL should fit him,"* he shouted to the sales assistant. Their sizes go up to 5XL but he instinctively knew I was much skinnier. I like his judgement. Ever the charmer and salesman, he knows how to please a customer, not just the crowd.

I gave him a man-hug and walked back to the Paris Métro with Van Morrison singing loudly in my head:

"You can't stop us on the road to freedom You can't keep us 'cause our eyes can see"

Perhaps Van wrote those lines for him?

Merci Jean-Ba, à la prochaine.

"He was a cool, charismatic guy, with quite a dry sense of humour, always up to mischief. Whereas someone like Sella would be super-focused and intense before a game, Jean-Ba would be very relaxed, almost nonchalant."

Franck Mesnel

PARIS   "IN MAY 1990, WE PLAYED AGEN IN THE FINAL OF THE FRENCH CHAMPIONSHIP, AND WORE PINK BOW TIES AGAIN. BAPTISTE HAD BOUGHT ONE EXTRA WHICH HE GAVE TO PRESIDENT MITTERRAND DURING THE TEAM PRESENTATIONS. INSTEAD OF ORANGES AT HALF TIME, WE SIPPED SOME CHAMPAGNE SERVED TO US IN CRYSTAL FLUTES BY YVON ROUSSET, DRESSED AS A PARISIAN WAITER. WE WON 22-12!"

BORN : 30TH JUNE 1961

CLUBS : RACING CLUB DE FRANCE

INTERNATIONAL CAPS : 56

POSITION : FLY-HALF OR CENTRE

GRAND SLAMS : 1987

NOM DE GUERRE : PARISIAN PANACHE

MY VISIT TO MEET HIM : THURSDAY 19TH APRIL 2018

Franck is every mother-in-law's dream – charming, articulate, intelligent, funny, chic, good looking and the founder of Eden Park. What more could a mum-in-law hope for? OK, he doesn't have my calves, thighs or wine collection, but he did play for France fifty-six times. Come to think of it, he wouldn't just be a mother-in-law's dream. He would also be your wife's, girlfriend's, boyfriend's, whoever's.

I tracked him down via Pascal and we managed to schedule a lunch in Paris in spring. How romantic, I hear you scream. My wife wasn't happy. Not because I wasn't having lunch with her, but because she wasn't having lunch with Franck.

I met him at Eden Park's HQ on Rue Mont-Louis in the 11th *arrondissement* in Paris and he greeted me warmly. He showed me around his design studio and introduced me to some of his staff. The place was buzzing and full of clothes, pictures and creative types sitting at tables looking at large drawing pads where they were busily designing next season's clothes.

"This is the design team David. I have no idea what they do."

They laughed and we were on way.

Of course, he knows exactly what they do. They are the very essence of his business. Here, I didn't see any accountants, compliance officers or box tickers. No, this business is about brand, products, customers and markets. This isn't a place for internally-facing nerds who tie businesses up in knots with their rules and financial jiggery-pokery. Franck's people innovate, create and develop, not inhibit, complicate and diminish. They actually make stuff. It is a proper business.

If you don't know it already, Eden Park is the clothing brand that encapsulates French style, flair, beauty and spirit. Franck, along with some of his former teammates at RCF (Éric Blanc, Yvon Rousset, Jean-Baptiste Lafond and Philippe Guillard) created it back in 1987.

But first, I was wondering where Franck and I were going for lunch. A sandwich in the local shop? No chance. Fortunately, he had seen me coming and chosen a fabulous, small Italian restaurant called Il Bacaro about ten minutes' walk from the office. It is nothing fancy but the sort of place an Italian village or small town would be proud of. Its food is seasonal, home-made and authentic. As we walked in, I noticed the corn-yellow painted wall on the left, glowing as softly as the autumnal Tuscan sun onto the exposed brick wall opposite. The oak parquet flooring is distressed herringbone, slightly worn by a thousand happy customers. It is the sort of neighbourhood restaurant

that has been nurtured over many years, built with labour and love, heart and soul, patience and practice.

We ordered the spring *risotto primavera*. The rice had a delicate bite, and the asparagus, broad beans and peas were firm and cooked to perfection. Franck wasn't drinking so we 'only' ordered one bottle of the Saint-Aubin white from Burgundy, which had a beguiling nose of pears and greengages. In the mouth, it had tension and refreshing acidity with a lively, lemony note. This is what spring should taste like – fresh, young, zippy and bright.

Le Show-Bizz

I asked Franck to tell me more about Eden Park and *le Show-Bizz*.

"We started with a beret in Bayonne, an idea dreamt up by Jean-Baptiste Lafond and Yvon Rousset on the physio's table in 1986/7. We played Bayonne at home and won, and in the changing rooms afterwards, Baptiste let Pierre Salviac, the rugby commentator from Antenne 2, know that we would be playing wearing berets for the return leg in January 1987. As soon as he was told, he reported it and that boosted our publicity across the airways. Then all we had to do was to buy eight of them for the backs, and win of course.

"Can you imagine wearing a beret in a game and then losing? Papa, our coach, was circumspect but let us do it.

"Little did we know what we had started. There was no

coming back from it after that! We started doing other funny pranks."

In April 1987, in a quarter-final of the French Championship against Brive, the backs decided to mark the event by running onto the field each wearing a blazer and bow tie. They won.

"Pierre Salviac said to us, 'Prepare something for the final at the Parc'.

" It was a day for celebration and we thought we may never return so we had to do something. We couldn't play in a DJ so we thought we'd keep the pink bow tie."

"The idea of wearing a bow tie at the final in 1987 arose during a dinner. The colour pink was already a team trademark because the team mascot was a pink panther. So, a pink bow tie became the epitome of Parisian insolence! One week later, 'le Show-Bizz' backs took part in the final against Toulon wearing their bow ties. Unfortunately, we lost.

"Unconsciously, we had created a logo, like the Lacoste crocodile.

> " The press picked up on our
> shenanigans and gave us access
> to a completely different market.
> There was this media tidal wave.
> We went on prime-time
> TV about forty times."

"The press picked up on our shenanigans and gave us access to a completely different market. There was this media tidal wave. We went on prime-time TV about forty times. Eddie Barclay, the famous French music producer, made a record with us. We like to think we were the first 'boy band', but only one of us could sing, and two of us thought we could dance because we went clubbing once a week!

"No one in the world of cinema had really heard of us or knew that we played rugby because it wasn't a very big sport back then in Paris. But they remembered the pink bow tie. The media really helped boost our profile.

"We did other silly things too. In 1988, in a match against Toulouse, we daubed ourselves in black body paint to celebrate the birthday of our African friend and teammate Vincent 'Momo' Lelano.

"In 1989, in a match against Béziers, Baptiste played wearing a bald headpiece to gently tease our international team mate and opponent that day, Didier Camberabero, who had just had a hair job.

"Then, in May 1990, we played Agen in the final of the French Championship, and wore pink bow ties again. Baptiste had brought one extra, which he gave to President Mitterrand during the team presentations. Instead of oranges at half time, we sipped some champagne served to us in crystal flutes by Yvon Rousset, dressed as a Parisian waiter. We won 22-12!"

So where did the brand name come from?

"I was at the end of my studies and about to go to the first Rugby World Cup in Australia and New Zealand. We all sat around a table and agreed that we had to do something to build upon the logo we had created. I started to think about the name, and was designing and drawing, thinking about Le Parc, Twickenham, Cardiff Arms Park, and so on.

I played the final of the RWC at Eden Park and we thought Eden Park would be perfect because it had an equal number of four letters and we could put the pink bow tie in between.

"I came back with the name. While I was away, the others had continued to be invited everywhere across the media. I spent eighteen months with an advertising and marketing agency thinking about the marketing strategy and what the brand stands for.

"We knew we had created a logo, but we wanted to build a business. I received some great advice from friends and experts, notably that people will come to you once but you need to get them to come back a second time, and for a lifetime. To achieve that, you need high quality products, great design and innovation. But we had to think about what our iconic products would be. Champagne? Wine?

"Baptiste was already involved in his family's wine business, Philippe Guillard was writing, Yvon a physio, I was thinking about becoming a pilot or architect. I decided to stop architecture and called Éric to tell him that I had reflected long and hard, and that our iconic product was invented by the English, but that we could adopt it in France with, of course, the links back to its history. I often joke and say that while our English neighbours had invented modern rugby and formalised the laws, the origins of the sport were actually French, based on the old game of La Soule, which was a type of sporting war between villages!"

Franck and his team have certainly created a very impressive business since those early days. It is stylish,

Wearing a pink bowtie during the final of the
French Championship, Racing 15 v Toulon 12.
Photo - Marc Francotte, TempSport, Corbis, Getty Images.

high quality and a lovely mix of rugby and French chic, with distinct colours and style. It weaves together tradition and originality, with a strong French influence running through it.

A lot of international teams have worn its clothing – France, Italy, Ireland, England, the British Lions.

The business also created a charitable association called Les Papillons du Ciel in 2011, which supports educational projects, leveraging the values and learnings from rugby.

"Rugby can be a metaphor for life in society. It has the advantage of being a game, but it is also an educational sport. Rugby is refereed by a respected person whose decisions are sacrosanct. It is governed by laws, but danger is always present so it seems to be close to real life, and requires trust, friendship, fraternity and discipline if we want to succeed in living together in harmony."

Early Years

I asked Franck about his early years and the basis for his love of rugby.

> " I was in love with the incredible Welsh team of the 1970s. I loved that era. If I had done a book like yours, it would have been on that Welsh team. Maybe I just loved their side burns!"

"I grew up in Carrières-sur-Seine, and when I was in my teens, I would play with my mates underground in the

quarries, messing about in the tunnels with head lamps. We'd come across these small underground tunnels that we would crawl through for thirty minutes. It was an amazing playground, hard work and sometimes scary.

"I did that all the time apart from four times a year, when my friend would take me to his house to watch the Five Nations matches. I joined the local club, Carrières, because they had red shirts, like Wales.

"I stopped rugby for a while but restarted at Saint-Germain-en-Laye where I played for pleasure until I was twenty-six. One day, a scrum-half left for RCF and told me I should really go and trial for them. I was doing my architecture studies, but I was very tempted by the adventure. I never finished architecture even though I had done six years.

"I remember turning up at RCF with my sports bag for a trial in 1986. I had trained really hard and we played a second division side called Sainte-Geneviève-des-Bois in what I regarded as the most important game of my life. All the current RCF players who would become my great friends were there with sand in their toes and taking it a lot less seriously than me! I remember Jean-Baptiste Lafond, who I didn't yet know, said to me, 'The fat boys should be over there with the other forwards'. I had to explain to him that I was actually a back. He looked surprised but reluctantly accepted."

"I messed up my first kick-off, but then played the game of my life - I was fit, focused and gave my opposite number a nightmare. I was nervous because I was going from

the third division to first, but I had trained hard for two months using the Rocky music to keep me going! I was fit and I had a chance."

Franck had a meteoric rise to the top. Within a few months of trialling with RCF, he was playing against the All Blacks, first at the Battle of Nantes, and within a year against the same team in the first RWC Final. He was also part of the team that won the Five Nations in 1987, and RCF reached the French Championship Final against Toulon.

"The French team realised that I wasn't a typical fly-half at 95kgs. Jacques said to me, 'I didn't pick you because you are a great fly-half. I picked you because you interest me as a rugby player. You tackled John Kirwan in the last line of defence in a provincial match, and on that action alone I will pick you. Let's see how you get on'."

My Inspiration

"Jean Gachassin, the former Lourdes, Bagnères and French player, was my inspiration. He said to me, 'Your opposite number must obsess about you. He must worry about you the whole match. Never get complacent and go through the motions. If you become predictable, you are dead'.

"Peter Pan, as he was known, told me that he was so small he had to be unpredictable to survive. Once Jacques took me to one side and said, 'Forget Gachassin. Why are you obsessing about him? You weigh 95kgs. Use your strength. Stop thinking you're a dancer at the opera."

Jacques was a real character and Franck told me an amusing story about him.

"In 1987 at the RWC, Jacques came to see Denis and me in our room a few days before selecting the team to play Fiji. Berbiz was there too. Jacques was full of original lines. Jacques said to Denis: 'Who is the best player in the Five Nations?'
Denis: 'Érik Bonneval.'
Jacques: 'Where does he play?'
Denis: 'On the wing'
Jacques: 'Who is the best player in the world?'
Denis: 'John Kirwan.'
Jacques: 'Where does he play?'
Denis: 'On the wing.'
Jacques: 'Great, that's where you're playing on Sunday against Fiji'
Denis: 'But Jacques, I have never played there before'.

"I started laughing, so Jacques said to me, 'I don't know why you are laughing. You are playing centre against them.'

"After the match, Jean-Baptiste Lafond told us that 'Denis and I defended like swinging bar saloon doors'.

"If the Fijian guy hadn't had dropped the ball, we would have lost against them. Eventually, Éric Champ said, 'Right, that's enough, we are playing this tight and marching all over them'. We scraped through after Lolo Rodriguez scored two tries from the base of the scrum."

Franck was very generous with his time and had given me a huge amount of material in the three hours we had

spent together. He is a very impressive man. What really struck me was his judgement, his eye for a gap and his composure. The way he has created a business on the back of a pink bow tie is a brilliant business story, the sort of thing that an expensive MBA would never teach you. They spotted a gap in the market and went for it. He and his mates came up with a simple idea, unconsciously, developed it, and then converted it into a 50m € plus turnover business. They backed themselves, took some risks and stuck at it through thick and thin. That requires courage, great judgement and resilience.

I am sure things haven't always been calm through the ups and downs, but you wouldn't think so listening to Franck's composed and humorous style. If you get a chance, get hold of a copy of their book called Rugby Papillon. It chronicles their wonderful story in words and pictures, while capturing the spirit and fraternité of a group of fun-loving guys who built Eden Park while having the time of their lives at RCF. Chapeau, les gars. Big respect.

Le Déjeuner des Interdits

There is a lot I admire about the French, not least their revolutionary spirit, hostility towards the establishment, blatant disregard for rules, independence of thought, and love of traditions, particularly the epicurean kind. This weekend encapsulated all of the above.

A wine grower friend of mine was visiting London back in 2014 when he invited me to a lunch that a friend of his has been hosting for his guests for some thirty years. It is called 'The Lunch of the Forbidden'. He elaborated a little, *"David, it consists of eating things that are, well, forbidden in France"*. *Ah bon*, I thought, that sounds right up my *boulevard*. The *mélange* of mystery, mischief and monkey business is the sort of thing that I find irresistible. He gave me the date and told me to be there, as though I needed persuading. I was already frothing with excitement.

But just in case the police are reading this, I must first give you the legal disclaimer...

"I think that the events depicted in this article are true. However, any similarity to any person, fish, bird or animal, whether drunk, dead or alive, is merely coincidental. In fact, as you will see, perhaps I wasn't even there and it was all a figment (or fig-roll) of my imagination."

Anyway, apart from a mysterious time warp, this is what I think happened.

I arrived on the Friday evening, the eve of the big lunch, and met the host in a restaurant. He is a tall, good-looking and charismatic man who has clearly lived a lot and enjoyed many a night out. You could tell from the lined forehead, deep tan, slicked-back hair and smart dress sense. We chatted about the next day and what might be in store although he didn't tell me much, other than the food would be exquisite and we would be joined by several world class *vignerons* and other stars from the epicurean world.

Wild Frontiers

He guided me through the menu and, like a naïve Englishman abroad, I accepted his recommendation of *pieds et paquets*. Now, this so-called 'dish' is at the wild frontier of French gastronomy, consisting of sheep's feet and stuffed sheep's tripe stewed together. It was like an *andouillette* on heat, or perhaps one that had spent too long in the heat. I like to think of myself as being at the adventurous end of the epicurean spectrum,

having eaten during my years in France *tête de veau* (deboned calf's head), frogs' legs, snails, *boudin* (black pudding), *tripous* (tripe), *gésiers* (gizzards, such as heart, kidney, liver and neck), *riz de veau* (sweetbreads), and *andouillette* (sausage made from intestines), but, had I known, I would have drawn the line in the pasture at sheep's feet and entrails. When it arrived it smelt like a Parisian *pissoir*. Not wanting to offend my host, I tried to eat some of it but nearly retched with every mouthful. Perhaps the chef had an off day, or perhaps I will never like it, but that evening it was rancid, sweaty, stinky and gelatinous. With hindsight, it was everything you would expect from an abattoir's left overs. It was tongue-curlingly awful.

It reminds me of a couple of near misses in other French restaurants over the years. Once, in Paris, in a moment of madness, I ordered sheep's brains (*cervelles d'agneau*). Its flavour was creamy and its texture lumpy and emetic. It was the sort of thing Hannibal Lecter would order for dinner. What was I thinking? That it would somehow make me more intelligent? It is the type of dish that you have to be drunk to think up and on drugs to order twice.

Another occasion, I was with three friends, Will Bentley, Jules Rimmer and Alun Griffiths MW (a Master of Wine and one of the world's great wine experts), in a restaurant in Alsace. Having just spent two hours tasting at the exquisite Domaine Ostertag, we were quite well-oiled and needed a hearty dish to fill us up. I quickly spotted *rognons* on the menu. Now, I adore *rognons à la moutarde*, the silky texture of the kidneys complementing the heat, acidity and richness of the

mustard, wine and cream. Three of us confidently ordered the aforesaid delicacies. However, Alun, the elder statesman of the quartet and by far the wisest among us, noticed that these *rognons* weren't any old kidneys. They were *rognons blancs*, or 'white' kidneys. We nervously asked what that meant: *"Ah monsieur, they are very nice. They are bulls' testicles."*

I swear she said it with a straight face, as though she meant it.

It was a near-triumph of menu marketeering, a close call of style over substance, cunning over clarity, jiggery-pokery over justice. I can see why the chef didn't market them on the menu as 'bulls' testicles', but we should have reported him to the local *gendarmerie de cuisine*. Instead we quickly back-tracked and ended up with something conventional like *entrecôte et frites*.

Snap, Crackle and Pop

So, back to The Lunch of the Forbidden. I went to bed hungry, but woke up with a clear head, although that wouldn't last long. We were wine tasting by 11am, making our way through a beautiful flight of wines, which spanned most parts of the Rhône Valley. When we eventually sat down about 1pm, I was placed like a prime piece of English *rosbif* on the head table, ready to be sliced and diced. I was surrounded by stars from the wine and food industry. The tasting had oiled the wheels so all the guests were already in full flow, talking loudly and at full speed, and all at the same time, lampooning me and the English for our base cuisine.

It was a classic southern French scene.

From the moment we sat down, the food flowed, a *smörgåsbord* of dishes from the sea, land and air, which teased our taste buds and extended my gastronomic frontier. Not all the dishes were forbidden and, where they weren't, they were decadent and luxurious.

The menu read something like this:

- *Rouget, poutargue et mélets* (red mullet, caviar of the Mediterranean and small fish aged and tenderised in brine)
- *Truffe en croûte* (truffles en croute / in pastry)
- *Petits oiseaux* (small birds)
- *Grive en cerises* (song thrush with cherries)
- *Oiseau au long bec sauce salmis* (long-beaked bird in a salmis sauce / when the game is sliced and reheated in a sauce to enhance the flavour)
- *Vieux comté millésimé 2011 et 2012 Anthony* (old comté cheese)
- *Vacherin vanilla et chartreuse* (meringue and cream with vanilla and chartreuse liqueur)

The dish of *rouget*, *boutargue* and *mélet* was pink, perky, refined and exquisite, its crispy skin complementing its sweet, soft flesh and salty caviar.

Then the *petits oiseaux* arrived. I was hoping these would be the infamous *ortolans*, the tiny, rare bird that used to be caught during their migration to Africa across the south west corner of France before the government banned the killing and selling of them in the late 1990s. Famed for their delicate flavour, Marcel Proust wrote

"Ah *monsieur*, they are very nice. They are bulls' testicles." I swear she said it with a straight face, as though she meant it.

about them, President Mitterand ate them, and some great French chefs still yearn for their reinstatement on the tables of France's restaurants.

If you are squeamish, vegetarian or belong to an animal rights group, just skip the next few paragraphs.

Traditionally, the tiny *ortolans* were kept in dark, enclosed cages for up to a month, which was believed to stimulate them to gorge on grain to double their weight. There are even stories of the Romans gouging their eyes, rendering them blind to encourage them to eat more, so the theory went.

Fattened up, the birds are then drowned in Armagnac, a technique that also marinates them at the same time. There are many ways to cook the *ortolan*, but gastronomes opine that the only way is to roast them in the oven or on a spit, and only in their own fat.

Except mine weren't *ortolans*. They were robins. Yes, those jittery, little birds with the red breast, known as 'rouge-gorge' in French.

Three of them were presented on my plate, their heads and beaks still attached to their thin necks and little fat bodies. I still have the photo, although it is blurred, no doubt due to my high blood-alcohol level and excitement at the time. I popped one in my mouth and devoured it. It tasted of wondrous flavours, like Armagnac, game, dark meat, salt and fat. I chewed the soft flesh and crunched the bones, like you would fleshy pork and crackling at a Sunday roast.

Snap, crackle and pop, and it was all over in a robin's heartbeat. To my large appetite, it was no more than a throat-tickler of an *amuse-bouche*.

Beggars Can't be Choosers

Next on the menu was the *grive* or thrush. When I tell people about eating thrush, I always preface it with 'song', as in song thrush, just to differentiate it from the vaginal infection. For me to simply say 'I ate thrush' sounds a bit weird, *non*? I think so.

The song thrush arrived on a plate, a hearty *tartine* spread thick with the dark, rich meat, its viscous juices dripping from the bread. Its head was placed in the middle of two round pieces of flesh, which looked so appetising that I could feel myself salivating. They were extraordinary. The combination of the salty meat, acidic cherries and floral red wine from Burgundy was impeccable. The wine had earthy notes of mushrooms, forest floor, truffles and black fruits. It was complex, decadent and sumptuous. I can't remember whether I ate the head…

A quick *vignette* for the linguists. The expression *'faute de grive, on mange des merles'* means 'beggars can't be choosers'. It literally means 'if there aren't any thrush, eat a blackbird', the poorer cousin of the richer, darker meat. I am not sure of the exact etymology of the expression, but you can imagine it emanating from pre and post-war France when song thrush were caught for food, and, if you couldn't catch one, you'd make do with a blackbird.

Next on our plate was the woodcock, a bird that you can shoot but only in small numbers in France. If you're eating, please stop for a minute.

Woodcocks empty their bowels before they take off, which means you can roast the whole bird, guts and all. This heightens the flavour of the flesh. Therefore, the bird is plucked but not gutted, and the breast covered with a slice of bacon and suspended by the neck with string attached to the mantelpiece of the fire. Under the bird, slices of bread rubbed with garlic and garnished with *foie gras* are laid out in a pan to collect the bird's fat.

Then after cooking, you can scoop out its guts including intestines and put them into a hot pan with a little stock and a touch of Armagnac, before spreading the roughly chopped and mixed offal onto some fried bread. Oh, how I love the French. Only they are creative and daring enough, in a culinary sense, to think of this.

At the lunch, the woodcock arrived in a similar form to the song thrush on a *tartine*, although the beak is much longer. The flesh melted in my mouth and the flavour lasted for minutes. I definitely didn't eat its long beak, fearing it would impale my oesophagus. I drank a delicious *syrah* to complement its rich, gamey and mineral tang, and the whole thing was so delicious that I was speechless, lost in a *fricassée* of gastronomic euphoria. How do they create those flavours? All three birds were head, shoulders and wings above any game I had ever tasted.

Time Warp

We continued through to cheese and dessert before, at about 5pm, the host opened his large humidor from which I chose a striking, long Montecristo, made from 100% Nicaraguan tobacco. And it was then that it happened. I lost four hours of my life. Following the postprandial cigar, I have no recollection until I was sitting downstairs in another room preparing to eat dinner at 9pm. Dinner? I can hear you shout. *Sacré bleu*! I had only just eaten lunch for God's sake. But as importantly, where on earth had I been? I'll be damned if I know.

I do remember that the intoxicating mix of alcohol and nicotine had rendered me as high as a kite, or perhaps a *rouge-gorge*, and as a result I was struggling to speak English let alone French. I fantasised about what might have happened. Unknowingly, during this time-warp, had I been seduced by the local dark, brooding bombshell, and lost myself in a world of make-believe and magic for four hours of ecstasy? I hoped so. I guess I will never know unless she comes forward to admit her benevolence.

From what I can remember, the whole day was a veritable *tour de force*. I can't wait for the next invite that is due in 2020.

I fantasised about what might have happened. Unknowingly, during this time-warp, had I been seduced by the local dark, brooding bombshell, and lost myself in a world of make-believe and magic for four hours of ecstasy? I hoped so.

Collioure, France. Photo - Pierre Carton.

Mediterranean & Provence

"FUNNY HOW I FIND MYSELF IN LOVE WITH YOU
IF I COULD BUY MY REASONING, I'D PAY TO LOSE
ONE HALF WON'T DO
I'VE ASKED MYSELF, HOW MUCH DO YOU
COMMIT YOURSELF
IT'S MY LIFE"

TALK TALK, IT'S MY LIFE, 1984

This area covers the vast expanse of Collioure, Perpignan, Narbonne, Béziers, Montpellier, Avignon, Toulon and Port Grimaud.

'Funny how I find myself in love with you'. It is such an apt opening line. If I had to single out a region in France for unconditional love and adulation, this would be it. It is where my heart is. Back in the late 1980s when I was about nineteen, I used to spend hours in Avignon and the surrounding villages chatting to the locals, soaking up the sun, chilling in cafés and making new friends. When I think about it now, I hear that line from Passenger's beautiful song 'When We Were Young':

We used to never say never
Used to think we'd live forever
Flying free beneath the sun

Les Baux-de-Provence.
Photo - Pierre Carton.

That was me; insouciant, nonchalant and a world-class fantasist dreaming my way through the south of France with not a care in the world. I am sure it is where I perfected the art of small talk, partying, flirting and procrastination, and learnt to appreciate fully the value of the *siesta*, one of southern Europe's greatest innovations.

This is the land of milk and honey with its warm climate, piercing sunlight, rolling vineyards, hearty food and wines, lavender fields, olive groves, abundant fish and fresh, luscious fruits. I love it. Did I mention that already?

When I first arrived in 1986 at the Collège du Mourion in Villeneuve-lez-Avignon, a sleepy village just outside Avignon, I understood very little of what the locals said to me. Their quick-fire dialogue and twangy accent bore no relation to the French I had studied for years in England. I remember being at the local market one Wednesday to buy some fruit and vegetables. I asked the farmer sheepishly, *"C'est combien?"* His response was almost incomprehensible, *"Quarainte-cinqe franges."* *Poutaing*, I thought. This is going to be tough.

But you get through it. Like love, there is no success, without sacrifice and suffering. Learning a language is like anything else you want to succeed at in life, whether it's sport, work, art, love, whatever. You have to be determined, resilient, committed and disciplined, then the benefits will flow, but it takes time. After a period of three months or so when I felt isolated and a million miles from home, I walked into a bar called Les Célestins in downtown Avignon and my fortunes changed

This is the land of milk and honey
with its warm climate, piercing sunlight,
rolling vineyards, hearty food and wines,
lavender fields, olive groves, abundant fish
and fresh, luscious fruits. I love it.
Did I mention that already?

immediately because I met a group of people who became life-long friends. The days out and parties with Claire (Dutch), Kara, Scott (both American) and Elsebeth (Norwegian) were raucous, exciting and perfect for a nineteen-year old learning his trade.

While meeting them solved the problem of loneliness, it didn't teach me how to speak French like the locals. I turned that corner when I met the dark, sultry Valérie, a local girl from Aramon near Avignon. She and her family changed me forever, and I am sure they bestowed more kindness on me than I ever deserved. Their generosity was boundless and I will always be thankful to them. I lived with them for a few months in the summers of 1986, '87 and '88, and was utterly immersed in the southern French culture, perfecting my language skills, learning about food, the importance of time together at the dinner table, wine and cooking, and visiting all the iconic sites in the region such as Le Pont du Gard, Cassis, Marseille, Arles,

Saint-Rémy-de-Provence, La Fontaine de Vaucluse, la Camargue, and so on. Josie, the mum, was hot-blooded with a strong Latin temperament who loved a few glasses of wine at dinner. As a result, meal times were often entertaining, loud and sometimes confrontational, and great for my French.

Roger, the dad, was born and bred Marseille with an *accent du midi* to match, and he would tell me jokes in the local slang, rib *les rosbifs*, correct my French and look wistfully at his home, the *départment* of Les Bouches-du-Rhône, across the great Rhône river. Frédéric, Valérie's brother, was a constant source of humour and taught me more swear words and French slang in three months than I had learnt in the previous ten years. I remember the summer of 1986 in particular because we spent hours watching the Football World Cup on TV. It took place in Mexico so we would watch the matches about 11pm during the warm Mediterranean nights while we drank ice-cold *pastis*. The family was full of wonderful

characters and southern French warmth and good humour. I was experiencing my first flirtation with romance so life was good and the days long and lazy.

The region is also home to most of my favourite wines in the world – Domaine de Trévallon in Saint-Eitienne-du-Grès, La Grange des Pères in Aniane, Gourt de Mautens in Rasteau, and Saint Préfert and Clos des Papes in Châteauneuf-du-Pape.

Beyond the luxuries of wine and food, it was the intangibles and nature's gifts that gave me so much joy. There is a place in the square near the Hôtel d'Europe in Avignon where I would relax for hours with the sun on my face, my mind soaked in harmony. Or I would head to Châteauneuf-du-Pape or Gigondas to wander among the vineyards and listen to the rhythmic cacophony of the *cigales*, noisy with desire. Or I'd go to Villeneuve-lez-Avignon or Aramon to watch the locals playing *boules* around the plane trees in the squares. I would love watching them dispatch the silver globe with a caress of the hand, and hearing the clean cracks of *boule* on *boule*.

For me, these pictures and sounds are so evocative of Provence. They are fragrant with vivid memories, as warm as oil and as sweet as childhood.

Anyway, enough of this descriptive and nostalgic stuff about Provence. Let's get back to the former players.

Didier Camberabero

MEDITERRANEAN
+ PROVENCE

"I WAS UNLUCKY NOT TO BE PICKED
IN THE ORIGINAL SQUAD FOR THE
RWC IN 1987 BUT THEN LUCKY
TO BE PICKED IN THE FINAL ONE.
THE PLANE WAS DEPARTING FROM
ORLY FOR AUSTRALIA THAT EVENING
AND AT MIDDAY I RECEIVED A PHONE
CALL SAYING I HAD TO BE ON IT.
I WAS IN BÉZIERS, MILES FROM PARIS.
I EVENTUALLY MADE IT ON THE PLANE
BUT THE PLAYERS WERE OBVIOUSLY
NOT EXPECTING ME. THEY LOOKED
AT ME AND SAID, 'WHAT THE F**K ARE
YOU DOING HERE?'"

I had spoken to Cambé during my long, lavish lunch with Serge so he was well primed when I reconnected to fix a time and place to meet. I flew into Marseille and drove to Béziers in the torrential rain to a restaurant called La Coupole, which is very near Béziers' rugby ground, Stade de la Méditerranée, and seems to serve as an unofficial clubhouse for the great club.

As I drove along the motorway, I gave a thought to Jerry Collins, the former great All Black flanker, and his wife, who were killed in a car crash in 2015 on the A9 motorway near Béziers. He joined several other great players to have been killed on France's roads: Raymond Albaladejo, Jean Othats et Émile Carrère (1964), Guy Boniface (1968), Jean-Michel Capendéguy (1968), Rene Berges-Cau (1983) and Pierre Lacans (1985).

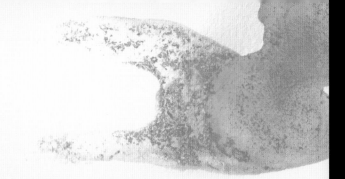

Didier came from one of the great dynasties of French rugby, the son of Guy and nephew of Lilian, who helped France to its first Grand Slam in 1968. They originally came from St-Vincent-de-Tyrosse in Les Landes, South West France before playing for La Voulte, in the Ardeche, where they won the French Championship in 1970. Guy is now eighty-three and still lives there.

Didier had many memorable performances for France too, but I will pick out two from my souvenir chest. First was his match-winning performance in the Rugby World Cup Semi-Final in 1987 when he kicked beautifully and was key to winning the game. The second was his role in that wonderful try at Twickenham when he chipped to beat a player and then delivered the cross kick to Philippe Saint-André to score under the posts in 1991.

Didier followed his parents to La Voulte where he played between 1980-1985, before enrolling at le Lycée Jean-Moulin in Béziers to study sport, then under the direction of the Sorcerer of Sauclières, Raoul Barrière, the highly decorated coach of Béziers in the 1970s. He had become an international in 1983 while at La Voulte, but felt he needed a bigger club to cement his place, and Béziers had the requisite stature. He stayed at Béziers for four years before joining Nîmes, then Grenoble before returning to Béziers. At the end of his career, he became the player-coach at USAP.

He was blessed with natural footballing ability. He was quicker than Sella over the first ten metres or so, could pass, kick off either foot, and had beautiful balance.

> "I had a real crisis of confidence. During this period, I didn't have the courage to fight back and defend myself. That only happened when I was about thirty-years-old in 1989/90."

Foxed by Fouroux

He was capped in 1983, but then he didn't play in the Five Nations between 1984-87. I was intrigued to know why.

"I played against England in 1983 and injured my shoulder, but because we had a two-week break, I recovered in time for the next match. However, I played poorly and missed all my kicks at goal even though I was kicking everything in the Championship.

"Jacques would constantly undermine me in my early years. I had a real crisis of confidence. During this period, I didn't have the courage to fight back and defend myself. That only happened when I was about thirty-years-old in 1989/90. In the changing rooms right before matches, he would say, 'If you miss your kicks, you're dropped, if you miss touch, you're out...' At twenty years old, I couldn't take it. His attitude foxed me completely because I wanted him to give me confidence.

"It came to a head after the first test match against Australia in 1990. In that match, I hit the kick-off straight into touch, which led to a scrum in the centre circle. In the ensuing ruck, Abdel Benazzi was sent off for stamping. In the video analysis after the game, Jacques blamed that on me. I was the reason why we lost the game!

"I went to see Serge and told him it had to stop and that we needed to meet Jacques immediately. We met and I told him everything that he had been in my heart and head for a decade. Jacques was at the end of his reign and therefore ready to accept what I said. Serge said that it was on the back of that conversation that I played fly-half regularly thereafter.

"When Daniel Dubroca became coach in 1990/91, he really understood me and I adored him. He was very intelligent and had great knowledge. That gave me even more confidence."

> "For Serge's try, I had to move all the TV cables to kick the conversion but I knew I would get it. For the first time ever, I felt invincible. Nothing could have put me off."

Fired Up by Fouroux

"Jacques could be quite complicated! He was a fabulous leader of men, but if I could reproach him for two things, it would be these. First, he never fixed on his style of play. He always changed tactics and so it could be difficult to find a rhythm. Second, his motivational speeches were so good that everyone would get worked up before matches. I liked to be calm and lucid, so it didn't suit me, but some of the players loved it and really responded.

"Once, we were in the changing room before a game against Wales, and Ondarts and Cabannes were working themselves up to a frenzy. Pascal suddenly shoulder charged me and I flew 3m back and hit the wall. I was quite shaken up and spent the first twenty minutes of the match not knowing where I was. We went on to smash them though, 36-3!

"Jacques had this strength and impact. At times, he could be very disrespectful, severe and intransigent during training and for the match preparation. Then afterwards, he would be very funny and charismatic. The team could really enjoy his company."

Le Come-Back

Didier was eventually picked in the French squad for the Rugby World Cup in 1987 and that was the start of his renaissance.

"When I came back in 1987, I played on the wing. He started to support me more, mainly because he knew they needed a good kicker.

"Jacques had a problem because the team lacked a reliable goalkicker. After the Zimbabwe game, Jacques changed everything against Fiji by playing Laporte at fly-half, Franck in the centre and Denis on the wing, but we nearly lost the game. After that, on the Tuesday before we played Australia, he came to see me and said, 'Listen, I need a kicker but I don't have a place at fly-half. The only solution is to play you on the wing'. I said that was fine. As long as he didn't play me upfront, I would play anywhere!

"In that week, training was pretty fiery. As we had been so poor against Fiji, everything and everyone was being challenged. Jacques had created a situation where the players were scared of losing their place, and they were fighting very hard. It became very competitive. I remember that Patrick Estève scored a great try and shouted, 'I'm going to play in the semi-final', but Jacques picked me instead. Initially, I think Patrick was very disappointed. We were a tight team though and we were all as one after training."

Invincibility and Press Anonymity

"When we played the semi-final at the Sydney Concord Oval, there was only one stand. The other sides were grassy knolls and mounds so the ground was exposed. There was a lot of wind and the balls were different to the ones we were used to. I missed my two penalties, but I kicked all the others including the conversions on the touchline for Alain's and Serge's tries. We were still 24-21 down and the clock was nearly in the red when I kicked the penalty to draw level.

"For Serge's try, I had to move all the TV cables to kick the conversion but I knew I would get it. For the first time ever, I felt invincible. Nothing could have put me off. The bloke next to me in the stand could have let off a bomb and I wouldn't have heard it.

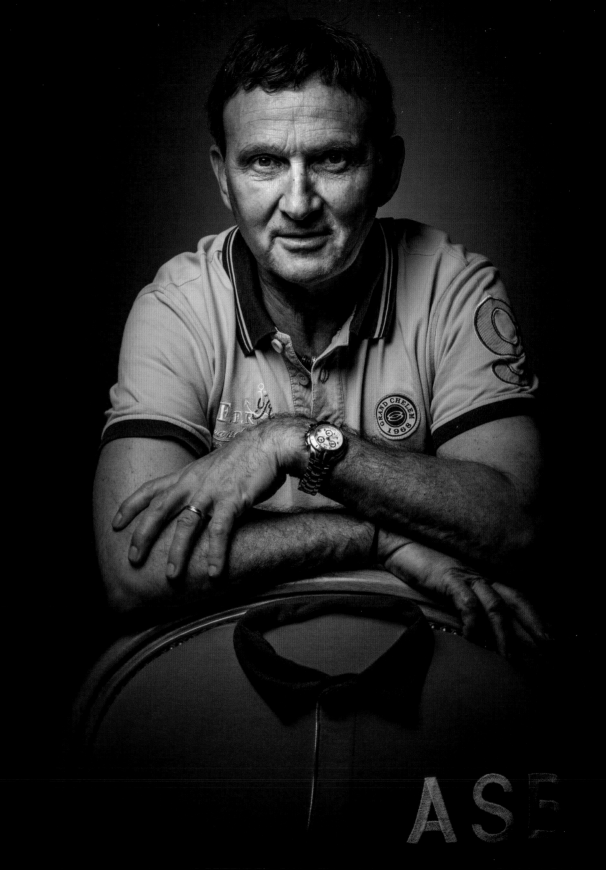

"I get so pissed off though because the press never gives me any recognition for that performance. At an event in Paris in 2017, they only talked about the tries. They didn't talk about all the kicks even though I scored fourteen of the thirty points including all four conversions and two penalties. If I'd been English, I would have been feted like Jonny Wilkinson. When I challenge journalists, they say, 'It is all about the spectacle!'"

Better Late Than Never

In the wilderness years between 1984-87, Didier wasn't picked in the original squad for the 1987 Rugby World Cup, but France had some injury problems, which meant he received a late call up.

*"I was unlucky not to be picked in the original squad for the RWC in 1987, but then lucky to be picked in the final one. Bérot, the kicker from Agen, got injured and they replaced him with Andrieu, a winger! The plane was departing from Orly for Australia that evening and at midday I received a phone call saying I had to be on it. I was in Béziers, miles from Paris, there were strikes everywhere and I didn't know where my passport was. I eventually made it on the plane but the players were obviously not expecting me. They looked at me and said, 'What the f**k are you doing here?'"*

It was just as well that he was selected. Not only was he instrumental in beating Australia, he also scored thirty points against Zimbabwe in one of the group matches.

When I went to meet Gavin Hastings as research for the book, he told me a story about how he broke

Didier Camberabero, Paris, 3rd March 1990, France 31 v Ireland 12. *Photo - Bob Thomas Sports Photography, Getty Images.*

the points record twice at World Cups.

"On 2nd June 1987 against Romania, I scored twenty-seven points. Our game kicked off at 1pm local time. After the game, I had to go and do some media interviews, and by the time I had left the changing room, Didier Cambérabero had beaten my record by three points against Zimbabwe! Their game had kicked off at 3pm.

"Then in the 1995 Rugby World Cup, I scored forty-four points against the Ivory Coast. I was cock-a-hoop. A few days later on 4th June, the All Blacks played Japan and Simon Culhane scored forty-five points including a touchline conversion in the seventy-ninth minute!

"**I had held the world record twice, but it was snatched away within a matter of hours and days!**"

Like the French, I have a huge soft spot for the Scottish, and it was very enjoyable meeting and speaking to some of their former great players such as Gavin, David Sole, Ian Milne, John Jeffrey, Derek White and Finlay Calder. I lived in Glasgow for a year in 1993 and played a season for Hillhead-Jordanhill rugby club in Hughenden. I was affectionately known as the 'English C**t' by my teammates. It was a term of endearment, so they told me. After a while, they simply dropped the word 'English' believing that using both is tautologous. 'Where's The C**t?', they would ask when I'd left the pub early. I genuinely loved my time there for its people, humour, scenery, rugby and of course their wonderful restaurants. I would spend many a night at places such as Rogano's, One Devonshire Place and The Ubiquitous Chip, where I enjoyed their fabulous cuisine with its refined Scottish influence.

Back at La Coupole, it was still pouring with rain as Didier and I knocked back our third espresso of the morning. We were in extra time and I needed to leave to drive to Sète.

It was a privilege to meet Didier, someone who is clearly as passionate about the game today as he was when he played. He fought his way through his crisis of confidence in his early years to establish himself as a regular member of the squad from 1987 until his last match against Ireland in 1993. When I think about French flair, Didier certainly comes to mind. He may not have had the profile of Sella, Charvet, Blanco, Lagisquet and others, but his skills, pace and vision were outstanding, and he is universally viewed by his peers as a player of real class.

When I left La Coupole, I headed to the mythical Stade de Sauclières - Raoul Barrière, Béziers' former stadium, across the river on the south side of the town. I stood in the stand imagining all its great players who once graced its weathered turf – Vaquerin, Paco, Palmier, Astre, Séguier, Lacans, Cantoni, Estève, to name a few. Between January 1969 and October 1981, Béziers were unbeaten for an astonishing ninety-five matches. La Voulte beat them 10-19 to end their run, ironically a team featuring Didier Camberabero.

Call me a romantic, but I love immersing myself in the nostalgia of places like this. Sauclières has no distinctive beauty or charm but that misses the point. It is far more than just grass and concrete. It is precisely the bareness that stimulates my imagination. Places like this have a soul long after the sporting glories have passed. You can still sense the spirit of the great Béziers - the passion, the feeling of belonging, the pride in the city. Sauclières is the immortal witness to that wonderful period of human endeavour and sporting achievement.

I had a busy week ahead of me with a diary full of star names, such as Codor, Champ, Gallion, Rives and Maso. Then I was meeting my great university friend Knoxy and his wife Kaidi in Avignon for a few days of hilarity. Knoxy spent time with the French rugby squad during the 2003 Rugby World Cup in Australia as a translator, famously improvising on live TV when Fréd Michelak was too tired to answer a journalist's question: *"I dunno Knoxy, say what you want, I can't be arsed".* Knoxy performed like the ultimate professional he is, kept a straight face and came out with some rubbish about the match being close. Knoxy is a big personality, an *animateur extraordinaire*, a *bon vivant* and a fabulous friend.

Marc Cécillon

MEDITERRANEAN
+ PROVENCE

HIS STORY SHOWS BOTH THE
BEST AND WORST OF HUMAN
ENDEAVOUR AND BEHAVIOUR.
IT IS A CELEBRATION OF A RUGBY
COLOSSUS FROM BOURGOIN-JALLIEU,
AND AN EXAMPLE OF HOW THE RUGBY
COMMUNITY TRIED TO SUPPORT HIM
AND HIS FAMILY IN THE AFTERMATH
OF THAT DREADFUL NIGHT. IT IS
ALSO A PROFOUND ILLUSTRATION
OF HIS AND OTHERS' SORROW.

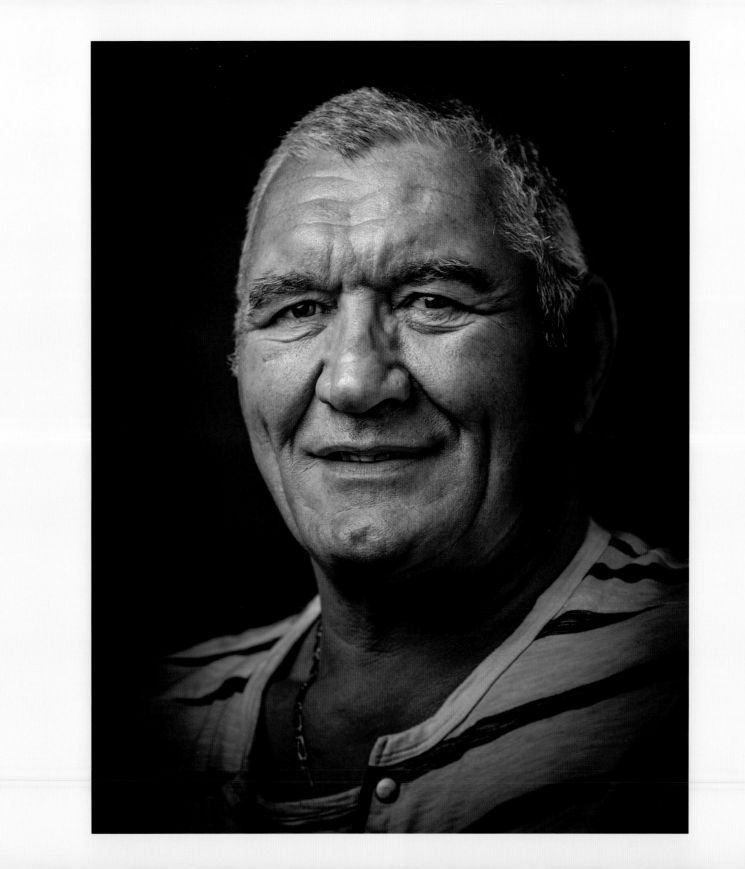

BORN : 30TH JANUARY 1959

CLUBS : CLUB SPORTIF BOURGOIN-JALLIEU RUGBY

INTERNATIONAL CAPS : 47

POSITION : NUMBER 8, FLANKER, SECOND ROW

NICKNAME : MARCO, ARNOLD

NOM DE GUERRE : THE GLADIATOR

MY VISIT TO MEET HIM : SATURDAY 17TH FEBRUARY 2018

Marc was a brilliant player and beautiful beast of a man, his 115kgs and 1.91m towering over the masses and turning heads everywhere he went. However, he struggled with alcohol and depression when he stopped playing, and this path took a devastating turn when he shot his wife dead in 2004. The French courts sentenced him to twenty-one years in prison for premeditated murder, subsequently reduced to fourteen years for manslaughter. His lawyer argued that it had been a crime of passion, committed under the influence of alcohol and depression. He was freed on parole in 2011 and has been living freely since near the French/Spanish border.

Briefly, I wondered whether I should include Marc in my squad, but my indecision only lasted a few seconds. I knew instinctively that I had to select him. That he had committed an awful crime is not in doubt. I did worry about how the other players might react to his inclusion, but this is my team and I am Chairman of Selectors, and the criteria for selection are clearly laid out in my introduction! Brothers in Arms includes former great rugby players, whatever their circumstances, whatever the rights and wrongs they have committed. Marc was a great player who won forty-six caps and played in two World Cups in 1991 and 1995. He was therefore part of the golden generation, and merits his place in the squad.

Once I had selected him, other practical questions remained:
- How would I get hold of him?
- Would he want to meet me?
- And if he did, how should I cover his story?

Unsurprisingly, it was Pascal Ondarts who put me in contact with him. The first time I met Pascal, he called Marc during our lunch and handed me the phone. Marc was keen to meet me, partly because his great mate had introduced me, but also why wouldn't he want to be in my book alongside the other greats of his era? His pride would have wanted that. But I also hope that he had considered how this could, in some small way, help his reintegration back into his rugby community and society more widely. Pascal was sure my visit would make him happy because it would rekindle great memories, and his association with other former great players would make him feel good about himself.

> A key part of prisoner rehabilitation is regaining some dignity and self-worth. If no one thinks you are worth anything and you have little respect for yourself, you tend not to respect others and therefore re-offend.

A Test of Loyalty

Pascal is a man with a huge heart, a magnificent human. He and other friends have never abandoned Marc or his family all the way through this trauma. This isn't about taking sides or forgiving Marc for what he did. It is about pushing cold logic to the side and being a kind human being, extending the hand of friendship to those who need it. Pascal elaborated:

"I first played against Marc in 1977. He is a friend of over forty years. On the rugby pitch, we grew up together. I have seen what a kind man he is. You can't just abandon your friends when they need you most. What he did was unforgiveable but what should we do, just leave him to rot in the gutter? That isn't how we should treat people who need help, not least your mates. It wouldn't help Marc, his girls, his family, society or anyone.

"On the pitch, he was a 'force de nature', but he was also one of those players who didn't know what to do after playing, a route that ended in tragedy."

Not all of Marc's teammates agree with Pascal. One said to me:

"I can't forgive him. I travel around France a lot and Marc's name has damaged rugby's image. It hurt us a lot. I have tried to defend the undefendable and I can't. We have all f**ked up in our lives, but he shot someone dead. That's different. He also didn't serve his full sentence in prison."

To declare my hand, I disagree with this. Marc's crime isn't unique to rugby. It didn't happen because he was a rugby player. He is a killer (what a brutal but factual descriptor) who happened to play rugby. There is no causal relationship between this specific sport and his crime, and I think the vast majority of the public would agree. Furthermore, the fact that he didn't serve his full term isn't Marc's fault. It is how the criminal justice system tends to work in a western democracy. People who commit such crimes typically serve about half their sentence as a reward for good behaviour and if they no longer pose a threat to the public.

Whatever people's views, what isn't in doubt is this. His story shows both the best and worst of human endeavour and behaviour. It is a celebration of a rugby colossus from Bourgoin-Jallieu, and an example of how the rugby community tried to support him and his family in the aftermath of that dreadful night. It is also a profound illustration of his and others' sorrow.

I think there are four chapters to Marc's story:

1. The Player
2. His Road to Tragedy
3. Prison and the Rugby Fraternity
4. His Reintegration

First, let me set the scene.

I was a little nervous about meeting him, not because of his notoriety but because how I would navigate my way through the conversation without mentioning that terrible evening when Chantal lost her life. I wasn't here to discuss that, but it would come up. How would he deal with it? How would I? However, one can also overthink things. Of course, you do your research and planning, but sometimes you just have to jump in and rely on your emotional intelligence to guide you through difficult situations.

I met Marc in the centre of Collioure on a bright winter's day. It was freezing cold and the plane trees were bare as I saw the man-mountain walking down the hill. He'd said to me in an earlier call, *"How will I recognise you?"* *"J'ai la tete d'un anglais"* I replied. *"You can't miss me,"* and he didn't. Marina, his partner, was with him. They married in October 2010.

I had brought a bottle of Domaine de Trévallon or Châteauneuf-du-Pape to give to each player, but I turned up empty handed for Marc. How could I bring alcohol to a man who has suffered from alcoholism, and with devastating consequences?

However, his first sentence to me was: *"Salut David, allez, on va aller boire une mousse,"* and we headed straight to the bar. So much for my thinking ahead. We sat at a table and chatted, but I was conscious to make my beer last some time.

1. The Player

Marc first played for Bourgoin in 1979 when he was seventeen years old.

"I was playing for Perpignan and the teams were fighting like cats and dogs. I was sent off with Jacques Tisseyre who was thirty-six years' old. Caseneuve was the selector for France A at the time and he ran after me shouting, 'It wasn't the referee who sent you off, it was me who made the referee send you off.' I was targeted by Perpignan, and seemingly by the selector too.

"As a result, Lolo Rodriguez, who is a year younger, was selected for France Juniors instead of me, and then for the French squad a year later, where he cemented his place.

"Due to that sending off, I was in the cold for ten years, until 1988 when I won my first cap."

One of the outstanding men who I met on my travels is Gilles Cassagne, the former Bourgoin player. Whenever Marc's name came up in conversation with the other players, Gilles' did too. They are all in awe of his patience, commitment and loyalty towards Marc. I went to meet him for lunch in Saint-Jean-de-Bournay near Bourgoin September 2018. Gilles and I were joined by Dominique Mazille and Alexandre Chazalet, other mates from the region who played for Bourgoin and so knew Marc well. Gilles told me:

> "He was a physical freak of nature, like Rodriguez, without doing any weight training. He was very gifted technically as well as being a huge physical presence."

He was the key man in the Bourgoin side, the enforcer and very much the leader on the pitch. He didn't punch much but he did have a very powerful jab, which he used effectively on Gary Whetton in a match against Castres!

"Both Marc and Lolo were head and shoulders above any other Number 8s in France at the time, with perhaps Loppy and Melville coming close. Today, players may be as strong and good physically, but they lack Marc's and Laurent's all-round ability."

Over the years, I have chatted to Dewi Morris a few times about Marc and he remembers him very well:

"My god, he epitomised what I wanted out of my forwards. Cécillon was so hard. In 1991, I remember Winters kicking him in the head. He just got up and

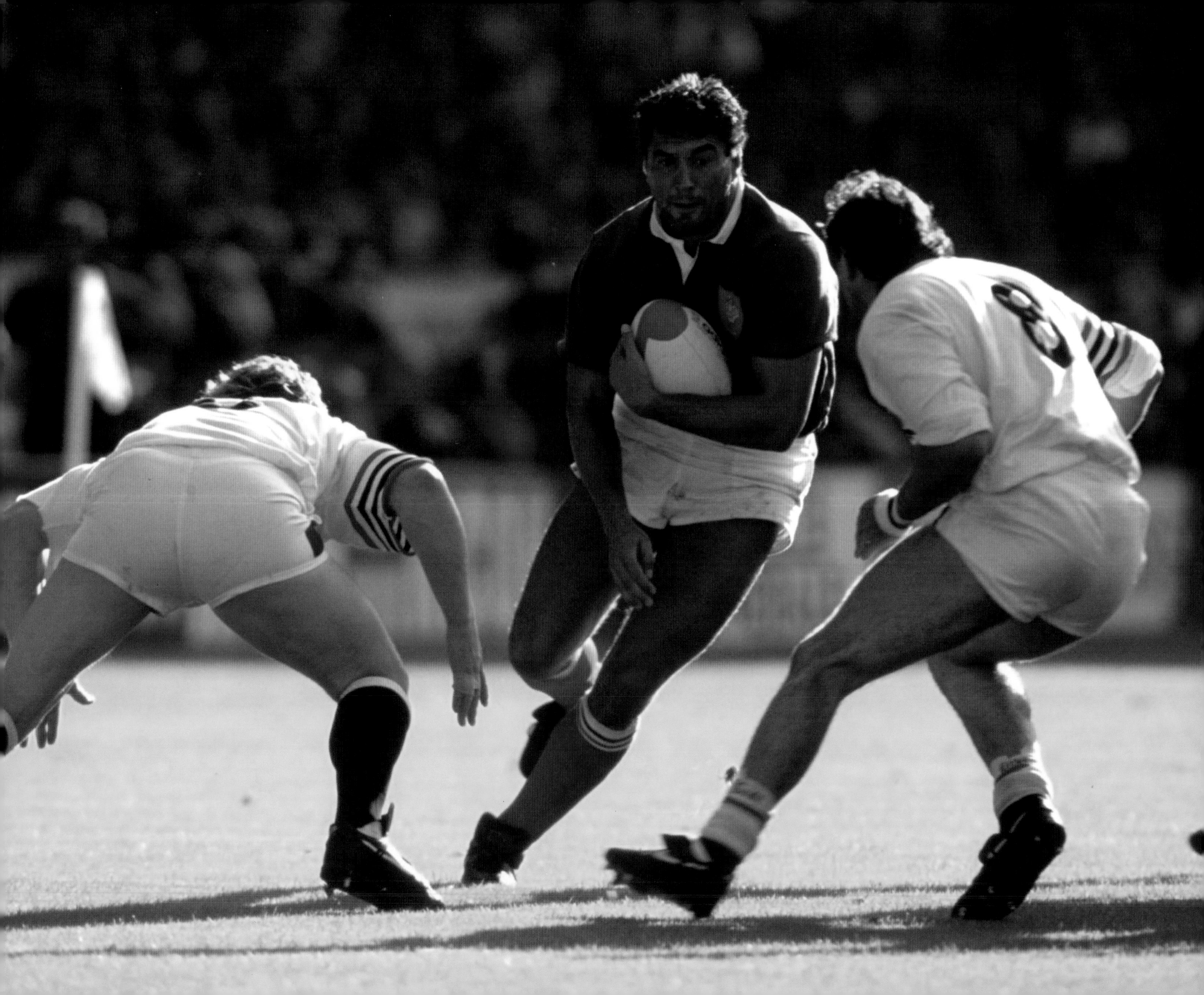

> "Both Marc and Lolo were head and shoulders above any other Number 8s in France at the time... Today, players may be as strong and good physically, but they lack Marc's and Laurent's all-round ability."

shook it off. He was like Dean Richards but far better looking of course! You needed someone to hold the side together and Marc was that man for the French."

I spent a couple of hours with Mickey Skinner and he described 'that tackle' on Marc Cécillon in the infamous 1991 Rugby World Cup quarter-final in Paris:

"The scrum was very near our line. I was very worried about their scrum-half but I also knew I had to cover Cécillon if he ran it. If he picked the ball up, I had to take him early because all he needed to do was pop the ball to Galthié and they might score. When he picked it up, I just smashed him, and it was only when I felt other people joining the tackle that I realised he must still have the ball. England won the penalty from the following scrum, but Pascal still managed to get a little Basque upper cut into Jason!"

Marc had many opportunities to leave Bourgoin for a bigger club, but his loyalty to his family, friends and teammates was stronger than his search for fame and fortune.

"In 1986, I nearly went to Toulon, but I stayed because my family was settled in Bourgoin. With hindsight, I should have gone. I would have enjoyed playing with all those big, hard men like Diaz, Champ and Louvet."

At his first trial, and in a chilling allusion to the past, the judge in her summing up said:

"You chose to stay on conquered ground where you think you could make your laws and where nobody could challenge you. Marc Cécillon's problem is that he arrived too late in front of his judges."

I showed Marc some old photos of the French and English players. He couldn't stop smiling. He loved reminiscing because it took him back to a former world when he was a kingmaker and star, and innocent of his crime.

2. His Road to Tragedy

How can the life of a top sportsman turn so bad? When I looked into the topic of idolatry, the thing that struck me was how one-sided the research is, focused on the person idolising, not the person being idolised. On the face of it, that seems to make sense. The idol's life is devoid of problems. He or she is special, superhuman, immortal, impervious to what we mere mortals have to contend with. The idol has it all, right? Wrong. For the sporting idol, their purpose has a cruel shelf life, a sell-by date after which the material deteriorates. Compare that to a singer, TV presenter, politician, painter, comedian whose fame and fortune aren't really constrained by age. For a sportsman or woman, post-career, the negative impact on the mind can be huge, when they are still very young, typically in their early thirties, when most people are just starting their arc to success.

Every player's circumstances are different, but it was fascinating to observe how the former players I met managed their own *reconversion*, as the French call it. Whether they were educated at university or not, many of the players seem to have mapped out their paths while they were playing, and therefore developed successful careers. Many of them come from humble backgrounds, such as Ondarts, Champ, Lorieux, Blanco, Imbernon and Codorniou, but they all have this instinctive intelligence, which means they don't make big mistakes in their lives.

They fall back on their values – inculcated by family, friends and rugby – and have the strength of mind to make the right choices (although no one is perfect of course). The sporting adulation they once enjoyed has been transformed into respect.

My reading of Marc is that he either doesn't possess this same instinctive intelligence or something was stopping him drawing upon it. I suspect the latter. After all, he was steeped in the culture of rugby and brought up by a loving family, but he still didn't make the right choices. Was it down to his mental health issues? It looks like it was.

In 2019, the PRA in England conducted some research on approximately 200 retired players, and 62% had experienced some sort of mental health issue. Clearly, Marc's manifested itself in an extreme way. Others find a way through. Others tragically take their own life, as was the case with Dan Vickerman in 2017.

Mark was a tortured soul after he finished playing. He played until he was forty years old and still regularly frequented the clubs and bars of the area.

At the trial, Marc admitted to his problems:

"When I finished playing, I never found my place in the family. I needed someone to look after me. I had always worked but I had no money. My wife managed it.

> " She would give me 200 FF each week so I could buy myself some fags. I had no cheque book. She would give me a shopping list and I would do the shopping and give the cheque book afterwards."

Reading all the testimony and newspaper reports, plus listening to the transcripts of the three hours that Marc and I spent together, this is the only example I could find where Marc looked fallible, real and humble, and admitted it. The court forced him to face the brutal facts of life and admit his problems.

Again, we see the juxtaposition in the life and behaviours of a star player. On the pitch, he was the captain and enforcer, in control and idolised by the fans. Off the pitch, his words make him sound pathetic, like a child incapable of taking responsibility and growing up.

The stories about Marc's philandering and drinking were well known, but he certainly wasn't the only player guilty of that. The violence was a big problem though. Several of the players told me that when he drank, he would become aggressive, but they were able to control him.

When he was in Bourgoin, they said that it was only his father who could control him, with his enormous hands.

Several of the former French players I met were critical of those 'friends' in Bourgoin who didn't control him when his behaviour was bad. Perhaps they let him get away with it because they were scared of him, and dumb-struck by this man who was the star of Bourgoin and won nearly fifty caps for France? Or perhaps they did try to control him, but he simply wouldn't listen to anyone other than his father and French international colleagues whom he regarded as his peers?

According to the press reports of the time, three months before the drama, Chantal had confided in friends that Marc would come home drunk more and more often. Ever the loyal friend, Gilles Cassagne said to me, *"I obviously regret not going to speak to Marc about this. Things might have turned out very different".* Gilles still questions himself about what he could have done differently. I am constantly struck by his commitment, kindness and loyalty.

On the night of 7th August 2004 when Marc killed Chantal, he used a gun that had been given to him by one of the body guards as he left a tour of South Africa in 1989. It is extraordinary to think about the chain of events that had to happen for Chantal to die as a result of that 'gift' fifteen years before. Fate moves in mysterious ways and can have devastating consequences.

3. Prison and the Rugby Fraternity

Marc's former rugby teammates can't forgive him for killing his wife who was also their friend. But they never abandoned Marc either.

He was in prison in Grenoble while waiting for his first trial and appeal, and was then sent to Muret prison just outside Toulouse in around 2008.

Gilles organised two games of rugby against the prisoners at Muret and a few former teammates went to watch, players such as Gilles, Erbani, Califano, Benneton, Chollet, Sadourney, Armary, Garuet, Bérot, Rodriguez, Ondarts. Dominique Mazille said it was 'un sacré souvenir'.

When I spoke to Finlay Calder and John Jeffrey, they told me they had written a letter to Marc following the murder. Fin told me, *"I can't remember what we said but it was a letter of support for him as a person. We have all f**ked up and gone through shit. His was an extreme version, admittedly, but life goes on and you have to support people. At times like this, you find out who true friends are."*

Derek White told me, *"I met him on the 1992 tour to South Africa as part of a World XV. I liked the way he played. He was hard on it but very friendly off it, in spite of the language barrier."*

JJ told me, *"Fin and I were part of a back-row with Marc, and part of an invitation team against the French. Marc slipped a box into his jock strap so Fin and I asked him what he was doing. He replied, 'You can't trust the French players not to grab them!'*

"Based on what I saw then, I liked him. He was quiet, unassuming and a great player. I can't remember what we said in the letter. It is the friendship and fraternity of this sport that make it so special."

Garuche talked to me about Marc:

"We were very good friends. He was a colossus, a supertalented player. He was like Jean Prat at Bourgoin. You get to know each other and I tried to help him manage the alcohol, how much he should drink and what he needed to do to eliminate it. Sometimes he would forget and I'd put him in his place. He always had great respect for the older players. We called him Arnold (Schwarzenegger) because he was magnificent. He was never injured."

Pascal and I spoke at length about Marc. He couldn't understand how a man he had known for so many years and who had been such a wonderful friend could have done such a thing.

"He is our friend, and I and others made sure we supported him and his family as much as we could. I call Marco regularly and always on 31st December to wish him well for the New Year.

"After we saw the rugby game at his prison in Muret, I wanted to go and see him afterwards in the changing room. To begin with, the warden said no. I explained to him: 'I want to go and see the player, not the man. A person who

kills his wife isn't a man'. The warden eventually agreed. Garuche was with me. I wanted to know how he was. We chatted a bit but I didn't really know what to say to him. I didn't want to hurt him. He was empty, without much reaction.

"I knew him so well, his wife and family too. I was thinking about his family when I asked him how he was. The prison director invited us to eat there, but we couldn't. We were heading off to watch Toulouse play Biarritz in Toulouse, and I was due to be staying overnight in a hotel. But I couldn't stop thinking about Marc and his family. I left at half time and drove back to Bayonne. We had made an effort to see him but I felt great pain. When I think about Marc, I think 'what a waste'."

Understandably and inevitably, Marc found prison very tough. He told me about it:

"There are a lot of people in there who shouldn't be because they are sick. I had my own cell, which helped protect me, but every time I left it, I couldn't be sure what might happen to me. Everyone is so tense inside, there are always problems and anyone could be targeted for any reason. That makes it is exhausting."

Some will judge Marc and Marina, a prison visitor, for getting married. I wanted to know how she came to fall in love with him:

"I didn't follow rugby at all, but I had a friend who did and he mentioned Marc. I saw them talking about the trial on the TV and I was shocked. I really felt for Marc. He was

"We were very good friends. He was a colossus, supertalented... We called him Arnold (Schwarzenegger) because he was magnificent. He was never injured."

> "In prison, everything goes slowly. When you leave, you are overwhelmed by everything – noise, people, traffic, shopping malls. You think everyone is looking at you. When there were fireworks, I couldn't stand the noise."

suffering terribly and my heart went out to him, so I started writing to him. Gradually he started responding. I asked the authorities if I could go and see him and they quickly granted permission.

"When I first saw him, I thought 'wow, what a giant'. He filled up the whole door frame. We were just friends to begin with and I helped him emotionally and spiritually. Then our relationship developed from there. It took time."

4. His Reintegration

"When I knew I was coming out of prison on parole, Gilles Cassagne was still there for me. He's always been there. With Jacques Brunel, they helped me find an apartment and job here.

"In prison, everything goes slowly. When you leave, you are overwhelmed by everything –noise, people, traffic, shopping malls. You think everyone is looking at you.

When there were fireworks, I couldn't stand the noise. I was traumatised by life. You have this sensation that everything is going so fast. I couldn't drive for a while and I didn't like speed. It is essential that you have an apartment and job so you can gradually reintegrate back into normal life."

When I met Marc in January 2018, he was working for a vineyard owner tying vines. However, after the harvest in 2018, he got drunk, assaulted the vineyard's owner and hit a truck while driving away from the scene before being stopped by police. He went to court again and admitted that he still has problems with alcohol, and received a suspended prison sentence.

When I saw Gilles, he was very angry after he heard about Marc's behaviour:

"I haven't called Marc because I want him to call me first. He hasn't had the courage to call me because he knows

I am angry. I have never stopped helping him, but he still seems in denial about his drink problems. When will he change?

"The problem with Marc is that he has never properly acknowledged his issues. If you ever ask him how he is, he will always say the same thing: 'Impeccable. Everything is great, no worries at all'. That never was and is still not the case."

I suggested to Gilles that he sit him down, like he had wished he'd done, and be clear with him, friend to friend, about what he needs to do to get his life back on track. I don't know if he did.

I occasionally swap messages with Marc, checking in to see how he is. I recently asked him whether he was still working at the vineyard, but he told me he was no longer there after the trouble at last year's harvest, that he was unemployed and would soon be retiring anyway. I replied asking him why he wouldn't coach one of the local rugby teams, and how that would be a great way of passing on his rugby knowledge and helping the community. He replied, *"I don't want to do that anymore"*. He needs to do something productive to occupy his time. He is only sixty and I am sure he has a lot he could be contributing to the community.

He goes back to Isère sometimes to see his three sisters and Mum. What about your girls, I ask? *"No, I don't see them."*

At the trial, Angelique, his eldest daughter, shouted

to him: *"I will never forgive you, but I still love you"*.
Céline, the youngest daughter told him she would
never forgive him and didn't want to see him again.
Now, neither sees him.

My heart beats with melancholy when I read Angelique's
and Celine's words. As Pascal says, *"What a waste"*.

Compassion

When I think about Marc and how I should describe
him, every adjective comes to mind – pathetic,
tortured, alcoholic, sad, timid, ashamed, stubborn,
empty, but also warm, friendly, even lovely. I enjoyed
his company very much, in spite of the moments of
intense sadness. At times, he spoke with a heavy heart,
his face coated with emotion and regret. Even when
he didn't say the words, his sorrow is palpable.

If you didn't know the crime he had committed and
you were having a drink with him in a pub, you would
think he was just another former rugby player who
was friendly and good fun, and who liked booze, fags
and girls. He won't be the last.

In spite of the dreadful crime he committed, my
overriding feeling for him is compassion. How can it
not be? Because of one terrible act in 2004, he has
destroyed the lives of his wife, children and family,
and seriously damaged those of his friends.

As we were leaving the restaurant after lunch, I asked
him my final question:

"What are your hopes for the future, Marc?"

He replied, *"I want to return to Isère, my home. I want
to get my girls back, but I don't know if I will ever see
them again. I hope so."*

It is a very understandable emotion. Does he have any
tangible plans that might go some way to redeeming
himself and building the necessary bridges back
to a reconciliation with his daughters? I don't know.
Marc, if you're reading this, that is where I would focus.
I think it will be a long road back, but I wish you the best
and I hope too that you make it.

*"Marc was a fabulous player, a monumental team
mate. Rugby had given him structure and meaning
to his life, but he suffered from depression and alcoholism,
and he eventually lost his way."*
Louisou Armary

The impressive Éric Champ told me:

*"He was a fabulous player, but one day your career is over.
You have the limelight for a period and then the light goes
out. If you don't have the right environment to support you,
things can turn sour. Those around him should have told
him some hard truths, given him some tough love, not said
'come and have another drink', and 'you're the best person
on the planet'."*

"Be careful because notoriety can happen to anyone"
Jo Maso

Éric Champ

MEDITERRANEAN
+ PROVENCE

" WHAT I HAVE LEARNT IN BUSINESS
AND IN SPORT IS THAT THERE IS NO
REAL LOVE OR LASTING FRATERNITY
OR GREAT ADVENTURE, WHICH
LEAVES AN INDELIBLE MARK, UNLESS
THERE IS SUCCESS AND VICTORY."

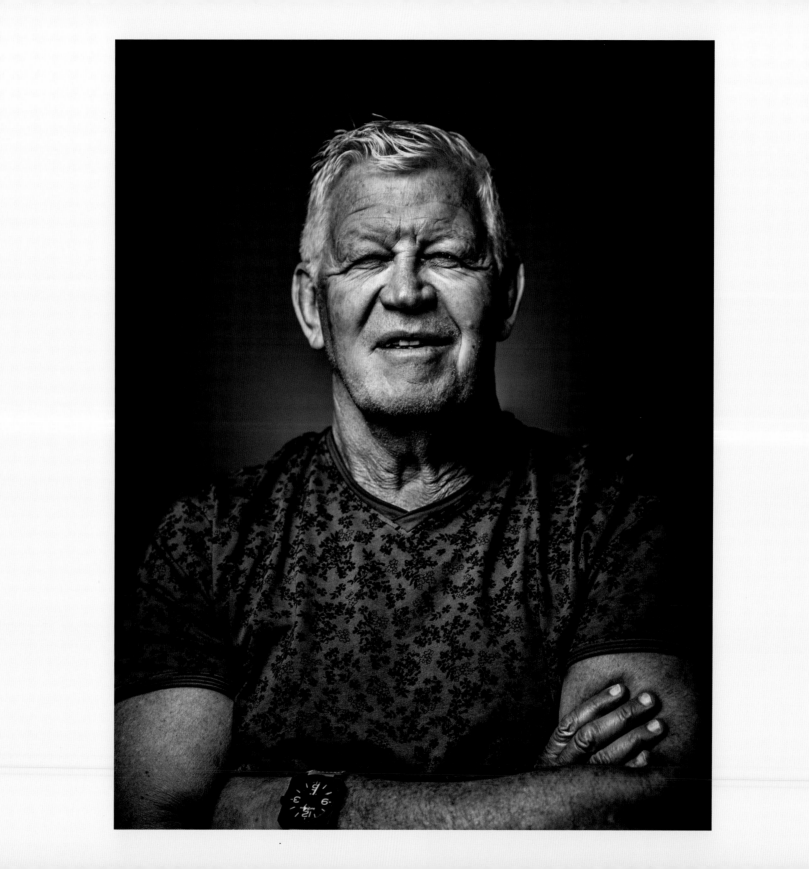

BORN : 8TH JUNE 1962

CLUBS : RACING CLUB TOULONNAIS

INTERNATIONAL CAPS : 42

POSITION : FLANKER

GRAND SLAMS : 1987

NICKNAME : LE BARBARE DE LA RADE

NOM DE GUERRE : THE GODFATHER

MY VISIT TO MEET HIM : TUESDAY 12TH DECEMBER 2017

I used to love watching Éric play. He was tall, lean, athletic and aggressive. He would push his chin and chest out in that Mediterranean way telling everyone that he was the boss of the town. He is from Toulon and would defend his patch to the last.

We scheduled dinner at a bar called Chez le Basseur in La Valette near Toulon. He was easy to spot because he hadn't changed much, other than his grey mane and a few more beauty lines around the eyes. He still looked lean and fit, but also much more friendly than he did during his playing days.

We sat down in the corner, near all his rugby shorts and photos, where he wouldn't be bothered by people seeking his autograph.

"You see all those rugby shirts on the wall, David. My girls aren't interested in rugby so I gave them all away! For some reason, the Scotland shirt is missing."

He launched straight into a discussion about the importance of winning.

"I experienced two great periods of French rugby with the Rugby World Cups in 1987 and 1991. In 1987, we had been together for six years or so. We had been through many tough games but we were winning a lot. When you have a team that wins, it naturally creates very strong bonds between the players. Of course, we had talented players and that helps. But on its own, it is an insufficient factor. Jacques knew which buttons to press. He created a formula that worked and it was winning that created our bonds of friendship. From 1991 onwards, it felt different to me. That human dimension wasn't as strong. Perhaps I was so well rewarded before and therefore had very high expectations. It wasn't because of the players. Whatever the reason, we weren't as successful as before. What I have learnt in business and in sport is that there is no real love or lasting 'fraternité' or great adventure that leaves an indelible mark unless there is success and victory."

Paté or Foie Gras?
Éric is steeped in the culture of Toulon, which is some distance from the South West of France where the majority of rugby clubs were based back then.

"I was brought up here in La Valette-du-Var. They created

a rugby school right behind Chez Le Brasseur where I started playing age seven. Dad played for Toulon and trained the colts. I did a lot of athletics and sailing in those days. Living right next to the water meant that my passion was really sailing. Dad sent me to play rugby to calm me down because I was boisterous at school. We lived on the third floor of an apartment and I would throw buckets of flowers on the people below! At the rugby school, we would pick up all the stones before training so we didn't injure ourselves. It is where RCT train today. I went to play for Toulon when I was about fourteen."*

Éric played all the age groups for France and remembers his first match for the French schoolboys' team against England in Dax when he was around sixteen.

"We won that game and Cambé and Sella were both playing too. What I really remember though was my discovery of 'foie gras'! My grandparents worked at le marché de Valette and every Sunday when we went to play

rugby, they would give us a slice of 'paté', which I loved. At the after-match dinner in Dax with the schoolboys, they served what I thought was the same sort of 'paté', but when I put it in my mouth, I realised it was completely different. It was 'foie gras' and it was delicious."*

Imbécile!
Éric started playing against the big international teams from 1981 when he was selected at Number 8 for a French selection against the touring All Blacks side in Clermont Ferrand in 1981. In spite of the tough competition at the time from Rives, Joinel, Rodriguez, Lacans and Erbani, he was in the mix, but then suffered a set back when he was banned from being selected for three years.

"I was captaining France Juniors and we won the Grand Slam, but I had to do military service. I didn't want to travel so managed to find myself a post in Toulon where

> "When you have a team that wins, it naturally creates very strong bonds between the players. Of course, we had talented players and that helps. But on its own, it is an insufficient factor. Jacques knew which buttons to press."

I could carry on quietly with my rugby at home. During the Five Nations, Le Bataillon de Joinville was the opposition for the French team in Paris on the Wednesday before the matches. Like an 'imbécile', I travelled to Paris with the French team, but the General of the Bataillon called the FFR to question how I could travel to Paris with the French squad when I wasn't able to travel for military service. So, they banned me from being selected for any French team for three years!

"I came back in 1984, but broke my hand at La Voulte so I couldn't play in the Five Nations. When Jean-Pierre Rives retired, I didn't succeed him, I simply borrowed his Number 6 jersey! Jean-Luc Joinel was also towards the end of his career and Pierre Lacans, poor guy, died in 1985 so I had more chance of being selected."

Éric was an athletic flanker who was particularly effective off the back of the line using his height to launch the backs, or off the base of a scrum where he would switch with Mesnel to cut through the opposition defence. I remember one try in particular when Champ burst through and passed to Érik Bonneval who scored against England in 1987.

"The games I really remember are the ones that were tense and close, like England in 1989 and 1991, or any game against the Scottish because they were so strong with players like Calder, Jeffrey and Laidlaw. Scotland won the Grand Slam in 1984 and finished joint first with France in 1986."

Eric Melville, a Great Player and Man

Éric Champ is born and bred Toulonnais, and he talked with great passion about his friends and teammates:

"At one point, I became President of RCT. When the team is promoted, it's great but when you stop winning, everyone starts searching for people to blame and they want the heads of the trainers. At the time, we had Thierry Louvet and Aubin Hueber, who are both former teammates and great friends. I said we could remove them but if they left, then I would leave too. In spite of the process, we never fell out. We lived through so many incredible experiences that we would never allow that.

"Another great friend was Eric Melville who played for us for many years and who died recently. He was a magnificent player and man, the most courageous and strongest of all of us. It gives me goose bumps when I speak about him. On a human level, he was a huge man who always sacrificed himself on the pitch for the service of his team. Once he played a match with a broken jaw.

"Eric Melville played for Stade Montois when Toulon first played against him. We fought and he really impressed us. Toulon was a team of fighters but he wasn't like that. During that match, Daniel Herrero saw what a player he was and what he could bring Toulon in terms of physicality, talent and character.

"Eric Melville was a practising pasteur and had a wonderful philosophy about life. He would often quote Churchill's line and say, 'We make a living by what we get, but we make a life by what we give'."

Daniel Herrero also spoke to me movingly about his great friend.

"He was exceptional as a player and man. He was tough, disciplined, energetic and skilful. He had this 'altruism absolu' that governed his life. He only played for the right reasons, for the team. Effectiveness was more important to him than brilliance. He had a great sense of responsibility. For him, everything was about sharing and sacrifice for the greater good. I miss him greatly."

The Herrero Brothers

Éric Champ was lucky to have some excellent coaches like André and Daniel Herrero, and Jacques Fouroux.

"All of them were exceptional with formidable intelligence. When I was young, I had André. He was in the same mould as Walter Spanghero and Benoît Dauga. He was very demanding, but he really helped me technically.

"Daniel worked differently and was a bit like Jacques Fouroux. He knew that to win, you needed to be physical and dominate your opponent, but he also appreciated that we had some real talent out wide such as Gallion, Bianchi, Carbonnel and others. So, he wanted us to play dynamic rugby. He also worked on the psychological aspects, leveraging our characteristics as a team of young guns and rebels, breeding a siege mentality against the other clubs of France. This is why we had so many great fights against teams like Lourdes, Racing, Agen and Bègles. Against Bègles in 1991, we deliberately kicked the ball out on the full from the kick-off so the scrum would form on

Mike Brewer jumps for a line-out with Éric Champ. Rugby Union, Toulouse, 8th November 1986, France 7 v New Zealand 19.
Photo - Bob Thomas Sports Photography, Getty Images.

the halfway line, followed by a mass fight, penalty against Bègles and three points for Toulon. It was great fun!

"Daniel still thinks deeply about things that happened a long time ago. For our thirty-year reunion recently, he said to us, 'If I had coached you differently, do you think we would have won more?' I replied, 'Daniel, who gives a f**k, it won't change anything!'"

Champ and Skinner Would Be the Best of Friends

One of the most famous photos is of Éric Champ nose-to-nose with Mick Skinner during the 1991 quarter-final of the Rugby World Cup in Paris.

"Everyone was on edge for that game. Geoff Cook had given me a video of Champ to study how he played, and it was full of all his good and nasty highlights. He could be one dirty player, including one clip when he stamps on someone. So, when I was nose-to-nose with him, it was because I thought he was going to stamp on Dools. After the ref had blown the whistle, I ran to the breakdown and Champ must have thought 'what the f**k are you doing?' I was the aggressor... for once! I spent the whole afternoon trying to mute anyone in a blue French shirt, but especially Cécillon and Champ.

"I'd actually love to meet him again. I am sure he is a top bloke, like the vast majority of players back then. Most of us were the same on and off the pitch. We just speak a different language, and there wasn't much time or emotion left to make friends after the matches!"

Peter FitzSimons, the former Australian second-row who played for Brive in the late 1980s, played many times against Toulon and knows the area well. He told me a couple of anecdotes that capture the spirit, emotions and humour in this part of France:

"Brive was playing Hyères in an early season match and one of our opponents was a jailbird, covered in tattoos and as hard as nails. He was violent and known for stamping, gouging, clawing, biting and kicking. Modin, our scrum-half, told me that we had to take him out before his thuggery got the better of us. I said to this thug, 'If you move, I will take your head off'. He put me down with a killer line: 'Oh really? Well I am going to f**k you dry'.

"Now, there are things that one man can say to another man, but I had never heard that expression before or even contemplated it. He caught me by surprise so I backed off and said, 'OK, no problem'.

"Another time, we were playing Toulon at Brive. I was momentarily pinned on my back and couldn't move, as Jeff Tordo stamped on my face. The red mist descended. I cocked my arm back ready to give him the right hook of my life. I was so f**king angry. He saw it coming and just said, 'Sorry'. How can you hit a man after he has apologised?"

Éric went to three finals for Le Bouclier de Brennus, losing in 1985 and 1989 against Toulouse, and beating RCF in 1987. Toulon also beat Biarritz in 1992, but Éric was suspended for the match following a sending off against Agen in the semi-final of the Yves du Manoir cup competition.

"Abdel Bennazi and I had a scuffle but it never stopped us remaining friends. I was disappointed not to play in the final, but my teammates spoiled me by asking me to lift Le Bouclier de Brennus. I say that I am twice champion of France, even though it feels a little false saying so!"

I used to love the adventure for the fans, typically from the south of France, when they headed to Paris for the Bouclier de Brennus final. It was a big carnival with the cars, trumpets and singing. I went to that final in 1992 and remember it well. It was 6th June and quite warm, at least that's what I recall. I had been at Willi's Wine Bar in Paris the whole afternoon before heading to La Porte d'Auteuil, next to the Parc des Princes, where we partied with the Biarritz and Toulon fans, Basque v La Rade, Cider v *Pastis*, Provincial v Provincial. It was a celebration for the great rugby communities in an atmosphere of conviviality and fraternity.

I watched a video recently when Éric said, *"In the play-offs, the beautiful game is replaced by hard rugby, by the taste of blood in the mouth".*

Those words encapsulate the Toulon spirit perfectly. It is a town of high emotion.

On N'est Pas Bien Là?

When I met Franck Mesnel, he told me what it was like playing with and against Éric:

"It was re-assuring! He was typically Toulonnais, with his big heart and strong personality. He never went missing. He was a hard man and good leader. Being Parisian at RCF, we always had a tense relationship with the Toulonnais at the other end of France. We would tease them a lot before and during matches. They didn't like us smug, arrogant Parisian boys!

" I remember one game we played. The scrum smashed together, I looked at Baptiste and winced just as a big fight broke out. Thierry Louvet, their flanker, and Michel Tachdjian, one of our hard men, were face to face, with blood all over them. Louvet's teeth were broken. Louvet just looked at Tachdjian, who'd smacked him, and said, 'Michel, isn't this great fun?' That was the Toulonnais. They were volatile but never took a backward step."

"English has held me back a little in my career so I really pushed my two girls, to learn it. I am too old to start learning it now. I'll rely on them for any translation!"

Suddenly, his friend Fred calls him. Éric hands me the phone and Fred says, *"Éric doesn't even speak French, let alone English!"* Just to be clear, Éric speaks perfect French with those guttural sounds so typical of the *accent du midi.*

Since he stopped playing rugby, Éric has had a number of business interests including Parlym, a major force in industrial engineering, as well as running sporting and business conferences and workshops. He is also a shareholder in Chez Le Brasseur.

Appearances can be deceptive and Éric couldn't be more different from that image he had on the pitch. He is charming, articulate, personable and smiley, and so typical of the people of the South of France. They live here because they love the space, sea and weather. When they can, they live outside and immerse themselves in friendship, discussion and, of course, rugby. I loved his company and will certainly look him up when I am next down there again.

"In the first final we lost in 1987, we were in the tunnel just before the game, wearing perfume, bow ties, our shirt collars up, and with perfectly coiffured hair. At least, that was 'le Show-Bizz' backs, as we called ourselves. The Toulonnais next to us were sweating profusely and chewing gum. We would drive them nuts.

"I used to wind Éric up and say,

'I can't smell you today Éric. Something isn't right. You're going to break something.'

"I always had a strong relationship with flankers because their job was to hunt me down!

"Of course, our forwards would be sweating before the games. We would refer to them as 'Le Gros-Bizz'. It would wind them up much to our amusement!

"Another time, we were at dinner and I started throwing some bread at Éric. I was next to Denis Charvet and we were chatting away. All of a sudden, I had a fork impaled in my arm. Éric had walked calmly around behind me and stabbed me with it. I had a scar for ten years!"

Like so many of the former players whom I met, Éric regrets not being able to converse with his former adversaries from the British Isles.

"I wish I could speak English. When I am with the same blokes I played against, with the same values of friendship, team work, respect and solidarity, I get so frustrated that the language gets in the way. I want to chat and laugh and share stories. I think I suffered so much from Skinner that I have never been able to learn English properly!

"*Brave and hard. He was a great player, a real warrior.*"
Patrick Estève

"*Champ was a big character, a fighter who could be very hard on the pitch.*"
Daniel Herrero

"*Champ was one of my toughest opponents.*"
Sean Fitzpatrick

"*He gouged me so hard that I could see my brain. It was big.*"
Peter FitzSimons, former Brive second row

"*Champ was a thug. Dirty on pitch and lovely off it.*"
Nick Farr-Jones

Didier Codorniou

MEDITERRANEAN
+ PROVENCE

"RUGBY TEACHES US TO
HAVE DISCIPLINE IN LIFE,
IT REMINDS US WHO WE ARE
AND WHERE WE HAVE COME
FROM. YOU LEARN ALL THE
VALUES AND VIRTUES WHICH
YOU NEED FOR LIFE – HUMILITY,
HARD WORK, SACRIFICE, TEAM
WORK, ENTHUSIASM, RESPECT,
GENEROSITY, CHARACTER,
ANTICIPATION, AND SO ON."

BORN : 13TH FEBRUARY 1958

CLUBS : RACING CLUB DE NARBONNE MÉDITERRANÉE,
STADE TOULOUSAIN

INTERNATIONAL CAPS : 31

POSITION : CENTRE

GRAND SLAMS : 1981

NICKNAME : CODOR

NOM DE GUERRE : LE PETIT PRINCE, LE PETIT MOZART

MY VISIT TO MEET HIM : TUESDAY 12TH DECEMBER 2017

I looked forward to meeting every player, but in my mind, there was something exceptional about Codorniou. He was my school-boy hero, this supremely gifted, diminutive player with fabulous balance who could throw beautiful passes and always evade contact while he had the ball. He was mesmerising to watch and undoubtedly one of the greatest rugby players of his generation. Now a very successful politician, I tracked him down via the Mayor's office in Gruissan near Narbonne, and we met for lunch in the beautiful coastal town of Sète, just south of Montpellier on the Mediterranean.

If you hadn't noticed already, I love France, and I especially love this part. This is the land of milk and honey, where the sun shines three hundred days a year, the *cigales* sing, the sea is warm and you can enjoy a light rosé, luscious white or full-bodied red wine with your *poisson du marché*, *entrecôte* or *Provençal* lamb. The sun is scorching at the height of summer, but the air is typically bone dry so you don't feel too hot in the shade. Furthermore, the winds can blow – not just the Mistral, but also the Tramontane, expelling the clouds and germs, which is why the sky is blue and the grapes rarely suffer from disease.

He was mesmerising to watch and undoubtedly one of the greatest rugby players of his generation.

I had arrived from Béziers the day before and I checked into Le Grand Hôtel in Sète. It has a slightly French colonial feel to it, showing more charm than grandeur. The food was excellent, but the standard wine list poor, a feature of many French restaurants these days – too focused on local wines or not enough variety of those wines, as though the restaurant can't be bothered to think about it. But fear not, I chatted up the *Sommelière* and secured a bottle from the *la carte spéciale*.

I was meeting Didier for lunch the next day so I took full advantage a night off from my busy schedule. For some, this might mean a walk on the beach, the cinema, a book and an early night. However, that wasn't my calling. I decided to do a trial run in the restaurant to ensure it was of the requisite quality for lunch the following day. I did and it was. I couldn't wait for lunch with Didier.

Broken Ribs

I slept well and was up early. I nipped out for a coffee and *cryssante* around 8am only to suffer what I would describe as a minor incident, but one for which I paid a heavy price in the following weeks. As I left Le Grand Hôtel, I wasn't sure whether to turn left or right so I stood there trying to find my sense of direction. Those of you who know Sète will be thinking *'this bloke is a cabbage, Sète is tiny, how can you not know?'* It is a fair question, but sense of direction isn't one of my strong points. As I say to my long-suffering wife, *'I can't be good at everything'*. Or as my friend Julian retorts, *'You're not good at anything'*. Anyway, let me explain what happened:

The pavement was narrow and there were people trying to get by, so as a thoughtful citizen, I stepped onto the road. As I turned left (which, by the way, was the wrong direction), there was a curb right behind my left foot and before you could say *'où est le meilleur restaurant de la ville s'il vous plait?'* I was on the floor.

Both my feet had become wedged behind this *putain de* random curb and I had belly-flopped onto the concrete, smacking my hands and chest on the ground. Not only that, but the glasses case in my chest pocket was clearly made of the world's hardest steel because it rammed into my ribs. I was reeling in pain but too embarrassed to admit it to the passers-by, who were all staring at the old bloke on the ground. A young lady helped me up and I said *'merci'*, before scurrying away in the other direction (which, by the way, was the right direction).

The next few days were agony, exacerbated by the fact that I was with Knoxy, the walking *soufflé*, who makes me laugh a lot, even though I have heard all his stories a thousand times. A few weeks later when I was having some fitness tests, my doctor friend, Dr David Burling, told me that I had broken a rib. Knowing now what it feels like, I finally have sympathy for the likes of Sean Fitzpatrick when they say 'Garuet broke my ribs'.

When I played, I only suffered from athletes' injuries such as pulling a hamstring, tearing a cartilage or breaking a toe nail.

The Mozart of Rugby

Anyway, back to Didier, one of my top ten centres of all time (see article on Philippe Sella).

Didier has had a very successful career, on and off the pitch. At various times, he has worked for a bank and Adidas before becoming Maire de Gruissan in 2001. He is now Vice-President de l'Occitanie, which encompasses thirteen departments from Tarbes to Drôme. He was a very busy man so I knew I had to make the most of the limited time we had together.

The best way to describe Codor as a player is through the eyes of his peers and journalists. When I met Denis Charvet, this is what he said about Didier:

"When Codor came to ST, it was the greatest rugby time of my life. I lived a real dream. I was playing with the player I wanted to be. He was the best player I ever played with."

"He had everything - the innate sense of the game, vision, anticipation, technique. He was a magician. Yes, when you take everything into account, he was the strongest. He was the Mozart of rugby."

Jo Maso told me: *"Codor was exceptionally gifted and so passionate about the game. He had the temperament to be the best because he was serious, looked after himself, ate well and liked training. Sometimes, I would miss him out in the matches to protect him, then I would give him the ball and he'd be off. He had a touch, a sense of the game, he read it beautifully. He was so good."*

When I saw Christian Montaignac, the great French sports journalist and writer, I could see the adulation in his eyes, for both the man and the player:

"He was the master, Le Petit Mozart. He could fix a player with a look. He shone a light around him and made it easy for his teammates. He was graceful and gracious."

Rugby's Lessons for Life

Didier arrived bang on time. He is such a busy man and I was grateful that he could spare me a couple of hours. I opened up about the book and he recognised instantly the Francophile opposite him:

"You speak super French! You have a mix of accents from England, and the centre and the south of France."

"The culture of rugby is very clear and precise. Rugby teaches us to have discipline in life, it reminds us who we

are and where we have come from. You learn all the values and virtues that you need for life – humility, hard work, sacrifice, team work, enthusiasm, respect, generosity, character, anticipation, and so on. All these ingredients are useful and help shape who we are.

"It's an inter-generational thing too. At any one time, there are four to five generations who played, are playing or who will play the game, so the transmission between them is vital. This notion of history, learning and handing down is vital. Wherever I played - Narbonne, Toulouse, France, abroad - I would know players of every generation. History is very important because that is how we learn. Players of all generations need to recognise how they became who they are and how to pass down those values to the next ones. Time passes very quickly.

"I worry that today's players don't think about the wider importance of the game outside of their bubble, that they don't recognise the important role they play in its integrity and future. Today's game is very different with all its marketing and money, but players will have the rest of their lives to live after they retire at about thirty-two years old. Life can be tough and lonely, and they need to have the right values to manage their way through."

Didier didn't go to university, but he too has this instinctive intelligence, which Jérôme Gallion spoke about when describing André Herrero, Éric Champ and Jacques Fouroux. They are highly intelligent people without being highly educated, and rugby has been key in developing how they think. Didier is clearly a deep thinker, which is understandable when you consider his political standing.

Adapting to Professionalism

We ordered lunch and I plumped for the same dish I had 'tested' the previous night – *le risotto d'homard*, plus a bottle of luscious white from Pic Saint-Loup, not far from Montpellier. The risotto had a firm bite and creamy texture while the lobster claws were plump and perky and romped concupiscent with clams, shrimps and some aromatic vegetables in a bright broth. Didier and I couldn't get enough of it. If I'd been on my own, I may well have ordered it as a starter, main and dessert.

"We need to make sure in France that they don't lose these rugby values. I don't want to sound like an old pro having a go, caught up in some romantic notion of yesteryear.

"It seems to me that the English have managed to preserve their way of playing with their discipline. They have adapted better to professionalism in terms of coaching, physical condition, developing the young kids coming through and maintaining their intensity. We in France have lost our French flair, trying to copy something from everyone such as the All Blacks, Australia and England. Some are starting to adapt and come back, such as Stade Toulousain, La Rochelle and Bordeaux Bègles. Everyone looks for collisions, encouraged by the rules, with defence getting the upper hand on attack."

Talking of the All Blacks, I wanted to hear first-hand

about the New Zealand tour in 1979 and that second test, which France won:

" That tour in 1979 was fabulous. The second test against the All Blacks was the greatest match I experienced for its intensity, pace and skill…"

...and the way Jean-Pierre Rives led the team. It was the first time we had beaten the All Blacks in New Zealand and it happened on 14th July. We were in a fragile period having lost the previous week."

Didier made a huge contribution that day, scoring a try and playing a key role in Averous' try. As usual, he had

anticipated where to support as he received the ball from Joinel bang on the halfway line. His line, pace and pass to Caussade were typically gorgeous. Caussade took the ball at pace and weaved right then left before passing inside to Averous who caught the ball at the third attempt before scoring. It was another moment of French flair, executed off-the-cuff.

For his own try, Averous picked the ball up about 40m out and passed it left to Caussade who sprinted down the left touchline. Didier could see the play before it happened so ran another exquisite support line inside where Caussade passed to him and he scored.

It was Didier at his best, encapsulating everything that his peers describe in their testimony. He was a beautiful rugby player to watch because he made everything look so easy. He instinctively knew where to run, when to pass, when to break.

"We need to make sure in France that they don't lose these rugby values in their bubble. I don't want to sound like an old pro having a go, caught up in some romantic notion of yesteryear."

"I was nervous about my opposite numbers. They said that Osbourne used to hunt for wild boar with only a knife, so I was a little intimidated!"

"We had the great platform for success. Costes, Blanco, Pardo, Dintrans had all played France U21s so we knew each other well. We celebrated Bastille Day twice, leaving New Zealand on the 15th, crossing the date line and arriving in Tahiti on the 14th!"

Taking Responsibility

Didier had a lot of success at Narbonne, winning the Bouclier de Brennus in 1979, but by 1985 he became disillusioned with the Directors over the extension of his contract so he joined Stade Toulousain.

"The team was already settled when I arrived so I had to win my place, which meant Érik Bonneval moving to the wing. I loved my time there. We had complete freedom to play as we wished. Villepreux and Skrela encouraged us to take responsibility and play running rugby. At Narbonne, we trained and played like the old school with lots of collisions. At Toulouse, the calm was striking. Cigana would just say a few words before we went on the pitch. I helped Denis develop his game there, introducing him to classical music and preparing mentally for the matches.

"Denis would try to do anything on the pitch. He had great self-confidence. We didn't need to go looking for each other. We really suited each other. Érik was also a brilliant player. If he hadn't been injured, he would certainly have been one of the best players of his generation. In fact,

he probably was anyway, in spite of his career being affected by a knee injury. He had everything – a piece of both Sella and Blanco. He was supertalented, fast, skilful and powerful. Even when he came back after injury, he was a superb player.

"I loved Pierre and Jean-Claude as coaches. Their focus was on getting the players to take responsibility for managing chaos and disorder in a match. We had to read what was in front of us, react and quickly find the space. We had to play off-the-cuff, within a framework, and adapt on the pitch in real time. It was how the All Blacks played. I spent three years there and they were three of the most enjoyable of my rugby career, along with 1979-80."

When I met Pierre Villepreux, he spoke about the signing of Didier:

"Some players were nervous because he would take their place, but you can't turn someone like Codor down. He is very intelligent and charming and he integrated really well. Noves was coming to the end of his career and Bonneval was such a great player and team player so he moved easily to the wing. Codor was very clever and technical. He wasn't big but he had a mastery of the game."

Talent Everywhere

I wanted to know about the other players Didier had played with.

"I've always considered Sella as the modern-day player. I first saw him play full-back in Toulouse when he was

about eighteen and I thought he was exceptional – fast, powerful, fit, brilliant tackler, great movement. He was the outstanding player of his generation. I thought the same thing about Dan Carter when I first saw him play. He could do everything. I was there with my son, Aurelien. When you watch an artist at work, whatever the discipline, you are blown away by their skill. That was both Philippe Sella and Dan Carter.

"I played with so many great players - Maso, Rives, Caussade, Sella, Bonneval, Charvet, Gallion, Estève - that I always had the conviction that I would one day play for France.

"François Sangali and I were similar types of players, relying on instinct and our audacity. His strength was his commitment, discipline and precision.

> "Jo Maso was my mentor. I would have liked to have played more with him. I felt his influence very strongly. I loved the way he would guide me during the matches and then replay the match afterwards. He had such wisdom."

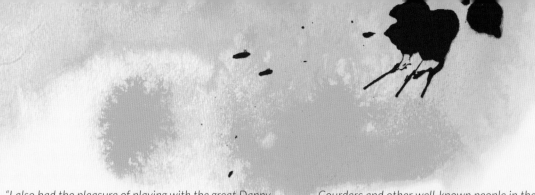

"He had a game of finesse, with his vision,
beautiful passing and judgement. He could immediately
see where the space was."
Jérôme Gallion

"He was one of the most gifted centres I ever played against.
He was silky smooth with pace, great hands
and an eye for a gap. He epitomised French flair."
John Kirwan

"He could mesmerise defences without the ball.
He would move towards the ball carrier, then drift
away, tricking defenders."
Bob Dwyer

"I also had the pleasure of playing with the great Danny Gerber from South Africa in August 1992 at Serge's testimonial. He was fast, skilful and so powerful. The experience was fabulous."

Narbonne and Béziers were great rivals in the 1970s and '80s and I asked Didier to tell me what he remembers: .

"I remember playing Béziers and seeing red and black everywhere. We couldn't find any space. There were three or four Estève or Senal or Palmié wherever you looked. It was a quarter-final in Toulouse and I was only eighteen. Those Bitterois were scary! At their stadium, Sauclières, they had 'le couloir de mort' that you had to walk through to get to the pitch. Something illegal always happened in the tunnel..."

Kiss and Make Up

What was the truth behind his fall out with Jacques Fouroux, which meant he didn't go to the Rugby World Cup in 1987? Jérôme Gallion told me that Fouroux 'n'aimait pas le talent pur'.

"Jacques was an inescapable force in French rugby. He had a philosophy about rugby that didn't match my skills. He wanted big, physical men. When we toured Australia in 1981, Jacques told me that I wasn't good enough defensively so he didn't select me for the first test match. From that point, we started to bang heads. I was very offended. I let a journalist at L'Equipe know how I felt and that it was all a big injustice. When the likes of Roger

Courderc and other well-known people in the media got hold of the story, they built it up and made it worse. The press was critical of Jacques' style and felt it betrayed France's history of running rugby, which they thought I epitomised. I was young and said some things that Jacques didn't like, so he eliminated me. When I went to ST in 1985, I disappeared a bit from the screens, but I was on good form there.

"At the time, I took it very badly and it went against all the values of rugby that I had grown up with – loyalty, respect, openness. But it also coincided with the first years of my marriage so I could spend time with my wife, Isabelle. For years, I was very resentful. It still hurts but you learn to manage it!

"In 1993, I was playing for the French Barbarians against the Australians in Clermont Ferrand. Jacques took me to one side and apologised for how he had treated me. It was a lovely moment. After the match, Horan, Little and Campese all asked why I hadn't been playing in the French side.

"After we reconciled, we became quite close and I would see him from time to time. We turned the page and life was beautiful again. I am a humanist; I like people and I don't want to be bitter. With Jacques, life came full circle."

Several of the players told me how Jacques would use funny and provocative images to explain why he picked big, physical players, one of which he often applied to his non-selection of Didier.

"If you put Mark Andrieu and Didier Codorniou in a room alone, and threw a piece of beef in the middle, who do you think would eat it first?"

Seeing and Feeling More

The lunch was over. We ordered a couple of coffees, prolonging the postprandial discussion for a further fifteen minutes when he had to leave to resume his Mayoral duties. I thanked him for his time and wished him well, searching for any excuse to come back to see him.

As I left the restaurant, my head was full of images of Didier's inspiring rugby skills. I went for a walk next to the sea and thought about those initials 'DC,' which seem to bestow the combined gifts of natural talent and requisite commitment onto a chosen few - Didier Codorniou, Denis Charvet, Danny Cipriani, Dan Carter. Didier, like all the other DCs, was a player who could see and feel more than most.

For the next few days, I hobbled around the south of France with my broken rib, but I was too excited to let it affect me. That week, I was meeting Éric Champ, Jérôme Gallion, Jean-Pierre Rives, Daniel Herrero, Jo Maso and Knoxy for a few days of rugby romance, food fantasy and vineyard veneration. *Que la vie est belle.*

Jérôme Gallion

MEDITERRANEAN + PROVENCE

"THE NOISE AND THE SINGING WERE INCREDIBLE. THEY SANG FROM THEIR CELTIC HEARTS, KNOWING THIS WAS GARETH'S FAREWELL. I WANTED TO SWAP SHIRTS WITH HIM, BUT I WASN'T SURE HE WANTED TO BECAUSE IT WAS HIS LAST GAME. I WENT TO LOOK FOR HIM IN THE CHANGING ROOM AND HE WAS TOO EMBARRASSED TO SAY NO!"

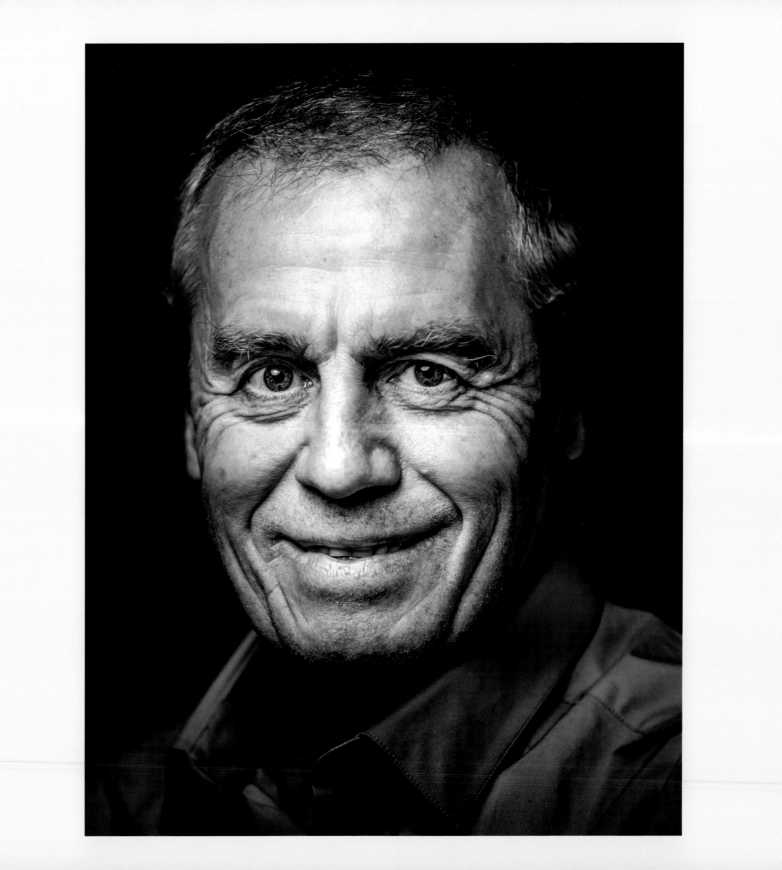

BORN : 4TH APRIL 1955

CLUBS : RACING CLUB TOULONNAIS

INTERNATIONAL CAPS : 27

POSITION : SCRUM HALF

GRAND SLAMS : 1981

NOM DE GUERRE : POCKET ROCKET

MY VISIT TO MEET HIM : THURSDAY 14TH DECEMBER 2017

As a former brilliant French scrum-half and now a renowned dentist, Jérôme is a man in demand, and I needed to be persistent and patient to schedule a slot to meet him at his surgery in an imposing old building on the main drag in Toulon. I arrived and the waiting room was full to capacity and hot. His assistant offered me a coffee and I knocked back a double espresso to sharpen the senses. It isn't every day you get to meet your childhood idol. I jumped the queue and went through to his office, right next to his dentist's chair.

Jérôme was one of my schoolboy heroes. Growing up in Bath, my brother and I would practise our sidesteps and passing for hours on the road in front of our house. He had panache and lightening pace, and would explode off the back of scrums and mauls, in the way Gareth Edwards could. However, there was something exotic and mysterious about the French team. While we saw and heard a lot from the great Welsh side back then, the French players had weird names, spoke a different language and emanated from foreign places called Toulon, Biarritz and Agen.

If you look at the photos of Jérôme back then, and indeed many of the other players, you notice that paradox of top sportsmen, a feature that I describe at various points throughout this book; they can be kind, modest and considerate off the pitch, but ruthlessly focused and unforgiving on it. They are winners, sometimes at all costs, driven by their fear of failure. The higher the stakes, the more intense they become, as though it is a matter of survival.

There is one photo in particular that captures Jérôme's speed, power, focus and intensity. He is playing for Toulon and passing to his left. Éric Champ is in the background, ready to support.

This intensity is what Éric Champ means when he talks about the high-pressure stakes of plays-offs and finals, *"... the beautiful game is replaced by hard rugby, by the taste of blood in the mouth"* and *"...what I have learnt in business and in sport is that there is no real love or lasting fraternity or great adventure that leaves an indelible mark*

unless there is success and victory."

I hadn't been back to Jérôme's part of France for a while, but I remember my visit to the area vividly because of the pain I endured. It was 1987 and my girlfriend at the time, Valérie, and I went to Cassis for the day. It was about 30°c, the sun was scorching and the air bone dry. I was sporting a trendy pair of budgie smugglers and I lived to regret it. After a few hours of 'sun-burning' (a well-known sport for pasty Englishmen), it was as though someone had fried my delicate bikini line with a Bunsen burner. The pain lasted for weeks. I learnt my lesson.

From Student to International

Jérôme has a very inquisitive mind and his first question to me was: *"What the hell is going on with Brexit?"* Suddenly, I had to snap into some technical French, one that I hadn't been practising. I was very adept

at talking about rugby, food, wine and engaging in general chit-chat, but Brexit was a test. In fact, I don't understand Brexit in English, let alone French, so I moved the conversation quickly on.

I wanted to know all about Jérôme's journey and road to the top.

"I was studying medicine at the University of Marseille, which was already hard enough, but I loved rugby and was playing for Toulon. I made my first team debut in 1975/6, and in 1977 I was selected for the tour of Argentina. I was very happy to go, not least because it was unexpected. I received my diploma and three days later I left for Argentina with the great Grand Slam team from 1977. I wasn't first choice but several others dropped out, including Astre, so Jacques and I were the scrum-halves. I was no competition for Jacques at all so I was very relaxed. I was there to learn and watch the master in action.

> "I wanted to swap shirts with Gareth, but I wasn't sure he wanted to because it was his last game. I went to look for him in the changing room and he was too embarrassed to say no!"

*"Jacques was an extraordinary person – diminutive,
charismatic, funny and a brilliant raconteur. He could
command the whole room with his knowledge, insight,
storytelling and humour. I felt very inadequate next to
him and all these other stars who I had been watching
on television.*

*"Then, in 1978, Élie Pebeyre, the Chairman of Selectors,
changed the half-back pairing. Out went Jacques and
Romeu, in came Bernard Viviès and me. Next to Jacques,
I felt inadequate and wondered what I was doing there.
This great pack was used to being led and driven by him.
How could I possibly emulate Jacques? I did what I could
and we nearly won the Grand Slam, but were beaten
by Wales in the last game, and they won it."*

Gareth Edwards

What was it like playing against the great Gareth Edwards?

*"It was intimidating, especially because we were at the
Arms Park. The noise and the singing were incredible.
They sang from their Celtic hearts, knowing this was
Gareth's farewell. The whole experience gave me goose
bumps. We had the chance to win another Grand Slam
but we were beaten. I wanted to swap shirts with Gareth,
but I wasn't sure he wanted to because it was his last
game. I went to look for him in the changing room and
he was too embarrassed to say no!*

*"It was the only time I played against Gareth. His was the
only shirt I kept. I hope he still has mine!"*

"This great pack was used to being led and driven by him. How could I possibly emulate Jacques?"

Beating the All Blacks

What about the shirt from the 1979 victory against the
All Blacks, the first time France had beaten them away?

*"I gave that one away too! That was another great tour and
memory. We arrived and it was pouring with rain, which
suited them. We wanted to run it but the weather and their
skill made it very difficult for us.*

*"The provincial matches were very tough. Jean Desclaux,
our coach, told me not to make breaks for fear of declaring
our hand before the test matches. I played against my
instincts, which were to attack. You can only play what
comes naturally to you, you can't play against your
instincts. When the first test team was announced,
I wasn't selected! Yves Laffarge was instead.*

*"We were smashed 23-9, and we lost the mid-week game
11-12. When Desclaux announced the team for the second
test, those who weren't selected had big smiles, driven by*

*relief, and the fact that they could go and party! We had
been there for six weeks and trained every day so some
people were exhausted. We had some brilliant players there
like Caussade, Codorniou, Aguirre, Averous and Costes.*

*"That week, Jean-Pierre led the team and he decided that
we would play according to our values of running rugby.
We wanted to show everyone that we could play in
our way and win. Béguerie couldn't play because of the
stitches in his hand so Salas from Narbonne came in at
Number 8. He had never played there before so I told
him how we should defend with me taking the outside.
Usually playing either prop or second row, he always
had his head stuck in the scrum so he wasn't familiar with
how the back row defended.*

*"He was so scared of missing a tackle that he ran and
tackled everything. I said to him, 'If you see a man in black,
tackle him'. He played brilliantly.*

> "He had this instinctive and intuitive intelligence that was remarkable. He instinctively knew the right answers to problems in rugby and life. He didn't need a university education or statistics to know what to do on the pitch and in the real world."

"We arrived at the stadium and it was already full. They really are connoisseurs of the game. We really liberated ourselves and scored four tries. It was like the old France of 1977, imposing itself with all its grandeur. We scored early and gained in confidence, playing some great running rugby. Joinel, Salas and Rives in the back row were extraordinary. The All Blacks came back and scored so it was close at the end. Jon West was the referee who I really liked. I told him it wasn't worth playing extra time!

"Winning the match changed everything – suddenly the tour was fabulous."

Jérôme scored the first try in the test, using his pace to charge down the fly-half's kick. When I think about Jérôme's pace and explosiveness, it reminds me of the other supercharged scrum-halves, such as Gareth Edwards, Richard Hill, Aaron Smith, Antoine Dupont, Dewi Morris, Joost Van de Westhuizen...

I have spent many a good night out with Dewi and he told me an amusing anecdote when he played the French at the Parc des Princes in 1992:

> "The French kept infringing and I was speaking to the referee in my best French *'le ballon, plaquage, les mains, hors jeu, en avant'*. After a while, he looked at me and said, 'Dewi, I'm f**king Irish, which means I speak English'. The referee that match was Stephen Hilditch."

I wanted to know what it was like having such brilliant leaders on the field such as Rives and Dintrans.

"Jean-Pierre was atypical and quite reserved, not a big orator before or during games in the mould of a Jacques Fouroux. But Jean-Pierre had that non-verbal form of leadership, a palpable and magnetic quality, which meant others always followed his example of hard work and sacrifice.

"He had this amazing energy on the pitch, but off the pitch, you always thought he might fall down and needed to take some vitamins! The role really made him and he took to it easily. It lit him up. He had this 'vitalité de folie' and he was always stuck to the ball. He tackled anything that moved. The opposition punched and kicked him and pulled his hair but he didn't care. Against South Africa in 1980, he must have given away twenty plus kilos but that didn't stop him.

"Dintrans was much more demonstrative, a real tough warrior who led the charge from the front. He was a 'capitaine de combat'.

"The coaches wanted me to throw the ball into the line-outs but I have little hands! I wasn't convinced about my skill to do it, especially when the ball was wet. I tried to throw it in straight but ever so slightly on the French side.

"Once I had my diploma, I was focused on building my practice so between my work and some injuries, I played for France on-and-off in the 1980s. Three times I played in teams that could have won the Grand Slam but I never managed it. In 1978, we lost against Wales,

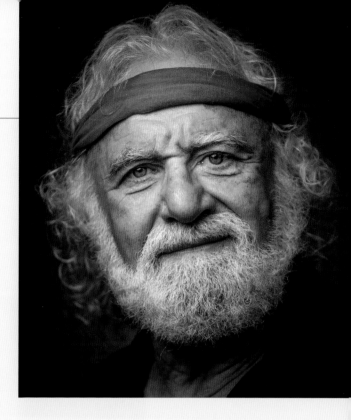

in 1979 we drew against Ireland, and in 1984 Scotland beat us in the Grand Slam decider.

"I was a replacement in the 1987 Five Nations and was due to go to the Rugby World Cup, but you had to be totally committed. By then, I had three children and the youngest was only one, and I didn't want to be away for six weeks. I was the only player to refuse selection. Of course, I would have loved to have gone but I had a real life to manage too. That year, Toulon won the Bouclier de Brennus so I had a great season anyway."

Jérôme, like Éric Champ and the Herrero brothers, are so intertwined with Toulon. I wanted to know more about André Herrero in particular whom I have never met.

"The Herrero family is full of big, smart characters. André was one of six children, four boys and two girls.

"He was a great player and captain, a hard man and very much the boss. He didn't go to university and worked in the dockyard in Toulon while playing for a small club, before being spotted by Toulon who recognised his talents and signed him. He has this instinctive and intuitive intelligence that is remarkable. He instinctively knows the right answers to problems in rugby and life. He doesn't need a university education or statistics to know what to do. He just knows. You need that wisdom and instinct on the pitch and in the real world, and André has it in spades. Jacques Fouroux and Éric Champ were and are the same. They also saw what rugby could give them and they capitalised on it. People like that don't make mistakes in their life. All three were and are so smart.

Jérôme has a very successful dentist practice with his brother Christophe who was a fly-half or centre for Toulon, so transitioning to life after rugby wasn't difficult for him.

" I felt great when I finished playing and I haven't touched a rugby ball since. To keep fit, I play football and tennis, and I cycle, swim, walk, ski and windsurf, basically everything except rugby. I cycle up hills and go so slowly that I can count the flowers."

"When I look back at my career, I felt good having beaten the All Blacks, played in the Five Nations, been Champion of France, toured with France and played in a few finals. I deploy my competitive instincts in my dentist practice now! You need to move on from your rugby career and apply your skills elsewhere."

There was a backlog of customers waiting in the changing room, who must have been wondering what treatment I was having that was taking so long. It was time to wrap the interview up. Jérôme is charming, engaging and as bright as a button with an outstanding memory for detail. It was the most enjoyable visit I will ever have to a dentist. He invited me back for dinner next time I was in town. I will definitely take him up on that offer.

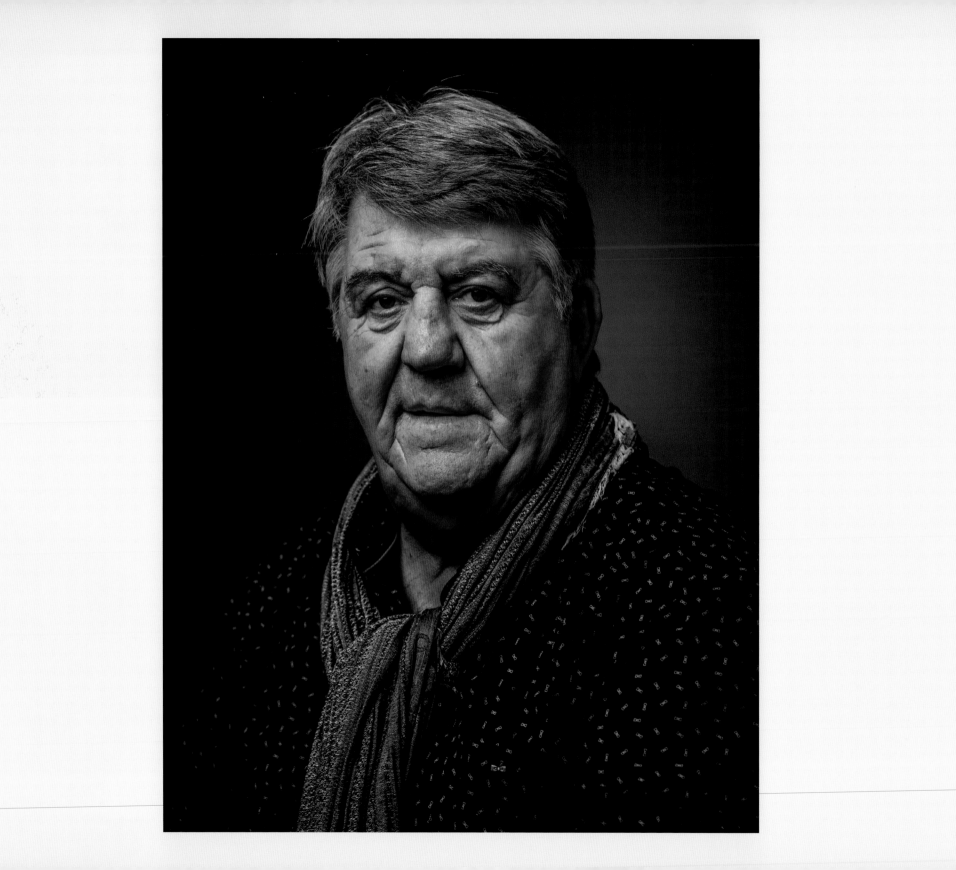

Jean-François Imbernon

MEDITERRANEAN
+ PROVENCE

"JEAN-LUC JOINEL SAID TO ME,
'IT'S ALL CHANGED, WE'RE
ALL FOLLOWING A DIET'. THEY
WERE EATING GRATED CARROT,
CELERY, BEETROOT, LEEKS,
CHICORY, SALAD, FISH. I SAID
GOODBYE TO JACQUES AND
PICKED UP MY BAG. I TOLD
JEANNO LESCARBOURA THAT
THERE WASN'T ANY ORANGINA
OR COKE SO HE WOULD HAVE
TO HAVE A RICARD INSTEAD!"

BORN : 17TH OCTOBER 1951

CLUBS : UNION SPORTIVE DES ARLEQUINS PERPIGNANAIS

INTERNATIONAL CAPS : 23

POSITION : 2ND ROW

GRAND SLAMS : 1977, 1981

NICKNAME : JEFF

NOM DE GUERRE : THE URSINE GIANT

MY VISIT TO MEET HIM : SATURDAY 17TH FEBRUARY 2018

I f Jean-François Imbernon were a bottle of red wine, he would be big, tannic, rustic and comforting. Here is a son of the Catalan people, a true product of the region and a giant, warm-hearted man too. We met on a cold winter's day right outside the stade Aimé Giral in Perpignan. As I arrived, he was puffing heartily on his fag.

"Hi David. How are you? Nice to meet you. Give me two minutes while I finish this and then we'll go inside for a long lunch."

Spoken like a true Frenchman, I thought. It's a good job I don't have an aversion to eating or drinking. I should really express that as a positive, shouldn't I? I was about to embark on a three-hour lunch with a giant of a man. It's a good job I love food and wine. There. That's better.

Along with virtually every other part of France, I love the Agly valley, the area that runs to the west of Perpignan. It is rural, sun-baked and rugged, and makes hearty, luscious, fat wines, but with some complexity too. I drove from Salies-du-Salat in the Ariège to Perpignan in the Roussillon, in the deep south of France near the Spanish border, passing kilometres of vines on the way. Gérard Gauby, based in Calce about 15km from Perpignan, makes wines that are a particular favourite of mine. Here, because of the heat, altitude is a crucial factor with most vines grown at about 500m. Hot days and cold nights encourage longer and slower grape ripening, and the result is more complexity and freshness.

Jean-François finished his Gauloise cigarette and we entered the bustling *brasserie*, a Mecca for foodies and rugby fans. The waiter brought over two bottles of the aforementioned Gauby wine, La Muntada white and red, his top *cuvées*. *Ah bon dieu*. The white was big but elegant with notes of honey, apricot and hazelnuts, and there was a clean line of minerality running through it. He decanted the red to let it breathe. The power of its *parfum* was intoxicating, like a handful of freshly crushed black fruits, all fleshy, juicy and lush. Tasting wines like these is like dating a voluptuous, smouldering *femme fatale*. Upon the first sip, you know immediately how the evening is going to end - horizontal, drunk and

> # Tasting wines like these is like dating a voluptuous, smouldering *femme fatale*. Upon the first sip, you know immediately how the evening is going to end - horizontal, drunk and satisfied.

satisfied. We drank a couple of glasses of the Catalan nectar before ordering *paté de campagne Catalan*, *champignons à la crème de fleurette, l'entrecôte and filets d'hareng*. I sensed we would be here for some time.

Cut From Catalan Cloth

Jean-François' regional accent is immediately recognisable, as it is with the vast majority of players who emanate from the South of France. The pronunciation, cadence, intonation and particular use of words allow you to fix their origins, or at least determine that they come from somewhere in the deep South. The *accent du midi* is the rhythmic, umbrella voice that stretches below the imaginary diagonal line from Bordeaux to Rodez to Orange and then down to Toulon and Nice. It varies a little between the Basque country, Bordeaux, Toulon and Marseilles but not too much. It is more the dialect (*peuchère, con, dégun*) and exaggerated movements of the hands, shoulders, mouth and eyes

that differentiate places like Toulon and Marseilles. As people speak, especially males, the chest is pushed forward, the chin out, the hands move vigorously and the facial expressions are contorted to reinforce the spoken word. I love watching them in action. These *provincaux* are animated, passionate, funny and loud.

I asked Jeff to tell me about his journey.

"I was born in the Pyrenean mountains in a village called Fuilla near Villefranche-de-Conflent, not far from Perpignan. Dad was Spanish, but he moved to France when he was about ten years old because of the Spanish civil war. There were thousands of Spanish refugees in the camps who were freezing and starving. There were some 100,000 who arrived in Prats-de-Mollo, south of Perpignan.

"Mum was from Cerdagne near Font-Romeu. They were simple people living off the land with chickens, eggs, rabbits and vegetables. They had no flour to make bread so

Jean-François Imbernon in his beloved USAP stadium.
Photo - Pierre Carton.

they would barter with the baker, offering eggs in return. Dad would cycle 40km each way. They worked so hard.

"We had an orchard where I loved working because I didn't like school. The magpies would eat the fruit so I would get 5 FF per magpie when I caught one. We would grow over 100 tons of apples so the boxes were very heavy, but a great source of weight training.

"I started my career at Prades before moving to AS Bages, south of Perpignan. They wanted to recruit the best local players and they told me I could go and do my military service there and they'd pay me 500 FF per month. It was all amateur but no one would ever know!

"While I was playing for them, I had an accident with a chain saw and lost my middle finger. I had just left the army at nineteen and I couldn't play rugby for six months. I played for Perpignan from the age of twenty."

At this point, he was clearly worried that I wasn't eating enough.

"Eat. Take loads, Take more. Have some mushrooms. Go on..."

Fighter or player?

"I had this reputation as a fighter at Perpignan and kept picking up suspensions. I missed the knockout stages in my first two seasons. One day, I realised that I could play and not just fight, so I stopped being an idiot and started playing. That was when things clicked. I was picked for the Five Nations in 1976."

Pierre Dospital told me, *"Cholley, Palmié, Imbernon - these were the hard boys. They were very big and strong. Jean-François was a rough diamond who was tough but fair. He had the face of a farmer and was quite scary if you didn't know him!"*

When I spoke to Bill Beaumont, he remembers fondly the encounters against Imbernon and Palmié:

"When you played them, you couldn't just use brute force because they were so big. You had to manoeuvre them around and use cunning.

"When you lined up in the tunnel, they just stared at you. They had these gnarled hands, and they were always unshaven, covered in tape and sweating. I loved playing at the Parc and against them, but you had to stand up to them. You had to make them respect you."

I asked what it was like playing against his French teammate Palmié when Perpignan played Béziers?

"Palmier was a hard man. We tried to avoid each other. I would target Estève or Senal and he would target Goze! Estève was big and hard, but not vicious or dirty, unlike Senal and Saisset."

The Greatest Grand Slam

I mentioned the 1977 Grand Slam. He beamed with pride and laughed heartily, with his gravelly voice.

That was the work of Jacques, the captain. He was an incredible leader of men. He had this charisma and confidence. He could both amuse and bore you too with all his chit-chat!"

At this stage. Jean-François was in full flow. He was tearing into his meat like a brown Pyrenean bear and gulping the Muntada back. He was enjoying a wonderful lunch and remembering his greatest days.

"After we won the first match against the Welsh in 1977, Fouroux went to see Ferrasse and said, 'Keep the same team. Change no one and we will win the Grand Slam, I promise you'.

"1982 was the year that France had lost all their games and Ireland had won the triple crown. However, we had had a month off, on the piss celebrating, and when we came back, we lost to them in Paris. They smashed us in scrums and rucks.

"In the following year, we were ready for them. Willie Duggan and Fergus Slattery warned us that we couldn't let them start otherwise we would be finished. We smashed them and took revenge although we finished joint first overall."

HUGO MACNEILL

Robert Paparemborde, Jean-Pierre Rives and Jean François Imbernon. 19 February 1983. Five Nations Rugby, Lansdowne Road, Dublin. Ireland v France. *Photo - Ray McManus, Sportsfile, Corbis, Getty Images.*

> "He looked at me and shouted, 'You f**king useless Catalan'. He saw Richard Astre warming up to replace him but there was no way he was going off. He told the doctor, 'Just put a bandage on it and f**k off'."

"His motivational skills were legendary. Before matches, he would get all the forwards into one of the hotel bedrooms and get us worked up. We won the Grand Slam using only fifteen players and didn't concede a single try.

"And boy did he have a temper. Against Scotland in 1977, we had a line out near our line and I tapped the ball down badly for Jacques at scrum-half. As a result, the Scottish pack broke his nose. He looked at me and shouted, 'You f**king useless Catalan, you f**k me off'. As the doctor tended to him, he saw Richard Astre warming up to replace him. There was no way he was going off. He told the doctor, 'Put a bandage on it and f**k off'. That was Jacques – tough, uncompromising, direct and very funny."

Le Come-Back and Eye-Gouging, Moi?

In 1982, the French team had lost all its games so Jacques contacted Jean-François.

"L'USAP were due to play against Toulouse and our coach André Quilis said, 'You will play. I know you can't run, but you cause havoc. Just throw a few punches'. In the Toulouse match, I slowed the game down and everyone was waiting for me at the scrums, but we won 6-3. Basquet watched and said, 'Jean-François, you played a great match'.

"A few days later, the dwarf (as I used to call Jacques) telephoned me while I was at my bistro. I knew what was coming so I messed around. 'What, you want me to come to Paris for a piss-up?'

"He asked me to come back and play the last game against Ireland. I told him I was huge and not fit, but he wouldn't take no for an answer. He said, 'Can you walk? Well you're selected then'. I only went to make him happy.

"I arrived at La Porte d'Auteuil and went to find a byrre (a Catalan wine). Jean-Luc Joinel said to me, 'It's all changed,

we're all following a diet'. What position does he play, I asked? They were eating grated carrot, celery, beetroot, leeks, chicory, salad, fish. Things like red wine, red meat, cream and cheese were banned. I said 'goodbye' to Jacques and picked up my bag. I was joking of course but he thought I was being serious. I told Jeanno Lescarboura, who was twenty years old and playing his first tournament, that there wasn't any Orangina or Coke so he would have to have a pastis instead!

"That night at the dinner table, Jacques had laid me a special place with my name next to it, alongside a plate of cheese and a bottle of red. What a coach he was!

"As for the game, I punched, stamped and gouged a few players, but I was knackered after twenty minutes. After the eye-gouging, I thought I was going to get sent off, but I held up my fingers to show the one that was missing and said to the referee 'look, it is not possible'.

"We went on to win the game 22-9. Ireland were deprived of Willie Duggan who had injured himself in a fight with some taxi drivers two days before!"

We'd been at the table for a good three hours. I had laughed all the way through as well as eaten and drunk my body weight in food and wine. Jean-François is a very kind man who is the epitome of old school French rugby – gaillard, dur, rugeux and généreux.

Afterwards, I walked into Perpignan to sober up and rehydrate. I was driving to Collioure the next day to meet Mark Cécillon.

Jean-Pierre Rives

MEDITERRANEAN
+ PROVENCE

"I GAVE AWAY ALL MY MEDALS.
I WOULD HAVE ENDED UP LOSING
THEM, BUT I REMEMBER ALL THE
PLAYERS I PLAYED WITH, AND THAT
IS MUCH MORE IMPORTANT THAN
ANY JERSEY. I DON'T WANT THE
PLACE TO LOOK LIKE A MUSEUM.
THE MEMORIES ARE IN MY SOUL."

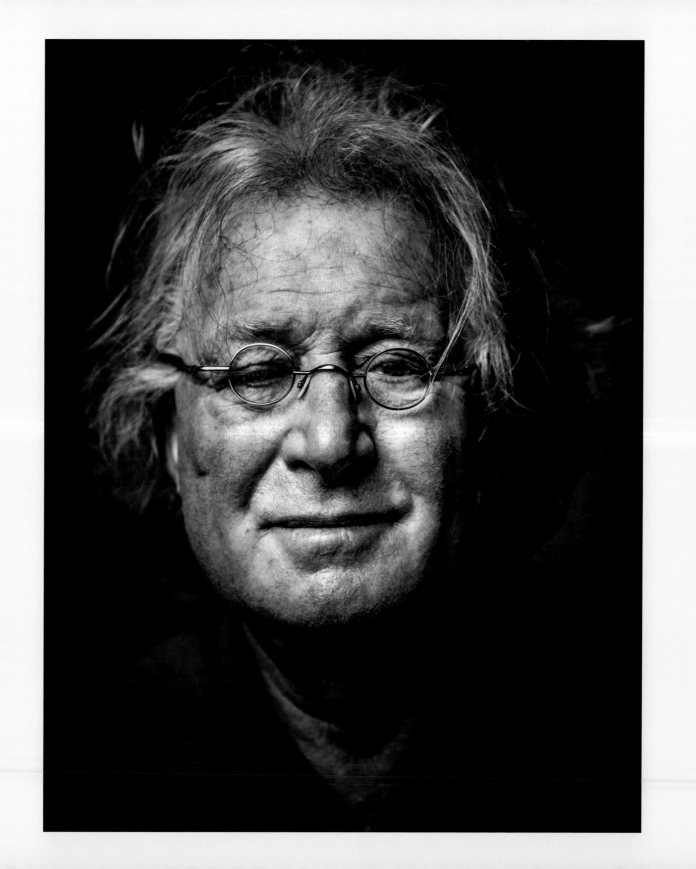

BORN : 31ST DECEMBER 1952

CLUBS : TOULOUSE OLYMPIQUE EMPLOYÉS CLUB, STADE
BEAUMONTOIS LOMAGNE RUGBY, STADE TOULOUSAIN

INTERNATIONAL CAPS : 59

POSITION : FLANKER

GRAND SLAMS : 1977, 1981

NICKNAME : LE CASQUE D'OR, LE BLOND

NOM DE GUERRE : THE LION KING

MY VISIT TO MEET HIM : WEDNESDAY 13TH DECEMBER 2017

I was having breakfast at home in Winchester on Tuesday 17th October 2017 when my mobile rang showing a French telephone number. I answered in French: *"Hallo"*. The person replied, *"David, bonjour. C'est Jean-Pierre"*.

His name and voice sent my adrenaline pumping and my heart racing. The great Jean-Pierre Rives had called me. I had sent him a comprehensive email about the book on the Monday evening asking him to participate and he had responded immediately, and in the most personable way possible.

He spoke to me in *franglais*, his American inflection coiling around the English words: *"Yeh, hi David, I'm in, we are a rugby fraternity aren't we?"*, his question being rhetorical. He has spent a lot of time near San Francisco so speaks English well.

As I discovered when I met him, his immediate response was the mark of the man, a fabulous human being, a *'homme'*-of-the-people, whose self-effacing and humorous, chatty style belies the steely determination and desire to win. Without those, he would never have been the player he was and, in my experience, a person never loses those instincts, whatever their age.

In spite of his quick response, it took a few calls before we arranged a time to meet:

"David, I am in Biarritz, call me back later this week."
"David, I can't do Wednesday to Friday because I am away."
"David, I can do Wednesday to Friday because I'm at home."

" David, I have such a bad memory that I can't remember whether I ever had one."

In the end, I thought the best plan was to travel to Toulon to meet their two former luminaries, Éric Champ and Jérôme Gallion, and then call him. I had blocked out a few days before I flew back to England so we could make it work, and it did. Jean-Pierre lives about an hour east of Toulon towards Saint-Tropez.

Bonds of Friendship

I travel to and around France a lot but I hadn't been back to this chic area since 1992. I remember that last trip well for the laughter, hospitality and fun. My friend, Pierre Kalfon, and I had flown to Nice for a long weekend to visit his family, which was on holiday at La Croix-Valmer near Cavalaire-sur-Mer. As we came into the arrivals' hall at Nice airport, his father, André, a salt-of-the-earth Marseillais, was waiting to meet us, sporting a skinny pair of blue budgie smugglers and flip-flops, his ample, sexagenarian paunch protruding, no other body-concealing garment on him. That was it, two items of clothing. So much for French style and sartorial elegance! He drove us to La Croix-Valmer, calling me 'John' the whole way, because he thought all Englishmen were called John, and rarely looking at the road, constantly chatting with his head turned sideways towards Pierre in the front passenger seat. Somehow, we arrived safely.

Pierre's house was right on the sea front, the beach a garden of fine, white sand. With André, his wife Nicolle and Pierre's two sisters, Michèle and Geneviève, we laughed, ate, drank (a lot of *pastis* from memory) and relaxed for three days, our bodies bronze from the long, brilliant sunlight and our hair matted from the salty water. For a few days, it was an idyllic French life, spontaneous, uncluttered and untarnished by city living. André was a very funny man, the patriarch of this wonderful *Provençal* family, and one of the reasons why the weekend is etched in my memory. I often think about how there are short moments in one's life that create disproportionately strong, long-term memories and bonds of friendship. This, for me, was one of them.

Back to the Future

Jean-Pierre had given me his address on a golf complex and the GPS took me to his road, but I couldn't find his house anywhere. I parked the car and walked up and down looking for his house number or name on the letter boxes. After twenty minutes or so, two ladies pulled into their drive and they guided me to his house on the other side of the main road. I drove down and saw a young boy with his mum in front of a house. The scene stopped me in my tracks. There was a young Jean-Pierre Rives, aged about ten, with long, blond, free-flowing locks, only it was his son, Kyno-John. The resemblance was remarkable, as if I had gone back in time.

He and his wife, Sonia, welcomed me into their warm, lovely, wood-framed home, festooned with a large Christmas tree, pictures, kids' drawings and models, golf clubs, cards, paintings and books. There are tree houses and play areas in the garden for the boys. Clearly there is no point in planting lots of pretty flowers as their heads would have been clubbed off by Kyno and his elder brother Jasper, a golf fanatic. This is a proper family home, not just a house, the physical embodiment of Jean-Pierre's warmth of character and love of people.

Physically, he is still a fit looking sixty-seven-year-old.

At 1.78m and about 90kg, he is a similar size to when
he played, which I tried to reconcile with his abilities
on the pitch. After all, he wasn't big even back then,
but no other rugby player in the world at that time
could match his bravery, and force of mind and body.

Blond, swashbuckling, committed, tough and fast,
he made his debut for France aged twenty-three,
captaining them thirty-four times and playing every
minute of every game. He would fizz around the pitch,
tackling anyone and putting his head where others
wouldn't in order to secure the ball for his teammates.
His great mentor, Jean Salut, a great player himself,
was in awe of his ability to tackle, get back up and
tackle again.

He has obviously aged, his blond hair thinning and his
body unable to do what it once could, but I could still feel
his strength of body and mind. He is in the third quarter
of his *aventure humaine*, as he describes it, hopefully with
plenty of road left to run, having sacrificed his body and
head for his team and country. His memory, like all of
us in middle age, may be fading but his thinking is razor
sharp and true to his values.

Don't Forget the Past

During the time I spent with all the former players,
I quickly realised that the key thing is to let them speak
and don't box them in with a set format or detailed list of
questions. You just need a few to set them off and then
let the conversation take its own course. Conversation
is the key word. It was important that it didn't become

an interview with simple Q&As. I remember the great
Michael Parkinson saying something similar and it
had stood him in very good stead. This approach was
particularly key with Jean-Pierre because he is
a freethinker and great talker.

Over coffee and some chocolates, he naturally instigated
the first topic of conversation. He went straight into an
articulate defence of traditions and how he admired the
English for sticking to what they believe:

*"Of course, you have to be open-minded, but what I love
about the English is that you have a certain attitude,
you respect the past and the importance of continuity. You
listen to your mothers and fathers and respect your history
and environment. Progress is important to a certain point,
but you can't just forget the past. If you don't know where
you have come from, you don't know where you are going.*

*"You, the British, especially the English, have a respect of
your constitution, where you have come from. You know it
works and what others say doesn't put you off. I have great
respect for that, whether it is which side of the road you
drive on, the food, smells, politics or whatever.*

*"It isn't about you handing out lessons in morality,
you just want to retain your independence and way of
life, and that means you have continuity in your journey.
I think that is great.*

*"Even though I am French and I played against the English,
I really admire the English and I love London, and think
Twickenham is a lovely garden!"*

Jean-Pierre is a great raconteur, quick-witted, distinctive
and a natural humanist with a high EQ. It is very clear
that he has spent much of his life observing and thinking
about people.

*"I wasn't so much in love with the game, but I loved the
blokes I played with and their friendship.*

> "The game was a pretext
> to make life-long friends.
> I loved the human adventure
> of it all. That is why I don't
> like all these statistics that you
> find in American Football.
> The game is about humans,
> not computers and rigid
> rulebooks."

*"If the game had been about statistics in my day, I may
never have been successful – I was too short, too light,
often late. This is one game that everyone can play –
short, fat, skinny, tall, fast, slow, and I think that is great.
All my friends come from rugby, and I have none from
school even though I spent so much time there."*

He isn't someone who remembers a lot of detail about specific games. His memories about the friends he played with are far stronger, and his focus now is on the 'here and now' – friends, family, art, living.

When he ran off the pitch after his last game for France in 1984 against Scotland, he moved quickly and smoothly into the next part of his life as an international artist. In his house, there wasn't a single rugby memento in sight.

"I gave away all my medals. I would have ended up losing them, but I remember all the players I played with, and that is much more important than any jersey. I don't want the place to look like a museum. The memories are in my soul."

We talked about my book and I explained that while its original idea was French flair, it quickly became a story about human adventure and a band of brothers.

"Of course. We don't know each other but we recognise each other because rugby is the common bond. Once, a man came to see me about a sculpture and he bored me senseless for an hour (Jean-Pierre impersonates him). After an hour he mentioned rugby and I said to him: 'F**k, you could have told me at the beginning'. Let's talk about that instead."

Jean-Pierre sits in that group of players who didn't conform to the norms. Their talent was innate and they could do things that no one else could, however much training and coaching they had. That was their genius. I would put Jean-Pierre in the same camp as sportsmen like Seve Ballesteros, George Best, Ian Botham, Kevin Peterson, Shane Warne, Andy Ripley, John McEnroe and Ronnie O'Sullivan.

Modern day sports science and statistics wouldn't have made him a better player, not materially anyway. He was the sporting equivalent of a musician who can't read music but can play anything by ear.

I spoke to Fergus Slattery who described the aura that Jean-Pierre commanded among his teammates:

"1984 was the first time Jean-Pierre's parents saw him play for France, and he was keen for me to meet them in a cocktail bar. I arrived and Jean-Pierre took me to one end of the bar while all the other French players waited dutifully and patiently at the other end. After twenty minutes or so, he left the bar and walked on to the team bus, and sat at the front, only then followed, again dutifully, by the French team. If I had done that, my Irish teammates would have told me to f**k off! But such was the deference for Jean-Pierre that he could get away with it!"

Rugby is an Art, Not a Science

Jean-Pierre wanted to discuss the current state of the French national team.

"The problem in France is that people can take things too seriously. Things don't weigh you, the English, down in the same way and you can take these things more lightly than we can. The situation with the French national side might be serious but it isn't a grave situation. We could have a bit of a joke about it, like you would. In France, we let serious things become grave, and we let grave things really weigh us down. They become a huge burden on us. Life with you is more light-hearted.

"You, the English, come out of a hole organised, we come out of one disorganised!

"Rugby is an art, not a science, and it is the players who are on the pitch and they should decide what to do on the pitch. They can't keep looking up at the stand for instructions. They have to take responsibility. Rugby is part of our education; it enables children to become men, and it enables men to become children by enjoying themselves on the pitch.

"The players should play how they want to play and not according to a rigid plan. This is particularly important for the French who aren't well organised and structured by nature. For us, everything comes from chaos! In that sense, we are completely different to you.

"Style comes from character, and character is being killed by rules and instructions. The ball should be the star, not the players or the referee. People want to see the ball.

"Rules tell you to do this and that, and don't do this or that. It's not a game anymore. We have talented players so let them play. I want them to be liberated.

"And I want to see passion and emotion and grandeur and pace. We have a Latin temperament, so instinctively, we are great at all of those.

"You have to be unpredictable. That's what makes the difference, that's what makes it enjoyable. Perhaps the pitch needs to be bigger? It is still the same size as when we played, but now everyone is bigger, faster and fitter, so there is less space. The ball should be the star and it needs to be passed and moved from one side to the other. That is what people want to see."

The 'globalisation' of the sport also bothers him.

"The game has become homogeneous. Before, you didn't need to see the colour of a team's shirt to know whether it was the English, Irish, Welsh or the Springboks playing. Now, everyone plays the same and it is the French that have lost out the most. We have removed the invention, enjoyment and improvisation. If Blanco were playing today, we would convert him into an assembly-line worker or a water carrier! Often, he didn't know where he was going but he went to the right places.

"Today, we take very talented players and artists and we turn them into workhorses. In rugby, some players are there to work hard, but others are there to make dreams and create fantasies. That is how it should work. You can't put them all into the same bag.

"Why would changing the French coach make a difference? Everything is formatted in the same way – the clubs, the national team, the FFR. We have some great players so I am not sure we need a coach, do we? What is a coach going to teach them that they don't know already? They train every day and have done for years – surely,

"Rugby is an art, not a science, and it is the players who are on the pitch and they should decide what to do on the pitch... They have to take responsibility. Rugby is part of our education; it enables children to become men, and it enables men to become children..."

at this level of competition, they know how to run, kick, pass, tackle, and so on.

"We need a charismatic, spiritual leader, a leader of men to make a great team and the simple way to do that is to take them to a bar and let them cement their friendships. Let them decide what time they want to leave and train the next day."

Bastille Day, 1979

I reminded him that he beat the All Blacks once in 1979 on French Bastille day no less (14th July).

"Haha! Yes, we did, although I don't know how. It was a miracle! I remember we were stuffed in the first game.

"Before the first test, Patou (Robert Paparemborde) and I were talking and we said, 'We are super strong,

we are going to put them on their arses'. At the first scrum, we went back five metres! Our strategy was f**ked and we had no plan B.

"In the second week, some guys were saying, 'Come on, let's go home', but I said, 'No way, we are going to play this f**king match. And we will do what we can to win it'.

"When the match started, we had some luck and things went well. Winning was brilliant, out there in the middle of the pitch. Graham Mourie, the All Blacks captain was magnanimous in defeat and a lovely man, even if he was as hard as nails on the pitch."

Jean-Pierre was being very modest when he described the game. Based on the testimonies of Codorniou, Joinel, Dubroca and Dintrans, Jean-Pierre had a huge impact on the team in the week before the second test, showing his qualities as a leader of men. Jean Desclaux was the coach

> " If the game had been about statistics
> in my day, I may never have been successful –
> I was too short, too light, often late. "

Free Spirit

Jean-Pierre was an artist and a free spirit when he
played rugby, and he has drawn on those skills and
instincts to guide him through life since he retired.
His art work has been a cornerstone of his life since
he left Toulouse for Paris in 1981.

*"I'll take you to my atelier later. It is outside and I only
go there in good weather. When the weather is cold,
I go to my art studio in the garden.*

*"I have always loved art and I wanted to go to the School
of Art (École des Beaux Arts), but at the time, when I was
about twenty, it was full of people with long hair and I was
from a family that was more conventional and serious
so I ended up doing law! I have never used it.*

*"One day I met Albert Ferraud, a French sculptor who used
reclaimed materials, typically from iron and steel, bending
them into the desired shape, and it changed my life.
I decided to move to Paris to live near him to do sculpture.
I didn't go to Paris because I particularly wanted to join
Racing Club! But it meant I could go and see him every day.*

*"I didn't train with Racing Club, I trained alone in the
Jardin de Luxembourg and then at Le Parc du Sceaux in
Châtillon. In fact, we were on the bus one Sunday going to
the game and there was a little guy next to us. I thought he
was the son of the driver, but he started getting undressed
in the changing room. I had to ask Denis (Charvet) who he
was and he told me he was the hooker! That is how little
I knew the club or the players because I hardly saw them."*

but he was quite authoritarian and not Jean-Pierre's
cup of tea at all. So Jean-Pierre took over, galvanised the
team and led them to victory.

*"We won but they were super strong and I actually felt like
apologising to them for winning. It was a strange feeling."*

I asked him about the games where France narrowly
missed out on Five Nations' Grand Slams by losing
a single game (1978, losing against Wales in the last
game; 1979, drawing against Ireland in the first game;
and 1984, losing to Scotland who won the Grand Slam).
Far from a Gallic shrug, he prickled, his competitive spirit
kicking in, notably about 1984 when he was captain
and in his last year playing for France.

*"We were refereed by a puny little Welshman who had
never refereed an international game before. The Scottish
player, John Rutherford, admitted to me that they were
constantly offside so they could suppress our attacks.*

*I was very angry after the game as it would have been
my third Grand Slam."*

At the after-match dinner, Ferrasse forgot to thank the
referee during his speech and Rives said that the most
important player on the pitch was a Welshman.

When I met Jean-Luc Joinel, he told me that Jean-
Pierre told a joke during his speech that wasn't properly
translated at the time, but is now: *"There are three
useless things in the world: a priest's balls, a nun's tits
and a bad referee!"*

Jean-Pierre is a very warm human being but one
who certainly doesn't suffer fools lightly.

*"While we had to congratulate the Scots, Jones spoiled the
match and the Scottish party as well. But listen, they won
and we didn't, and we had to respect that."*

When Jean-Pierre moved to Racing, he was given what was called a 'licence rouge', which meant he couldn't play for the first team for a whole year. The system was meant to dissuade international players from moving clubs.

"When I trained alone, I would run around the parks with the local fire brigade who also trained there. They would run and run, fast, and I used to get knackered, so would go back to my house for a sleep. I would also do Tai Chi with some Chinese folk in the park. It was good fun! It was the end of my career so I was very relaxed about the whole thing.

"But a few weeks before the tournament, the selectors wanted me to prove my fitness so I ended up playing for the 3rd team at Colombes on a crap pitch in front of a lot of people and cameras, and in a few inches of water and mud. Every time I got the ball, four blokes would jump on me! I was knackered. The ref was also pissing me off so I pushed him over and he fell in the mud. I said to him, 'Go on, just send me off, put me out of my misery and that'll be the end of it'. He didn't dare!

"That year, I played all four games in the Five Nations without getting my head kicked in every week playing for Racing Club, and I loved it."

Family and Friends

He moved on to talk about his family and friends.

"Sonia and I had kids late, she was forty-two when Jasper arrived and forty-five when Kyno arrived. At fifty-four

years old today, Sonia is super fit, more so than me!"

He met Sonia in Paris via a friend in the Castel restaurant where he went every evening near his home in La Place Saint Sulpice. His friend told him that Sonia was, and still is, a very good golfer, who would drive the ball further than Jean-Pierre. In denial and with his competitive instincts (and attraction) piqued, he took up the challenge.

> "We arranged to meet. She won the driving competition but I made the kids with her!"

For all his career in rugby, surrounded by men and parties and women, Jean-Pierre has never really drunk, simply because he doesn't like it.

"I have only ever been drunk twice in my life. Once with the Irish, which is, of course, quite normal (he says smiling), and another time I ended up being sick on my mother's shoes after a match in the UK. Mum and Dad had come to watch me play and later I went to see them where they were staying. She was so lovely that she said to others who saw it happen: 'Oh, he has run so much today, he is tired and not feeling well!'

"In England, I didn't want to drink but at an after-match dinner, they were serving port. The Archbishop of

Westminster, who spoke French, was there and he was surprised I didn't drink, especially as we had won. I told him that if the church was ordering me to, then like a good Catholic, I would! I do like sugary alcohol so I drank quite a lot and struggled to do my speech afterwards!*

"My father, Jo, was a pilot in the air force and spent a lot of time in Africa and we were a family of tennis players originally. I had a cousin who played rugby and my dad found me apathetic and not giving a toss about much. He thought rugby would smack me about a bit to wake me up. In matches and training, I ran about like a mad man. It woke me up on the pitch but I returned to my normal self afterwards! It was a bit of a shock for him because I remained the same."

We move onto discussing some of his favourite people and Jean-Pierre beams with emotion. He has some very close friendships, and Denis Charvet is one of those.

"I worked at Pernod-Ricard and had helped Serge get a job there, and I wanted to help Denis get one too. I worked with the then Director of Communication, Michel Mouillot. Denis asked him, 'What would you want me to do?' Michel responded, 'You see Jean-Pierre and Serge. They do nothing. You can help them!'

"Michel was a great friend and he really helped us at a time when we were all amateur. Denis came to Paris and took a while to get settled. But now he has become a real Parisian and lives next to Parc des Princes.

"I have many Basque friends and learned to play pelote

basque. In Paris, we used to play a similar game in the cellar of my house called Rives-Ball. Oh, it was terrible. We played with Jokari type rackets and squash balls, and everything was permitted. It was war and I was very strong! It was in my house and I was world champion, and if I ever lost then that person was banned from playing so I would still be the champion.

"We played every evening – Yannick Noah, Denis Charvet, Laurent Pardo, me and others. If Denis tells you he beat me, tell him that he must have been dreaming!"

He loves the Pays Basque very much, home to many of his great friends like Serge Blanco, Pierre Dospital and Laurent Pardo, and near to where his great, late friend, Robert Paparemborde, the Bearnais from Pau, played before he joined Jean-Pierre in Paris and played for Racing Club.

"I love the Basques. Many of them look the same because they interbreed! Just look at Doxpi – there are many people who look like him in Espelette! Pardo is a real character and he must have fallen out of his cradle and banged his head when he was little. If I were Laporte, Pardo is the sort of player I would get involved with the national team. He is mad but charismatic, like a clown, but the clown is so important for the spirit of the team. He is key to the French Barbarians. OK, you might need a couple of people around him to calm him down."

Another great friend and hero of his is Jo Maso,

"Every rugby-loving child wanted to be like the very gifted Jo Maso, right up until recent generations – Sella,

Codorniou, Charvet, Castaignède. He was a wonderful player and he should have won far more caps for France. The press was always on his back for his good looks and long hair, and the FFR and Ferrasse bowed to the press. They were old fashioned and fixed in their views and were too serious. It was a hard generation and Jo was, and still is, a charming man.

"I got away with long hair because I stood up to the FFR. Once Ferrasse told me to get my hair cut. I said I would if we lost. We didn't lose for about two years so I didn't cut it."

More Graft Than Craft?

He then hit me with a line I wasn't expecting.

"I was not a gifted rugby player. I couldn't do anything other than clear the ball out, tackle people, clean the loose balls up and put my head where others didn't dare venture. In short, I wasn't very good."

I challenged him on his incredible modesty, but he was convinced he wasn't a great player.

"The great players in my day and before were players like André and Guy Boniface, Jean Prat, Jean Salut, Jo Maso, Serge Blanco, Philippe Sella, Gareth Edwards and Phil Bennett. They could run, pass, kick, score tries and make tries. When I played with Gareth Edwards for the Barbarians, it was easy. He ran and made breaks and I just supported him."

Let's just pause for a second and think about what Jean-Pierre achieved. His bravery, tenacity and

toughness were legendary. There are many games that stand out: his debut in 1975 when the crowd started chanting his name, recognising there was a special talent on show as the previous generation of Maso, Spanghero and Trillo were retiring; every game of the Five Nations in 1977 when his play was unassailable; 1979 v Wales, 1981 v England, 1982 v Scotland, 1983 v Wales, bloodied and bruised. But the one that stands out for me is in 1980 against the Springboks. Rives was knocked out cold. Coming around, he refused to leave the pitch and was bandaged up, spending the remainder of the match running, tackling and linking, which led to the Dintrans' try. Even after his injury, his performance was a remarkable one of technical skill, speed and bravery. Take your pick from any of the games he played. He never gave anything but 100% commitment.

He spoke with great affection and emotion about his friend Jacques Fouroux:

"Fouroux was also a huge figure in my life, an enormous companion on the road, and a great friend, as a player, captain and coach. He was our leader and a huge personality. Jacques had a different approach to humanity, a permanent circus, a great storyteller, a man who animated us and welded us together as a team. It was me who advised Ferrasse to appoint him as a coach. He had enormous energy and we were always great partners. I had no interest in coaching or managing, that was his skill, and I was leading on the pitch so we complemented each other perfectly. He was a fabulous man.

"We played rugby liked we lived life. For the code of rugby

> " There are a few different ways to lead men – you can be alongside them and love them and they follow, or you can be authoritarian. We, the French, need love. You have to love each other to take punches and protect your teammates"

should be the code of life. I have so many memories in my soul. I don't need the physical things. It is the memories, that make me happy."

All the players reflected the same sentiments – you built your life around your teammates, as much off the pitch as on it. You had a bond of loyalty, respect and friendship with them that would last forever.

The Art of Leadership

It was lunch time so we headed to La Table de Didier in Grimaud, one of those great local restaurants run by its owner, Didier, who takes loving care over every aspect. Jean-Pierre called ahead and asked for the big round table. They eat there very regularly. *"If Sonia were a better cook, we would eat more at home!"*

Sonia, Jasper and Kyno joined us. Jasper is thirteen and a superb golfer with a handicap of three. He can drive the ball nearly 300m already. Kyno finds golf boring and prefers sailing although Jean-Pierre says he has great pace and could end up playing rugby. If I were a betting man, and looking at his features and hair, there might just be a future Jean-Pierre Rives mark II in the making.

The lunch arrived quickly as Didier already knew what the family wanted. Sonia, Jean-Pierre and I had their roast chicken that was juicy, sticky with a little caramelised sweetness. It was delicious and accompanied by a simple green salad, tossed in a light, salty vinaigrette. Jean-Pierre and I fought the temptation of a dessert, but we couldn't resist. We decided to order a *tarte tatin*, but share it. *"I am too fat, he told me."* Me too, I said.

Sonia, Jasper and Kyno left to head back for more sport so Jean-Pierre and I carried on chatting like a couple of ordinary blokes in a pub.

"The Grand Slam team of 1977 was so hard and talented, and we were driven and directed by the inimitable Jacques Fouroux. Palmier and Imbernon would impose themselves and never take a step backwards. They played hard - you could get away with anything in those days. They would warm-up in the changing rooms by smacking each other around! Cholley was massive and would smash opposition props about too. He may not have been the most technical scrummager, but he had Palmier behind him so always went forward. And you had Patou and Imbernon on the other side. My God, what a team. Pierre Lacans was exceptionally gifted too, a fabulous athlete, a tough rugby player and strong leader who complemented the brute force of others."

Jean-Pierre was being very modest again, but he was right up with the best and toughest of them all. His ability to run, tackle and withstand pain was unrivalled at the time.

"There are a few different ways to lead men – you can be alongside them and love them and they follow, or you can be authoritarian. We, the French, need love. You have to love each other to take punches and protect your teammates. We are tender and tactile because we are Latin and emotional, and we need these emotions to go to war. We close our eyes, think of France and consider it war. You are different. It has always worked like that and it couldn't work another way."

Wordplay

Jean-Pierre loves inventing adages and playing with words.

"I always come out with the same bollocks but they make me laugh."

Here are a few of his favourites:

"I have forgotten half of rugby and the other half has changed a lot."

"It isn't by eating three salad leaves washed down with a glass of water that you become a rugby player. On that diet, rugby would be sad. Going out onto a pitch knowing you are going to suffer means you have to love life. Without this love, rugby wouldn't last long."

"If you want to interest the British in war, tell them it's a sport. If you want to interest the French in a sport, tell them it's a war."

"I wasn't cut out for rugby but I played it for fifteen years. Were it not for being blond, then I wouldn't be who I am. And if I hadn't been who I am, then maybe I wouldn't have played rugby. Therefore, the likely reason I play rugby is because I am blond."

In one of his books, he thanks his family at the beginning revealing his light-hearted humour. It goes something like this:

"To Sonia, Jasper and Kyno-John,
To my mother for washing all my shorts,
To my father for buying her a washing machine,
And to Philippe, my brother."

We stood up to leave the restaurant and Didier and other guests gathered around Jean-Pierre. He is still feted as an icon, even though he doesn't find this comfortable or believe it is justified. We walked outside into the cold, but the sunlight was dazzling and the sky a bright winter blue, a typical *Provençal* day.

On the way back in the car, he reiterated his distrust of structure and authority, his free spirit fighting against conformity and what he called 'the imprisonment of rules'. Ever the artist, we went via his atelier, a locked-up, open-air area that is full of rust-coloured, bent pieces of iron and steel, the raw material for his *objets d'art*. Since retirement, he has become a world-renowned sculptor, twisting metal into works of art. He has exhibited all over the world. This has been his life for thirty years and where he still seeks inspiration and an outlet for his creativity.

Jean-Pierre is such a fluent speaker, a creative force and powerful independent thinker. He is an artist, preferring in all walks of life a game plan that is fluid, relying on the senses and responsibilities of the participants to succeed. His life since rugby reflects these traits; his chosen friends show that he loves positivity, free thinkers, audacious people who can see opportunities, invent and take risks. His nemesis is, and always has

been, conformity, a life constrained by rules and conventional wisdom that would suppress his intuition and freedom of expression.

Back at the house, we drank another coffee before I said goodbye. I'd had a wonderful day, thoroughly enjoying the warmth of their generosity, humour and stimulating conversation. I high-fived the kids, kissed Sonia à la bise and Jean-Pierre and I embraced each other in a big man-hug. I was sad to leave but promised to come back soon.

However, every cloud has a silver lining. I headed back towards Toulon where I was due to meet the great Jérôme Gallion the following day. And what a player he was.

"What is rugby?
You need love in your heart
and a kick in the head."

DOMAINE de
TRÉVALLON

ATELIER
CENTRE
FRANCE

Trévallon's Top Ten

BY ELOI DÜRRBACH OF
DOMAINE DE TRÉVALLON, FRANCE

"Trévallon wines are stunning examples of power and poise, labour and love, heart and soul. Not only is Eloi a man of unstinting kindness and patience, he and his brother, Balthasar, are the godsons of Albert Gleizes and Pablo Picasso."

Eloi Dürrbach, creator of the world-renowned wine Domaine de Trévallon in Provence, is a rebel, artist, visionary, pioneer and a genial, gentle man. Admonished by his father in 1973 for leaving university before completing his architecture studies in Paris, he returned to Trévallon in his beloved Provence to pursue his dream of planting vines and making wine. Born in 1950 and with forty years of winemaking under his beret, he has built one of the great *domaines* of France, competing with the magnificent whites and reds of the North and South Rhône, Burgundy and Bordeaux.

Art and artistry are the *fils conducteurs* that transcend Eloi's life. His father, René, and mother, Jacqueline, were both artists and sculptors who met in Marcel Gimond's atelier, and counted among their friends some of the world's most celebrated artists – Picasso, Gleizes, Léger and Delauney. Gleizes and Picasso were Godfathers to Eloi and his brother, Baltasar, which must have made for a fascinating christening.

Today, there are musicians and actors who visit Trévallon and enjoy their fabulous red and white wines – Bono, Paul McCartney, Anthony Wilson (the jazz guitarist and composer), Carole Bouquet (the French actress and former partner of Gérard Depardieu who starred as Melina Havelock in For Your Eyes Only) and Paul Arditi (the French actor who dubbed Christopher Reeve on the French-language version of the first three Superman films). McCartney visited and his name is written in chalk on the first *foudre* on the right as you walk into the cellars.

How did it all start? Back in the 1950s, Picasso asked Jacqueline to weave a tapestry of his famous Gernika painting and, with the proceeds made from selling it to Nelson Rockefeller, the couple bought Trévallon in Saint-Étienne-du-Grès in the Alpilles, just west of Saint-Rémy-de-Provence. Eloi's path to destiny was set. He is bestowed with the same artistry and independence of spirit (what his daughter, Ostiane, calls *anticonformisme*) as his parents, shown by the work of his wine-making and organic farming.

Their methods are artisanal but precise, and have been developed and refined over the last forty years. His wines require minimal intervention and are about as natural as you can get for wines made for ageing, although he never describes them as 'natural'.

I spent two memorable days at Trévallon, hosted by the wonderful Eloi, Floriane, his wife of nearly forty years, and Ostiane, their lovely daughter. As you can imagine, after nearly half a century of emotional and physical investment in the business and pleasure of wine, Eloi and Floriane have enjoyed some spectacular bottles. I asked them to recall their memories, which they did with great passion over a fabulous dinner of chicken, *girolles* and asparagus, cooked by Floriane in their *Provençal mas*.

Our dinner was the epitome of traditional *Provençal* living - modest, simple, delicious, hearty and warming, what the French would call *chaleureux*. The whole scene evoked powerful memories of the time I lived in the area as a student in the mid-late 1980s, when I regularly shared similar experiences with friends who nourished me through my lean years and taught me much of the

French I know today. We washed the tasty food down with some silky, rich Trévallon 2007, which revealed notes of wild strawberries, *cassis*, rosemary and thyme, flavours and fragrances that are typical of the *garrigue*.

The descriptions below are a summary of the transcript from several hours of recordings. Eloi and Floriane spoke and debated with great fluency, in spite of the free-flowing Trévallon wine, sometimes disagreeing on the vintage or venue or people they were with but never on the quality of the wine or experience. The words are written as though Eloi is speaking.

1. 1945 Château Rayas, Châteauneuf-du-Pape

There are many reasons why you remember a wine – the wine itself but also the love, friends and ambiance you share it with and this whole experience was magical. We drank it at La Beaugravière in Mondragon in around 2000. It was so memorable - the wine was delicate and fine with notes of *sous-bois*, cherries, game and liquorice. It had body but also fine tannins and great freshness, with aromas of kirsch and smoke.

2. 1961 Drouhin Griotte-Chambertin, Côte de Nuits

Drunk at L'Oustau de Baumanière in Les Baux at least thirty years ago. Floriane gushes with great excitement: *'I have never drunk a wine that gave me so much pleasure. It was so floral. It was my first time drinking a great burgundy'.* There were hints of nutmeg, cherries,

leather and game. It was another great memory, a beautiful wine drunk among friends. My memory of the whole event is what gave me the pleasure.

3. 1961 Jaboulet La Chapelle, Hermitage.

We have drunk it on three occasions and each time the whole experience was unforgettable, all with friends amid great fun and laughter. As for the wine itself, it was classic *syrah* from this part of France displaying olives, pepper, meat and black fruits. It had notes of leather rather than *sous-bois*.

La Chapelle is more powerful, less delicate than the 1947 Rayas. We loved it. Remington Norman had fifty odd cases of it before it became so expensive. Then Gault et Millau did a tasting at a well-known, three starred restaurant called Comme Chez Soi in Brussels where La Chapelle was entered as a *vin pirate* (a ringer) in a blind tasting against the very best Bordeaux wines. All the great tasters of the world were there and La Chapelle came first! Before that day, Pic in Valence had it on the menu for 500 FF, but they next day they added a zero!

4. 1962 Beaucastel, Châteauneuf-du-Pape

Drunk with friends at La Beaugravière, the greatest restaurant in the area, and Guy Julien, the restaurant owner. I remember it was in January 1989. Floriane was there. It was an extraordinary, unique evening for

so many reasons, not least because we were at the table for nine hours!

Guy decided to do a special meal called *Le Repas de la Truffe à la Gloire des Vignerons du Rhône*. They only served truffle-based dishes. Many big-name Rhône growers were there – Gérard Chave, Marcel Guigal, Jacques Reynaud, Bernard Burgaud, Jean-Louis Grippat, Robert Jasmin, François Perrin. Every wine we drank was memorable. Marcel brought La Mouline 1967, Gérard his Vin de Paille 1955, we brought a Trévallon red 1983.

Then the party really started. Floriane was on Marcel's knee and I was on Madame Chave's. All very innocent of course, but we were all worse for wear after nine hours!

I remember they served a rib of beef with truffles and paired it with the Beaucastel 1962. The match was sensational. The quality of the wine came from the perfect pairing. François was so happy, he brought Guy two cases of 1962 the next day.

It was very special to see François so moved by his wine. He is like a brother to me. I remember when we first arrived forty years ago, he was very kind, helping us in the business and introducing us to his US importers.

5. 1978 Guigal, La Mouline, Côte-Rôtie

This is one of Marcel's great wines. It has an oriental, spicy side with smoke and *cassis*. Extraordinary. François and I have had many memorable dinners with this wine.

Trévallon's casks and vineyards.
Photos - Pierre Carton.

generous and loved Trévallon so we always used to swap forty-eight bottles each, and they always included six bottles of their Montrachet plus Bâtard, Les Ruchottes from Chassagne-Montrachet and others. In 2005, Noël gave him an extra bottle, which was the 1983 magnum of Montrachet. It was powerful, rich, full bodied and buttery but fresh and mineral with layers of fruit and spice. It was outstanding.

We also drank his very first Montrachet of 1978 at La Beaugravière at a special dinner. It was so memorable because it was Pierre's first vintage.

6. 1978 Clape, Cornas
August Clape was one of the great growers of the Rhône Valley and the 1978 was everything you want from a Cornas – beef blood, granite, dark fruits, herbs, minerality.

7. 1955 Chave Vin de Paille, Hermitage
In addition to drinking it at La Beaugravière, we also drank it with Kermit Lynch in about 1995 in Berkeley, California. I remember that we had it with truffle ice cream, which I had only tasted once before at La Beaugravière. Floriane said, 'It smelt of flowering peonies'.

I remember the trip well because we travelled all over the USA, dining at a great restaurant each evening in places like Boston, New York, Denver, Dallas, Washington, Chicago and San Fransisco. Once I saw an American *sommelier* in a top restaurant filtering a bottle of red Trévallon through a kitchen towel. Fortunately, I stopped him just in time.

You know David, there is a lot of rubbish spoken about wines, especially by some of the wine critics. The whole experience is what makes a wine memorable – friends, ambiance, laughter - it isn't just about the wine itself. Gérard Chave always used to pull the critics' leg. There is a famous book written called Le Monde du Vin, Art ou Bluff by a former Figaro journalist called Guy Renvoisé who has now passed away. He once told a *sommelier* in a top restaurant that a wine smelt like a hare's sperm, just to see his reaction!

8. 1983 (in magnum) Ramonet Montrachet, Côte de Beaune
All the Ramonet Montrachet we have drunk have been fabulous. The grandfather, Pierre Ramonet, was one of the first to bottle Burgundy in the 1930s and for fifty years he had wanted to buy some Montrachet, which he eventually managed to do in 1978, all paid for in cash. His two sons, Noël and Jean-Claude, were very

9. 1998 DRC Montrachet, Côte de Beaune.
We drank it at the Domaine de la Romanée-Conti in 2009. It was another extraordinary wine. It was exotic but not flamboyant. It had some spice and was rich and honeyed. We drank it in the cellar and it is my greatest memory of white.

10. 1906 Crème de Tête, Château d'Arche, Sauternes.
We drank it over dinner at L'Oustau de Baumanière in 1985. You could still taste it the next morning. It was brown, almost black, with notes of clove, orange, cinnamon and spiced bread. It still had refreshing acidity even after all these years. We couldn't stop speaking about it for days.

Independent
Thinking

J érôme Bressy of Gourt de Mautens in Rasteau is a *brave mec*, the sort of man I connect with instantly. He loves wine, food and rugby. I wonder why we have become great friends?

He is self-taught, committed, honest, down-to-earth, independently-minded, entrepreneurial and utterly unpretentious. I often think he is a model for French rugby, the sort of *esprit de corps* that they need to clone. Dear FFR, please ditch the conventional wisdom, stop copying the Anglo-Saxon way and play to your instincts. Your best rugby is played by artists not scientists, crafters not grafters, rule breakers not rule takers.

In fact, society in general should take a leaf out of Jérôme's book of life. He is a triumph of substance over style, in contrast to the shallow 'celebrity' culture, as practised by those halfwits who appear on reality shows.

of at least 25% each of *syrah* and *mourvèdre* and 10-15% of other varieties, neither of which he has. He wants to use some varieties because they make great wine, but they are banned by the bureaucrats.

Rules are for fools. He just wants to make a *Vin de Terroir* and have the freedom to do so.

Moreover, the politicians, intelligentsia and myopic bureaucrats in Paris could learn a thing or two from Jérôme on how to create value and appeal to the common people. He is a genuine force for good, a sort of vinous *gilet jaune* without displaying the aggro.

The man can do no wrong in my eyes. Jérôme is here for the long haul, carrying out his work diligently and honestly, knowing that manners maketh man and from tiny acorns great oaks grow. Or, to adapt this into vinous form, from great *vitis vinifera* and *terroir* great wine can be made. And in this field and *terroir*, Jérôme is a genius.

A deep thinker, Jérôme told me, *"The hardest is always best and from that comes the best wine. There are no short cuts".* He reminds me a lot of Laurent Vaillé of La Grange des Pères and Thierry Allemand of Cornas. All three of them have a punishing, Lutheran-type work ethic that frames their lives, based on hard work, determination, frugality and a never-ending search for improvement.

They are never satisfied. I love that commitment and intensity, the foundations of all high achievers. Jérôme doesn't want to make more wine, he just wants to make better wine. Neither does he want to cultivate publicity.

He is a passionate advocate for authentic, naked, artisanal, but not faulty wines. Like a Gallic gladiator, he protects his land and practices from the meddling bureaucrats who add nothing but try to take something. He is determined to uphold the traditions and protect wine-making from those who he thinks are destroying the culture. He says to me wistfully, *"Ça me fait si mal."*

Like the producers of so many great wines in France, he has declassified his wines from Appellation d'Origine Contrôlée (AOC) to Indication Géographique Protégée (IGP) because he doesn't want to comply with local rules. He feels they stop him making great wines. The Rasteau Appellation requires the use

All these hard-working growers know that pursuing their passion demands relentless, hard work. Looking pensively at *moi*, this fat cat from London swanning around France, Laurent, Thierry and Jérôme have all said the same words to me: *"My work is never finished, David."*

If they think I am a *gros chat*, they should meet Tristram and Rupert in their red pantaloons from Corduroy, Brogue and Tweed, a fictitious but entirely believable London-based wine merchant. For them, lunch simply rolls into dinner and yet more fine wine. I am an under-nourished kitten in comparison.

In my opinion, Gourt de Mautens is the greatest *domaine* in Rasteau, with Jérôme using organic farming and employing natural and authentic methods, which result in wines of extraordinary concentration and *terroir*. The grapes are situated on Rasteau *terroirs*

whose soil of chalky clay and marl regulate water
and give the wines minerality and character.

There is no sophisticated laboratory equipment here
to help him. He constantly tastes them and completely
relies on his palate to make the best wines possible.

His reds are made from *grenache noir* (typically 50-70%
depending on the year), *carignan*, *mourvèdre*, *syrah*,
counoise, *cinault*, *vaccarèse* and *terret noir*.

His whites are made from *grenache blanc*, *clairette
blanche*, *bourboulenc*, *picardin*, *picpoul*, *roussanne*,
viognier and *marsanne*.

If you get the chance, whether in Rasteau or in a
restaurant, check them out. They are fabulous.
Vive la liberté.

Dear FFR, please ditch the conventional wisdom, stop copying the Anglo-Saxon way and play to your instincts. Your best rugby is played by artists not scientists, crafters not grafters, rule breakers not rule takers.

My Favourite Idioms

IN ENGLISH + FRENCH

English	French	Literal French
Beggars can't be choosers	*Faute de grives, on mange des merles*	Lack of thrush, eat blackbirds
End of the world	*La fin des haricots*	The end of the beans
Hair of the dog	*Le poil de la bête*	Hair of the dog
I don't know whether it is true or not	*Je ne sais pas si c'est du lard ou du cochon*	I don't know whether it's lard or pork
It's game over	*Les carottes sont cuites*	The carrots are cooked
Like father, like son	*Bon sang ne saurait mentir*	Good blood can't lie
Love at first sight	*Un coup de foudre*	A strike of lightening
Old habits die hard	*Les vielles habitudes ont la peau dure*	Old habits have hard skin
Stop pissing me off !	*Arretez de me casser les couilles !*	Stop breaking my balls
The apple doesn't fall far from the tree	*Les chats ne font pas les chiens*	Cats don't make dogs
The straw that broke the camel's back	*Le goût d'eau qui fait deborder le vase*	The drop of water that made the vase overflow
To arrive like a bull in a china shop	*Arriver comme un cheveu sur la soupe*	To arrive like a hair in a soup
To be be stuck etween a rock and a hard place	*Être pris entre l'enclume et le marteau*	To be caught between the anvil and hammer
To be full of energy	*Avoir la pêche*	To have the peach
To be hungover	*Avoir la gueule de bois*	To have the wooden gob
To be starry eyed	*Avoir les étoiles dans les yeux*	To have stars in the eyes

English	French	Literal French
To be starving to death	*Crever la dalle*	To burst the slab
To bear a grudge	*Garder le chien de sa chienne*	To keep the dog from his bitch
To call a spade a spade	*Appeler un chat un chat*	To call a cat a cat
To cost an arm and a leg	*Coûter les yeux de la tête*	To cost the head's eyes
To drink like a fish	*Boire comme un trou*	To drink like a hole
To go ballistic	*Péter les plombs*	To explode the lead
To have a drink	*Boire un coup*	To drink a blow
To have a frog in your throat	*Avoir un chat dans la gorge*	To have a cat in your throat
To have a lie in	*Faire la grasse matinée*	To do the fat morning
To have your cake and eat it	*Avoir le beurre et l'argent du beurre.*	To have your butter and the money from the butter
To hear a pin drop	*Entendre une mouche voler*	To hear a fly take off
To jump from pillar to post	*Sauter du coq à l'âne*	To jump from the cockerel to the donkey
To put his oar in	*Mettre son grain de sel*	To put one's grain of salt in
To speak terrible French	*Parler le français comme une vache espagnole*	To speak French like a Spanish cow
To turn over a new leaf	*Dépouillier / tuer un vieil homme (en nous)*	To skin or kill an old man (in us)
You can't kid a kidder	*On apprend pas à un singe à faire sa grimace*	You can't teach a monkey to pull a face

Homeward Bound

Pulteney Bridge and weir on the River Avon, Bath.

This has been a wonderful trip, a twenty-month tour with my fantasy rugby squad. It was an ambitious project from the outset, but I approached it with gusto, chutzpah and a Panglossian spirit. I told myself: don't doubt yourself, trust your instincts and your capacity to last the distance, and here I am at the final whistle.

Here are my top ten thoughts from my *tour de France*...

1. Rugby is like a brotherhood.

There is no love without suffering and sacrifice, and this team epitomised this.

"There is no place for emotional or collective mediocrity. To be successful, you have to love each other." Patrick Estève

"I wasn't so much in love with the game, but I loved the men I played with and their friendship. The game was a pretext to make lifelong friends." Jean-Pierre Rives

"What I have learnt in business and in sport is that there is no real love or lasting fraternité or great adventure that leaves an indelible mark unless there is success and victory." Éric Champ

"We really loved each other, we still do and we would do anything for each other now." Serge Blanco

2. Back then, some players were so rough and uncompromising on the pitch, but are now so warm and kind off it.

Éric Champ personifies this beautifully. In England's eyes, when he played, he was the villain of the piece and pitch. When talking about 'must-win' games, he said, "The beautiful game is replaced by hard rugby, by the taste of blood in the mouth." I love the way those words perfectly encapsulate both him and the Toulon spirit.

I can't think of another sport or activity that allowed, back then, such contrasting behaviours on and off the pitch. Other players across the globe demonstrated this too, whatever the nationality.

3. Never underestimate the intelligence of the front row.

Most have this finesse – the way they think, talk, interact and manage. Garuche, Dintrans, Armary, Paparemborde, Doxpi, Ibañez, Fitzpatrick, Moore...

4. Rugby is a great metaphor for life.

Rugby teaches us to have discipline in life, it reminds us who we are and where we have come from. You learn all the values and virtues that you need – humility, hard work, sacrifice, teamwork, enthusiasm, respect, generosity, character, anticipation, and so on. All these ingredients are essential and help shape who we are.

5. In the amateur game, rugby is surely the most democratic and democratising sport in the world.

Socially, it levels the playing field. Players turn up on a Saturday or Sunday, and whether we're a banker, baker, butcher, prince, teacher or whatever, we are all equal. We are one team with a single collective goal: to beat the opposition. Then there is the physical side. There is a role for everyone, whatever our shape and size – tall, big, fast, skilful, powerful, skinny. It doesn't

matter. Everyone can contribute and feel part of the team. What an inclusive sport and brilliant framework for society.

6. We should eat more, not less.

I love the bars and restaurants in the Basque Country. They are pictures of societal bliss with locals of all sizes, ages and backgrounds chatting and laughing. I witnessed Spain, France, the Basque Country, the world at its best, watching the way food and wine can be such an equalising, democratising and unifying force. As I enjoyed countless hours immersed in French, Spanish and Basque conviviality, I concluded that we should all be eating more, not less.

However, and I may be leading with my chin (but remember Reader, I have eaten in a lot of restaurants), I find there are fewer places of the requisite quality to lunch and dine across France. Years ago, you could roll up to any village or town and find a decent place to eat. Now, I find myself seeking reassurance through personal recommendations, and that's if you can find a brasserie that hasn't been converted into a pizzeria or simple bar selling spaghetti carbonara and the like. On the other hand, the opposite seems to have happened in Britain. We seem to have benefited from a renaissance in cooking and eating, and the quality of our restaurants reflect that. I know this is going to wind up all my French readers... *desolé*!

7. Back in the 1980s, was French rugby really so beautiful or was it an illusion?

I have seen all the videos again and talked to all the players... it was definitely as good as I remember! The pace, power, guile and unpredictability really are woven inextricably into my memory like a first love.

8. Be kind to people because you never know what lies beneath.

Don't judge them too quickly. Don't think they are any different to you and me, and somehow impervious to pain and suffering. Everyone is having to deal with their own demons, whatever or whoever they are.

Denis Charvet suffered from depression and low self-esteem following a stellar career. Fortunately, his strength of mind and his friends helped him through it. Buy his book, it's a brilliant read. I love him as much now as I did when he played.

Conversely, we have seen how Marc Cécillon went from rugby star to murderer. How can someone as seemingly calm and lovely as Marc commit such a heinous crime? His mental illness had a devastating effect. I am in awe of his former teammates and how they have never abandoned him. I talk about a few in the article on Marc but let me mention again here both Gilles Cassagne and Pascal Ondarts. They are truly magnificent men.

In the amateur game, rugby is surely the most democratic and democratising sport in the world.

9. Had I been French, I would never have been good enough to get in their side.

I knew this already, but writing Brothers in Arms was the only way I could get close to becoming one of them. In that, I think I succeeded!

10. My wife can't wait for me to finish this book.

Well Jo, the match is over...
Mais on a la 3ème mi-temps d'abord!

À très bientôt. Over and out.

David Beresford
June 30th 2019

Philippe, David, Sean and Pascal, enjoying a night out
at Pascal's restaurant, Le Royalty, in July 2019.
Photo - Pierre Carton.

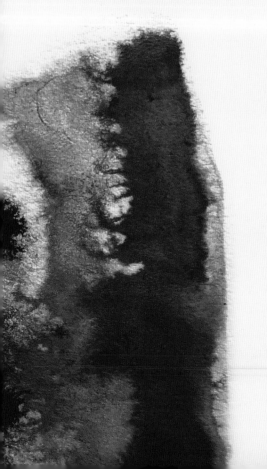

Any profits I make personally from the sale of my book (English and French versions) will be divided between four chosen charities that are dear to me. They are all UK-based, but of course their research is shared around the world among the medical community who change and save lives everywhere.

The UK Sepsis Trust

Why? Because septicaemia almost killed one of our twins, William, when he was two. For seven days, we thought we'd lost him. Somehow he survived. We have never forgotten that traumatic week or the people at Southampton Hospital who saved his life. Sepsis (also known as blood poisoning) is the immune system's overreaction to an infection or injury. Normally our immune system fights infection, but sometimes, for reasons we don't yet understand, it attacks our body's own organs and tissues. If not treated immediately, sepsis can result in organ failure and death, yet with early diagnosis, it can be treated with antibiotics. It is estimated that sepsis affects more than 30 million people worldwide every year, potentially leading to 6 million deaths. It is estimated that 3 million newborns and 1.2 million children suffer from sepsis globally every year.

sepsistrust.org

The Stroke Association

Why? Because my mate Michael Lynagh, the former Australian fly-half, suffered a stroke in 2012. It is estimated that there are 4.5 million deaths a year from stroke in the world and over 9 million stroke survivors.

stroke.org.uk

The British Heart Foundation

Why? Because Dad died of a heart attack when he was thirty-four. The British Heart Foundation's vision is a world without heart and circulatory diseases. They raise money to research cures and treatments so we can beat heartbreak forever. They fund research into all heart and circulatory diseases and the things that cause them: heart diseases, stroke, vascular dementia, diabetes. They're all connected.

bhf.org.uk

40tude: Curing Colon Cancer

Why? Because my father-in-law died of bowel cancer when he was 40. Since 40tude was founded by brothers-in-law, Gordon and Fraser, in September 2011, we have raised close to £1.2 million to help cure colon cancer. St Mark's Hospital is a world leading centre for research and treatment of bowel disorders and 40tude is helping to fund pioneering research projects that are targeted at the early diagnosis and treatment of colon cancer. If you like cycling or paddle boarding or walking or climbing, come and join us on one of our events in the UK or abroad.

40tude.org.uk

Enivrez-Vous

BAUDELAIRE,
LE SPLEEN
DE PARIS, XXXIII

Il faut être toujours ivre. Tout est là : c'est l'unique question.
Pour ne pas sentir l'horrible fardeau du Temps qui brise vos épaules
et vous penche vers la terre, il faut vous enivrer sans trêve.

Mais de quoi ? De vin, de poésie ou de vertu, à votre guise.
Mais enivrez-vous.

Et si quelquefois, sur les marches d'un palais, sur l'herbe verte d'un
fossé, dans la solitude morne de votre chambre, vous vous réveillez,
l'ivresse déjà diminuée ou disparue, demandez au vent, à la vague,
à l'étoile, à l'oiseau, à l'horloge, à tout ce qui fuit, à tout ce qui gémit,
à tout ce qui roule, à tout ce qui chante, à tout ce qui parle, demandez
quelle heure il est ; et le vent, la vague, l'étoile, l'oiseau, l'horloge, vous
répondront : « Il est l'heure de s'enivrer ! Pour n'être pas les esclaves
martyrisés du Temps, enivrez-vous sans cesse ! De vin, de poésie
ou de vertu, à votre guise. »

Be Drunk

You should always be drunk. That's all there is to it: it's the only way.
So as not to feel the horrible burden of Time that breaks your back
and bends you to the earth, you have to be continuously drunk.

But on what? Wine, poetry or virtue, you chose. But be drunk!

And if sometimes, on palace steps or the green grass of a ditch,
in the mournful solitude of your room, you wake up, the drunken
haze already dwindled or gone, ask the wind, the wave, the star,
the bird, the clock, everything that flees, everything that groans,
everything that moves, everything that sings, everything that
speaks, ask what time it is; and the wind, wave, star, bird, clock will
answer you: "It is time to be drunk! So as not to be the martyred
slaves of Time, be drunk, be endlessly drunk! On wine, on poetry
or on virtue, you chose."

Dominique Erbani and Laurent Pardo, July 6th 2019.
Photo - Pierre Carton.

"Only someone with a deep love, respect and knowledge of France could write such a book. David packs thirty years' worth of stories and memories into this wonderfully researched work. But it is also a masterpiece of personal joy, generosity and compassion, which has at its core his ability to connect easily with people, understand them and communicate their stories."

« On ne peut écrire un tel livre si l'on n'éprouve pas de l'amour, du respect pour la France et si l'on n'en a pas une bonne connaissance. David a rassemblé quelque trente ans d'histoires et de souvenirs dans ce formidable ouvrage particulièrement documenté. Mais il s'agit surtout d'un chef-d'œuvre d'enthousiasme personnel, de générosité et de partage qui trouve sa source dans sa capacité à entrer facilement en contact avec les gens, les comprendre et à restituer leurs histoires. »

LAURENT PARDO

Acknowledgements

Writing a book is harder than I thought and more rewarding than I could have ever envisaged. I had the genesis of an idea in September 2017 and it quickly developed a life of its own and into a full-time project. I selected more players, interviewed more people, spent more time in France, travelled more miles, shed more tears, expended more emotional energy, ate more food, drank more wine, incurred more speeding fines and made more friends than I could have possibly imagined. I could never have achieved this without the support of a lot of people, all of whom are named on the following page. However, I wanted to thank a few people in particular who have been there every step of the way or at key moments:

Jo, my wife, who has the patience of a saint. Your common sense, support and indefatigability never cease to amaze me.

William, Ollie and Marcus, our beautiful boys, who calmly continued with their studies and sport while looking after their Mum, as I was gallivanting around France. Well done, I am so proud of you.

Julian Rimmer, Alun Griffiths, Andy Peterson and Gordon Peterson, a quartet of great friends who corrected my almost perfect grammar and spelling, and tried to eliminate the clichés! Your commitment to editing my English manuscripts was unstinting, and your feedback often humorous. *Merci, les gars*. Readers, if you spot any errors, please write to them.

Pascal Ondarts, Diego Minarro and Lolo Pardo, three magnificent men whom I adore. Your support, friendship and humour have been unwavering and essential in helping me connect with the former players and their families.

Olivier Villepreux whose knowledge, humour, skill and contacts were essential in securing a book deal in France. You're another great Frenchman who helped an Englishman, thus strengthening the *entente cordiale*!

Bertrand Pirel from Hugo Sport who believed in me and gave me my break in France. You have great judgement, *mon ami*! I love your love of life and sport, especially rugby.

Mathieu Lauverjat, my editor from Hugo Sport in France. Your diligence, brilliance, charm and patience make you a pleasure to work with.

Mel Brown who introduced me to Aggie, and who gave me several master classes on social media. You have a flair for marketing that is extraordinary, inspired by your instinctive intelligence, charisma and human touch.

Aggie Bainbridge who designed the book and website so beautifully. You have shown tremendous commitment, fortitude, skill and patience, and there is no way I could have done this without you.

Pierre Carton whose photography is simply *magnifique*. You have a real gift and I love your work. *Vive les Basques!*

Sean Fitzpatrick, whose insight into the dark arts of playing the French is unparalleled. You have given me access to so many former All Black players as well as being such a great *compagnon de route* over the last seventeen years or so, not just during the writing of this book.

Merci à tous et à toutes. I love you all.

Aggie Bainbridge
Al Lukies
Alain Lorieux
Alain Paco
Alexandre Chazalet
Alexis Saint-Martin Peguela
Alison Martin
Alun Griffiths
André and Guy Boniface
Andy Haden
Andy Peterson
Anne Baret
Benôit Papy
Bertrand Baret
Bertrand Pirel
Bill Beaumont
Bob Dwyer
Brian Moore
Buck Shelford
Celine DeMaesschalck
Charlotte Courcelle-Labrousse
Carsen Russell
Christian Montaignac
Clare Beresford
Clive Woodward
Daniel Dubroca
Daniel Herrero
David Sole

Denis Charvet
Derek White
Dewi Morris
Diane Belugou
Didier Cambérabero
Didier Codorniou
Didier Sanchez
Diego Minarro
Dominique Erbani
Dominique Mazille
Elie Vaquerin
Eloi Dürrbach
Elsa Paparemborde
Eric Champ
Erik Bonneval
Fergus Slattery
Finlay Calder
Franck Mesnel
Françoise Van Den Berge
Fraser Moore
Frédéric Maddeloni
Gary Whetton
Gavin Hastings
Gilles Cassagne
Gordon Moore
Gordon Peterson
Greg Sherwood
Harvey Robinson

Harvey Thorneycroft
Henri Nayrou
Hugo MacNeill
Ian Milne
Ian Robertson
Ieuan Evans
James Sparshatt
Jason Leonard
Jean Condom
Jean Courcelle-Labrousse
Jean-Baptiste Fouroux
Jean-Baptiste Lafond
Jean-François Imbernon
Jean-Luc Joinel
Jean-Patrick Lescarboura
Jean-Pierre Garuet
Jean-Pierre Rives
Jérôme Bressy
Jérôme Gallion
Jill Beresford
Jo Beresford
Jo Maso
John Hall
John Jeffrey
John Kirwan
John O'Driscoll
Julian Rimmer
Keith Prothero

Kevin Beeston
Laurent Pardo
Laurent Parquet
Laurent Rodriguez
Laurent Vaillé
Louisou Armary
Marc Cécillon
Marcus Beresford
Martin Hepworth
Maryse Lacans
Mathieu Lauverjat
Matt Perry
Melanie Brown
Michael Lynagh
Michel Marfaing
Michel Roux
Micky Skinner
Nathalie Tonon
Neil Loft
Nick Farr-Jones
Olivier Villepreux
Ollie Beresford
Ollie Campbell
Ostiane Dürrbach
Pascal Ondarts
Patrice Lagisquet
Patrick Estève
Paul Beresford

Peter FitzSimons
Phil Orr
Philippe Dintrans
Philippe Sella
Pierre Berbizier
Pierre Carton
Pierre Kalfon
Pierre Dospital
Pierre Villepreux
Rachael Dalzell
Rachelle Healy
Raphaël Ibañez
Richard Pool-Jones
Roger Maddaloni
Sean Dinnen
Sean Fitzpatrick
Serge Blanco
Simon Jones
Simon Wilde
Steve Meredith
Stuart Evans
Valérie Maddaloni
Valérie Paparemborde
Virginie Hovanessian
Wade Dooley
Will Bentley
Will Carling
William Beresford